# Keep on Walkin'
# Keep on Talkin'

An Oral History of the Greensboro
Civil Rights Movement

by

Eugene E. Pfaff, Jr.

Tudor Publishers
Greensboro

Keep on Walkin', Keep on Talkin': An Oral History of the Greensboro Civil Rights Movement by Eugene E. Pfaff, Jr. © 2011

All rights reserved. This book, or any portion thereof, may not be reproduced in any form, other than for brief review purposes, without the written permission of the publisher.
For information, email: Tudorpublishers@ triad.rr.com

All photographs courtesy of the Greensboro*News-Record*.

First Edition

Library of Congress Cataloging-in-Publication

Pfaff, Eugene E., Jr., 1948—
  Keep on walkin', keep on talkin': an oral history of the Greensboro civil rights movement by Eugene E. Pfaff, Jr.—1st ed.
    p. cm.
  Includes bibliographical references.
  ISBN 0-936389-36-2  (alk. paper)
1. African Americans—Civil rights—North Carolina—Greensboro. 2. Civil rights workers—North Carolina—Goldsboro. 3. Greensboro (N.C.)—History—20th century. 4. Greensboro (N.C.)—Race relations. 5. Greensboro (N.C)— Biography. 6. Oral history—North Carolina—Goldsboro. I. Title.
  F264.G8P44  2011
  323.1196'073075662—dc23                                    2011025525

# Contents

Acknowledgments ........................................................................ vii

List of Interviewees ....................................................................... ix

Preface ........................................................................................... xv

Chapter 1: Conundrum .................................................................. 1

Chapter 2: The Greensboro Sit-ins ............................................... 61

Chapter 3: Greensboro CORE ..................................................... 144

Chapter 4: Direct Action Begins ................................................. 183

Chapter 5: Juggernaut .................................................................. 198

Chapter 6: Counterstroke ............................................................. 243

Chapter 7: Crescendo ................................................................... 279

Chapter 8: Resolution .................................................................. 305

Chapter 9: In Retrospect .............................................................. 352

Afterword ..................................................................................... 396

Sources ......................................................................................... 399

Ain't gonna let nobody turn me 'round,
Turn me 'round, turn me round, turn me 'round.
I'm gonna keep on walkin',
Keep on a-talkin.
Marching on to Freedom Land.

> — Ain't Gonna Let Nobody Turn Me 'Round

# Acknowledgments

The research and writing of this book has been a very moving journey of discovery into the human heart and soul. In the process I have gotten to know a number of people harboring a diverse range of beliefs about the complex and emotionally volatile issue of race relations. To each of the interviewees I would like to extend my gratitude for sharing their memories in a sincere and generous amount of their time.

My first and most profound gratitude must go to my parents, Eugene and Kathleen, who inspired me with a love of history. I am indebted to my family in their unstinting patience and encouragement to persevere in the completion of a project that proved to be more involved and arduous than I could ever have imagined.

I also wish to express my appreciation to George Viele and Shirley Windham of the Greensboro Public Library, for their enthusiastic support of the project as a part of the Oral History Program., and to Helen Snow of the Reference Department of the Greensboro Public Library, and Hermann Trojanowski of the Jackson Library, University of North Carolina at Greensboro, for access to the original material in the archives and the Community Voices Program. I am grateful to Diane Lamb of the *Greensboro News-Record* for graciously granting permission to use the photographs contained in this book.

A special thanks goes to my sister and soulmate, Pamela Cocks, for many hours of patient proofreading and serendipitous suggestions that contributed immeasurably to the improvement of the manuscript. This book is as much hers as mine.

I join all of the interviewees and all those that participated in the Civil Rights Movement in the hope that this book will add a chapter to the history of truth and justice.

# List of Interviewees

Numbers indicate chapters where interviews appear. Titles indicate positions held when the events occurred. The married names of female interviewees are in parentheses.

Helen Ashby  1
    Executive Secretary, Greensboro YWCA

Warren Ashby  1
    Faculty, Woman's College of the University of North Carolina

Joseph Asher  1
    Rabbi, Temple Emanuel

Cecil Bishop  7, 9
    Minister, Trinity AME Zion Church

Ezell A. Blair, Sr.  1
    Teacher, Dudley Senior High School

Ezell A. Blair, Jr. (see Jibreel Khazan)

Gloria Jean Blair (Howard)  2, 3
    Student, Bennett College

Josephine Boyd (Bradley)  1
    Student, Greensboro Senior High School

Lewis A. Brandon  2, 3, 4, 5, 6, 8
    Student, A&T College

Gordon Carey  2, 3, 8
    Director of Field Secretaries, Congress of Racial Equality (CORE)

Vance C. Chavis  1
    Principal, Dudley High School

B. Elton Cox  3, 4
    Minister and Field Secretary, CORE

Ann Dearsley (-Vernon)  2
 Student, W.C.U.N.C.

Lewis C. Dowdy  6, 9
 President, Agricultural & Technical College (1962-1980)

Ima Edwards  2
 Employee, F. W. Woolworth & Company (Greensboro, N.C.)

Herman Enochs  6
 Municipal-County Court judge

George Evans  8, 9
 Physician

James Farmer  2, 3
 Executive Director, CORE

Warmoth T. Gibbs  2
 President, A&T College (1955-60)

Evander Gilmer  3, 6
 Student, A&T College and Treasurer, Greensboro CORE

William L. "Lody" Glenn  1, 9
 Assistant Principal, Greensboro Senior High School

Charlotte Graves Burroughs (-White)  2
 Student, W.C.U.N.C.

Leonard Guyes  4
 Greensboro businessman/member of the Zane committee

Otis L. Hairston, Sr.  1, 2, 9
 Minister, Mt. Zion Baptist Church

Otis L. Hairston, Jr.  5, 6
 Student, Dudley High School

Clarence L. Harris  2
 Manager, F. W. Woolworth & Company (Greensboro, N.C.)

Frances Herbin (Lewis)  2, 3, 9
   Student, Bennett College

Howard Holderness  2
   President, Jefferson-Pilot Insurance Company

William H. Jackson  5, 6 9
   Captain, Greensboro Police Department

Hobart Jarrett  1, 2
   Faculty, Bennett College

Ralph Johns  2
   Greensboro businessman

Marion Jones  3, 4, 5, 8
   Minister, United Church of Christ

Sarah Jones (Outterbridge)  3, 5, 9
   Student, Bennett College and daughter of Marion Jones

Jibreel Khazan [Ezell A. Blair, Jr.]  2, 3, 4, 5, 6 ,8
   Student, A & T College/member, "Greensboro Four"

John Marshall Kilimanjaro  1
   Faculty, A & T College

Elizabeth Laizner  4, 5, 6, 7, 8
   Faculty, Bennett College

J. Kenneth Lee  6
   Attorney

Ralph Lee  8
   Student, A&T College and Chairman, Greensboro CORE

Lois Lucas (Williams)  2, 3, 4, 5, 6, 8, 9
   Student, A&T College

Clarence C. Malone  6
   Attorney

Clyde Marsh 9
: Fire Marshal, Greensboro Fire Department

Franklin McCain 2, 9
: Student, A & T College/member, "Greensboro Four"

Neil McGill 5
: Manager, Carolina Theater

Floyd McKissick 3, 4
: Attorney

James C. McMillan 3, 5, 6, 7, 8
: Faculty, Bennett College

Joseph McNeil 2, 9
: Student, A & T College/member, "Greensboro Four"

Furman M. Melton 5
: Greensboro (N.C.) Police Department

Jack Moebes 2
: Photographer, *The Greensboro Record*

David H. Morehead 1, 2
: Director, Young Men's Christian Association

Boyd Morris 5, 9
: Owner, Mayfair Cafeteria

Franklin Parker 1
: Faculty, W.C.U.N.C.

Jennie Parker 1
: School teacher

Robert (Pat) Patterson 2, 3, 4 ,5 ,6, 9
: Student, A&T College/Vice-Chairman, Greensboro CORE

Willa B. Player 1, 6
: President, Bennett College (1956-66)

David Richmond 2
    Student, A & T College/member, "Greensboro Four"

George Roach 2
    Mayor, Greensboro, N.C. (1957-61)

David Schenck, Jr. 7
    Son of Mayor David Schenck (1961-63)

Arnold A. Schiffman 2
    Greensboro businessman/member of the Zane Committee

Eugenie [Genie] Seamans 2
    Student, W.C.U.N.C.

Frank O. Sherrill, Jr.  2, 9
    Assistant Manager, S&W Cafeteria

Hal Sieber 9
    Publicity Director, Greensboro Chamber of Commerce

George S. Simkins, Jr. 1, 2
    Dentist/ Chairman of the Greensboro NAACP

McNeill Smith 2
    Attorney

Willliam L. Snider 1
    Editor-in-Chief, *Greensboro Daily News*

Jo Spivey 1
    Reporter, *The Greensboro Record*

A. Knighton (Tony) Stanley  3, 4, 5, 6, 7, 8 ,9
    Faculty, A & T College and Bennett College

Marvin Sykes 2
    Reporter, *The Greensboro Record*

Alvin Thomas 5, 6, 8
    Student, A & T College/Chairman, Greensboro CORE

William A. Thomas   3, 5 6, 7, 8, 9
   Student, A & T College/Chairman, Greensboro CORE

Geneva Tisdale   2
   Employee, F. W. Woolworth Company (Greensboro, N.C.)

Elizabeth (Betsy) Toth   2
   Student, W.C.U.N.C.

James R. Townsend   2
   City Manager, Greensboro, N.C. (1947-61)

Ben Wilson   2, 9
   Faculty, Greensboro College

Edward R. Zane   2, 9
   Businessman/Chairman, Zane committee

# Preface

Oral history has several limitations as a research tool. It is impressionistic, subject to confusion over events many years in the past, and frequently not supported by documentation. But when it is used in conjunction with traditional research, it may be a useful means of capturing valuable historical moments from the past. Its very impressionistic nature may reveal hidden motivations of individuals. Perspectives of the moment may be reviewed over the years. Private conversations or secret arrangements, too delicate to be written down, may be revealed with the passage of time. Perhaps most important of all, it can be the means for every side of a historical event to receive a fair hearing, whereby such an event may be understood as fully as possible.

As such, oral history is uniquely suited to analyze the subtle aspects of the Civil Rights Movement. There are many oral history repositories, most of which focus upon the prominent personalities involved. However, a significant omission in these collections is the testimony of thousands of individuals about the grassroots nature of the Civil Rights Movement. To understand how this phenomenon succeeded, it is necessary to hear the voices of anonymous participants from communities throughout the South. Each individual and every community provides an essential piece to the complex tapestry of this remarkable social revolution.

Greensboro, North Carolina, is an excellent example of the confluence of disparate contending forces that battled for the political and social future of the United States in the second half of the twentieth century. In attempting to understand how the struggle took place and its ultimate resolution, it is necessary to view the motivations and actions of all parties: government officials; influential members of both the white and black communities; student and adult African American activists and their white sympathizers; police forces charged with maintaining law and order; owners of segregated businesses; attorneys for the opposing sides; and the members of the society at large, confused by the turmoil that had forever changed their world, and the anxieties of the unavoidable future. As members of each group reveal their motives, actions, fears, doubts and adherence to principle, the reader will gain a more sophisticated concept of what was at stake: the preservation of a traditional way of life by the white political and business community, and the aspirations of African Americans, spearheaded by a new, dynamic generation determined to achieve the constitutional rights of African Americans within their own lifetimes.

The confrontation involved both time-tested and innovative tactics: the sit-ins and mass marches of CORE harkened back to the labor movement of the 1930s, now guided by the Gandhian discipline of passive resistance, presented a challenge to the white power structure, which sought to maintain its authority and traditions without resorting to repressive brutality. Both CORE and city officials sought the sanctity of favorable public opinion in a contest of creative action and response that at times took on the aspects of an elaborate chess game. As each side sought some middle ground between the perceived victory of the Establishment in Albany, Georgia, and the moral supremacy of civil rights activists in Birmingham, Alabama, the Greensboro struggle in many ways set the tone for future confrontations in the Civil Rights Movement in the South.

With a reputation as an economic and educational center, and possessing a strong business and political elite and a vibrant black middle class, Greensboro contained dynamics that made it virtually unique among Southern cities. Although Greensboro was unique in one sense, in another sense it was representative of the mores of hundreds of Southern communities in the 1960s. Faced with the choice of peaceful change or violent resistance, Greensboro citizens struggled to resolve their racial dilemma. The solution lay deep within the diverse elements of the community. The ensuing drama could either result in encouraging social progress, or destroy any chance for an enlightened resolution.

It is my hope that the narratives will stimulate the creation of other repositories of local oral history of the Civil Rights Movement. Only then will the complete story of that time be understood by future generations. There are cases of repetition and confusion of chronological order, inevitable as people seek to reconstruct events of the distant past. I have tried to leave much of the narratives as conveyed, for this reflects the subjective emotional verve that the events hold in memory. To see them through the eyes of the narrator is the only way to capture the meaning of that moment in history. To that end, I ask readers to view the narrators as individual human beings, embued with all the passions that made up the spirit of the time. Whether or not one identifies with their perspectives, they may at least come to understand them. If so, then I have accomplished both the purposes of the narrators, and my own.

Eugene E. Pfaff, Jr.
Greensboro, North Carolina
June 2011

# Chapter 1

## Conundrum

To the casual observer, Greensboro, North Carolina, seemed to be a contradiction. A history of small farms with few slaves and an active Underground Railroad station, presented Guilford County as a center of moderation in the antebellum South. The presence of two black colleges and the practice of black voting rights suggested an area of twentieth century Southern progressivism. Yet there were elements of regressive regional traditions: a rigidly segregated urban transportation system and residential pattern; a black population whose members, including a higher-than-average percentage of college graduates, earned a much lower annual income than whites.

But there were notable exceptions to the prevailing Southern racial pattern. In 1951, the cover of *Time* magazine featured a Greensboro physician as the first African American to be elected to a Southern city council. A small black community located within a block of a white female college, the purpose of which was to locate cafeteria and laundry personnel close enough to arrive at work on time, existed in defiance of racially segregated housing customs. While African Americans were not served at restaurants, they were patrons at a number of retail stores; local theaters admitted blacks, but they were required to sit in separate balconies. Unlike other Southern retail establishments, a number of stores would allow female African Americans to try on clothes, and even take them home and return them, if necessary. In 1954, the Greensboro school board gained national attention for its decision to voluntarily cooperate with the controversial **Brown** decision mandating public school integration. There were interracial meetings of liberal white and black citizens to discuss social issues. African Americans voted, although white "vote buyers" were an aspect of the political process.

So Greensboro presented an image that was at once traditionally conservative and progressively advanced in terms of race relations. While acknowledging the influence of individual liberal white intellectuals, businessmen and political leaders, black residents also recognized a subtle de-

*termination of the white power structure to simultaneously present a public image of moderate racial attitudes, while quietly maintaining traditional Southern mores. As the nascent Civil Rights Movement grew in the South in the 1950s, it was a community that presented the opportunity for revolutionary social change. In the 1960s, it would confront that conundrum with dramatic consequences.*

## Vance Chavis

Greensboro was a typical Southern city in terms of racial attitudes of the white power structure; there were some progressive white citizens and some narrow-minded, prejudiced people. Blacks had to sit in the "peanut gallery," a separate balcony high up in the theaters. I was one of the leaders of a group of blacks that boycotted the two white theaters at that time—the National and the Carolina Theaters. The National subsequently brought Fats Waller here, and a lot of people went back. But we refused to pay our money, and then go upstairs and be segregated. In my classes, I often teased the students about going to the theaters; I'd say, "You going to go up those four flights of stairs to be segregated?" Some of my students got the message, but most people went back to the theaters.

About 1941, we had an organization called the Guilford County Race Relations Commission, which had no status. But there were a few white people we called "liberals" on it. We had Dr. Wilson who was a retired minister at a United Church of Christ; Dr. Richard Bardolph; the Bensons, several other people, and one white lady who was really more avant-garde than I was. We had a group called the Southern Brethren [Organization of Southern Churchmen] and we used to have dinners, discussions, and lectures at the old YWCA, because it was the only place at that time that integrated groups could eat.

Long before the sit-ins, Mrs. Raymond Smith, Mrs. Angeline Smith, Dr. Bardolph and I went to all of the stores in Greensboro that had separate black and white water fountains, to ask that they be removed, and we were surprisingly successful. Carson Bain, a County Commissioner, told me, "Vance, we're going to paint the county courthouse in two weeks, and when we paint it, we're just going to paint out those signs." I went to the A&P stores, Woolworth and Kress and Duke Power and they all agreed to remove their signs. So we got the signs removed from many of the water fountains in Greensboro by going around talking to the owners.

Dr. Bardolph made a study of segregation laws in North Carolina. The State did not require separate water fountains and had very few segregation laws in general. For instance, if a black woman was accompanying a white child and she had on a white uniform, she was able to go into the theater or sit in the front of the bus or train in North Carolina, simply by being a servant.

But the others usually were relegated to the rear of the vehicle.

There wasn't a great deal of communication between the City Council and the black community. They communicated with us, because, although blacks did not vote in large numbers, they had been significant in the election of the City Council and, more importantly, in the passing of most of the bond issues. If they had not received the black block vote, many of these things would not have passed in Greensboro. We observed representatives of white politicians coming into the black community to buy votes at election time. Sometimes the candidate's people collected the money and didn't do anything. On one occasion, they found a man who was giving out a lot of cards at the precinct for his candidate's opponent. That's how bad it was. I've had some candidates tell me, "Vance, we can buy our votes," hence, they never bothered to bring about any improvements. In a situation like this, if you pay someone to deliver you the votes, if you are elected, you are finished, you don't owe them anything. You've paid them in money rather than in improvements. No one ever knows how much they got under the table. A lot of it was given to them, and it stopped there. The honest candidates did pay workers five dollars to give out cards at the black precincts. However, I felt that the black people in the community had been done a great injustice by these practices.

I talked to several people—Esther Jenkins, Grace Lewis, William Hampton, George Evans, W. L. T. Miller, Kenneth Lee and others—about how to stop this practice. We formed an organization called the Greensboro Citizens Association. Membership was open to every individual, club fraternity, church, and there was a small fee for the affiliation. We started as a small group, but we became successful in the very first election after we were formed. The politicians who usually elected the governor in North Carolina, sponsored a man named Johnson, but Kerr Scott opposed him. People told us that Scott couldn't win, but we went along with him, because we thought he was the better of the two. To everyone's surprise, he won, even though the "vote buyers" in the black community had backed Johnson. The community chose to go with the man who they thought was right, rather than the one who was paying for votes. We also worked for Frank Graham's campaign for senator [1950]; in fact, we *gave* money to his campaign. We sat up there at the Hayes-Taylor YMCA until two or three o'clock the night of the voting, counting the ballots.

I also worked in the 1951 campaign of Dr. William Hampton, a black physician, for the City Council. He was president of the Greensboro Citizens Association, and that gave him a leadership role in the black community. Because of the block vote in the black community, and a lot of white voter support, he came out first in one of the primaries. Dr. Hampton was a very capable and personable man, the kind of person that everyone liked. He spoke for what he thought was right, without antagonizing others; he was honest and he had no intemperate habits, so that whites felt comfortable supporting him. I think that the white community was not upset at having such a black man on the City Council.

In 1952 Dr. David Jones was the first black member on the school board. I think that this came through the influence of Dr. Hampton, since the City Council appointed members of the school board. We have to look back at the time that they served. I knew both of them well, and neither one would do something that was against his own philosophy. In order to get half a loaf, they may have done some accommodating, but half a loaf is better than no bread, and I feel in both instances they were able to make some achievements for the people whom the represented. No one can say that either of them was an Uncle Tom-type of personality.

At that time, integration was not a problem. We were trying to get back to the *Plessy* decision [*Plessy v. Ferguson*], that is, more or less, equal facilities. Dr. Jones was interested in seeing that Dudley [High School] and other black schools got their share of whatever expenditures were made by the school board. Dr. Hampton was primarily interested in the streets on the south side of Greensboro and other problems that we had at that time in improving the city of Greensboro. I doubt that there was any genuine perception by the white community of the needs of the black community, because they lived on their side and we lived over here. White people never came into our area, except the sheriff or the police. Occasionally, a candidate might come into our area, but usually the people who were paying "vote buyers" didn't see the black people, so they weren't aware of the conditions in the black community. If some lady from Irving Park was bringing her cook or maid home, then she could see these conditions. The sewage odor was terrible out here, but it wasn't a problem in the southwest or the northwest, so the white citizens there didn't know that it existed. We had a fertilizer plant and the city abattoir next to the black community, creating noxious odors, but most [white] people weren't aware of the problem, so it didn't concern them. And if they didn't have to do anything, they didn't.

I have found that if you have no power behind your request for change, you get very little. You need some kind of weight to throw around, and for the black community, that was the amount of votes that we could deliver to a candidate. I think that this is where the power comes from. When it came to paving streets, we were the result of "benign neglect." I remember when they paved some streets around A&T College, the City Council allowed them to stay half-done throughout the entire winter, and the people couldn't get in there on account of the mud. I know of another instance when Dr. Hampton was on the Council, in this same area, it wanted to build a housing project, but some of them wanted to build some homes similar to those around the Bessemer Shopping Center, and a group of us went up and protested it. Dr. J. W. Hines, pastor of the Providence Baptist Church, and some others spoke to the Council on that day. We were able to prevent the rezoning of that property, and today it is the only section on this side that is comparable to the highest zoning in the Greensboro. But that is a fight that we won because we protested to the Council.

There was not much resentment in the black community over this type of neglect. In Greensboro, we had it better than most places in North Carolina, to the extent that the antagonisms weren't there; people were living and they were eating, some of them had nice homes, but they took having the vote for granted. In North Carolina, blacks often did not vote in a large percentage, because they have typically never known what it is to not have the vote. People in Greensboro who could read and write never had any trouble registering. I think, primarily, it was the influence of the people who settled here in the beginning. Guilford County did not have large plantations with a lot of slaves, and related to that was the Quakers. We had an Underground Railroad here, and I think that the Presbyterians probably brought about a very good influence; but I think the people in that church were the leaders. I've never had many racial epithets hurled at me since I have lived here. Although there was some racial hatred, it was subtle. Many people may have privately supported the Klan, but they didn't do so openly—but they didn't vehemently disapprove of them. Sometimes silence gives consent.

Blacks in Greensboro have sought things that have taken quite a while to accomplish. Although during the 1930s we were able to build Windsor Community Center through WPA [Works Progress Administration] funds, trying to get black policemen in Greensboro was more difficult. A group of black people led by Dr. [John] Tarpley, Dr. Windsor, and Reverend Weatherby, had several meetings with Police Chief Jarvis in the old Carnegie Library on the Bennett College campus. Jarvis said that we would never have a black policeman, unless it would be over his dead body. But as the Citizens Association became stronger, and as time passed, Police Chief Jarvis did appoint two black police officers—Penn and Raeford. That was significant, because this was long before any other city in the South had black policemen. We had the same thing when we started integrating employees in stores and the sit-ins, and all. A lot of people said, "We'll lose all of our white patronage." And they also made pessimistic statements about violence if black children were bused to schools, but so many of the things that people feared never happened. All of these things have brought about positive results; at least they have brought people together and they have learned to live together.

There was a great deal of back patronage of white stores in downtown Greensboro prior to 1960. Unlike Winston-Salem and Durham, Greensboro has never had many first-class black stores. And black women in most places could try on clothes, which was not true in most places of the South; in some instances, they could bring them home and return them. There was one store that didn't wait on blacks, and that was Montaldo's; they didn't wait on blacks until after 1964, after it was required by law. I never had any trouble. Most white merchants welcomed you, if you paid your bill.

But blacks were not completely dependent on white merchants and professional people. There was a strong black middle class in Greensboro, because of A&T and Bennett Colleges being here. I think that we have always had a larger portion of the middle class and college-trained black people in this area, more so than in most cities in North Carolina. The black community stuck with the black middle class. Take Dr. [George] Simkins, for example; if ever a black man was born with a silver spoon in his mouth, he was. His father was a dentist before him, and his father was well thought of and was a candidate for the City Council. Dr. Simkins himself is a dentist. He didn't have to become involved with the NAACP. And the Greensboro Men's [Club] is made up of professional people—doctors and teachers and businessmen— they were instrumental in the fight for civil rights. They have always supported the causes from the blacks, sometimes more than the poor.

You take the poor, sometimes they don't bother to vote. I think that they are sometimes at fault for their conditions, because they accept it, and they have been sold on class hatred. And they are jealous of blacks who were successful, or were afraid to join the NAACP. Greensboro has always had a strong NAACP, but we didn't have more than about ten people in it. Of course, A&T and Bennett were small, but most of the leadership came from the schools, and often times, I hear criticism about the middle class not being members of the NAACP. I heard Dr. Martin Luther King say that over at Bennett College chapel in 1958, and it didn't please me at all, because I had been working all my adult life, trying to get people to become members and involved, and most of them were teachers. They have supported the NAACP. I found it inactive when I came here, and a Professor Nelson, who was working for North Carolina Mutual, was the President; Dr. Faison, a teacher at Bennett; and Dr. Simkins, Sr., were about the only active officers. Then Mr. N. L. Gregg came here—he worked for North Carolina Mutual Insurance Company—was president for a long time as an insurance agent. He contributed significantly to its growth. Because of the efforts of these individuals, the NAACP has been increasingly active everywhere in the black community in Greensboro.

Even among the teachers, there was a reluctance to join the NAACP. Every year, I went around to canvass them to collect membership fees. My principal, Dr. Tarpley, knew what I was doing, but I was never discouraged from doing it. This wasn't done in all of the schools, because all of the teachers and principals were not that courageous. I don't think that they were afraid of losing state funds; they must have just been afraid. A lot of people were afraid of many things. Some of the teachers were afraid when we were trying to fight for equal salaries. One of the fellows said to me at Dudley, "Vance, we'll never get equal salaries." We had a salary differential for a long time. He didn't believe it, and we even had a black principal who wrote a letter to the newspaper, saying that it didn't take as much for us to live on as it did for white people. I wrote a letter to the *Greensboro Daily News*, in which I said, "No one said, 'Well, you are a poor school teacher, and black at that, so I'm going to give you a discount.'" In many instances, blacks paid *more*, in rent and food. But because enough black people protested, led by the Greensboro Citizens Association and the NAACP, we succeeded in getting a more balanced wage differential. That's how [Greensboro] got this good name, but they saw which way the wind was blowing; they didn't want a lawsuit in North Carolina. I joined Dr. Tarpley, who was high in the echelon of the Teachers Association, and a fellow named James Taylor from Durham and some others to talk to Governor Broughton. He agreed to gradually raise salaries for black teachers. It was several years before they actually reached equality; it was done in steps.

Starting with [President] Roosevelt, black people in Greensboro were made conscious that there was an opportunity for a better living, and there was an opportunity for political involvement. There was a gradually increasing activism and bonding between the economic classes in the black community. This was especially true with the Gillespie Golf Course case involving Dr. Simkins and three other gentlemen. Most of them were not professional people; one man shined shoes. It was a conglomeration of citizens, not just the professional people involved. The same thing was true when we asked the City Council to integrate the swimming pools. They filled up the swimming pool at Windsor Community Center, because people asked [for] it to be integrated. All of these things happened before the sit-ins, and I think that this is significant. George Simkins also entered a suit against the hospitals because the hospitals weren't integrated.

Many black citizens, particularly the young people, were activists long before the sit-ins of 1960. I don't believe that the sit-ins could have taken place in Wilmington, Greenville or Raleigh. That was the propitious moment and this was the propitious location, because of the leadership that we had in Greensboro, and also the attitude of the whites who would tolerate more from black activists than other parts of the South and North Carolina.

I remember when black women called for the integration of the YWCA pool. Caesar Cone offered to build a new pool if those calling for use of the YWCA agreed to use the black YMCA. I was on the board of the Hayes-Taylor YMCA, and we turned down the proposal. It was hard, because Caesar Cone was one of the biggest contributors to Hayes-Taylor YMCA, but it must have been due to the discussions concerning combining the two at that time. It was rumored that it was an attempt to keep the YWCA segregated, or he may have been sincere in his belief that it was more efficient to have one pool for both male and female blacks in Greensboro; I don't know. Mr. Cone may have been honest in his belief that they could have a bigger facility at Hayes-Taylor.

The Interracial Commission was far from being militant on integration. When I first came here it was the opinion in the black community that it was made up mostly of the "yes" people in its community, and they were there to agree with the "powers-that-be" in Greensboro. They were satisfied in meeting with these people, and they were there to keep racial problems from arising, rather than to solve them. People my age at that time had very little respect for the Interracial Commission, because it believed in the status quo and this is what they preserved.

Very few of the public facilities were integrated in Greensboro during the 1950s; the YWCA and the airport, but not the railroad station or the bus station. Blacks could ride on the city buses, but they had to sit in the back. There was an area on the west side of the railroad station and one on the east side, and there were separate entrances. The main entrance was where the white people went in, and the black people entered on the west side, and there was a waiting room there. The only time you got close enough to touch white people was when you went down this viaduct to board the train at the upper level. There were separate "Jim Crow" cars on the trains, but the black porter would see that blacks got on the white train car in many instances. [Laughs.]

I think that there was an absence of overt racial violence in Greensboro until the period in which Kenneth Lee was active in the NAACP, and at that time, the Ku Klux Klan raised its head in Greensboro. They did have some marches; they came by Benbow Road once. There was a man called [C. J.] Webster who was their leader here just prior to the sit-ins. But you could not say, by any means, that this is Ku Klux land. I think that there is a lot of good in Greensboro, and the Klan has not been encouraged too much.

The feeling in the black community when the *Brown* decision [*Brown v. Board of Education*] was announced in May 1954, was one of great satisfaction, almost euphoria. I never saw anyone that was in opposition to it; they felt that it was a long time coming. But I don't think that there was a large number of black parents who wanted to make application for their children to attend white schools, because of the experience of those that did go to Gillespie and the young lady who went to Grimsley Senior High School [Josephine Boyd]. The children did not want to subject themselves to that kind of embarrassment. The people were afraid that their children would be abused verbally and physically molested. I think that the people were looking forward to what we have today.

But the black community never agreed with what was called the "Pearsall Plan" or "Freedom of Choice." It's difficult to evaluate the thinking of the board members, as to how conscienciously they tried to implement the Supreme Court's decision. A lady on the board, Mrs. Clarence Brown, was one of the finest people in this city; she was one of the few whites that I ate with at the YWCA. Another member, Dr. Raymond Smith was a good man. The Chairman, D. E. Hudgins, was a courageous man. I believe that these people were sincere. I talked with Mr. Ben L. Smith, the Superintendent, on many occasions. I remember making a talk once at the YWCA on four reasons why segregation was wrong, and he asked for my cards, because he wanted to make use of the notes that I had. These people received unimaginable criticism and vilification after making the decision to comply with the Supreme Court decision. I understand that some of Mr. Hudgins' long-time friends, wouldn't speak to him. Most of these people were not reappointed to the school board again, and the composition of the school board was changed entirely. I believe that any delay in implementing the Supreme Court's decision in Greensboro was due to the pressure that was put on these people, more so than their own inclinations. I believe that they wanted to do what was right. The pressure came from the people in the community: the City Council, the Chamber of Commerce, and insulting anonymous telephone calls.

I think there was discouragement in the black community over the slowness in integrating Greensboro schools, because there were so few people who wanted to attend the predominately white schools, and those who did experienced such difficulty. As this message spread in the community, and as people read in the paper or saw on the television what was happening, this discouraged a lot of people from even attempting to do so. We also felt that we had pretty good black schools. I know that we did at Lincoln Junior High School, because one year that I was there, the state Board of Education evaluated the city junior high schools, and over sixty percent of [our] teachers had masters degrees. I tried to see that each person worked in his or her field of specialization. In addition, we had a high experience ratio for the faculty, because the people usually stayed. We had good schools, so few parents clamored to get their children into white schools; most of those who did were the affluent.

## George Simkins, Jr.

Years ago, if you were black, you'd go into a department store and could not try on a dress or a suit because you were black, and you had to drink water from a separate fountain from whites. You had to sit in the back of the buses for transportation. You had a segregated car on the trains that you had to sit in that was usually right next to the engine where all the smoke would come in there. You couldn't go to any white church. The churches were segregated. You hardly came in contact with any whites at all. My mother would go into Meyer's Department Store. They had a little tea room up there, but she couldn't go there. And I told her, "Mama, I'll go with you," but the reason I didn't want to go in the store was because Mama was picking over everything, because the store wouldn't let her try on clothes or go into the Tea Room, because she was black. I said, "I'll just sit out here on the street and wait on you to come out."

The movie [theaters] were segregated; some wouldn't even take blacks. And those that did take you, you had to walk up the back steps and sit in the balcony. None of the white hospitals would take you. You could be bleeding to death, and they wouldn't take you in. The jails were segregated. They had no black policemen on the force. There were no black lawyers in town.

Greensboro had a segregated golf course called Nocho Park Golf Course. We had been trying to get the city to fix it up, and they never would do it. There was another course for whites called Gillespie Park Golf Course, and they were always fixing that up. So we asked that we be allowed to play at Gillespie Park Golf Course. As a result, they leased it for one dollar a private group to keep blacks from playing out there.

One afternoon six of us decided to go out and see if we couldn't play at Gillespie. We went out and put our money on the counter and tried to sign the book. The caretaker snatched the book from us and said, "You can't play here." So we said, "Well, we intend to play," and we put seventy-five cents down to play eighteen holes, and proceeded to tee off on Number one tee. About the fifth hole, the pro came out and started cursing us and telling us that this was a private facility. We said, "We know better; the city owns this facility. And since we're taxpayers, we have a right to play out here and enjoy the recreational facilities provided by the city."

He cursed us and threatened us and called us everything under the sun. So I said, "Well, we're out here for a cause." He said, "What damn cause?" I said, "The cause of democracy." He turned red and his lips got blue. I had to keep a club in my hand for protection, because I thought any minute that he would hit me. I didn't intend to hit him, but I wanted to make him think I was going to do something.

He followed us around. I would try to hit the ball down the center, but I was so nervous I was hitting it to the right. And so we left. That night the police came by the house and arrested all of us for trespassing out at Gillespie Park Golf Course.

We went into city court and we got a lawyer. The judge said, "If you agree to plead guilty to trespassing, I will give you a light fine, and we'll forget it." I said, "Oh, no, no. We're not going to do that. We're not guilty. And we're going to take this all the way to the Supreme Court if necessary, because we think the city is wrong." He fined us fifteen dollars and court costs, and we appealed it to the Superior Court. We got in Superior Court and the judge was from down east, and he said, "If you'd come out on my place like you did, I think I would have gotten my shotgun. You're guilty." We had a jury trial, and they had gotten rid of all the blacks on the jury. We found out that two of the members of the jury had played at Gillespie. So we took them out of the jury box and had them take the stand. The management claimed that you had to be a member or the invited guest of a member to play at Gillespie. These two jury members testified that they were not members, nor were they the invited guests of any member. All they did was pay a fee and play out there.

So they found us guilty of trespassing. In the meantime, our lawyers had gotten a declaratory judgment in federal court. Judge Johnson J. Hayes said we had a right to play out there, and the only reason they arrested us was because we were black. He also said that anybody who has to defend this country in an act of war and has to pay taxes, ought to be able to enjoy the recreational facilities provided by the city. As far as he was concerned, the city was still in the saddle. It had this course, and couldn't even show where these other two individuals had paid one dollar for the lease of this course. He ruled that the course must be integrated, and he gave the city a certain date to integrate. Two weeks before integration was to take effect, the clubhouse mysteriously burned down. The fire marshals condemned the whole course because the clubhouse had been burned down. It stayed condemned for seven years.

We appealed the trespassing decision. Our lawyers, unfortunately, left the declaratory judgment out of the trespass case appeal when we went to the State Supreme Court. You have so many days when you make an appeal to get all your evidence in. They forgot and left that out, which was the most important thing in our case. So we were found guilty in the State Supreme Court.

We appealed it to the United States Supreme Court. And in the meantime, we went up to Thurgood Marshall, who was the head of the NAACP Legal Defense and Educational Fund out of New York, and asked Thurgood for some help. Thurgood looked at the record and said, "Your lawyers ought to be the ones to go to jail instead of you, for messing this case up like they have." We had been given an active thirty-day jail sentence at that time. So he said, "I am not going to ruin my win/loss record by taking this case, but I will help you all with your printing expenses." Our expenses were exorbitant, because when you go to the Supreme Court, you have to have so many briefs printed. He said, "You're going to lose this case, because the lawyers have messed it up. Tom Clark [a member of the Supreme Court] is going to vote against you."

We went to the Supreme Court, and my father-in-law argued the case for us. The first thing that Earl Warren, who was the Chief Justice, wanted to know was, "How could the lawyers leave something so important out of the case?" My father-in-law said, "I don't know, but it was left out." Thurgood Marshall was right. We lost by a five-four decision; Tom Clark voted against us. All the justices said if that declaratory judgment had been in the case, we would have won the case unanimously. Chief Justice Earl Warren wrote a very strong dissenting opinion, which said he couldn't understand why any citizen would be denied the use of recreational facilities provided by the city. Governor Hodges commuted our sentences and gave us a fine so we wouldn't have to go to jail. And that ended the golf course case.

Well, we decided that we needed to get political, because at that time we had only 5,500 blacks registered to vote in the city. We found that there were teachers at A&T and Bennett colleges, and at Dudley High School were not registered voters. I went over to Dr. [Samuel] Proctor, president of A&T at that time, and told him, "Dr. Proctor, look at all these people that you have on your faculty who are not even registered voters." He was just amazed, and it made him mad. He sat down and wrote each one of them a letter and told them if they stayed there, they had to become a registered voter.

I went over to Bennett College, where we found Ph.D.s teaching political science, who were not registered voters. And Dr. Player was amazed. She sat down and wrote them a similar letter.

I went to Dudley High School where Dr. Tarpley was the principal. And I said, "Look at all these teachers that we have on the faculty here that are not registered voters." And he was amazed. He sat down and wrote each one of them a letter and told them that they had to become a registered voter.

I became a registrar myself. We went from house to house in certain areas and got blacks to register. We increased the roll of registered black voters from about 5,500 to over 12,000. And then we started writing letters, telling them who were the best people to vote for. We made one of the campaign slogans was that "Do you intend to open up Gillespie Park so that everybody can play there? Otherwise we're not going to vote for you."

So we got rid of all the City Councilmen who had voted to close down the recreational facilities. They not only voted to close Gillespie down, they closed Nocho down. They closed all the swimming pools down. And the City Council said that it was going out of the recreation business rather than integrate. We were fortunate enough to get rid of every one of the Councilmen that had that opinion, and put a new City Council in there. It took us seven years to reopen Gillespie Park as a nine-hole course on December 7, 1955.

That's how I got started in civil rights. The experience I had in the state courts, where the judge knew that these people were lying, and they found us guilty on lies, made me want to devote my life to civil rights. Seeing the solicitor and the judge were in cahoots and laughing infuriated me. And the fact that they deliberately got rid of all the blacks on the jury, so that we didn't have a chance. And so I said, "I'm going to devote my life to civil rights and see if I can improve something in this city."

Greensboro is a very strange city in that [blacks] have to fight for everything that they get here. I mean, they don't give one inch. And you have to picket, demonstrate, take them to the court to get anything done. Other cities around Greensboro—Durham, Raleigh, Winston-Salem and High Point—were opening up their recreational facilities to people of color, whereas Greensboro was closing down everything. They would knock us down, and we'd get back up and continue to fight.

I said, "Well, if you're not going to let us play golf, maybe you'll let us swim." So we sent somebody out to Lindley Park swimming pool, and they immediately closed that down and decided to sell it. The pool was just two years old, and it cost two hundred and fifty thousand dollars to build, and they sold it for about sixty-some thousand. They sold it to someone from out of town. They were not going to zone it so he could make a profit, so he said, "Well, I have no use for it then." Then they sold it to Dr. Taliaferro, who was chairman of the Parks and Recreation Department. And he formed a little group, and he tried to operate it as a private structure. It stayed in business for a couple of years, but he decided to give it back to the city because they couldn't make it. After about seven years, the city decided that it would open it up for everybody.

And we went to the school system and protested that a lot of the black teachers didn't have any equipment to work with. I remember a typing teacher telling me, "I certainly hope some of my students are absent today, because I don't have enough typewriters to go around." Teachers would tell us that they didn't even have crayons or chalk, things like that. So I got my daughter to be one of the plaintiffs along with some of the neighbors in a suit against Greensboro Public Schools to integrate the schools. As soon as the judge ruled that they must be integrated, the school board start fixing up the black schools, painting them, building fences around them and everything. I got threatening messages over the phone, that they were going to kill me if anything happened to their child.

After that, the hospitals came along. I had a patient in my office; the boy's jaw was [swollen]. He had a temperature of a hundred and three. And I called up L. Richardson [the black hospital], and they had no room over there. They had a waiting period of two to three weeks. People were lying in beds in the hallways, they were so crowded. I called Cone and Wesley Long, and they wouldn't take him, because he was black. They had room, though; beds were available.

I called Jack Greenberg, who was head of the NAACP Legal Defense and Educational Fund at that time. I said, "We've got to do something about these hospitals, because you could be dying and they wouldn't take you in [if you are black]." Jack said, "If you can organize the doctors, I will bring a case. What you need to do is find out whether these hospitals were built with federal funds." So I went around and found out that both Wesley Long and Moses Cone [hospitals] had been built partially with federal funds. I said, "We got a good case, Jack."

I contacted black doctors to go along with me. I had a petition, and I wanted to collect fifty dollars from each one so we could pay the lawyer. I said, "I want you to agree to be a plaintiff." Well, the young ones agreed, but some of the old ones wouldn't go with me. All the dentists went along with me. And I got this boy who had come to my office with a swollen jaw and a temperature of a hundred and three to be a plaintiff in the case. We went into Middle District Court and brought suit. We had a lawyer who took the case, but he kept prolonging and prolonging. Finally I decided that maybe he was scared to take this case.

So I called Jack. I said, "I think we might have a scared lawyer on our hands." And Jack said, "I understand." He called Conrad Pearson, who was a NAACP lawyer in Durham, and Conrad came over the next couple of days and filed the case for us. Judge Edward Stanley ruled against us in Middle District Court. He said the hospitals were private, and they had a right to discriminate and decide who they wanted to take and this type of thing.

We appealed the case to the Fourth Circuit Court of Appeals, and Bobby Kennedy, the Attorney General at the time, came in as a friend of the Court. He wrote a brief in our behalf, saying that since taxpayer money had paid for these hospitals to be built, and they should be integrated. We won it on a three-to-two decision in the Fourth Circuit Court of Appeals. The hospitals appealed it to the United States Supreme Court, and the Court would not hear it. So it ended up as a landmark case in that any hospital in the country had to integrate their facilities as well as admit blacks, physicians and dentists, to their staff and take blacks as patients in the hospital. This was probably the most important thing I've ever done in my life, because health means so much to everybody.

I think that the young people should be aware of where we have come in our struggle for civil rights and human dignity.

## David Morehead

The Hayes-Taylor YMCA in the Forties and Fifties was concerned with serving all of the people. It was the hub of the black community; this was the meeting place for people: civic meetings, forums, breakfasts, luncheons, that kind of thing. We developed informal education classes, teaching a lot of people reading, writing and arithmetic. We didn't have a gymnasium or a swimming pool at that time, but we used the city recreational facilities until we were able to get some physical facilities. The YMCA was unique, because we had a dormitory. At that time, African Americans could not get a room in the hotels uptown. On the second floor we had meeting places and a place for meals. Until the YWCA held interracial meetings, this was the only place in Greensboro where blacks and whites could meet together over a meal.. So white political candidates were able to come down and plead for blacks to vote for them. If we had a program that was appealing, they would ask if they could come. Until the YWCA held interracial meetings, this was the only place in Greensboro where blacks and whites could meet together over a meal. The black YWCA was started later; it originated in the old Dudley home that was across from A&T's campus. James B. Dudley, the second president of A&T, was one of the first presidents. Then the YW was able to get a building up on the corner of Lee and Elm; they finally merged, and they became one uptown. But that was during the civil rights in the Sixties. The YMCA started in the basement of the old Carnegie Library. We had a woman's auxiliary at the Y, with a mothers' club and a parenting group, where the parents of the kids we worked with participated in their activities

Some of the older men would serve as counselors to a group of youngsters on Sunday afternoons. They didn't have any funds except the money they would put in the offering. So they finally announced that they were going to try to get a building, and they got it in the paper. Caesar Cone read it, and decided to make a contribution. It was announced in the paper that the black citizens wanted to build a building, and found a piece of property for five thousand dollars. Mr. Cone made a challenge that if African Americans would raise the money, he would make a donation of sixty-five thousand for the building, provided it would be named after two servants that had worked in his household: Mrs. Hayes, who was the cook, and Mr. Taylor, who was the chauffeur and the butler. The African American community raised four thousand five-hundred dollars, so he went on with the donation of sixty-five thousand dollars. That's when the dormitory was added on the second floor, and a meeting room, the lounge and offices and game room were on the first floor, in December 1939. No gymnasium, no swimming pool. The Y hired the first sectary, Thomas Hummins. I came aboard in 1942 or 1943. At that time the Y and a city recreation center on Benbow and Gorrell streets, built with WPA funds, were the only two places where blacks could recreate. The other recreation centers were segregated, which we had to accept, but it was always on our minds. In February the city had a Brotherhood Month, where blacks went to the white First Presbyterian church for joint services. They'd invite the choirs from Bennett and A&T to sing. But when that was over, you'd go back to your respective places.

At the downtown stores, there were white fountains and black fountains. You couldn't stand and eat food or sit and eat food; if you got anything you'd take it out in a bag and eat it in a car or somewhere, but not in there. We were concerned about having to take lunches out of the stores, because it meant that whites felt they were better than blacks. We were also concerned that there was a difference in pay scales and job opportunities. You had blacks working side-by-side with whites and the whites made more money. Although it was a concern, it was also one that, what could you do about it except wish that something better would happen? There were individuals and organizations receptive to integration. Mrs.Frances Herbin, of the American Friends Service Committee, began to have interracial meetings at the Hayes-Taylor YMCA.

But most of the black community leadership would not challenge the status quo. I never shall forget, I had a father and son banquet scheduled from the Y, and I had invited Ezra Charles, the former heavyweight champion of the world to speak. I had secured Murphy Hall, A&T's dining room. Ezra Charles was due to fly into Greensboro at eleven-thirty. That morning it came out in the *Greensboro Daily News* that we were having a father-son banquet, open to whites and blacks. I received a call about seven o'clock from Dr. [Ferdinand D.] Bluford, president of A&T. He said "Mr. Morehead, you won't be able to have a banquet with us tonight." And I said, "Why, Dr. Bluford?" And he said "You have an ad that whites will be able to eat with Negroes. I can't go along with it." I said "Do you know what you are doing to me? The banquet is tonight." He said, "I know that, but you should have thought of that before you got it in the paper. I won't be able to get any money from the General Assembly down in Raleigh if they learn of this." And I said, "I don't see it, Mr. Bluford." He said, "I know you don't; you're not the president of the college."

Because he was on the board of the Hayes-Taylor Y, I felt a lot of pressure from him. In terms of Dr. Bluford's fears that funding might be cut off for A&T, I think that he was overreacting. He could have stood tall and said, "Yes, somebody might try to ridicule me. But I will be able to stand and fight this thing." Bluford did some good things at A&T, like getting the land where the stadium is now. All of that was at one time an army base. When the war was over Bluford was able to get the land for little or nothing, as a donation to the college. Each president has a chapter in the history books, and Bluford's was long.

So now where was I going to have it? We didn't have facilities at Hayes-Taylor large enough to take care of two hundred-fifty people. A&T was the only place. I could have it downtown at the other Y, but I couldn't eat anything down there. They wouldn't even invite me to eat down there and I was on the staff at the other place and we were a branch. Shows you how ridiculous that thing was. So I called the recreation center. And Mr. Levette, who was in charge, said "David, we don't have equipment. You'll have to get the meal catered." So I was able to get the meal prepared downtown at the Central Y. I hauled tables and chairs all day on a truck and in my car, and finally got it set up down there. I got it on the radio and in *The Greensboro Record* that we had moved it from A&T to the Windsor Center. Those are some of the kinds of things that I ran into

I tried to make Hayes-Taylor Y the best Y possible. We had a campaign to add some additional facilities at Hayes-Taylor. We were going to add a gymnasium and a swimming pool. Through the Community Chest [now the United Fund], we were able to raise enough money for the gym and to remodel some parts of the old building. But we didn't have enough for the swimming pool. That's when I made contact with Spencer Love of Burlington Industries. His secretary called me one day and asked me to assist them in hiring two chauffeurs and two cooks for the Love family. About two months later they called and asked me to help them again, which I did.

I wanted to meet Mr. Love, and his administrative assistant, Joe Hamilton, arranged it. He came out of his office, shook my hand, and asked me to come in. Here was a man with sixty-five thousand employees, and here I am with nothing except the Y [laughs]. He said, "I've looked forward in meeting you. What can I do for you?" And I said, "Mr. Love, I think the great thing that you could do for our people is to help us get an indoor swimming pool. It would be a monument that would be there a long time." He asked "What do you think it will cost?" And I said "About a hundred thousand dollars." So he said, "Caesar Cone is the original donor, I'll have to talk to him." So he called me one night about eleven o'clock, and said, "I've got your swimming pool. I got in a bridge game with Caesar, and I told him that I would give fifty thousand if he would give fifty, and he said he would do it." So that's how we got the pool

He did many other things. The City of Greensboro got out of the golf course and the pool business because George Simkins and others went to play golf, and later a black woman wanted to go swimming in Lindley Park pool. The city officials said they would get out of the recreation business if blacks came where whites were going to play with them. So they closed down the golf course and the pool. They also closed down Windsor Center for two summers. So Love and his wife bought it and reopened it. I had two pools that I was operating, the one at Hayes-Taylor and the one down there. I'd operate it every summer with only the swimming fees. He promised me that he would pick up the deficit, and he did. He said, "Don't turn anybody away. If any whites want to come down there they can swim down there."

Mr. Love would give me one day a year. I would pick him up at his office and we would ride out in the country, and he would ask me, "What can I do to help the causes on your side of town?" I had his private phone number at the office that I could call him anytime. I was able to get him to give twenty-five thousand to the Boy Scouts. The[ black] Boy Scouts had an old rundown camp, Camp Carson, out there at Brown Summit that was deplorable. Camp

Greystone, the white Boy Scouts camp, was beautiful. And the white YMCA had a beautiful camp out here that they would go to in the summer. We couldn't carry our kids out there, and yet we were a branch. So we ended up having to use Camp Carson whenever the Boy Scouts was not there. Our kids didn't have a camp. But I started a day camp for them, where they would come in at eight o'clock and bring their lunch, and they would stay with us at the Y until six. We would hike from the Y, out in the field somewhere, eat, and then they would go home in the evening. The next day they would come back. We improvised a lot of things. We couldn't go out to the white camp, so we developed our own things.

Black children were aware that they couldn't go to nice places like the white children. The parents just explained it bluntly to their children: "You know you're not supposed to go to that fountain and drink, because that's for whites. They'd go up to Woolworth to buy something, and a white girl would treat them hateful. After she waited on everybody white, then she'd come ask them, "What do you want?" Like they were trash. Those things stayed with them as they grew up. And it would bother the older people, too. But they looked at the [white] people and said, "We feel sorry for them. They're ignorant, and they don't know any better. This is what they've been taught, so let them go their way with it. If they're that foolish and simple, then we're not going to bug them. We'll do our own thing." But the younger people got tired of going into places asking to be served, and they wouldn't be served.

But there were always some good whites. Caesar Cone, Spencer Love, and the American Friends Service Committee wanted to do something. They knew that racism and segregation were wrong. But they also wanted to be a part of what was going on. But despite his philanthropy to the black community, Spencer Love was like other big manufacturers. He was very much against hiring blacks in good jobs in his mills, and was just as astounded as other mill owners at the request. He wanted to make money and be socially accepted. What was he going to do, come in here and fight against his business associates and social peers? He said to me, "I pay good wages, more than anybody in Irving Park." But had that gotten out, they would have criticized him because, "We aren't paying this kind of money. You're going to mess things up. You're going to have them making all kinds of demands on us."

The city government built a black fire station with twenty-eight black firemen on Gorrell Street, when Waldo Falkener was a member of the City Council. That was the one thing that he was able to get over on this side of town. They couldn't fight the fires uptown, but they could fight them over here. That's how foolish and expensive segregation was.

## Otis L. Hairston, Sr.

In 1954 the state government and local school systems sought to evade public school desegregation by the Pearsall Plan, but some citizens of Greensboro made an effort to get the school board to comply. We've always had a few progressive people in Greensboro, but as a whole, the city was not willing to move in that direction. Ed Hudgins, who was Chairman of the school board, supported superintendent Benjamin L. Smith, and was able to get the board to approve a resolution saying that Greensboro would desegregate that fall. But pressure came from the folk who did not want to see Greensboro move ahead, to force these people to change at a slow pace.

The Pearsall Plan was conceived by Governor [Luther B.] Hodges [and State Senator Pearsall] to find a way to avoid integration. It was designed to make it difficult for black parents to apply for their children to attend white schools. And they were also intimidated by telephone and personal threats on the job. We had a few blacks courageous enough, in spite of this, to do it. In our church we had two families, the McCoy family and the Blair family. The Blair family was unique in that both parents taught in public schools, but they had the courage to apply to send their kids to formerly all-white schools. The McCoy family had to have their telephone number unlisted, because of the calls that they had throughout the night. Families were encouraged by the leaders of the black community, but no pressure, because we felt that this was a dangerous thing, and black leaders and institutions did not pressure them, if they didn't feel comfortable doing it.

After the Supreme Court decision, a few whites and blacks got together to talk and plan and to try to get the climate right for integration. But there was little interaction between the races. Blacks were not employed as skilled laborers during that period; it was a master-servant type of relationship, for the most part

The city government thought it would be useful to have a token number of black officers on the police force. The first two officers, Samuel Penn and Conrad Raiford, had more education than the average policeman at that time.

We have had a black middle class group in Greensboro in what they call the Warnersville area, as far as I can remember. The first black supervisor of schools was a person who owned twenty to twenty-five homes. We had doctors who could be classed as middle class. We had principals of schools, a few who had reached that status of moderate income. You also had one or two lawyers, and some businessmen. The professional blacks were very concerned about the well-being of the other blacks and they became involved in efforts that would upgrade the blacks not on their level, on an educational basis as well as other ways.

Blacks would petition the City Council for something they needed—streetlights, paved streets. Dr. Hampton, the first black member of the City Council, was a very bright and dedicated person who impressed everybody in such a manner that, even folk that were prejudiced had to vote for him for a second term. At his funeral service Mayor George Roach said he had never known a person who did his research on a problem like Dr. Hampton. He was a scholar and a student of city government. That's why I think he led the ticket; it was not that they loved Dr. Hampton, but he was so impressive, that they had to forget about race in his case. The presence of a black on the Council helped a great deal. In petitioning for things that the blacks had not gotten, and this at least disturbed a lot of the members of the Council that did not vote to give them to blacks. In later years, perhaps, they acted more quickly than they would have had Dr. Hampton not brought attention to some things.

The Greensboro Citizens Association controlled the voting of the black community by block voting as the only way that you can develop any power. In 1959 the Citizens Association organized, with Dr. Hobart Jarrett as president. At that time, it was thought that they needed to influence the outcome of the election to find the best candidate who would support black causes. This was not bossism, because the citizens were involved in the decision. The sentiment was that they expressed themselves after listening to people. It was a representative group of black people in Greensboro from all social and economic levels. Those folk knew what others felt. It was a case where people were involved. A list was sent out—not to all of the voters at the time—some of the lists were circulated in the churches and at the polls. Most of the candidates who ran came to the black community to get support. Even fairly strong white candidates were defeated because they could not get the support of the black Citizens Association.

Whites used to call blacks by their first names, but more and more blacks began to demand that they would put a handle on black names. This surprised many whites, but I think that they should not have been shocked, because blacks were becoming more courageous about protesting things that degraded them. I don't believe that you had too much violence between the races. I think that you didn't have that much contact between the races, period. They were not in schools, together, they didn't live in the same communities. Perhaps on the job, occasionally, you'd have some violence.

I think that in one sense it's accurate to say that Greensboro was progressive in getting rid of slum housing on Lee Street during the 1950s, in that it was done. But I'm not too sure whether the motive was really to get rid of slum housing or an opportunity for the folk who were in the construction business to take advantage of building. But, it benefited folk in the black community who were making money, and they had no interest in trying to upgrade the living of people. Unless urban renewal moved in, I doubt whether we would have gotten rid of the slums. I think this is always the case. You need the outside pressure to get folk to make the changes that will upgrade the living standard of people. We don't volunteer to do too many things to help people; it takes outside pressure.

Dr. David Jones, president of Bennett College, was on the school board in 1954, when the Supreme Court decision came down. Being a talented educator, he probably influenced the board to make its resolution supporting public school integration. Dr. Jones retired from the board and Dr. Hampton was appointed to replace him, because the black community said, "We need a person strong enough to succeed Dr. Jones." We talked him into accepting the position to come off of the City Council in order to accept a position on the school board. When Dr. Hampton died, Dr. [George] Evans was appointed in his stead. This was fortuitous, because he could be flexible enough to deal with the blacks, but also deal with the whites.

## Dr. Willa B. Player

When I came to Greensboro, the city was pretty tightly segregated. The women in the black community were having problems with being called by their first names; no blacks were allowed to eat in the restaurants in the department stores downtown, drinking fountains were marked "white" and "colored," and the railroad station had a "white" and "colored" waiting room. But, there was persons in the white power structure with whom the president of Bennett College, Dr. David B. Jones, had good rapport, so that we never had to go in and out of Greensboro in segregated railroad cars. We always rode on Pullmans, although when we got in the dining area of the Pullman car, we had to wait until everyone else was served. Later on, they put up curtains and had a segregated section. The buses were segregated; we had to ride in the back of the buses. It was a pretty segregated situation.

I think that it was erroneous to think of Greensboro as a liberal city. It did just enough to appear to the outside world to be less segregated than other cities in North Carolina. For instance, I was the first person in Greensboro to receive an award from the National Conference of Christians and Jews, but it remained pretty conservative for a good while. It was not until the 1950s that we began to see Greensboro branching out as a more liberal city. I think that it came about because there were people in the black community who were courageous and upstanding people. There were people in the professions and ministers who really had to work with the city fathers at getting some of the situations changed in Greensboro. They were backed up largely by the faculties at Bennett and A&T Colleges. David D. Jones was a particularly forthright person, who just dared to do a number of things that were unheard of in the community.

One instance of his character was when Mrs. [Franklin] Roosevelt was invited to speak on the campus. She was introduced to Dr. Jones by Mary McCloud Bethune, who was president of Bethune-Cookman College, in Daytona Beach, Florida. At that time, this was so unusual that Dr. Jones put in the newspaper that the school children were invited to attend. The school children of the white schools wanted to come to Bennett campus to see and hear Mrs. Roosevelt. There was a great deal of pressure put on Dr. Jones to cancel this and to put a notice in the newspaper correcting this invitation, saying that it was only extended to the black school children. He refused to do this, and the program went on as scheduled, and some white school children came.

Bennett College was able to resist pressures to conform to the prevailing practices in race relations because it was a Methodist School, and it was supported by the northern church. There were a number of white women on the Board of Trustees of the college who helped by bringing meetings to the campus of people from all over the country, so that it could never be said that the campus was isolated from exposure to other races and groups.

I do not know of any significant communication between the white power structure and the black community before I got into the activities of the sit-ins. I think that Dr. Hobart Jarrett, head of the Humanities Division, was a thoughtful, forthright, level-headed person in his dealing with the white community in Greensboro. He was always able to articulate the reasons for activities that took place in the community, and was highly respected. And, there were some outstanding white people who sat on the board of trustees, like Mrs. Julius W. Cone. Some members of the Cone family were behind the YMCA effort in Greensboro, the Burlington Industries people, [Spencer Love] and the Babcock Foundation people, who had the lines of communication between the black and white communities.

There was a differential in the salaries of the teachers, in which the black teachers were not making as much as the white teachers. There was an effort in the public school community to get black teachers to go north to universities to get masters degrees, which they did in large numbers. It was on the basis of this kind of strength that they eventually got equal salaries with the white teachers. The large number of public school and college teachers, combined with the ministers, dentists and doctors accounted for a fairly solid black middle class in Greensboro. Unlike other cities in the South, a number of them had white clients. However, there was not a strong political climate in the black community; I don't think there were many registered black voters in Greensboro. I know at one time Bennett College conducted a voter registration drive after the 1957 Civil Rights Act, where numbers of people were registered to vote. It was at this time that people like Dr. William Hampton, who was a physician at that time, was very much on the political scene. He was the first black councilmen in the city of Greensboro.

At the time of the Supreme Court decision of 1954, there were women of the black community who were very valiant in supporting desegregation by doing a great deal of volunteer work to help the segregation effort. They had carpools to carry black children integrating white schools [Gillespie and Greensboro Senior High School]. I thought that Greensboro reacted pretty positively, in that there was not the violence connected with school desegregation that existed in other communities. There was a behind-the-scenes group that kept some things from happening that would have happened under ordinary circumstances. It was just a group of five or six people in Greensboro that were adamant on toeing the mark. I think that there was a contradiction in the school board's announcement and the delay in desegregation, but I don't know who was actually responsible for slowing the pace. I doubt that the white churches or the newspapers were helpful at all in urging desegregation. I don't think that the newspapers were in the forefront of trying to promote desegregation. In fact, the press was pretty conservative.

Greensboro was a rather ambivalent community. I think that it was a city that wanted to be known for being liberal on one hand, and cautious on the other, in terms of how far they really wanted to go. I don't think that everything was within the frame of reference of "moderation," but more subtly trying to hold back. There were, or course, exceptions to this attitude. I think that Mrs Julius Cone, Mrs. Spencer Love and the president of Duke University and head of the Babcock Foundation were sincere. I think there were people in the community who were sincerely trying to help their community to rise.

This was facilitated by certain leaders in the black community. I think there was great respect for Dr. Hampton, and a feeling that he would be poised enough in a difficult situation, to be able to influence the black community. I think that he was elected because the time had come for the Greensboro community to demonstrate that it had a better face than some people were saying that it did have. I think that both Dr. Hampton and Dr. Jones worked hard and courageously at it. I don't think that Dr. Jones was ever anybody to do anything in the community other than what he thought was right, and he had the courage to do that, and I think that the community would listen to Dr. Jones and Dr. Hampton, when they wouldn't listen to anyone else in the community. I don't think those men would have been elected if they had been looked upon as playing an "accommodation" role by the white power structure.

Dr. [Edwin] Edmonds was a sociology teacher at Bennett College. I think there was a cross burned on his lawn once for his activism in civil rights. But I don't believe that he left Greensboro because he was forced to leave, or that he left under tension. He was a scholar and he was impatient for social change, and I think that he didn't see himself as being able to bring that about in the Greensboro community, so he decided to leave it. Dr. Julius Douglas, minister of the Presbyterian Church, Dr. W.L.T. Miller, a dentist in Greensboro and Mr. Mateena were leaders of the black community during the 1940s and

1950s. To my mind, Dr. Tarpley was a moderate; I don't think that he was one of the people who were out in front.

One incident that exemplified the hesitant attitude of the black community on activism was when Dr. Martin Luther King, Jr., was invited to make a speech in Greensboro in 1958 by members of the black community, but one institution after another denied him a forum. He had been invited to speak at the Dudley High School, and then the message came through the school administrative offices that he couldn't speak there. So the individuals that had invited him came to the Bennett College administration to request that he be allowed to use our auditorium. I thought that Dr. King was a person who had achieved such greatness, and who was so courageous, and he had a message for American young people, that he had to be heard. He was a man of stature and was so unusual in his fervor, and yet in his ability to articulate very honestly what that civil rights struggle was all about, that there wasn't any harm that could come from presenting him on the campus. He was, I thought, a very warm, friendly person, who had a deep commitment, and a deep concern, that he would have an opportunity to fulfill that commitment.

Therefore, I said that Dr. King could use our auditorium. However, it wasn't large enough, so they said, "What shall we do?" I said, "We will allow Dr. King to speak; he has to speak, so he can speak in the Chapel." So, we set up the assembly room loudspeakers in all the rest of the building and the students were encouraged to go to the buildings as far as possible, except that the seniors were to come to the auditorium. Loudspeakers were put up in the Science Building and the Library. I asked the city to provide a police guard to surround the campus to protect the students from any possible threat, and Dr. King spoke.

## Hobart Jarrett

There was a subtle racism in Greensboro, under the guise of "moderate" behavior to maintain the white-dominated status quo. I think that the racism was there. I remember once that there was a movement to get black people to stay away from the segregated movies. There was one art movie in the city near W.C. [Victory Theater; later the Cinema Theater], and there was a white faculty member at my college who took a black faculty woman along with his wife to this art movie, and I remember the consternation that caused, but there was no publicity about it. I remember that a black man, who at one time was responsible for distributing the *Greensboro Daily News* or *The Greensboro Record* in the Negro community, he was over the boys who delivered the paper, was told that Woman's College, Guilford College, and Greensboro College students bought the newspaper, and that Bennett and A&T students didn't buy the newspaper. The spokesman for the newspaper did not understand that the Woman's College students were pictured in the newspaper, and he thought that the Bennett students were not as interested in the news as these other people, and it had to be pointed out to him that these are well-educated young women.

I remember many incidents like that. I myself went to a specialist on occasion. I sat in his waiting room, and immediately the nurse came and escorted me back to a small, very neat room, and said: "This is the colored waiting room. You will be comfortable here." I told her that I was quite comfortable right where I was, and I had to come back to the specialist on more than one occasion. Every time that I got there I was immediately taken into the examining office. But the white community was kind when Bennett College was raising money, and I worked in the drive with the late president, David Jones, to collect money. I was the person who collected money from the white people. While this was a wonderful contribution that was being made to our college by the city, at the same time, it was inconsistent with the city's segregated practices. Sometimes it was quite pronounced, and sometimes it was an undercurrent that you sensed rather than one that you could actually put your finger on. For instance, blacks could come into the bus station without the indignity of having to go to a particular spot. The Bennett girls began to sit in the white waiting room sometime in this particular period. This kind of experience, I could mention many times. I never went to a movie, for example, because I could not bring myself to subscribe myself to the segregation then in force. For me, it was self-selected segregation for me to go and sit in a seat that set me apart from everyone else.

There was a legacy of a rising level of black protest in Greensboro during the 1940s and 1950s. Such things as what was happening in the railroad station would be evidence that people were kicking their heels a bit. Bennett girls refused to wait in the Negro waiting room, and they waited in the white waiting room without incident. When we bought tickets to get on the train, we were supposed to go to a particular window, and we refused to go to that window, and sometimes the clerk would be a little nasty about it, but by being calm and standing up for what we believed, we were able to do this many times. People would try occasionally to sit in the bus in the places where they were not supposed to sit. I remember that black people periodically stopped riding buses to protest segregated custom. There was never any concentrated drive, but this was the day-to-day reaction.

There was a fairly consistent determination of black people in Greensboro to change things. William Hampton's election was a black revolutionary activity. I had just come to Bennett College at the time, and the Greensboro Citizens Association had just been established, and its one purpose was to campaign, to organize, to articulate the demands that this man would have a fair shake. As a result of the forcefulness of the Negro people, he was elected. Of course, he would not have been elected without white votes, but the community of Greensboro was of such a nature that cooperation could be counted on in many instances. Nevertheless, the subtle effect of race relations or prejudice, was still right there.

The success of the Citizens Association was due to the idea of bloc voting. The only way we knew that we could be effective in getting candidates that we wanted in office was to line up the vote. This we did unabashedly. Newspapers in Charlotte were criticizing the Greensboro Citizens Association for the stand that it was taking, but this was tommyrot. It was a small political machine, but it was well-oiled, and we did whatever we had to do. I was never a member of a political party in an executive position. I became involved in Greensboro politics when I discovered that there was a black person who was running for City Council. It turned out that I had already met Dr. Hampton, and he was a fine person, a member of the Greensboro Men's Club, which I eventually became a member of, and from that time on, I was associated with people with a great deal of savvy like John Leary, who was principal of a junior high school. We were all quite politically minded. The Hampton situation drew me in, and I was amazed that in the South in the late 1940s that there was the opportunity for this kind of political move. Hampton was a good man. I would not have been amazed if Hampton had been someone whom I could have with integrity supported, and all of our decisions were made like that. We had no personal vendettas.

The Greensboro Citizens Association, once the election over, did not disband. We became a political force, and I am very proud of that fact. When people in Greensboro were running for City Council, white people in Greensboro came to us for our endorsement; they asked us for the opportunity to speak to our group. In some cases we granted them the opportunity. We were visited by Terry Sanford's forces, and we heartily endorsed Sanford. I recall that we met in the Presbyterian Church one evening about fourteen of us, to talk with representatives of Sanford, and in the course of the conversation it turned out that this man had no idea that black people in Greensboro were members of the NAACP; he thought that the NAACP was something radical and communistic. We assured him that we had been long-term members of the NAACP, and this surprised him.

Whenever there was an election we were accused of bloc voting, and the accusation was completely correct. The only way that we could be effective was to organize ourselves, and this was our way of protesting. We continued to work politically until the day that I left in the mid-Sixties. I was happy upon leaving, to know that Attorney Henry E. Frye was my successor as president of that organization.

## Ezell A. Blair, Sr.

In the late 1950s race relations were very cordial in one sense: it was going along with the old status quo of many years. It wasn't that we particularly liked the situation, but we had learned to live with it to survive.

One of the things that really got close to me was a Christmas parade downtown in Greensboro. My youngest daughter and I happened to be on Greene Street in front of the Gate City Savings & Loan Building. Mr. Jack Stevens, who was director of Gate City Savings & Loan, and some of the staff knocked on the window and asked us to come on inside to see the parade. It was so cold. And we did. Shortly after the parade passed, we went to Woolworth to get some hot chocolate. We went to the counter and the supervisor, Mrs. Rachel Holt, kept one of my ICT students from serving us. But the girl served us anyway. She said, "We got a special counter for you up here." I said, "You don't have a special counter for me." This didn't sit too well with Mrs. Holt, so she went upstairs to get the manager. I believe his name was [C. L.]Harris. He emphasized to me that he was going to build a place in Southeast Shopping Center on Asheboro Street. They were going to put a F. W. Woolworth down here. I asked him not to do it if he wasn't going to fully integrate it, because we were not going to participate. I also told him that I was very comfortable where I was sitting at that time, my daughter and me, and that I would not move from there. So I ate my pie, and my daughter drank her cocoa. Then we left.

When the white power structure in Greensboro said that it was a moderate city in terms of race relations, I think they were overlooking a lot of things. And I think it bore on their conscience that they were wrong to make a statement like that, because there's no way in the world a human being could grow up in a society like Greensboro at that time and think that everything was all right. They just went along with the status quo, what they thought was the law at that time.

I think interaction between the races in Greensboro could be positive on an individual basis, or where the races lived in close proximity. Blacks in the Warnersville community had a close rapport with the white community in Glenwood. I know old families in the Glenwood community—the Wagoners on Florida Street, the Teagues on Aycock Street, the Melvins, who used to run Melvin Coal Company, the Kimbreys on Dollard Street—we were close together. The McGibleys, a black family, worked for the late Francis Brooks's father; he was the mill man there. The Eddinger Lumber Company, which is a Jewish family, had the Kimbreys work for them. And they did things together; It was a cooperative thing; just like a barn-raising.

But I don't know of any attempt to desegregate Greensboro prior to the Woolworth sit-ins on February 1, 1960. I think they accepted the status quo.

And I think that the NAACP at that time was keeping a very low profile, and they just didn't push it too much. The public library, the airport, the bus station may have had black employees by 1960. I know the police department did, because that happened during World War II, or a little bit prior to that. I know some of the officers during that time, some of the first ones employed. But that did not mean that the black community felt that there had really been major steps to integrating society in Greensboro. For example, the airport didn't have anyone in first-class jobs there. They might have been custodial workers, but not in any responsible position at the airport at that time. But by the time that my son [Ezell A. Blair, Jr.] was born in 1941, on the eve of World War II, it was a time for economic advantages in the black homes. We were beginning to make incomes where we could go and buy from the best stores downtown, like Vanstory's, Younts-Deboe, Belk's, Meyers, and Ellis-Stone. Blacks had a segregated place to drink water from and we didn't have bathroom facilities in many stores at all. I think that because economic conditions were getting better, and the fact that we had one of the best high schools in the state, Dudley High School, it was a good time to press for the things that we wanted.

*A key factor in the ability to integrate financial, social and educational institutions in Greensboro was the willingness of the city at large to accept a trend against entrenched Southern mores. As a large city in the Upper South, Greensboro had a reasonably good opportunity to realize this ambition. Crucial to the success of this effort was effective communication between the races and the perception of the black community by whites. At times this perception was keen and facilitated greater interracial cooperation; at others it was naive and counter-productive. But a small group of dedicated moderate-to-liberal whites in the educational and business sector risked social ostracism and financial ruin to create a positive atmosphere to enhance such communication. It was a slow, awkward process requiring patience with the incremental progress, often frustrating to the black community and its white allies. Each seemingly insignificant advance in the progress of this process carried with it the specter of retrenchment and failure.*

## Joseph Asher

I came to Greensboro in 1958 from a congregation in Tuscaloosa, Alabama, where I became involved in the integration fight at the University of Alabama with the first black student, Autherine Lucy. I succeeded Rabbi Fred Rypins, who was rabbi here for over thirty-five years. I was born in Germany and lived there until 1938, when I became a refugee from Nazi oppression. And it was precisely because of my own background, as a victim of the restraint on my own civil rights, that I became active in the civil rights struggle. I not only could not stay away from the Movement, but sought every opportunity to involve myself in it. This attitude was typical of many Jews, particularly rabbis, in the South. Many of them have been in the forefront of the Civil Rights Movement. Not every Jewish community in the South supported its rabbi in this effort, but my own congregation was most forthcoming. I hoped that I had earned the trust and respect of my congregation, so that when I did involve myself in the Movement, while some individuals were perhaps embarrassed by my involvement, the leadership in the congregation supported me, and that was a part of the tradition of the congregation. My predecessor, Fred Rypins, was also a man devoted to human rights. He made it very clear that he was a non-discriminatory person, and had association with the black clergy here in the city. So when I came, the congregation had already been primed for this situation. Rabbi Rypins had laid the foundation for it. I made it very clear to my congregation that I could not stay away from this, because I had been a victim myself. Not to the same degree, of course.

I preached on civil rights from the pulpit, and in my relationship with several of my colleagues within the ministerial association at the time; it was called the Ministerial Fellowship. I remember that we used to have prayer meetings, but I was not satisfied at leaving it at that. Initially, it was not integrated. Gradually one or two or three of the black ministers came into it. One clergyman who was most supportive of this was Monsignor Dolan. The Catholic church was committed to this. He had the support of his hierarchy, and so whenever the black clergy wanted to have a white clergyman to participate in any of these things, it was Monsignor Dolan and I that the black clergy was more than eager to call upon. And they called upon us quite frequently.

Also, there were many of the leaders in the community. I remember the chairman of the Board of Education at the time of the 1954 Supreme Court decision, Ed Hudgins, wanted to comply. In the beginning it was tokenism, to be sure, but it was compliance. The City of Greensboro did not want to say, "We're going to be among the Rejectionists. We will comply." In my own little way, I tried to encourage the desegregation of the public schools in Greensboro. There was an examination in my confirmation class at the end of the year. These were kids in the tenth grade, and that particular year, when the controversy over integration became intense, I said, "There will be no examination this year for confirmation class. The only test for confirmation will be that when these young black children come to the school, at lunchtime, invite a youngster to sit at a table with you. That will be the test. If you don't do this, then I won't confirm you." I told my confirmation class when the black student [Josephine Boyd] came to Greensboro Senior High, I said, "If I hear that you have taunted her, you will not participate in confirmation, I will not have it." After I told them about my own experience in Germany, I think that they were persuaded to be more tolerant.

I must say that my congregation was very exceptional. You had the top leadership in the city who were members of my congregation, prominent people in the community, like Herbert Falk and Stanley Frank, the Cones—Ben Cone and the younger Cones, in particular. These people were very supportive of me, and because they were supportive, the congregation didn't wish to rock that particular boat, either. They advised me, sometimes with great perspicacity, to tread a little more softly than I would perhaps otherwise have done. But they supported me; so much so that we even had a black family as a member of our congregation, which in those days was unheard of, in any church in Greensboro. The man was a professor at A&T College and his wife was a librarian. They are still members of the congregation, and their children come to Sunday school, and there was not a single person in the congregation who said, "This cannot be." I was very proud of that when the man's membership came up before the board of directors. When this man's name came up, one member of the board asked, "Is this the black professor?" The president of the board said, "That is not a question that is appropriate for this board. The question should be: 'Is the man Jewish or is he not Jewish?' " and the persons who asked the question apologized for the record. That night I was probably the proudest rabbi in America at that time. Don't forget, that was a period of great tension.

I don't think anyone among the clergy of Greensboro was overtly critical of me. I think that they were all supportive, but in a quiet kind of a way. I don't think they were quite willing to go out on a limb; some of them much to their own embarrassment. They would have done it, but either their congregations were not as supportive as my congregation was of me. I don't think there was a single clergyman that I know that was opposed to reaching out to the black community, but there was a difference in being opposed to my being an activist. I was told by several white clergymen, "It's all very well for you to urge the integration of our churches. How many blacks are you going to get in your church?" They misread everything. I am not claiming any particular insight on this. I am saying that because of my own personal experience, although it was on a different level, I figured, one can sin in a situation like that. The reason why the Jews lost in Germany was not because the Nazis were so strong or the Jews were that weak. The reason why this happened was because the vast majority of citizens didn't say anything; they stood there silently.

I spoke to a number of people in positions of leadership in the Jewish community. I said to them, "Isn't it time for you to be up front and integrate your business?" I achieved only a limited success, because they were also bound by the mores of the time. They were all, perhaps sympathetic, but they were not quite willing to go out on a limb. There weren't that many people that went out on a limb; there were some people, and of course, you had a very open administration in the state. You had men like Luther Hodges and Terry Sanford, who were in principle committed to civil rights. But the rank-and-file had to make a living here, and there were difficulties; there was no question about it. But the very fact that the sit-in movement started here was because there was a fertile ground for it. They knew that there wasn't going to be any serious violence. The reason for that was that the people were by and large reasonably forthcoming to integration. They weren't ready to say, "Now we're going to uproot this whole town and do it this way," but on the other hand, they weren't going to condone violence. I've always been fascinated by this community. It's a very sophisticated community. You had people like McNeill Smith, Ed Hudgins and William Snider; these are sophisticated men, and men who wielded considerable political power in the community, and there was no doubt where they stood.

At the time of the question as to whether or not to integrate the hospitals, there was a black hospital, L. Richardson. I spoke to people at Moses Cone Hospital—again, demonstrating the Jewish presence in the community. The black community was at odds over whether integration of the hospitals would mean the closing of the traditional black hospital due to the number of black patients going to the white hospitals. On the one hand, they wanted to integrate Moses Cone Hospital, and on the other hand they didn't want to give up L. Richardson Hospital. So the black community didn't have a uniform opinion on the issue, except that they resented the fact that black patients could not get admitted to Moses Cone Hospital. They were caught between a rock and a hard place. On the other hand, they didn't want to have patients in need of medical attention restricted to an exclusively black hospital. I wanted blacks to be admitted to Moses Cone Hospital, because I wanted to be proud that such a highly-visible Jewish presence in Greensboro would be responsive to the rights of black citizens. In contrast to other cities in the state, there were more Jewish professionals here than any other city in North Carolina, and they have overwhelmingly supported the aspirations of Greensboro's black citizens. The Jewish community did not say, "This is none of our business."

The Jews may not have been wholeheartedly in the forefront of the Civil Rights Movement, and I am not saying that every member or many in the congregation at Temple Emanuel would have said, "All right, I'll be more assertive with regard to civil rights, but I don't think there was a Jewish person of any consequence in this city who would say, "Let's keep the blacks down." I don't think that there was that kind of racial prejudice in the Jewish community in Greensboro.

## Warren Ashby

I think there were certain groups in the 1950s, and even farther back, which came out of a natural development in sensitivity toward civil rights. First, the YWCA, which I suppose more than any other group has a history of interracial activity and provided the only place in the late Forties and Fifties where blacks and whites could meet, certainly over a meal. In addition, I think that, particularly because of certain persons, the American Friends Service Committee should be mentioned. Sometime in the late Forties the headquarters of the Southeastern Region moved onto the campus of Woman's College [now the University of North Carolina at Greensboro]. There were other groups that were antecedents to the Greensboro Fellowship. There was the Fellowship of Southern Churchmen in the early Fifties that met irregularly in town. It went back in the South to the Thirties. It was a liberal interracial, explicitly non-Communist organization. Many people considered it radical, but I doubt there was any suspicion of Communist sympathies of this organization. The founders had some bitter experiences with Communists in other organizations, and they wanted to be explicit that members couldn't hold to the principles that they maintained, and at the same time be Communists.

The YWCA suffered for its liberal attitude toward interracial meetings in Greensboro. It faced the loss of income and came under pressure from the community when it wanted to hire a black secretary. Also, it agreed to let the integrated Fellowship of Southern Churchmen meet there. My guess was that there was no real radical stance being taken in the community by anyone, and they were not so much taking a stance in terms of social community action at that time, but its position was very clear, I thought. The same may be said for the Southern Churchmen. My memory was that just the bridging of the racial gap was itself an issue for them.

When the Supreme Court made its decision in 1954, I don't know if any stand was taken. Indeed, in advance of the Supreme Court decision, it was through the Fellowship that the superintendent of the school board, Ben L. Smith, was persuaded to have his school board to meet with George Mitchell, the Executive Secretary of the Southern Regional Council, who was quite familiar with legal processes and knew that the decision was coming. In advance of that, he met with the school board and told them to be sure to be prepared for it. While this was just one minor event, I would suppose that this meeting and the Fellowship's arranging for that meeting, was a minor factor in the decision that the school board made on May 17, 1954. So, rather than being activist in specific areas, its role was to facilitate communication between various segments of the community. This had been done earlier on a South-wide basis in the desegregation of transportation when the first Freedom Ride [Journey of Reconciliation] occurred in North Carolina in the late Forties. It was contacted about that, although it was not a sponsor.

There was clearly a certain amount of both physical and financial risk to church officials or members of educational institutions for being active in civil rights. Sometimes it was easily identifiable, as in the case of Ben Smith, who experienced intense social criticism, cross-burnings on his lawn, and telephoned threats. And I could mention other persons for whom there was real punishment. In other words, things happened, but they happened quietly, so that people didn't know about them. I know of one person who was dismissed by a church group. A young woman, Jo Lee Fritz, the Director of the Wesley Foundation at the Woman's College, was a member of the NAACP in the early to mid-fifties. There were fascinating problems in that. Jo Lee was a wonderful young woman who aggressively took stands. I think that she was also seeing a Negro friend in her apartment, but it was mainly her relationship with the NAACP and her active membership that caused persons on the board of the Wesley Foundation to ask for her resignation. One of the key people in this was Ed Zane, a member of the West Market Street Methodist Church, where the Wesley Foundation was located. The Foundation felt that she had just gone too far in terms of what she had done. I want there to be no doubt about his integrity. Subsequently, he was very important in easing the transition to integration of the lunch counters in Greensboro, but there was no doubt in that case that he was one of the key people in the Fritz situation. He was not alone in that, of course.

The higher educational institutions in Greensboro approached the issue of interracial communication forthrightly. The Woman's College faculty and student body took a very bold moral stand regarding integration at that time. The faculty passed a resolution which got a lot of publicity, advocating that the University should admit students solely on the basis of their credentials, regardless of race or creed or ethnic background. Interestingly, the University of North Carolina at Chapel Hill and the North Carolina State University faculties refused to pass such a resolution. The W.C. faculty in the early and later Fifties was predominantly female, and they did not want to take a public stand on the issue of integrating the College. But once the issue was brought to their attention, they refused to back down. Long before any other branch of the University was willing to do it, W.C. voted overwhelmingly that the University should be open to anyone. The Student Government unanimously adopted this resolution.

At some point in the early Fifties, a faculty fellowship was formed of the faculties of Greensboro College, A&T College, Bennett College and Guilford College, and it met slightly into the Sixties; it was organized at W.C., with persons coming over from the other campuses. It was a small group that would meet monthly during the academic year. The main purpose was simply to open communication between people; it was not primarily to address social issues, although there were times that it did. Paul Green talked to the group about 1954-55, when the State was having a reaction to the Supreme Court decision. He came and talked about the Pearsall Plan, and when he talked, there were well over 100 people that attended. Through that kind of contact, a fairly large number of the faculty of the individual units, got to know each other and the white faculty certainly knew where the black faculty stood in terms of the desegregation of public facilities and economic opportunities.

There was an interracial student group that went back to the Twenties. It began in Southern places where there were different white and Negro colleges. That was not a social action group; but it lasted through the years here in Greensboro. Raymond Smith of Greensboro College was a key person during the years on that, and it was explicitly to build bridges between white and Negro students. I think that it lasted longer in Greensboro than about any other community in the South, well into the Sixties. It was known as "College Interracial." These organizations were antecedents to the Greensboro Community Fellowship, and some others developed after Anne Queen came to Greensboro in 1950, as Secretary of the Friends Service Committee College Program. There began a regular weekly luncheon meeting, mainly of W.C., Guilford, A&T and Bennett faculty members. This was always a very small group—twelve or fifteen people would go down to the AFSC with a bag lunch. All of these things made it natural for the Greensboro Community Fellowship to emerge.

Tart Bell, who was Executive Secretary of the AFSC called some people and said, "Let's get some people together and talk about the YWCA." The first time that they got together, there were a large number of establishment people there, persons who were concerned about what was taking place. Certain steps were made to open communications with the mayor, and with the black leadership, who were informally meeting at A&T at the time. Out of that, John Taylor [owner of the Greensboro Holiday Inn] and his wife Betty were very much involved in the YWCA. Because of them, the Holiday Inn was among the first businesses to desegregate.

It was a bold thing for John to do. Desegregation was early at that Holiday Inn, and I have no doubt that they suffered from that. After things cooled down, there were some persons who said, "Let's keep meeting." And at that time, most of the establishment people tended to drop off—the businessmen, newspaper editors, and certain of the clergymen of the leading churches. Father Dolan was active very early in the group, as was Julian Douglas, and Rabbi Rypins of Temple Emanuel. I would not say that any of those took leadership in the early days of the Greensboro Fellowship, but I would say they were certainly active and always there. After the school desegregation issue declined, John Taylor picked up chairing a meeting from Tart Bell. McNeill Smith was another prominent member of that group.

In the early Fifties Marc Friedlander and I started the "Conversation Club."

It was all white for a few years, but in the late Fifties a few Negroes were invited to become members. I got people like Mac Smith, William Snider and Ed Hudgins together to meet with some of the black leaders at the time; this was at a time when most of the white political leadership had little contact with the black leadership. We started meeting at the YWCA because some of the people wanted to meet interracially, and the YWCA already had a policy of interracial meetings; it was the only place that we could go. We could make arrangements at some of the local churches, but that was a great nuisance. I made it a point to go see some people in both the white and black communities; I had been close to Bennett College, largely through Dr. David Jones. He used to invite me to speak to the students and faculty once a year, and I got to know Willa Player then, too. Part of my main reason for talking to those persons was the feeling that they were isoated, and they really didn't know what other people, literally, on the other side of the tracks, were thinking. I also spoke with other people in the black community, like Vance Chavis, George Evans, Henry and Shirley Frye, Joe Shaw, Leonard Robinson, Hobart Jarrett, and a number of others at Bennett. It was a very pleasant and wonderful relationship from my side, but I can look back now and see that we didn't push things hard enough.

The Faculty Fellowship was another interracial group that met on a regular basis in the Fifties. The smaller the group, the more directly that we talked about issues, the more frank we could be. This meant that the larger the group, such as the Service Committee on Tuesday for lunch, many times the conversation was just chit-chat. But at other times, they had real complaints about racial policies of the City of Greensboro and what was going on. From these discussions I became aware of the attitudes of the black community to the white power structure. Very early, it was pointed out to me by black members that they viewed Greensboro as a "nice-nasty" town and when they would say "nasty" any white person would know that it was a lot "nastier" than it was "nice" for them. For instance, the housing situation in the early 1950s was unbelievable. Most of East Market Street just beyond the railroad bridge, where the black community began, was in absolutely deplorable condition, and the only way to make that area decent was to bulldoze the dwellings down. Of course, this forced the people out to fend for themselves somewhere, which did not overly concern the city officials. When you think back, you wonder how Greensboro's black citizens could be as patient as they were with all of us.

We had a certain strategy with what we tried to say to area businessmen. First, we hoped that the owners of local businesses would say that they were ready to desegregate, but we knew that not many would be ready for that. So the second strategy was, "Would you be willing to desegregate if other restaurants would desegregate?" I don't know that there was any success from that at all, except as a softening up process with the theaters, restaurants and hotels. The Fellowship was involved in the successful campaign to get the separate signs at water fountains removed very early. I remember that some person went to the Sears & Roebuck management; some of the most obvious separate water fountains were in the downtown store. But they did it. About the same time, the Fellowship would also make contact with certain flash points of difficulties. When the first black student who went to Greensboro Senior High School in 1957 [Josephine Boyd], the Fellowship of Southern Churchmen tried to make some sort of contact with the school board to ease the situation, but it didn't accomplish much.

Vance Chavis was involved; he was a school principal and he thought other people ought to communicate with her family. And the Franklin Parkers were involved. Franklin Parker's daughter became a friend of that female student. The Parkers attended the regular meetings of the Fellowship of Southern Churchmen—they would have done it on their own—but I think that what happens in groups like that, you reinforce one another's conscience. Kay Troxler was very active in the Greensboro Community Fellowship; she got involved in school desegregtion matters. I was involved in it, but nothing like as active as she was. And because of her, the Greensboro Community Fellowship became involved in tutoring black students. This was designed to ensure that the black students in white schools could keep up with their studies, because of the intense emotional pressure that they were under. If you are going to do it, you needed to have friends that were going to receive them, but they also needed to receive support to do as good work as they could possibly do. Looking back on the Fellowship, the main contribution that it made was not so much the social activism—there were always persons who were engaging in that, but nobody quite knew how to do it, and what steps to take. The main effort was to keep lines of communication open between whites and the blacks.

I wouldn't say that the black leadership deferred to the white liberal leadership in the Fellowship. I think from the position of white persons there had been real cooperation and understanding. But whites never really knew, except occasionally, how strongly the blacks felt, how much or, how long they had been hurting, in ways that you could only experience second-and-third hand. If there was any kind of communication and reception, the blacks were much more intelligent and responsive than the whites were. I am sure that there was some suspicion on the part of the black leaders as to the motivation of even sympathetic whites, whether or not they were really concerned that the goals of the black community were realized. But I am not surprised; I would say that constituted the mentality of almost all of them.

There were no really influential businessmen in the Greensboro Fellowship. John Taylor was a wealthy businessman, but John was certainly not "in the know." Ed Lowenstein [local architect] was "in." Ed was married to a Cone, and what his relationship to the Cones was, I have no idea. But Ed was always supportive of civil rights, and he must have communicated the genuine aspirations of the black community to the Cones. He understood that what the blacks were demanding was equality, and he was absolutely sympathetic.

It is my clear impression that the white power structure and business community refused to acknowledge the real demands of the black community. There was no telling what they could understand, but the signals were there. I think that the editors of the newspapers in town have always been ignorant of that, too. How much Bill Snider [editor of the *Greensboro Daily News*] had understood of all of this. The white power structure and business community operated from certain preconceptions of presuming to know what the black community wanted, without really knowing what it wanted. And almost always there is some side issue that can justify any of us from seeing the real issue.

There was something really missed in all of this: Going way back, these individuals had been addressing these issues over the years, not in a frontal attack upon segregation, but in the sense that they knew that it was coming. They just didn't know when or how. The people "in the know" saw it in the Thirties, when the NAACP started taking its cases to the courts; and I think there were people who wanted that. Most people were not even aware that segregation existed. That may seem a strange thing to say; I think they knew that it was there, but it was never a moral issue for them. They didn't know how to bring it about, and were caught at times between various forces.

# Helen Ashby

Warren and I came to Greensboro in 1949 from Chapel Hill, when he came to W.C. to teach in the philosophy department. There was little that I observed in race relations intercultural or intereducational things at all. I had made it a rule that I would not join anything that wasn't interracial. Anything except the church. I found the YWCA, and I had a lot of experience with the YWCA before that. In 1947 the national YWCA had vowed to become completely interracial.

So immediately on coming to Greensboro, I got on the Y board, and I soon was elected president. The unsung heroines of any race relations movement in Greensboro are the women of the YWCA in the early Fifties and Sixties, when it was really tough to do it. In 1949 the board at the YWCA decided to become interracial in the governance of the organization and our activities. The YWCA at that time was the only place in Greensboro that served interracial meals. Some of the churches may have sponsored interracial meals, but I didn't know of any.

It was a radical thing to do at that time. The Greensboro Council of Social Agencies had no place to meet but the YWCA; anybody that wanted an interracial meeting had to go to the YWCA. And we came under a great deal of criticism from the power structure. There was a great deal of pressure that our funding might be cut or removed completely. The male money power structure of the community was particularly vocal in informing us that we should not be doing it, that it was detrimental to our program. So we really felt under great pressure from the community to stop this and to be "normal women."

But it didn't deter us. Any history of race relations in Greensboro should take into account the work of the YWCA, and the United Church Women, which shortly after became interracial, too. Later, some churches opened up for meals but very slowly. There was just not much doing at all, other than the Greensboro Fellowship, which was interracial. I went to the meeting when they tried to encourage the Greensboro Ministry to become interracial. In 1951 or 1952, Tart Bell, head of the American Friends Service Committee invited me to address members of various organizations. I spoke to them about how easy it was to have integrated meetings at the YWCA, and that it would be no problem for them. But they turned down the proposal; it just wasn't done.

There had been a separate black YWCA, although it was subordinate to the white Y board. Before I came, there had been a white board that had conducted the affairs of the black YWCA, which was in one of those big old homes near Bennett College. The programs were separate, but the uptown Y oversaw the black program. The black YWCA had a board, but the white board was predominant. Between 1947 and 1949, the YWCA voted to become interracial. The two boards were joined, so it was all one board, but usually the president was white. I don't know who the first black president was; I know that Shirley Frye was president sometime later. But there was always a good representation of black women on the board. Funds and personnel were administered through the downtown YWCA, but the board met interracially and made the decisions.

Merging of interracial activities came only gradually. For example, there was a swimming pool at the Davie Street Y and the other YW didn't have one, but we were coerced into having a program at Hayes-Taylor when that swimming pool was built. The donors of the building insisted that the Pearson Street YWCA have a swimming program there. We were discouraged from having interracial swimming. We were told that we had to have our black girls' programs at the Hayes-Taylor YMCA. Eventually, the annual meetings and many programs gradually were integrated.

During my presidency we built the Lee Street building. A lot of the black program was down there, and the white program went down there some. The black program came up to Davie Street, so we didn't need the building. The Lee Street building was turned back over to the United Way. The black program eventually had its own executive.

It seemed to me that the women who worked with the YWCA, the United

Church Women, were the most forthright in trying to move race relations along. They held the fort all those difficult years while the rest of the community was not only dragging its feet, but making it very difficult for us to do it. There was a lot of trust between the races on the YW board. I think all those women really liked each other, and everybody knew we were trying to move ahead on this thing. Margery Lane, Betsy Taylor, who are white; and Mrs. Westerband, and Mrs. David Jones, who are black; all are among the finest women you'll ever meet in your life. And Margaret Headen, who was the executive of the black branch. There was a real feeling that we were working on something important.

Warren was very interested in trying to promote as many interracial contacts as possible. So we devised a scheme of having a group of girls from Bennett and a group of girls from W.C. and Greensboro College, to meet at our house periodically. But some of our neighbors called us to say that they didn't want any interracial socializing in the neighborhood And we got some nasty telephone calls, too, asking us if we'd like to buy a piece of property on Benbow Road [in the black community]. Any kind of interracial social contact was just not done, but we kept it up. Woman's College and Greensboro College were all-female instituions. For young Southern women to be engaged in that sort of activity was frowned on and not permitted. Sometimes we discussed serious issues, and other times we just had something to eat and talked. I don't remember an organized study program. It was just fairly informal.

John and Betsy Taylor helped a lot. John was in real estate and construction. They were both very active in promoting interracial understanding. Betsy was president of the YWCA and very active on the board for many years. In the late Fifties they had a big house in the country, with a lake. They hosted interracial gatherings which included picnics and swimming. But they ran into a lot of difficulty from community opposition.

Warren was very active in the Fellowship of Southern Churchmen, and I was too. It was a southeastern organization based in Chapel Hill. The Fellowship of Southern Churchmen was a group of like-minded people in the South and Southeast. It was interracial, interdenominational and across all sorts of outreach groups. Its primary purpose was to provide contact between people who were like-minded on race relations, labor unions and other liberal economic, political and social issues. It really provided a wonderful bolstering for everyone that was in it, because you didn't feel so alone, that you weren't the only one trying to do this. There were people all over the South—not many, but a few—that would meet together., and had a conference For a while the executive office and key people were in the Chapel Hill area: Nell Morton, Charlie Jones of the Presbyterian church, and Frank Graham. Neil Hougley, who taught at North Carolina Central University. From Greensboro there was Ed Burrows from Guilford College. There were people all over the South who were trying to push things ahead, and felt lonesome if they didn't have a little support. It was a great group and a really fine thing. It was based in Chapel Hill at that time, but it would meet in various places, including Greensboro.

There was a black girl, Josephine Boyd, at Greensboro Senior High, who had a tough time. Jenny and Franklin Parker's daughter was a good friend to her, and suffered a great deal of trouble as a result. Very few people in the community came forward to offer their support for her, or other racial issues. The slow pace of school desegregation was due to the same thing that the members of the community have done all along. Just dragged their feet on every issue of racial cooperation and harmony; tried to put every block in the way that they could to keep it from happening. Following the 1954 [*Brown*] decision, the white community put every block in the way they could think of, and then finally it had to work out. There wasn't anything else they could do.

Everything was rather measured in remarks; there was little violent talk, no Ku Klux Klan-type thing. It was just a very slow kind of thing; if one thing they were doing to delay integrating local schools was ruled wrong, why then they would think up something else that they would try. Gradually integration just came along and there was no way to hold it back. The community was tense and there was a great deal of discussion.

One night Warren went out to Guilford College and spoke about school integration, just saying that it ought to be done. No other way was right, and no matter what they might feel about it, it had to be done. I remember Bill Snider, the editor of the newspaper [the *Greensboro Daily News*], saying he was almost persuaded. But the newspaper and the community really dragged their feet as long as they could. For the most part, it was a very civil type of thing and outside of the poor black girl who was over at Greensboro Senior High all by herself, it just proceeded on its own. But like a juggernaut, it had to come.

The *Greensboro Daily News* and *The Greensboro Record* were good newspapers, but on this subject they were very slow in their editorials. There was some person in the state that devised a plan that he thought would keep this thing from coming so fast. And the newspapers approved of the Pearsall Plan. That's what Warren was talking about out at Guilford. I don't remember the details now, except that it just wasn't any use for them to keep building these little hurdles, because they got torn down, which is a good thing.

Dr. David Jones, the president of Bennett College, was a gentleman of the old school in many ways. And Mrs. Jones was just a marvelous lady. We belonged to a small Methodist church over here near the campus, and one day I was going to a meeting of the women's society at the church. I saw Mrs. Jones sitting outside of the door of the meeting room. A charming, educated, cultured, lady, and she couldn't go in because they were eating. She was going to speak about Bennett or something, but she couldn't go in. So the churches were way behind on integration.

Under Dr. Jones, Bennett College was an interesting place. It was teaching those girls to try to live in a white world. The next president, Dr. Willa Player, did a good job of teaching those girls free in the early 1960s to be leaders in the black community, rather than just trying to function in a white-dominated world. Not that the college wasn't doing a wonderful job with the girls before that, but the atmosphere changed. Bennett College was not a location or scene of black and white contact in the 1950s. Warren went down there once a year and spoke at chapel, but I don't recall Dr. Jones being invited to any white college here to speak. So it was a one-way thing, and that was too bad.

The churches dragged their feet as badly as any other organization in the community. Just held off and wouldn't do anything, except the United Church Women, which integrated in the Fifties. The Council of Churches may have been integrated, I'm not sure. It, was a state organization, and the United Church Women was associated with them. It was the women's branch, and then there was a men's branch. Their board and officers became integrated in the early Fifties shortly after the YWCA did. All of their meetings and social functions were integrated.

*[Note: One afternoon Helen Ashby was confronted outside of a room at the YWCA, where she was conducting an interracial art class for children, by several men who may have been members of the Ku Klux Klan. They told her to send the black children home, and never conduct integrated classes again. Helen closed the door behind her, and ordered the men to leave. After several tense moments, they did so. This was just one example of many instances of personal courage that she demonstrated in her efforts as YWCA president to encourage interracial contacts in Greensboro. This incident was related to the author by Helen Ashby's son, Paul A. Ashby.]*

## Franklin Parker

My wife and I came to Greensboro in 1951 to teach at the Woman's College of the University of North Carolina. By coincidence, a black colleague of mine from graduate school came to Greensboro the next year, to teach at A&T. I suggested that we swap lectures; he would lecture my classes one day, and I would do the same for his classes. I went to check and make sure it was all right with the W.C. administration. The chancellor [Walter C. Jackson] wrote me what I considered a very threatening letter, saying that anyone who invited someone from A&T to come over and speak, was either wanting to hurt the institution, or didn't want his job, something like that. So I explained to my friend, and he said he understood, and I withdrew the invitation. That made me very sad, but a number of other impressions we had were very positive. From what we had heard about the South, I didn't expect to see any whites being friendly with blacks in public places. I went to a service station to have work done on my car, and while I was waiting on my car, the white owner of the station and another white man were joking with a black fellow, as though they were really enjoying each other's company and having a good time together. That amazed me; I didn't think anything like that ever happened. Little things like that delighted us.

And we had a number of good experiences through inter-educational institutional activity, mostly because we became acquainted with Warren and Helen Ashby. They were close friends of ours, and they invited us to this and to that. The Fellowship of Southern Churchmen, an interracial group, was active then. That was not tied in any way to the universities, but all the others were. We joined another group, just people from different walks of life, including several university teachers, would just eat and talk together once a month. My wife and I were delighted to see that something like that existed. We were glad to be able to take part in it. There was an inter-campus faculty group that met then, and we attended over a long period of years.

Most of these things folded up after the Supreme Court decision in '54 [*Brown v. Board of Education*]. The reason, I think, is simply that the various colleges and universities began slowly to become desegregated. And with students on campus who were black, or in A&T's case, with more students who were white, there wasn't as much emphasis to look for other means to get together. But the teachers used to get together. The campuses eventually became very busy, and it was more difficult. But in the early days it was easier to schedule things that affected people from several different disciplines and expect them to come, because there were always so few things on the calendar. That inter-campus faculty group grew and grew until, in the latter days of its activity, there would be meetings of, say, two hundred, two hundred fifty people, and a very good program. Randall Jarrell read poetry one evening to a mixed group, about half-black, half-white, at Guilford College that night. We'd meet at one campus and then the other. But beyond that, there was a student group that met in the early days. It was sponsored by Dr. Raymond Smith, professor of religion at Greensboro College. He was the leading light in this inter-campus student group. Jennie and I attended meetings on various campuses regularly, and encouraged students that we knew to come. We were very happy to see things like that occur.

I was in charge of the students from W.C., and my friend, Charles, in charge of the ones from A&T. We met on campus property. No problem. There was a black speaker. The principal of Dudley High School, spoke at W.C. in a lecture hall about the second year we were here. He said the way he really felt about things. Again, no problem. But it was a special occasion. It wasn't a class where students were supposed to be there. The idea was to require students to listen to a black teacher; the administration didn't like that idea. His name was Vance Chavis, who later served on the City Council. The story he told that made the greatest impression on me then was that he was waiting for a bus downtown, and a drunken, disheveled white man came up to wait for the same bus. As he stood there, he reflected that this drunk could legally sit beside the finest dressed white lady, while he, well dressed and well behaved, would be expected to go to the back of the bus. He said that made him feel bad, and he resolved to never ride a public bus again.

Dr. David Jones, president of Bennett College, was invited to speak at our church, the College Place Methodist, one Sunday evening. He told us how back in the old days when he would ride the trains, he would usually be the only black on the train. Whites would make up the rest of the passenger list. And, except for the porters, he'd be the only passenger who was black. He said that they didn't want to have the expense of setting aside a whole car for him, so they carefully pulled curtains around him, so it'd be like riding in a separate car. He told how at Bennett, the students used to come to the college with little training and so little preparation for life. He said in those days a Bennett student sometimes didn't even know how to take care of her hair, and faculty members would teach her that, among other things. He said that, "We took students who needed help, and helped them in any way we knew." That was a very impressive talk for us. We were members of groups later on, but Jennie more than I. She was a member of the Interracial Commission.

## Jennie Parker

I'm not sure what point in time that the Interracial Commission was organized. But it was organized for the purpose of trying to get certain things done in the community. Things that bothered blacks and some of the rest of us, like separate restrooms, "colored" water fountains, and theaters, which blacks could not go to unless it had a balcony for them. Annie Simkins [wife of Dr. George Simkins, later president of the local NAACP chapter] was one of the major ones in the group. Mrs. Amos Troy was the one that did all the nitty-gritty work for the group. I was secretary-treasurer. Rabbi Fred Rypins, of Temple Emanuel, was very, very active in that group. The YWCA was only one place in town where blacks and whites could eat together. We would have meetings at the YW and try to apply pressure for interracial communication in any way we could. It was like chipping away, because it was awfully hard to put any pressure at all on organizations. I remember one person who was working so hard on the [Victory] Theatre on Tate Street, because they didn't have a balcony. And he was trying to get blacks admitted into that theatre, but he never succeeded until after civil rights laws were passed. He regularly wrote letters to the editor of the *Greensboro Daily News* and *The Greensboro Record* about it, and kept talking to the owner, always very busy trying to get that theatre opened to blacks. And so, we just chipped away at instances of segregation in the 1950s.

I remember talking about transportation. One of the things that struck me when we first came was the buses. My daughter and I always used to ride in the back. There happened to be somebody I knew on the bus, and she said, "Well, you can't go back there. You can't sit in back." The buses in Greensboro weren't legally segregated, but it was the prevailing social custom. In any event, I didn't try to talk to her. [Laughs.] In Greensboro, as far as transportation was concerned, blacks seemed to accept that, although I'm sure that underneath it, there was a good deal of resentment. I think many older blacks kept on sitting in the back a long time after the court ruling on the Birmingham [Alabama] bus boycott. It took the younger blacks to sit up front at first. The older blacks didn't want any trouble. We left Greensboro from 1955 until 1956. One day shortly after we returned, I rode the bus. I just sat down in the first seat I noticed and wasn't thinking about color. I sat down beside a black girl, but I didn't realize it until I got close up to the W.C. campus and was ready to get off. I looked around, and I was pleasantly surprised, because I was so used to blacks sitting in the back. And then I realized for the first time the buses had been integrated by coming to the awareness that she was sitting there beside me. It made me feel good to think that that had happened.

And all these things that we'd been chipping away at for such a long time, it seemed like they happened almost overnight. I thought maybe it wouldn't even happen in my lifetime. I was glad that that black girl was adventurous enough to do that, and I was happy that she was at my side. In regard to the intercampus student thing, the most advanced point which we reached before that began to fold up was a play that was given with some blacks and some whites, males and females. It was Jean Paul Sartre's "No Exit." And it was given on our campus in the music building auditorium. Students came from all the different campuses around. It was all integrated seating; we wouldn't even have considered anything else. That was sanctioned, because the college did not mind us having meetings on its property. That was because attendance was voluntary. But they didn't want us taking kids who had come there to attend an all-white school and forcing them, as in a classroom setting, to listen to even two words.

We were impressed with our daughter's experience when Josephine Boyd desegregated Greensboro Senior High School in 1957. Students were permitted to choose which school they wanted to attend within a particular school district. And one lone black girl, Josephine Boyd, happened to live in the district for Greensboro Senior High [now Grimsley Senior High School]. She had gone to Dudley High School before, but she decided that she would go to GHS her senior year. If her parents hadn't supported her, she wouldn't have done it. And there were other black parents we knew who would have liked to have done the same thing But they were afraid of the things that might happen to them or to their children if they allowed them to go. But Josephine Boyd's parents were willing to take the chance; they did lose their grocery store. The first night she attended Greensboro Senior High, their grocery store was burned down by people who were in protest against the mixing of the races in the public schools. Josephine was very much alone for two or three days in the school library, where the librarian, Miss Herring, let her eat in the library as sort of a refuge. When she was in class, it wasn't too bad. But lunch hour was the most difficult time for her.

Our daughter, Ginger, Julia Adams, whose father, Charles Adams, was the librarian on the W.C. campus, and Monica Gelkin, a German exchange student living with McNeill and Louise Smith, went to Josephine and told her that they would like to eat with her in the lunchroom. I wrote a letter to Josephine. I told her how we applauded what she was trying to do, and we wanted to do anything we could to help, and how I was a former teacher at the school, and if I was still there I would help her. I said that we had a daughter who wanted to become friends with her.

And then it just all worked out. Ginger was able to juggle her classes a certain way, and she was able to get the same lunch hour. They started eating lunch together; then the week had gone by. Our daughter knew Miss Herring, because they both sang in the choir at College Place Church. So they knew that by the end of that week, when the library would be open, then Josephine would have to have some place to eat her lunch. That's when they made a sort of pact. They got together and let Josephine know that they wanted to eat lunch with her in the lunchroom, because that would be the most difficult time for her. And the first week was the hardest. At least one day during the week I went out and sat with them. Things were thrown, marbles, all sorts of things like that. Our daughter and Julia received threatening phone calls saying things like, "How does it feel to be a nigger lover?" and so on. They never knew who made these telephone calls, but the abuse at school did not come from the majority of the school kids. I think that's important. But there were students who were trying to force Josephine out. They threw eggs on her. Her father would bring her, to school, and they would throw rocks at the car. We felt that the school authorities took that attitude, also. We talked to the Superintendent and the Assistant Superintendent. We thought their attitude was, "We wish she would give up." Our attitude was that if we could get at least one black successfully through the year at a white school, then some others would follow. I felt the teachers in general probably were either supportive or didn't take sides.

She did well academically, and graduated at the top of her class. She had been an honor student at Dudley. And a teacher, Mrs. Angie Smith, helped her a lot with her studies. I think the Boyds received a great deal of support from the more sophisticated members of the black community, but I don't know if the black community at large were all that gung-ho about it. She was middle class, not from the ordinary working class environment. She did well at getting scholarships after she left high school, because her academic record was so good and because, of course, she had received considerable publicity.

Some Greensboro Senior High students who were members of the West Market Street Baptist Church formed a protective ring to keep any hostile students at a distance from Josephine. And they did, although they didn't eat with her because their parents just wouldn't permit it. But they could sit around her table and not let the students opposed to her attending their school get close to her. And they did that as a group undertaking. After the first week, some others joined them. It was a bit easier for Josephine then. But the ordeal remained very hard for her during the whole year. I'm sure she felt under pressure; she lost a great deal of weight during the year. But the extreme things, like the egg throwing, didn't keep up. We knew the vice-principal, Lody Glenn, quite well, and we spoke to him about the situation. He told us about some of the things that occurred in the administrative offices of the school. He said, "We get mail from hate groups. They send pictures of white women with black men to show us what this is going to come to. They're fearful of all those things." And then he told me about the phone calls he would receive in the middle of the night. His phone would ring through the night, night after night, with people saying things like it was the coal company, and they wanted to deliver a ton of coal. It was about three o'clock in the morning when they would arrive, or something like that. The idea was that coal is black. Silly little things like that.

I'd say that he really underwent quite a bit, being brought up in the Southern tradition. He didn't find it easy to think that it was important for her to continue in school there. With all that pressure, he would have been happy, I'm sure, if she had left. But eventually, though, he and principal A. P. Routh disciplined the students that were making trouble. But I think it took him quite a long time before that happened. It was a few months, at least. I think generally the kids must have felt that way for quite a while, at least a couple of months. They hoped to discourage her and make her drop out of school. And, of course, it is true that when she finished that year, there wasn't any success the next year. Although there was an opportunity for meaningful school desegregation, the school districts were still drawn to keep schools segregated.

There was a black minister whose family we knew quite well, who had twins, a boy and a girl. And they would have been excellent ones to follow, because they were very outgoing and very intelligent. And we had hoped that there would be a "snowball effect," whereby we could get Josephine through the year, and then others would follow her, and do well, and it would just keep growing. But the school board redrew the boundary so that those twins were not able to go to Greensboro Senior High School. So it just fizzled then. And it was several years, then, before all the schools were all forced to integrate. Josephine was a remarkable young woman. I know her mother well, and I admire her tremendously. Her mother still lives here in Greensboro. Josephine now lives in another part of the country.

The experience convinced us that that kind of integration wouldn't work. It just gave too many people who were opposed a chance to keep it from happening by putting pressure on people who had the nerve to send their kids to previously all-white schools. It sounds fine to say, "Let the kids go wherever they want to." And eventually I think they did that for the whole city. Maybe I'm wrong. But it still was a voluntary thing, and somebody had to be very strong-minded in order to do it until they began to change the whole system.

We've been impressed by housing in Greensboro, as far as blacks are concerned. When we first came here, the shacks in which the majority, of the black people lived were hovels. We just couldn't imagine so many people living in such terrible places. They've all been mowed down long ago, and the people who lived there have all moved to public housing or cheaper housing somewhere else now. On the other hand, there was a very affluent section on Benbow Road and Ross Avenue, where you would see blacks out in very nice houses and yards. You could be black and get somewhere in the world, if you were born into the right family or got into the right occupation. But it wasn't true for the mass of blacks. Educational and occupational opportunities were closed to them when we first came here.

When we first joined the church, one of the ushers was always talking about, "What if a black person comes to the church service? What would we do?" Another usher said that he wouldn't let them in. I was amazed. There was all this fear.

## William B. Snider

When I came to Greensboro in 1951, as associate editor of the *Greensboro Daily News,* the city seemed rather progressive and forward looking in its social work and community problems. It seemed to me that Greensboro was doing some pioneering work in local government. It was a manufacturing town, but at the same time it had an interesting, diverse population, a very strong Jewish population which was influential in the community, and a splendid educational community.

Greensboro, of course, reflected the traditionalist views of the South as far as race relations were concerned. "Separate but equal" was considered to be a way of life. And while we had a strong black community, focused and coalesced around A&T College [now North Carolina A&T State University], there were here all the manifestations of the South that we're familiar with. At the same time there was a strong academic flavor here of the state colleges and universities, and private institutions like Guilford College and Greensboro College, which made this community rather open to new ideas than perhaps other communities might be. It seemed to be in those days that Greensboro might be ready to move somewhat out of the traditional attitudes. In addition, the *Greensboro Daily News* was a very strong and influential newspaper. And in those days, might be considered liberal and progressive by Southern terms. It had a series of editors who led the community, rather than reflecting it. And it was my view that the community could handle a great many things that perhaps other North Carolina communities could not handle within the context of the situation as existed in those days.

This proved to be the case, because in 1954 when the *Brown v. Board of Education* decision was handed down, there was quite a bit of activity in that area to support the Supreme Court decision. I remember vividly a group of people who came around to my house—I was a man of just thirty-two or thirty-three—and it included Edward Kidder Graham, chancellor at Woman's College and Edward Hudgins, who was the general counsel of Jefferson Standard Life Insurance Company and head of the school board, among others. We decided that we would try to do all we could to persuade Greensboro that we ought to at least not take the negative position on this issue, which of course would be taken widely across the South.

This committee worked with newspaper editors and school board members in Charlotte and Winston-Salem, to do what we could to accomplish the first step in desegregation of the schools in the three communities simultaneously. This was to be done in September of 1957; ironically that was the same time that President Eisenhower sent the troops to Little Rock, Arkansas, which dominated the news. We succeeded in getting the three school systems to begin the process. Each of them decided that black students would be admitted to individual schools in each of the communities. Thus the three communities of Greensboro, Winston, and Charlotte broke the mold of total segregation. This didn't seem to be much of an achievement now, but if you go back in those days it was a considerable one.

That first step was to allow a black student to enroll in a predominately white school in each community that fall. They had a rough time. Ben Smith, the superintendent of schools here, had dreadful things happen to him, such as cross-burnings and deliveries of coal and flowers and other things to his door. There was harassment from the Klan here. All of us, in fact, were so identified with this that the same kinds of things happened to us. I had crosses burned in my yard. I was away the weekend when this happened, so my wife called Mr. Hudgins. And the group that burned the cross smashed the windows out of our house, in fact, where our small children were sleeping. So we had a rather interesting time in those days. Of course, it was not of much significance, because there were larger things happening on the national scene. But that experience sort of dominated my view of how things were working in Greensboro in those days.

I think the community tended at first to be somewhat tentative, but mostly negative. There were varying views. There were numbers of people here, in the academic community particularly, and some in the business community and elsewhere, who thought that there should be some effort to comply with the law of the land. And while I think that the predominant view perhaps was negative, I think there was a certain force of leadership here which allowed at least the initial breakthrough from completely segregated schools. That created a lot of turmoil in those days. I think that Greensboro was perhaps a little more open than the average Southern community to allowing this kind of change to begin even in a very small way. My view is that this might not have happened, and indeed did not happen in certain other communities. But there was in North Carolina, unlike states where massive resistance took place, a certain openness or feeling of fairness about perhaps trying to move a little bit in this direction.

North Carolina Governor Luther Hodges supported a plan for school integration known as the Pearsall Plan, put forth by State Senator Pearsall. It was ostensibly proposed to avoid as much unpleasantness as possible, but it came to be viewed differently by both sides of the school integration issue. This was seen by knee-jerk liberals as just a way to keep the schools closed to blacks. But actually there were two sides of the coin to the Pearsall Plan. It allowed communities like Greensboro to move tentatively forward, but at the same time allowed an escape valve for those communities which were not able to do it in more rural areas of the state. The newspapers supported the Pearsall Plan in Greensboro; some other papers did not. We did, because we felt it allowed a freedom of action and a right to choice about a very difficult subject. And therefore, we in North Carolina, unlike Virginia, did not close our schools. Later of course, many people said that it took us longer to complete the desegregation of our schools, because we didn't break the egg thoroughly, that it would have been better if we had just desegregated the schools all at once. But it always seemed to me that it was far better to make a start at something that needed to be done than to keep all the doors closed.

I knew Governor Hodges and Mr. Pearsall well, and I knew what they were attempting to do. Both were rather traditional in background, but they were not unenlightened. In some ways they were looking out for what they thought were the state's best interests. It seemed to me that Governor Hodges was a genuine moderate. So it was my view that North Carolina had a fairly good moderate kind of leadership for the South of those days. The Pearsall Plan worked in North Carolina for its time; there were no schools closed as a result. The process of desegregation moved pretty slowly in North Carolina, but it did not create a massive confrontation of the kind that you had in Virginia. People differed as to whether or not it was better to go ahead and do the job immediately and get it done. My feeling was that the leadership of North Carolina did a pretty successful job. Greensboro was representative of North Carolina in those days in that it seemed to me always to take the middle way. Rather than being strongly liberal or strongly conservative, it tended to take a point somewhere between those two points, and its government has certainly shown that.

I think the Pearsall Plan represented the mood of the community, which was one of civility in community relations, of trying to make things work out rather than to have massive confrontations. There was some communication at the upper levels in the black and white establishment communities. Willa B. Player, the president of Bennett College, was very active in the field of race relations. The City Council had black leadership in Dr. William Hampton. There were thoughtful doctors and lawyers and other professional people in the black community who were in touch with the white community. I served on what was called the "Conversation Club," founded in about 1953, and we had black and white membership. Many people in the white community didn't know what was going on in the black community, and they didn't care to find out. But I think there were some individuals who broke that particular mold, and there was some contact. The work of people like Ed Zane, the vice-president of Burlington Industries, who took such a leading role in trying to bring together the community in terms of race relations and the desegregation of public accommodations, represented a force in the community which made it possible to move forward in a positive manner.

I felt that Greensboro was a remarkable kind of community. It was comprised of somewhat diverse elements for a Southern community of that size. The Quaker and the Jewish influence was substantial. The black and the white colleges here made what might have been just a textile manufacturing town, something a little different. So I felt that we had here a good combination of practice and resources which made this community capable of doing something a little extra or a little different from the normal tradition of Southern towns. These were educated, intellectual, cosmopolitan people, who brought a different tone to Greensboro. And this community had both the wonderful elements of intellectual and artistic talent, and business acumen. And I thought that some of the leaders in the black community were extremely able, dedicated and involved people. I look at their contributions as being sizeable in trying to move this thing a bit. And I think that was very important.

Following the initial desegregation of the Greensboro public schools, black students did attend predominately white schools but it took Greensboro quite a long time to complete the job of school desegregation. The "Southern Manifesto" came out in those days, which Southern senators and congressmen wrote criticizing forced integration of Southern schools. The view of the *Greensboro Daily News* was that we ought to move along with this, to obey the law of the land. Desegregation was very difficult. We had labored under the idea that "separate but equal" really meant that separate racial communities were equal. And, of course, everybody knew that it wasn't. From the time of *Plessy v. Ferguson* it was pretty obvious that it wasn't, and yet we had failed to confront that problem, just as we had failed to confront the fact that blacks were people two hundred years ago. But it took time. *Plessy v. Ferguson* served a certain purpose of holding back what was coming, but it provided perhaps the time for it to happen. And it didn't happen until finally in 1954, when we were able to move into a new era.

## Jo Spivey

There were not a lot of interchanges between the races in Greensboro. There had been, for a good ten years, some effort on the part of members of the black community to integrate facilities in the city. In the early 1950s, from time to time, small groups would go to restaurants or places of this sort and sit down. No one would wait on them, and then they would leave. I had a feeling that they probably were spontaneous; however, most leaders in the black community did belong to the NAACP. Because the NAACP was not looked upon too favorably in the white community, there was another organization, the Greensboro Citizens Association, that was organized, but when you got into it, you would find that the membership of the two organizations were generally the same. I would assume that this was more or less, a way of getting around the resentment of the white community against the NAACP.

My first detailed association with any of the Civil Rights Movement was in 1955, when six black men with Dr. George Simkins, Jr., who later became president of the Greensboro branch of the NAACP, were arrested for attempting to play golf at the all-white Gillespie Park Golf Course. Subsequently, a black professor at a university in Louisiana, Dr. Amy Gibbs, went to Lindley Park Swimming Pool, asked to be admitted to swim and was turned away. There had also been some effort to get the white public library integrated; there was a black library here called the Carnegie Library for Negroes. In the aftermath of all these activities, the city closed down the golf courses and sold the swimming pools. The city government integrated the libraries, and the Dudley High School football team was allowed to play its games at Greensboro High School [now Grimsley] stadium. But those were the only major concessions.

In describing the black middle class in Greensboro in the late 1950s, it depends on what you refer to as "middle class." By white economic standards, there was not a typical middle class. You found black persons with college educations running elevators, things of this sort, but in the black community itself, there was a small but very strong middle class, just as there is in the white community. There was a group of black professionals—educators, doctors—who were the top echelon and exerted a significant influence in the black community. And there were persons who were mostly domestics or in custodial jobs, but still they were a strong middle class; they were well educated. Then you had your laborers, which would have been your lower class. The majority of black people in Greensboro were in menial jobs, even if they had college educations.

As regards the city government and the black community, it was pretty much two separate societies. I think that city officials felt that the blacks should not be making a lot of demands for services in the black community. They may well have had a naive idea of black aspirations. Most of the people in government were older; they had been brought up in a genteel Southern tradition, very polite and kind. They were not of the type that would go out and beat up black persons with a tire chain, but they still felt that blacks had their place. In their view, the "good" blacks observed the traditional standards of segregation, and the "bad" blacks were the activists and the malcontents.

I think that Greensboro has been so fragmented that there have not been any overall leaders. Since I came to Greensboro, I have not noticed any particular families or groups that dictated the way that the city should go. I understand those years before, the Cones were a very powerful force in the community. But in the 1950s, there was no leadership elite; it is pretty fragmented.

## Arnold Schiffman

There was a difference between the younger blacks and the older blacks. A good many of the older blacks recognized that while they didn't have equal rights with the whites, the whites did treat them right. They were treated really well here. If we ever found out that a black family needed help, we'd make it our business to see what we could do to help them. And the older blacks knew it. My relationship with older black leaders was at the top. I was the first one to establish a student aid fund at A&T, so that youngsters in school who couldn't have funds to continue could secure funds. That was in the Fifties. Later, I established the A&T University Foundation. And I was able to secure funds from big corporations, like Burlington Industries and Jefferson Standard. We raised better than a half million dollars in the first drive. Today, the Foundation is an integral part of the university. I was president of the Foundation for about eleven years.

# William "Lody" Glenn

The black teachers had their own separate association on the state level. White teachers belonged to the North Carolina Educational Association, and the black association had a different name. But I came in contact with black teachers for city-wide meetings involving the total city school system. Nothing in a big way; not anything at all like it was after we were totally integrated.

I was teaching when the *Brown* decision was announced in 1954, and the students asked a lot of questions. Did it mean that the Dudley students would go to Greenboro Senior High, or would Senior High students would go to Dudley? Because in 1954, there was one white high school and one black high school in Greensboro: Greensboro Senior and Dudley. I don't recall anybody being too upset about the *Brown* decision, as far as students or teachers were concerned. I think most people were thinking, "This won't happen here." This was something that happened out in the Midwest. It'd be a long time before we really see results. There was a question whether or not it would ever be enforced. It wasn't something you heard about every day. The first two or three days after the decision was announced in the paper, there was some comment, but then after that I didn't hear anything until weeks or months later. I don't recall any sort of planning by the school board, although the superintendent of schools in Greensboro at that time, Mr. Ben Smith, was quoted in the paper that the Greensboro city school system would comply with the law. I think most teachers at that time felt that the schools should comply.

A black student named Josephine Boyd lived on Pisgah Church Road, and she enrolled in Greensboro Senior High School, because all kids who lived on Pisgah Church Road went to school there. She was there her senior year, and the administrative staff and faculty were determined to make it work. We knew that the rest of the city, the state and the country were looking at us. But there were people at school and adults in the community who didn't want her there; what I called the "redneck element." At first she wouldn't go in the cafeteria; she used to eat lunch in the library. But some of the teachers talked to her, said, "You're going to eat in the cafeteria just like everybody else," which she eventually did.

I was assistant principal then, and I took it upon myself to be close by during the change of classes to be sure that no one committed any violence against her in any way. We in the administration and faculty felt we ought to do everything we could to be sure that these people that didn't want her there did not make life miserable for her. But the majority of students really didn't pay a whole lot of attention to her. They just went on their daily routine.

Nevertheless, there were ugly comments made to her. I never did hear any, but she told us about some comments like, "Why don't you go to your school?" as she would walk down the stairwell or something like that. One afternoon there was a rock-throwing incident, although she didn't get hit. We caught those people and we made sure that we never had anymore trouble with them. That all happened in the early weeks after she enrolled. By the spring of the year her attendance at school became normal daily routine for the other students. They just didn't care, and some were friendly with her.

It was some people in Greensboro, members of the Ku Klux Klan and others, who were causing us problems. But they never came on the campus during the school day. They arrived outside on graduation night, and paraded in front of the gym with their Confederate flags. But we had the police there and they were not allowed in the gym where we had our graduation ceremony. They saw they were not going to be allowed inside the gym, so they decided to leave. The leader of the Klan at that time in Greensboro, George Dorsett, had two sons enrolled here in the high school. He lived in the Glenwood section. And the fellow who was carrying the flag that night, his last name was Webster. I think they caused more problems at other schools than they did at Senior, particularly at Gillespie. The principal at Gillespie at that time was Banks Ritchie, a fine gentleman, and he really had a rough time. I think that all of the stress at that time eventually caused his death.

The Klan was fairly active; I wouldn't say it was very active. It always appeared to me to be kind of a half-hearted thing. It seemed to me like it was just an effort on the part of a few people to get a lot of media attention. I don't recall any other groups who were organized in any way to oppose the integration of the schools. Of course, a lot of the opposition was kind of subtle. For instance, the first day that Josephine was in school, it came out in the paper that I followed her around to make sure there was no problem. I started getting threatening telephone calls. People would call me on the phone at two or three o'clock in the morning, calling me an "S.O.B." and "nigger lover." Then pretty soon a black-owned taxi would show up in front of my house. And the next day, a load of coal came from a black-owned coal yard, which I hadn't ordered And one time I got a postcard threatening my life. It was just a sporadic type of thing.

Josephine had support in the black community, and some in the white community as well. The NAACP was very instrumental in selecting her for her grades and behavior. Some students in the school who befriended Josephine, made her feel at home. I'm sure it was a hard year but she apparently made it all right. Mr. Routh [A. P. Routh, principal] talked to her more than I did. I was always kind of on the outside of the circle, making sure that nothing happened, trying to find out who might try to do something to her. She had the full support of the administration. We were determined that no one, inside or outside of the school, was going to commit any acts of violence against her, or do anything to try to close down the school.

## Josephine Boyd (Bradley)

As my mother and I walked from the street to the Administration Building of the school, I felt the hatred. While the people did not physically attack me, their hostile feelings, were very raw and slowly wrapping themselves around me. I was terrified, because I had never seen so many white people gathered as a crowd before, and I had heard about the treatment of the five students at Gillespie the day before. About 200 whites had stood on the other side of the street, shouting "Go Home, Nigger!" as some were doing now.

My mother sensed my fear and grabbed my hand; it felt warm and safe. It was during this walk, which never seemed to end, that I wondered, "Why do these people hate me?" Once I thought that I would gag on the hatred, what I called "silent hatred," which for me was more threatening than the open vile screams of "Nigger, Nigger, Go Home!" I wanted to turn around, dragging my mother with me, run back to the car, where it was safe, secure and warm, and go home. But I knew that if I turned around and went to the car or if I went into the building, I had the protection of my family. Yet, I knew they would be disappointed if I quit before I started. So I walked up to the door, holding my mother's hand, but inside I was alone and frustrated.

We were met at the door by the principal, [A. P. Routh]. He appeared tired and had an expression on his face that seemed to say, "Welcome to Greensboro Senior High School. Come inside, please." He acknowledged Mama and said, "Good morning, Mrs. Boyd." As we stood there, I heard some students yelling,"Nigger Go Home." I worried about Mama's safety as I watched her walk back to the car, and my own safety as I entered the school's administration building.

It was at this moment that I developed my first survival strategy for dealing with the situation. I began retreating into myself, listening to my own song: "We came this far by Leaning on the Lord, Trusting in his Holy Word, He's never failed me yet!" Being stubborn and proud, I refused to embarrass myself by letting the enemy see any fear. I kept my fear under control all day until I returned home. I could not control my environment, but I did have control over myself. As I walked to my classes under the walkway leading from one building to the next there was a rainfall of eggs coming from the classroom building. Most of them landed on me. But I wiped my face, looked in disgust at my new dress and walked on to class. Some of the students jeered and called out "nigger." Some tried to look disinterested, but periodically made side glances to see if I was still in the room. Some students yelled, "You know we don't want you here. Go back to your own school. This is our school!" These were words that get inside your safety zone that we create for ourselves; words that hurt the psyche primarily because we did not understand the rationale for them. The five black students at Gillespie were greeted by a crowd of hecklers saying, "Go Home, Nigger" and "Go Black Sambo." This is difficult to explain to a ten year old or a seventeen year old.

At home, the telephone calls started. Unidentified people called, saying such things as, "How could you go against God's teachings? The Bible states clearly that blacks and whites should not mix." When these calls started, it really frightened me, and the calls also were very upsetting to my family.

A boy pushed me into the lockers one day and said lewd and vulgar things about my mother. My mild manner faded, my survival strategy retreated within myself and did not work. There was a scuffle and I pushed him into the locker. A teacher came out of a classroom and took me aside, telling me as she did, that if I was involved in another altercation, I would be dismissed for disciplinary reasons. As I tried to explain what happened, she made me understand that I would be considered the perpetrator of any future incidents. I still have trouble understanding that to this day.

There was a strange call from a man who identified himself as the Grand Wizard of the Klan. He said, "You are helping to destroy all that is sacred to the Southern way of life. If you go to Senior High, you will live to regret it." All I could think of while I listened to him condemn me to hell, was that I wanted to smother him. This ongoing harassment was joined by others who identified themselves as members of the White Citizens Council; they talked mostly about how the "good Lord did not intend for blacks to go to school with whites." My brothers told me later that members of the Ku Klux Klan and other groups threw things down our chimney. We were lucky that nothing exploded when it landed in the fireplace. We were not allowed to be in the yard at night, because white men would come by and cut up or puncture the tires to our car and truck. Many of our animals were killed and we mourned the death of our beloved dogs. A tree was cut down across our driveway, making it impossible for us to get out until my brothers cut it up into logs.

Our calls to the police were in vain. They did not provide any significant protection and said, "There is nothing we can do to prevent these disasters from happening." This was their attiude if we reported any rock throwing through our car windows. The policeman who regularly sat in his car across the street from the school would come over after a rock throwing episode and say, "I can't do anything unless you can tell me who threw the rocks." Students would regularly throw rocks at our car on a daily basis. I found tacks in my seats in the classrooms, or someone walked by and "accidentally" spilled ink on my notebook or on me.

We received emotional and financial support from various civic, fraternal and church organizations, particularly from our church, the Mt. Carmel Episcopal Methodist Church. The Methodist Youth Fellowship, the Friendship Club at Dudley, and the YWCA Y-Teens were particularly important, because my association with other blacks my age was limited. Some of the parents in the local community or other black areas were reluctant to let their children associate with me for fear it would affect their families. Some people in the immediate community where we lived asked, "Why did they have to send someone that black to Greensboro Senior High? Why didn't they select someone lighter in complexion?" Dating became rare because people did not want to be seen with me. My brothers lost their yard work jobs because I was attending Senior High.

The incident that hurt the worst was the loss of my father's snack bar, across from J. C. Price School. People rode by and threw rotten eggs against the windows, and it inexplicably burned down. That was the only time that I saw my father cry. He just said, "Why this? Why this?"

I found three girls at Senior High who had the courage to speak and eat lunch with me. They were Ginger Parker, Julie Adams, and Kitty Gervais.

I was curious about the "white students" who could learn what I could not. I wanted to know why they were considered to be superior to me and why I was considered inferior. I wanted to know what was it about being black that made it necessary to have separate restrooms and water fountains for us in Woolworth and other downtown stores. One day my mother and my five-year-old brother Michael were in Woolworth after the 1957 school year had started. The white saleslady asked Mama, "Are you the lady whose daughter is going to Senior High?" Mama answered, "Yes, I am." The saleslady responded, "Well, you know we don't serve niggers." Mama replied, "Well don't worry. My son and I don't eat niggers." Thus, the harassment occurred both inside the school and outside the school.

This was my senior school year. There was no senior prom for me as a graduating senior from Greensboro Senior High School. Finally, on June 4, 1958, graduation arrived. I remember very little about the ceremonies. My mother made arrangements for me to leave from the house of a neighbor, Miss House, because she did not know what to expect from the KKK and the White Citizens Council. Mama arranged for a black taxi company to take me to the school. She asked the driver to make sure that I was safely inside, and to bring me back home. My mother made arrangements for me to leave from the house of a neighbor, Miss House, because she did not know what to expect from the KKK and the White Citizens Council. Mama arranged for a black taxi company to take me to the school. She asked the driver to make sure that I was safely inside, and to bring me back home. After I got back home, the driver told her that a teacher was assigned to stay with me until we marched in. Mama asked the driver how much she owed him, and he said, "You don't owe me a thing. We should have paid her to go there."

As for me, it was an unclear memory. Right up until they called my name, I still anticipated that anything might happen. When they called my name, you could almost hear 4000 people breathe a sigh of relief. It was over and I had remained at the school for the entire year. I had also been on the honor role.

## J. Kenneth Lee

Race relations in Greensboro sometimes took a peculiar turn. As virtually the only black attorney in Greensboro that took civil rights cases, I received anonymous hate calls. One night, at the time of the Gillespie School integration, my wife and I went over to the next-door neighbors. When we returned, our six-year-old son was hysterical. Someone had called and graphically described what they were going to do to his daddy. We had to take him to the emergency room of L. Richardson Hospital to get him calmed down.

On the other hand, there was the time when C. W. Webester, head of the Ku Klux Klan and a local carpenter, repeatedly threw objects through my office window. One night, my friends hid in the bushes and caught Webster. We called the police and he was arrested.

One day I was sitting at my desk and looked up to see Webster standing over me. Not knowing what to expect, I moved my hand near the drawer where I kept a gun. He said, "Mr. Lee, my boss is building your house, and the court said that I can no longer come onto your property. If you'll tell the court and my boss that I can work on your house, I'll promise I'll do the best job I can." I thought, "Why not?" and did as Webster asked. He not only kept his word, but made suggestions that saved me a lot of money.

On the day of his trial, I testified as to the arrangement with Webster and the good work he had done. The court gave him a two-year suspended sentence. As I was walking down the courthouse steps, I saw Webster and some other men approaching me. I thought, "Here it comes." But he said, "Mr. Lee, I want to thank you for what you did for me. If anyone in this town [expletive] with you, just call us." I thought, "Now ain't this something? I guess this makes me an honorary member."

## John Marshall Kilimanjaro

A&T College was celebrating Founder's Day, and Governor Hodges was invited to address the student body. Dr. [Ferdinand D.] Bluford [A&T president] told him that the community was in upheaval about the "integration situation" [the *Brown* decision]. The Governor came into Harrison Auditorium and everything was going fine as he got up to speak. He congratulated A&T on how much progress had been made. Then he closed his manuscript and proceeded to talk about the integration/segregation controversy. He warned the students that they were "being led down the primrose path" and were unwise in what they were doing. As he went on, he pronounced the word "Negro" as "nigra," and the students and faculty, including myself, began shuffling our feet. He stopped and turned to Dr. Bluford and he said, in essence, "Shall

I continue?" Dr. Bluford said, "Yes, yes, go right ahead." And the Governor continued. He again used the word "nigra," and the shuffling of feet continued. This angered him, and he cut loose with the word "nigger."

He closed his manuscript and he left the stage. The next thing we knew, Dr. Bluford was in the hospital by that evening, and he died. The nurse or orderly reported that all he could say was, "They called me Uncle Tom." And this was the result of thirty-six years of bowing and saying, "Yes, sir, I'll do my best to do what you want me to do," when he wanted to say, "Go to hell."

In the schools we were brought up to look forward to achieving freedom, justice and equality; it was the capstone of our lives. One of the expressions in the schools and colleges was "We got to get ready, because integration is coming." But in the late 1950s, we had very little real leadership [in the black community]. Dr. Simkins was only beginning to become the leader we came to know later. The ministers in the community, like in almost all Southern communities, were, generally speaking, people who were quite conservative. So the ministers' attitude was, "We're going to do what we can, but we don't want to rock the boat too much, because I can be removed and replaced with somebody else who doesn't have the radicalism that I have, and where would the poor [black] people be?" So they did not take a political tack. But while we condemn these ministers, we have to stop and consider that the fire marshal is also a political figure. If the mayor called him and said, "Go down and inspect that church." And if he found that they didn't have "Exit" lights up over the doors and so forth, he could close up the church.

It was only with the advent of Martin Luther King, Jr., that we had black ministers coming up against the white opposition. The most dynamic, aggressive black minister we had in Greensboro was Reverend Julian T. Douglas, of the Presbyterian church. He had been president of the NAACP and he had run for City Council several times. He had incurred the enmity of the white power structure, because he was so outspoken. Reverend Douglas was an outstanding man in the town.

Hobart Jarrett, who was chairman of the Humanities Department of Bennett College, and Sociology professor Dr. Edwin Edmonds were brilliant and the quintessential professor that President David D. Jones and, later, Dr. Willa B. Player would have as professors there. Dr. Edmonds petitioned the school board unsuccessfully to have his daughter admitted to Curry School in 1957. For his outspokenness, the state legislature forced Dr. [Warmouth T.] Gibbs [successor to Dr. Bluford] to dismiss him as head of the Wesley Foundation at A&T College. I had been dismissed from the A&T faculty for suggesting that the money for a bronze bust of Dr. Bluford be used instead to help the NAACP pursue its protest of a black student who had been killed by a white policeman. However, I returned to the faculty four years later. But most of the NAACP was not disposed to argue about segregation. They said, "This is a moral issue, and we stand on moral grounds." This was the image of the NAACP; we had not yet evolved into confrontation, as we would later come to think of it. The Greensboro chapter was very small, only about fifteen members. The Greensboro Citizens Association membership had grown because people would join that organization, who would not join the NAACP for fear of losing their jobs, and the NAACP in many places across the South was under direct assault by state legislatures. And we had hostile white groups in Greensboro. In addition to the Klan there was the North Carolina Patriots, a suit-and-tie Ku Klux Klan, but who were just as determined to break this resistance movement to segregation. People say that we had a special leadership, but it was a leadership that went in the back door.

Langston Hughes had written a poem "Freedom. Who said free? Not me." Paul Robeson could really sing it. When he came to A&T College during the McCarthy period, people wouldn't come out to see him, there in front of the Dudley Building. I was told that people were standing behind the drapes, looking out, and he's standing out in the middle of the campus, wanting to talk. And just a few students came out there to talk to him, the greatest black man to ever wear a pair of shoes in America, in my opinion. That's why I named the theater at A&T State University the Paul Robeson Theater I bought the marquee and commissioned the painting of Paul Robeson that stands inside. I couldn't have done it if I didn't know that Dr. Dowdy was sympathetic toward what I was talking about. He said, "Just don't fix it so that it's impossible for me to let you do these things. What you're trying to do is right, is good, and I agree with you." I also spent $3,000 on the bust of Paul Robeson. It's a block of black African granite on the campus.

Then in 1958 we brought to Greensboro a young Baptist preacher from Montgomery that we had heard about: Martin Luther King Jr. We brought him here because we needed someone to galvanize and unite our people, and it did. I would mark that day as one that changed Greensboro.

# Chapter 2

## The Greensboro Sit-ins

*The undercurrent of discontent over the racial status quo by adult members of the black community resonated with their children. Influenced by years of listening to school teachers, ministers, and family members, young black citizens in Greensboro grew to maturity determined to effect change in their lifetime. On February 1, 1960, four freshmen male students at the traditionally-black Agricultural and Technical College, walked into the F. W. Woolworth store in downtown Greensboro to demand service at the lunch counter. Although African Americans could shop in the store, service at the lunch counter was restricted to white patrons. African Americans could order food at a stand-up counter, but they had to take the food out of the store to eat it. Although there had been individual attempts to obtain service at "5-and-10" lunch counters in the country and in North Carolina (Durham in 1958), there had been no sustained effort to desegregate such facilities.*

*Ezell Blair, Jr., Franklin McCain, Joseph McNeil, and David Richmond, quickly dubbed the "Greensboro Four," created a sensation when they remained seated at the counter after being refused service. Several hours later, they left when the store closed. Word quickly spread at A&T College and the nearby all-female black institution, Bennett College, and the so-called "sit-in" was the featured story on the local evening news. Over the next few days hundreds of local black students flocked into the downtown area to sit-in and picket the Woolworth and Kress department stores. A few white students at surrounding colleges also participated.*

*Within weeks, due to national news coverage, African American college students were conducting similar sit-ins in cities throughout the South. The Congress of Racial Equality (CORE) and the NAACP offered varying levels of support to what was rapidly being called "The Movement," but the students preferred to function independently through their own ad hoc organization, the Student Executive Committee for Justice. They did, however, accept advice from individual members of the black community and bail money raised by a local mortician and a physician. This unprecedented example of mass demonstration by mostly black college students, resulted in the formation of the Student Nonviolent Coordinating Committee (SNCC) at Shaw University in Raleigh, North Carolina, in the spring of 1960.*

## Robert "Pat" Patterson

In January of 1960, about eight of us fellows at A&T, including Joe McNeil, David Richmond, Ezell Blair and Franklin McCain, were studying for chemistry examinations in the dorm, and the question came up concerning a boycott that was being conducted in Wilmington, involving the Pepsi-Cola Company. Joe McNeil came from Wilmington, and as we asked him questions about it, one of us asked, "Why don't we do something like this in Greensboro?" We decided at that time to do something. I thought that it was kind of a half-hearted decision and didn't think anything more about it until the next day. I was walking to electrical engineering class, as Joe McNeil, Ezell Blair, Frank McCain, and David Richmond passed me going to class. They indicated that they were going to go downtown and sit-in at the Woolworth store, and invited me to join them. I said, "Fellows, I really don't have time to go downtown to jive around if you're not going to do it." Clearly, I didn't believe that they were going to do it.

## Joseph McNeil

There was not too much a question of motivation; it's there. You're going to face it every day to the extent that you have a sense of self-respect. At that time we were emerging into a sense of wanting to do something in our own context, of making a contribution, albeit a small one. Outside influences certainly had an effect on anyone who did any reading. We lived in a time when many found it easy to shun events that happened around them. But, to have a sense of self-respect required that you read and, if you did, you saw certain things that you couldn't ignore. I don't think that there was anything unique about our student body that you wouldn't have found at other institutions. It could have happened at Southern University in Louisiana; Orangeburg in South Carolina; or N.C. Central in Durham. I think that it was a problem that faced us all. We were aware of the integration of Little Rock High and the Montgomery bus boycott. We knew that black people were doing something about the problem, and we should do something in Greensboro as well.

Each of us had grown up under a dual-policy educational system. We were all raised in the South, and we all grew up at the time when public accommodations were generally refused to blacks. I think that we had all been refused service at one point in time, either restaurants, hotels, or the use of restaurant facilities. It was just a number of things that we called to mind that we needed to do something about. I didn't perceive race relations in Greensboro as being so different from any other location in the South. Certainly, the demonstrative things you see in race relations were the same: separate water fountains, in the public accommodations area, the things that hit you right out in front, were no different.

Before going to college, we had talked about doing sit-in types of things. The concept was not a seed that was suddenly born in somebody's mind. We were freshmen at A&T College at the time, and I think that at least some of us were in the same algebra class, and we lived on the same floor of the dormitory. We found some things in common, discussed many things: we discussed problems in the world, and then reduced those problems down to the level where they directly affected us. What led us to act that particular night was that we had met, we had talked, discussed the need to do something like this.

I had talked previously about that with Ralph Johns [a local white merchant active in the NAACP], who said that he would be helpful to us if we would do something like this. Ralph was a good man, in the sense that he did an awful lot of things in the community and with the college. He was helpful to us in the initial stages in getting things going, giving us a shoulder to lean on. He also was a local businessman in the community, and he knew things that, perhaps, we didn't know; he would have the press connections that we didn't have, things of that nature. He was also an adult, and we were students. It wasn't the case where we had a series of meetings with him, and I don't think it was a one-time conversation. I think it was something that we discussed in passing.

We [four] talked about it the night before, a discussion of the things that might take place, and we tried to figure out a response for every possible statement that could be made, or every action that could be directed against us. I think we expected a lot of things to happen.

## Jibreel Khazan (Ezell A. Blair, Jr.)

Frank, David and I knew each other at Dudley High School in Greensboro. Joseph McNeil went to Wilson High School in Wilmington, North Carolina. All of us were pretty good students. We came to A&T College already having established our personalities and being known by different people in our communities. Joseph McNeil was one of A&T College's $1,000 scholarship winners. It gives four scholarships every year, and he has won four. I have always admired Joseph McNeil as having an exceptional mind. I was in class with Frank McCain, and I always felt that he was a leader in his own right, and he was a scholar in high school. He had a brilliant mind. Although people regard him as quiet, David Richmond was very popular and an established leader from the time that he was a kid. He was not only known in Greensboro, but other places throughout the state as an exceptional athlete. He was an All-State high-jump record holder for North Carolina, and his record stood for ten years, but he wouldn't talk about it. We all respected each other, so it was like one of those "once-in-a-lifetime" relationships. We didn't always agree on everything; we might argue until the wee hours of the morning. But when all of that was over, we always respected each other, as we do today.

I was always a shy person, and so I felt pressures, once we had decided to sit-in at Woolworth the next day. I wanted to check with my folks. I wanted to make sure that I wouldn't do anything to embarrass them, because both my parents were working for the public school system. I checked with my father first, then I went to see my mother. I said, "Ma, we're going to do something tomorrow that's going to change things in Greensboro, and maybe around the nation. Would you be against me if I did this?" She said, "As long as you don't do anything that's going to bring disrespect upon the family or yourself, you have our support." So, with that I felt at ease, because I had the backing of my parents.

## Joseph McNeil

We went to the lunch counter at Woolworth, sat down and asked for coffee. We were told that they could't serve us and that we would have to leave. We discussed the fact that they had just finished serving us at a counter across the aisle, where we bought toothpaste and other items. I think that they suggested to one of the black help at that time that she come over and talk to us. She said that we might get ourselves involved in trouble and asked us to leave, that this was something that we might not want to get involved in. We continued to sit there, experiencing an intense sense of pride, and a bit of trepidation.

I thought that we might get arrested the first day, but I didn't know. On that particular day, I can't remember any patrons saying anything. The police may have showed up, but it was near closing time. I think there was an ongoing dialogue with the store management, but not an argument. I had a sense of "Damn it, we're going to do it. We're going to see where this thing goes." More so, a deep overriding sense of pride. We expected anything to happen, and we prepared for the worst, including arrest, if it came to that.

Upon reaching the campus, I think we felt the need to get others involved in what we were doing. I can't recall who we talked to first. One of the things that became critical was the campus leadership. We went to the various elements of the college community where we thought there was leadership potential—the student government, the air force and army ROTC programs, the football team, the college newspaper—soliciting help, and it was forthcoming. Despite a number of supportive people in the community, we considered it more practical for students to do it. The adults had families to support. We weren't breadwinners yet. No one stood over us, saying "You're going to get fired." So it made sense for us to do it. But it was a student movement; we had pretty much decided that.

## David Richmond

There were many things that occurred in our childhoods that influenced our decision to sit-in at Woolworth. Things from the time that we were first able to observe indignities inflicted upon black people: riding in the back of buses, going to the back door of restaurants to get food, officials from the white power structure coming to our house and calling our parents by their first names. All of these things were present in Greensboro where I lived as a youth.. There were many things that motivated me.

I'd known Ezell before coming to A&T. Frank came to Greensboro and attended Dudley High School his junior year. Ezell, Frank and I went to Dudley. Ezell and Joe were hooked up as roommates. During freshman orientation, we all met and the four of us really jelled; we had classes together. Joe, Frank and Ezell lived on campus and I lived at home, but I stayed on campus more than I did at my house. We talked about a lot of things in the dorm. We talked about everything but our studies; things happening around the world, things that were happening in Rhodesia, the Montgomery bus boycott. We talked about everything.

We had talked from September on about segregation, and we went over all sorts of possibilities, anticipating things that might happen if we sat down at the counter at the Woolworth store. We didn't know what to expect, but we knew all of the possibilities that existed. That Sunday night we were talking about it again, and about four o'clock that Monday afternoon, we said, "Let's do it," and we walked downtown. When we went in and sat down, one of the waitresses came over and asked us what we were doing sitting at the counter. And then we saw the manager and shortly afterwards, we saw two police officers standing there, but they didn't do anything; they just stood there. The store closed and we walked back to campus. As freshmen, we didn't know that many students, so we contacted some students that we knew and asked them to return with us on Tuesday morning. Then it hit the six o'clock news, and that's when we started organizing with other college leaders on campus. We did not encounter any criticism from anyone.

## Gloria Jean Blair (Howard)

I knew that my brother and his friends were going to sit in at Woolworth on February 1, 1960. He wasn't living at home at that time; he was living on campus at A&T. Before getting involved with that, he came home the two evenings before—he and Joe McNeil and Jack Ezell—it wasn't the original four—came by the house to talk with my father. There were some other students who lived in the dorm at A&T who came by and talked with my father. The night before the sit-ins, Ezell came by the house alone and talked with Dad and told him that he was really going to do it, and how they were going to do it. My father told him that he had the full support of the family. He did not show any fear of what was going to happen to his job, because my father was very supportive of anything that we did that we thought was right. If he felt it was right, he was very supportive. But he had a very natural feeling that a parent would have. My brother was very small and we often thought about his size and if he ran into the opposition physically, what would he do, and we did have feelings at times that something would happen to him. That didn't last very long. Ezell was very good in organizing people. He was very good with being on the front line and being out there. His greatest strength was being able to organize people, getting other people to do things and get things going.

## Ralph Johns

*[Note: Ralph Johns' interpretation of the origins of the sit-ins differs from that of the "Greensboro Four," not in overall concept, but in detail. All four credit Mr. Johns with having an influence upon them, but insist that the idea was their own.]*

Back in the late Forties, I would go to Woolworth and Kress to eat lunch, and I couldn't understand why I could sit down and eat, and yet the blacks had to stand up or take their food and leave. Here, in a place where they could go to all of the counters and buy merchandise, and yet be denied service at the lunch counter. I would go to the S&W or Mayfair cafeterias and watch my black friends walk by the window where I sat eating, and yet they could not enjoy the same privilege as an American, many whom had fought for democracy in the war. My conscience bothered me, and it broke my heart to see this indignity heaped on a human being of another color than white.

I lived in Greensboro and I decided to do something about this. So from 1949 until 1960, I approached black salespersons who worked in my store and students from A&T College to go to those businesses and break the law and try to get served. There were many over the years: Ira Kelly, Kathy Garrison, Turner Coggins, Dave Price, Martin Luther, Ed Stradford. For eleven years, I tried to get students and members of the NAACP to break these segregated barriers. I was vice-president of the local chapter of the NAACP a number of years, and week after week, I would bring this subject up to the members. They felt it was too radical then.

Woolworth became the target because I chose it. In December 1959 I finally approached a student who was a freshman at A&T University in my store buying shoes. I told him what I told the others. "Joe McNeil, you got any guts?" "What do you mean?" he asked. Then I told him to get about four students to go to Woolworth. I would give them money to buy at different counters and get a receipt for everything they bought, and then go to the lunch counter and sit down to get something to eat. I told him that he would be told by the waitress that they don't serve Negroes—the word "Negro" was used then, not "blacks."

Then I told him to call her a liar, that Woolworth does serve Negroes; that he was served on four counters, and he had the receipts to prove it. Then I told him that she would call the manager, and he would try to evict them or call the police. But I said, if he does, then call me on the phone and I would call Jo Spivey of *The Greensboro Record* to send a reporter and photographer to the scene at once. Well, Joe McNeil did not come back to my store. Dorothy Graves, a clerk in my store, said, "He's like all the rest you talked to. He ain't coming back." But Joe did come back, on February 1, 1960, with three more freshmen: Ezell Blair, Franklin McCain, and David Richmond. And they said, "We are here, Cuzzin,"—that was a nickname I used in my letters to the editor in the newspaper protesting segregation. Dorothy yelled, "Praise the Lord!"

For one hour, in the back of my store, I planned strategy, telling them what to do, and gave them money to use. And I told them if trouble started, to call me on the phone. That day was the beginning of the sit-ins that swept America. I told Jo Spivey what the plans were and when it would happen. I called her to send news reporters. Jack Moebes, the *Record* photographer, went to Woolworth that afternoon to take pictures of what was the beginning of the sit-ins at the Woolworth Five-and-Ten. George Simkins knew what I was trying to do, but he did not know that it had started until I phoned him and said, "George, four A&T students are up at Woolworth, sitting at the lunch counter, trying to get something to eat. The manager is trying to throw them out. They called me and I told them to sit there. I've already called Jo Spivey, and the *Record* has sent news reporters on the scene." I said, "George, if they get thrown in jail, I want to go bail and the NAACP must fight their case." George replied, with a laugh, "You finally did it, huh, Ralph? Go ahead, and the NAACP will back it up." I told him that since I was on the executive board of the NAACP, I'd keep him posted.

## Clarence "Curly" Harris

They came into the store at 4:30. The luncheonette was closed. They asked for a cup of coffee, and the employee behind the counter said that the store did not serve colored people. They continued to sit at the counter. I was inspecting the kitchen, and that same employee came to tell me what had happened. I told her to go back to the counter and to do her job. I said, "Don't talk to them in any fashion. Don't approach them in any way. Ignore them."

I walked to the police station and talked to Police Chief Paul Calhoun. He said, "The only way that you can get them out of there is to have them arrested for trespassing." I said, "I'm not going to do that. That's not my policy. I will serve anybody that comes to my store, if they're properly dressed." I returned to the store, and it was near empty. No one was sitting at the lunch counter, other than the four boys. Segregation was the policy of the city. There were separate "white" and "colored" signs in all public buildings and restaurants. I had taken such signs down in the store in 1958, after Dr. George Simkins came in and asked me to take down the signs. He said that he had talked to the people at Belk's, and they said they would, if I would. I contacted the home office in New York. I told them that "It won't amount to a hill of beans. There will be no reaction." So they said that I could.

We turned out the lights in the store, but they continued to sit there until 6:15. I would not serve them, because it was Woolworth's policy to abide by local custom. My supervisor was in town, at the Northeast Shopping Center store. He said, "It will blow over." I said, "I don't think so."

## Geneva Tisdale

When I began working at Woolworth, all the kitchen help were black; the waitresses were all white. The girl at the fountain and the one at the sandwich board, they were black, and the ones that washed glasses were black. There was not a place at the counter or near it where black people could get something to eat. There was a snack bar in the middle of the floor, and blacks could order food at the counter and take it to the snack bar or take it out, but not sit down and eat.

On February 1, 1960, when the four young men came to the counter and sat down, I was on the back steam table. It was a L-shaped counter in the back, against the wall. That's when I saw the young men sitting there. I thought they didn't know that Woolworth didn't serve blacks. So I kept on doing what I was doing. There were a few other customers at the counter.

As somebody passed by, they would ask if they could be served. They asked if they could have a cup of coffee and a piece of pie. Everybody just ignored them and kept walking. Later on one of the black girls told them that they couldn't serve them. Then I left and went upstairs. I wasn't anxious on that particular day, because I didn't think anything of it.

## Ima Edwards

On February 1, 1960, I was head of the bakery department, which was right next to the lunch counter. I remember that the four young men came in and sat down in the back, which was a counter away from me, but I could see them there. They asked to be served, and of course the waitress told them she was sorry, that she couldn't serve them. And then they demanded to be served, and the waitress got the manager, and the rest was handled through him.

I wasn't nervous; I just thought they didn't know that they couldn't be served. But when I was told that they would be back the next day, then I realized that they were demanding to be served. I couldn't hear what they said to Mr. Harris, because I was at the bakery counter. They weren't causing a commotion; customers at other counters were just coming and going as usual. In fact, most of the customers that day did not even know it was going on.

## George Simkins, Jr.

I first heard about the sit-ins when Ralph Johns called me. He said, "I've got four freshmen going down to Woolworth's now. I gave them money and they're going to buy hamburgers or something." He was very excited, and I knew what he was talking about. He had been trying to get me to do it for years. Whenever he would ask me to be a part of that in the past, I would tell him, "Ralph, I just can't do it right now." So I left my office and went down there. I watched them through the window as they sat at the counter until they left the store. There was a little crowd, but nothing like what there was in the next few days.

## Jack Moebes

Jo Spivey was a friend of George Simkins, so Simkins called Jo about it at home. She called Floyd Hendley [managing editor, *The Greensboro Record*], and he called me on my beeper; I was on another assignment. I didn't know what Curly's reaction was going to be. I said, "Floyd, I'm trespassing, and I could be arrested. You may have to get me out of jail."

I looked through the doors at Woolworth and saw them sitting at the counter. I didn't know which door they would come out of, so I stood on the corner of Sycamore and Elm Streets. It turned out that they left by the side door on Sycamore Street. I asked them if I could take their picture. The first one that I took had them walking by twos, and there was a black lady passing them. So I asked them to walk back, four abreast. They were very cooperative. That was the picture that would become famous, but the paper wanted pictures of what was going on in the store. So that picture remained in the files for ten years.

## George Simkins, Jr.

The NAACP had a scheduled a regular meeting that night at the Hayes-Taylor YMCA, and the four young men came to us, asking for our support. We gave it to them, along with a round of applause. They said that they were going back the next day. They were very excited, and felt that they had done something important. I knew Ezell Blair and David Richmond; I knew their parents from the neighborhood.

I had read about CORE doing that kind of thing in Chicago, I called them, and they sent Gordon Carey down. There is no question that Greensboro was the springboard for the sit-ins throughout the South.

## Jo Spivey

I got the call about 4:15 [p.m.]. I had just gotten home. It took me five or ten minutes to get Floyd Hendley and [Jack] Moebes started. So, it must have been ten minutes after five [p.m] when I got back downtown. The four students were at the back counter, so I couldn't tell what they were doing.

There were a few people out front but not an unusual number. So I went across the street from the Dixie Building, at the corner of February One Place [formerly Sycamore Street] and Elm Street]—there was a ladies' dress shop there then called Prago-Guyes. I stood underneath the canopy there so I could see. I never did see Jack Moebes. It really didn't occur to me to go around on the Sycamore Street side

The first thing I saw was Ezell Blair, [now known as] Jibreel Khazan. I knew him by sight. And he was leading the other three up Elm Street and everybody was just standing on the side of the street. I never saw anybody raise their hands or say anything. I was across the street, but the four went on up to the Jefferson Square and turned right and presumably went back to the college [A&T]. I later found out that John Erwin, who was a vice-president of the Greensboro branch of the NAACP had gone into Woolworth prior to the four men arriving, because the branch felt that if they got arrested for trespassing, or if they got beaten up, then somebody needed to be there to protect them. So he was already in Woolworth, and I found out later that George Simkins was up in front of Belk [Department Store], on the corner of Market and Elm. But I never saw either one of them, so I just went back home.

The next day I had to write stories about City Hall, so Marvin Sykes went down to cover the second day. And there were the two [original] sit-inners and two others at the counter. I think some more came later in the day. But after that I was able to clear my schedule and everything, or plan ahead to where I could cover it all. So everyday I was there.

I think most people in Greensboro would not have thought much about it if the lunch counter had just opened up, because they thought keeping it segregated was kind of silly. City Councilman Ed Zane were very concerned with getting it done without anybody being hurt. I think others were, too. General Townsend [City Manager]was quoted as saying, "There won't be any blood in the streets on my watch." I think that he saw the writing on the wall. He wanted it done without anybody being hurt. He wanted it done legally. I guess some of the Council members and other public officials couldn't have cared less. Some of them probably didn't want it to happen at all.

We never had any supervision [over what we wrote] at all. What the *Daily News* did, I have no idea. Floyd Hendley was sort of like General Townsend. He was a conservative, but he was a newspaper man first. And he could see that this was a news story, because a couple of hundred of years of practice was beginning to fall, and he knew this was a big story. So Robert Register, who was the city editor and who had the same feelings that I did about this subject, never gave me any supervision because he figured I knew what I was doing. I knew these people and they would talk to me, and there wasn't anybody else on the staff that they would talk to. So, as far as I can remember, nothing I wrote was ever changed one word.

I talked to General James R. Townsend—he was a retired general—he was the city manager here. And he was sort of conservative, but he was a good guy and I told him that I was concerned that some of these picketing students, particularly the girls from Bennett, might get hurt.

And so he said, "Well, Jo, you don't need to worry. I have talked with my people and I have told them, "There is going to be no bloodshed in this town. There's not going to be anybody hurt or killed, and if any of you cannot live with that, resign." So I didn't worry so much after that, because he had told all of his public safety-type people, and firemen, and everybody who might be called out that they were to protect these students. Of course, if the students had done anything that was breaking the law they would have been arrested. He said that no blood was going to run in his streets. So I think that he has never been given much credit for what he did. He actually put my house on a police survey route, too, so they would check this house every time they went around, so that I wouldn't be bothered.

## Robert "Pat" Patterson

The next day is when I got involved directly. There was a lot of demonstrating; it had a mushrooming effect. The Bennett College kids got involved. I remember one specific incident where things were getting a little tough in the city, and A&T had just won the CIAA championship. All of the football players put on their CIAA jackets and they sort of patrolled the marchers that were picketing. Things were tense for a while, but they eventually settled down.

## Jack Moebes

I went to Woolworth the next day [February 2], and Curly said, "You can't take pictures here," and held up his hands so that I couldn't get a shot of the counter. I said, "Well, Curly, they sent me down here to take pictures. I'm just doing my job. I'll have to do what I have to do, and you'll have to do what you have to do." Curly put his hands up, so I raised the camera and clicked; I didn't know what kind of picture I was getting. Then he went back upstairs to his office.

## Marvin Sykes

On February 2, 1960, I was on the staff of *The Greensboro Record* as business editor and feature writer. And I reported on racial matters, because I was filling in at A&T College when they had special programs. The sit-ins had started the afternoon before. Jack Moebes had gone down that afternoon and took a picture of the four original sit-in students as they left the store. So I went down with Jack about ten o'clock the next morning. Jo Spivey had heard that something was going on and had started the ball rolling.

We found black students in the store. We spoke with Mr. Harris, the manager. Of course, he didn't care for us taking pictures or asking questions. After about a half an hour, Harris acquiesced and told us what was going on without engaging in much conversation. Jack took photographs, and I talked to as many of the students as I could. The students, most of whom were freshmen, had very little to say at that time. In those days, the reporter's opinion never was a part of the story. I just asked them their names and home addresses, and whatever they had to say regarding their purpose, without going into opinion. We were criticized thirty years later for not having realized the depth of it. But at that time it was not up to the reporter to forecast or interpret what he is getting.

It was not very tense. Greensboro people were tolerant, more so than other cities. Captain William Jackson of the police department stationed men at the end of Elm Street and Greene Streets, to prevent known Klansmen and roughnecks from causing any trouble. These individuals were stopped and detoured away from the downtown area. It went very smooth, and there were few problems. Since my deadline was about 12:30, Jack took pictures quickly, and I asked questions as rapidly as I could. At the time that we left, there were no demonstrations, no cat-calling out on the street. People were looking, but they weren't making any commotion. I was told later that there were one or two radio reporters there, but at the time, Jack and I thought we were the only newspeople on site, and it was our exclusive story. The city editor sent me down there, and the staff knew that it was going on. The staff had copy ready as fast as they could, because in those days the *Record* enjoyed beating the morning paper [the *Greensboro Daily News*] to a story; the competition was fierce. The *Daily News* didn't pick up the story until the next day. Even so, it only played on the front page of the second section, because there was no inkling that it was going to be, what you might call, "the cradle of the Civil Rights Movement."

These students had to have guts to do it. They were well-mannered and well-dressed. They knew what they had in mind. They didn't go into any emotional tactics. They came to do a job, and they did it beautifully. And there were no large scale massive counter-demonstrations; most of the large crowds that formed downtown over the next few days were merely curious spectators. So there was only a small number of hostile whites. I'd say it was the behavior of the police, and even more, the goodwill of greater Greensboro at the time that prevented violence. In a way, people did support it. A feeling of, "It's about time" permeated through many people who saw it in those days.

## Ima Edwards

The next day [February 2] about four more black students came back about eleven o'clock, and sat down at the counter. I wasn't nervous, because they weren't threatening or anything. I never was really afraid, as far as being scared of what was going on. They just sat until later on that afternoon. I'm not sure whether they were joined with a few more that day or it was the next day, but, as it built up there was more and more that joined in. Finally it got to the point, with all the hassling from the Ku Klux Klan and so forth, that the decision was made to close the counter.

There were white men, probably Ku Klux Klansmen in the store, heckling the students sitting at the counter. I think police came and escorted them out. It didn't affect the relationship between white and black workers at Woolworth at all. We had a good relationship. I can't really remember that much about how I felt then about the people sitting at the counter. I think it was sort of tough on the black women working in the kitchen, because the students heckled them about working back there. I didn't hear it, but I have heard rumors that they did. As the years passed, I got to know David Richmond. He seemed like a nice fellow. I didn't think about it being a historic event.

No one was laid off when the counter was closed. We all worked; we had different jobs. I kept working at the bakery counter. Since the bakery counter and the snack bar were standing service, we served both races there. Some of our best customers were from A&T and Bennett. The ones in the kitchen, most of them were connected in the baking department, because they baked the cakes, baked the pies, did the donuts, and all this. So it really did not affect our operation that much. It affected overall business in the store. I think people were nervous about coming downtown and coming into the store.

## Ralph Johns

The next day twenty students went to Woolworth. Ezell Blair, Jr., was to keep in touch with me and meet with me at the store and notify me of happenings as we planned strategy. Dorothy went to Woolworth daily to keep tabs on what was going on. I went up and bought some items. As I walked by the students, I nodded my head, saying, "Good luck" and left. On the third day, hundreds of students came to Woolworth and overflowed into Kress. I went among them and told them to buy popcorn and go to lunch counters and eat the popcorn there. They did. They jumped over the railings when blocked by those who would prevent them from doing so. Hundreds and hundreds of students from A&T and Bennett joined the movement.

## John Hatchett

The sit-ins did not come about in some sort of political or social vacuum. The Bennett College students who were members of the college chapter of the NAACP have never received credit for their contribution to the idea behind the sit-ins. They had asked me to become their advisor, and I agreed. One evening in November of 1959, we sat down to discuss and plan what course of action we could take, as we put it, to make Greensboro a more open and receptive city for blacks. We researched carefully what was being done in other parts of the country at that time, specifically in Oklahoma, where sit-in demonstrations had been occurring. We took this idea to the president of the college, who was at that time Dr. Willa B. Player. She was receptive to the idea. But she cautioned us that, since Bennett College was a residential college and the holidays were approaching, what would happen if we started the sit-ins, and then all of a sudden most of the people involved had to go home on vacation? We saw some merit in her advice. And it was at that point that the young women from Bennett College invited some young men from A&T College to come over and participate in the planning. The young men who sat down at the Woolworth lunch counter on February 1, 1960, were participants in our discussion. And actually, we urged them to seriously consider doing this kind of action, in the event that the young ladies at Bennett could not participate fully, but that we would back them up.

There was a long period of discussion and planning that took place prior to January. The idea that those four young men were the sole initiators and the major participants, in the sit-ins is inaccurate. At least two, possibly three, of the four young men who ultimately went down to sit-in were at some of those meetings. I'm positive that Mr. [Ezell] Blair was there. I can't recall the names of the other gentlemen at the meeting. I have no personal axes of any sort to grind here. It's just that I felt that credit should be given to those young women who were courageous enough to at least want to start doing something at that time in North Carolina. But we weren't surprised. We were surprised by the statement that was made. But in order not to create any confusion about what was happening, we agreed that we would not say anything about the role that we played. We just simply became active participants, in order to not create any conflict between the women at Bennett and the young men at A&T. And that's one of the reasons for the long-standing silence about that.

A number of Bennett students participated in the sit-ins, in spite of the fact that Dr. Player had cautioned them about the holidays; that did not stop them entirely. In fact, sit-ins occurred after part of the holidays had ended. And they were the major supporters. It was very difficult at that time to get the bulk of the students at A&T to participate. So the young women at Bennett carried almost the full brunt of those day-to-day marches in front of the Woolworth store.

At that time, I was trying to function mainly as an advisor to the NAACP group on the Bennett campus. My role, to a large extent, was to offer some sort of protective and comforting influence, because there weren't that many young men involved at that particular time. It was good that I was there, because threats were received. There was a great deal of harassment. In fact, one young white boy accused me of being the leader, and said that he would like to do something to me. I didn't reply to him, because I didn't feel that he was going to do anything. But there was a great deal of verbal and very subtle mental harassment that took place during that period of time.

There were large numbers of people outside. It could have been crowded at times on the inside, but the days that I went inside, I didn't see that many people. Of course, each day that we would sit in, the counters were virtually empty. There were a lot of people who were curious about what was happening, but I didn't notice a large crush of people inside. But there were a large number of people outside who were either participants or onlookers in terms of the demonstration.

I don't recall any dumping of condiments, burning the students with cigarettes, or pulling them off of stools. I'm sure that if I had seen it, I certainly would have remembered [that] very vividly. Most of the accounts shared with me centered around a great deal of psychological pressures that they felt and experienced as they did this, because, obviously, that was there. These were pressures engendered in part by a very real fear of certain things that could have happened to them. There was no widespread protection on the part of the police, to my knowledge. They may have been there. But essentially, in terms of a demonstration of that nature, I would say that we were basically very vulnerable. And I think a lot of the young women, especially, experienced this kind of sensation. But I didn't see a heavy presence of police protection.

I did not believe that the Zane Committee was a sincere effective committee, because most of the participants from the Greensboro power structure were not sincere in either listening to or wanting to meet the demands put forth. They were essentially businessmen accustomed to power and influence, and not accustomed to dealing with black people who were, at that time in their eyes, very "belligerent," very outspoken.

And I think that initially we had a tremendous communication problem, because we were making demands. And they were not in a mood to listen very sincerely and openly to our demands. So I was not very happy with that particular committee, and not very happy with certain subsequent things that came out of it. Either Mr. Zane or the mayor [George Roach] called Bennett College, and put pressure on the president to silence me. The president called me into her office and said that she had received such a call, and that the person [who] made the call had suggested that, because I was too outspoken. I was an outsider by their standards. I did not know the social mores of Greensboro. I was not a part of the local black establishment here, and because of that, they did not feel comfortable negotiating with me. The president assured me that she had no intention of honoring their request. Not only did she commend what I did, but she gave me full rein to continue. I have to commend her for that.

But I felt that in the best interest of progress, that I should stay in the background, not because of any pressure brought. It was not necessary for me to negotiate with people who did not want to negotiate with me or with us. After those initial meetings, I made a decision to play a less active role in terms of negotiations.

I saw no evidence of resentment [by Bennett College students] at not being on the Student Executive Committee for Justice at A&T. I think what they really were concerned about was trying to make Greensboro, in their words, "an open city." Many of the Bennett women were from areas where eating facilities were not closed to them. And I think that they resented the fact that they had to live in a city where they could not attend a movie unless they sat in a certain area, or could not eat at a lunch counter, or could not participate in other social activities that they were accustomed to doing from the areas that they had come from. So their main interest at that time was a desire to open up the city in terms of activities that they could participate in.

But at some point, there was a disenchantment between the students at A&T and Bennett College. This could have grown out of a number of factors that had nothing to do directly with the sit-in demonstrations. There has always been a rivalry between the two schools. There could have been some resentment on the part of certain of the young women at Bennett who had been in the forefront of the struggle and the young men at A&T. And this could account for why that organization [SECJ] was composed primarily of the young men [at A&T], at least in terms of the leadership. Although there were certain differences of opinion and approach, it did not stop us from doing those things that we felt committed to, and did not stop us from continuing to work with the students at A&T. But my activities were confined mostly to the Bennett women and the NAACP there.

One reason that the negotiations were successful was that the national office of the five-and-ten stores knew that, because of nationwide sympathy to what was going on there, they had suffered very heavy losses economically. And that it was this kind of pressure, along with what was happening in Greensboro, that forced them to capitulate and open their lunch counters. So that it was this dual kind of thing that was operative at the time. The sit-ins had captured the attention of the nation, in part because of the media coverage. And people nationwide had made decisions to boycott Woolworth and Kress stores. And because of that tremendous economic loss, they decided to capitulate.

The NAACP chapter at Bennett College, was not satisfied with just the opening of lunch counters at Woolworth and Kress. We tried to determine what other activities could we participate in that would open the city up even more. These targets were places like bowling alleys, the movies, and other eating establishments that were throughout the city. Initially they were basically tests. No one agreed that we would challenge to the extent of being arrested, not at that time. A few individuals from both Bennett and A&T campuses participated in that. Many of the meetings occurred on the campuses. I do not recall any meetings, other than some strategy sessions, being held at anybody's home. Some of the larger churches opened up its doors for us to hold meetings there. I believe it was Providence Baptist Church. A few of us served in various capacities to call meetings to decide on what places we would attempt to test.

We basically asked that they [the owners of segregated businesses] honor an age-old American tradition of offering fair and equitable service to whoever presented themselves at their doors. I don't recall any incident in which we approached these negotiations and these discussions with any air of frivolity or lightheartedness. We were very serious in what we were asking. Their usual response was that, because of the mores of the area in which they were located, they could not honor our request, because to do so would mean that they would lose their white clientele and that they would eventually go out of business. We didn't think that would happen, but that even if that did happen, we were operating on principle and not solely on economics. We thought it was our right, our duty, to attempt to desegregate these particular places. That was basically our approach.

I think that once we were able to prove that we could do certain things and that we were "responsible," we wouldn't have to go through the whole sit-in type procedure in order to persuade some places to open. I think there were a few places that opened voluntarily once we approached them.

## Robert "Pat" Patterson

I can't say that the city was involved, but some very influential members of the community were involved. They were concerned about it. I think to a great extent the city fathers in Greensboro played a very important role in terms of how long it took us to get those places to open up. And at some point I think they played a role in getting them to open up. I think at first, the city fathers did not want to see Kress and Woolworth open up, because of what they believed was going to happen. If Woolworth and Kress opened up, then that was going to put pressure on a lot of local organizations and restaurants. And so I think they fought it to some extent. I don't have any way of proving this, but I think they had a part in the decision that Woolworth eventually made. But at first I think they were saying, "You can't afford to give in to this." And I think they were looking out for the business people here in Greensboro, which is understandable. If you're a politician, you can understand this.

We wanted to put pressure on local stores of national chains, because it would hit their bottom line. And I think they knew that if we targeted one small restaurant in Greensboro, we could probably quickly affect that bottom line a lot quicker. Although I think when we really started putting the heat on them there, then they had to start thinking about how it was going to affect local people. So at that time we were using a lot of different techniques to try and get what we wanted, what we thought was right then.

## Robert O'Neal

I went down to Woolworth on February 1 1960, with two other male students because we supported the sit-ins. We saw the "Greensboro Four" sitting at the counter. We went in and sat down, told them we were from Greensboro College and that we supported them. We sat there for probably about an hour, talking to them. I think they were shocked at first, and then pleased that there were some white students that would be supporting them.

By the time we left, there were twenty or thirty people in the store. There were several young white guys, what we used to call "greasers." When we went out they made comments, and tripped one of us. Another tried to punch me. I had polio as a child and I wore a long leg brace. I turned and he hit the top of my brace. I felt a jar, but it hurt him more than it bothered me.

The students on campus didn't know we had been there until the next day, when our names appeared in the paper identifying us as students at Greensboro College. Our names appeared in the newspaper the next day. We were in the second section. So even the newspaper didn't comprehend at that point how important the event was. On February 3 each of us was individually called into the dean of students' office. He told us that if we wanted to attend Greensboro College we should not do anything more with the sit-ins. All three of us asked why, and he said because two members of the board of trustees who were among the largest benefactors of Greensboro College, had called the president and put pressure on him. We had been asked to attend some meetings on the A&T campus. If I continued with that and I was caught, then I would not graduate in May. So I didn't have anything else to do with it, and neither did the other two. But two other guys went to A&T for meetings.

Most of the people at G.C. either didn't say anything, meaning they were opposed to what I'd done, or congratulated me. On February 2, after our names had appeared in the paper, I was walking in front of the campus, and a Greensboro College student drove past me. He stuck his head out of the window and said, "Rick, you son-of-a-bitching, nigger loving bastard, I'm gonna get your ass!" and drove off. I never saw the guy again. That's when I knew that maybe I had gotten myself into a little more than I had realized. But that's the only major thing that happened.

I'm sure the campus was made aware that the three of us were directly involved, and that it probably made some people reconsider. My relationship with a sociology professor was never the same after that. He probably was under pressure from the administration for his job because at least two of his students were involved in that. I'm sure for the rest of that semester, he was working under a cloud as far as his job was concerned.

I had applied at two major employers in Greensboro, Cone Mills and Burlington Industries. The interview with one of them didn't go well, but I was called back for a second interview on the other one. I thought that probably I would be offered a job, but I got a call from the assistant director of personnel. She said that something had come up, and they didn't think they could hire me. Of course I will never know, and it's not important in the long run.

## Anne Bisher

Somebody came in my dorm room and asked us if we would support the Bennett girls by sitting down at the Woolworth lunch counter. My roommate and I decided to walk uptown and sit in. I think that she was doing it because she thought it was fun to be a little rebellious, but when we got to the store, I finally realized what I was doing. I was holding space so that nobody could just sit there and order. The counters were full of black students, but nobody was eating anything. They were studying, and they ordered water with a toothpick; it was called a pine float. I went down there every day for several days. I'd take my books and I'd go up there and I'd sit and study. I don't think anyone else ever went with me after that first time. I told my daddy so he would know, and he said, "Do what you have to do."

I remember walking uptown and going in and seeing a bunch of people sitting around, all black kids and white kids sitting at the counter, and I went in and sat. What the black students wanted us to do was stagger it so that people weren't doing it all at one time. I only remember one girl in particular. One day, we were outside the front of Woolworth's picketing and carrying signs. I don't even know where the sign came from. I think somebody just gave it to me. We were marching with the signs, not saying anything. Somebody jerked me back; it was my aunt's lady that helped her, Mabel. She said, "Anne, what are you doing? You are up here causing trouble. I'm gonna tell your momma and daddy." I said, "Momma and Daddy know I'm up here." And then she jumped on the girl, the little black girl, who was her granddaughter. She was in college somewhere; I don't even know her name. But she said, "When you get home, you're gonna be in trouble." She was really mad at us.

Nobody did anything except maybe cat-called us or said things to us. I didn't see any violence. Most people just stood back and watched, maybe said things to us, but nobody ever started a fight.

I'd go down there and stay maybe an hour or two and just sit and study. But I was also watching people, fascinated. The waitresses weren't allowed to serve any of the black students at all. So nobody was getting food, and people behind us were razzing and cursing us, because they couldn't get food. A black girl told me, "We walk from A&T to Woolworth to get our supplies, just like you do from Greensboro College. And you can sit down and you can eat, but we can't. We don't think it's fair." And I said, "No, that's not fair."

It was very peaceful, and Greensboro probably led the way in that. The police stood around, but they didn't knock anybody around. They just kind of kept it quiet and peaceful. I think maybe they thought it might go away, but it didn't.

It probably didn't have any impact on the campus. I didn't ever tell the faculty or anybody, that I was going up there and sitting in, because I didn't know whether or not I would get in trouble doing it. But I still felt strongly enough about it to do it. My roommates and my suitemates knew it, but I don't know if anybody else did. I didn't realize until years later that three guys from G.C. had been in. I don't remember seeing them there.

Most of the G.C. girls were from middle-income homes and they were very sheltered. I think that they were all good Christian girls, but I don't think that any of them ever really realized the injustices that were done. But I'm sure every one of them would do anything they could to help, because none of them that I was ever around were prejudiced. I don't know how many of them ever sat in. I didn't go up to look to see if anybody else was sitting, so I didn't notice.

The Ku Klux Klan burned a cross in our front yard when I was home one weekend. It terrified us. When we looked out the front window, there were probably about a hundred Ku Klux Klanners standing out in the road.

I was proud to do it. And I'm proud of Greensboro for being one of the main places for the Civil Rights Movement to have started. At that point, those [black]kids had a hard time. They got their education, but it was more or less self-satisfaction. But as far as getting to use it, they couldn't use it, because people weren't hiring blacks.

## Edward Bryant

After the sit-ins there was a lot of discussion about civil rights among the students, but not a whole lot before. There were few blacks on campus, other than custodial work. It wasn't a point of discussion, but I would assume [the general attitude on campus] was segregationist. But we didn't discuss it as a topic. I think the faculty was a little ahead of us, generally. One faculty member was inspirational in getting this started. He mentioned to us one day in class that there was some activity in town that we ought to check into.

Several of us went down to the Woolworth store, and it was packed with people. When we got in we tried to get up to the seats at the fountain. Once we got there, they were all occupied by black students, mostly males. The crowd was mostly white, and I think most people were trying to figure what was going on, except for a contingent of hecklers. It had an immediate impact on me.

We spoke with black students and some white people and then a reporter asked for our comments, and they appeared in the paper. And that's when it hit the fan.

There were two other G.C.men with me, Lowell Lott and Richard O'Neal. We couldn't sit down [because] all the seats were occupied by the black students. We talked with them about what was going on. They were very well organized. There were shouts and derogatory comments being made generally, but I don't recall anybody zeroing in on us. The black students did, but I don't recall the crowd doing it. I'm not sure we went back to Woolworth, but I had subsequent meetings with some of the black leaders.

After it came out in the press, a lot of the G.C. students were ticked off. The administration—at lower levels, anyway—was kind of outraged. Dean Wold, the dean of students, and I had a working relationship, because I was involved in student government. After three or four days, certain members of the board of trustees called him. He suggested that I withdraw from the college, and I refused to do that. Then the next day, the president of the college intervened and said that he would sustain our right to speak personally on any issue.

After the story came out in the newspaper, my father was a little upset, but he held his tongue. His company had a plant in Greensboro, and the manager made sure my father knew what was going on. [My father] contacted me, but he just cautioned me to be careful. I don't recall anyone on campus accosting me, but there were signs put up about "nigger lovers." Frankly, we didn't give a damn what they thought, because it was painfully obvious to us that, something positive was happening.

I can remember after talking with some of the black students, that they were just a great bunch of people, depending on who they were and what they were, as opposed to just being black or white. So that was a very transforming moment for me.

## William Jackson

I was in the juvenile division at the time, and there were lots of kids uptown. There was a Junior Ku Klux Klan, and they were trying to get some of the kids stirred up. But we knew who was involved in that, and it really never really got off the ground.

For instance, in front of Kress's, which was half a block south of Woolworth on Elm Street, had a demonstration in front of it. There was a young man in there who was a fifteen-year-old leader of this Junior Ku Klux Klan. Before he realized what was happening, I had him out of there. I think by getting him out, we averted trouble on that particular day, because it was beginning to get a little nasty. I walked in the line with him, and when we got to the end of the street, I bumped up beside him, told him who I was and said, "Just keep on walking." I always believed that the easy way was the best way, if you could possibly do it. But it didn't amount to anything; In regards to the Klan stuff, most of our troubles were with white teenagers.

There was a danger of violent eruption to a degree, but not great. You'd see grown people in there crying over the situation; actual tears coming out of their eyes. But it worked out to the point where it wasn't a whole bunch of trouble. I saw a time within the store itself that looked like it was going to be very explosive, but we were able to get in there and get those that were kicking up, ease them out and got it over with.

We had people brought in here for that particular thing. There was one [white] young lady who was arrested in this store, and I carried her to the police station myself. She was college age, and the first thing she did was call an official in the state of New York.

## Jibreel Khazan

The protest was originally designed to be carried out just at the Woolworth lunch counter, but I remember Frank making a statement as the protests developed during the first week, "We didn't want to set the world on fire, we just wanted to eat." But behind that we had an idea, a hope, that this would catch on and spread throughout the country. Fortunately, it went even beyond our wildest imagination. The main emphasis was on Woolworth, and by the third day the counters there were filled to capacity. Perhaps over three hundred people were in that store. We decided to expand the sit-ins to the Kress store down the street.

I didn't have much time to think about being a celebrity, because my folks kept reminding me who I was: "You are our son, and you will have to go to work this summer." There was no way to sit down and think about it. My sisters reminded me, "You're nobody special, you're just our brother. We're proud of you, but I don't want to hear all of those weird theories." My older sister told me, "Get away from me with all of that civil rights talk. You talk about those things too much."

My mind was dwelling on that, but we knew the people on campus respected us and we respected them. That gave us an advantage in some ways that we were a part of this movement, but there was no advantage any other times. The teachers didn't ease off on our school work. The four of us—Frank, Joe, David and I—in sitting down at the lunch counter on February 1, 1960, didn't do it for personal recognition. Later, we were asked to represent the students nationally, but it was always as symbols of the Movement, not as celebrities. I would say to Frank, "You go to Chicago to represent us at the Catholic Interracial Human Rights Award Dinner." Another time Joe might go to Washington." The Bible speaks of the "body of Christ," meaning the Messiah has many parts, so we were one body with many parts. For the organism to function, we had to achieve equal rights. The ultimate goal was, hopefully, to get Congress to pass a comprehensive civil rights bill.

The Movement allowed us to meet at Shaw University in Raleigh over Easter weekend. We talked with Hank Thomas, Julian Bond, Marion Wright, Raymond Barry, John Lewis, Dionne Diamond, Laurence Henry and John Henry, as SNCC was formed. No one knew that we were there, because events had moved beyond Greensboro at that point. We were observers, just watching everyone. They talked about "This is the way it should go," but nobody talked about Greensboro; as far as they were concerned, we were not there. In Greensboro, we made a decision on Saturday, February 6, to suspend demonstrations to negotiate. So we stopped picketing for a week, but it turned into almost two months. Students around the country said, "The Greensboro Movement is dead, so we have to pick it up." But the Greensboro Movement was not dead; we knew that eventually they would have to do the same thing that we were doing.

## David Richmond

We were not aware of any threats by the state to cut off funds to the College at that time. A&T has always been on the low end of the totem pole as far as appropriation of funds from the state legislature. They were getting the maximum that they were going to get anyway. So I don't think that they could have cut funding. By law, they had to give us something, but the legislature always gave [the school]the least they could.

Our focus from day one was centered on the A&T campus, which was the source of our inspiration and our strength. The only thing that I could say would be that it started with the sit-ins and it continued from 1960 to 1963. Then the freshman class of 1964 carried on until 1968. So during those years, there were always some students on campus that had participated in the dialogue and the interchange of ideas involved in civil rights, and they communicated with each other. So, definitely, there would be a continuity of protest activity at A&T.

All of the students involved with the sit-ins were determined to maintain some sort of control over subsequent events. We were walking a thin line between getting our education and being expelled and, perhaps, going to jail. Because our futures were at stake, we decided that it had to be a student-led protest. And we believed that we could most effectively work with our fellow students to prevent things getting out of hand and eroding into violence.

## Gloria Jean Blair (Howard)

My brother never placed a lot of emphasis on himself being in the limelight. He was excellent at supporting other people when they had doubts and fears about doing things. He was very supportive, and on many occasions when people did not see him out there in the limelight, he was encouraging others in a quiet way that impressed them and kept the spirit of the sit-ins alive. Ezell was always talking to students who were fearful that their parents were going to lose their jobs, kids who wanted to help in some other way. If they could not march on the picket lines and be active in the demonstrations, he was very supportive of why they could not be involved, and he was always willing to make recommendations on other ways that they could support the Movement, other than being on the front lines and sitting down on counters.

He spent a lot of time doing that. And there were a lot of telephone calls that had to be made, a lot of paper work that had to be done. There were people coming in who wanted to interview students who were involved in the sit-ins. People from the national and local news media. There were guest speakers who came to town, people wanting to talk with the students who had to be housed. There were students who were working on that, entertaining them, helping them with their schedules, people doing a variety of things regarding the sit-ins.

I was not involved in the sit-ins at Woolworth, because when the first sit-ins occurred at Woolworth, I was a senior in high school, and it was more college-oriented. Probably after five or six days, I went down there with my father, but I was never there with my brother and his friends when they were deciding how to organize the sit-ins. Initially, the focus was on getting the college students there, because they had more flexibile schedules. There were some who were free mornings, some who had no classes on certain days, whereas high school students had to be in school from 8:00 in the morning until 3:00 in the afternoon. So high school students did not participate on an active basis in the sit-ins until the summer months.

## Warmoth Gibbs

It was significant. It was unusual. It was something we had not heard of at A&T, in the handling of students and question of relationship with the city. It was a new situation in that the students apparently had the thing well in mind as to what they wanted to do, but they hadn't made known very much—at least I hadn't heard much of anything about it. And I don't believe many, if any, members of the faculty knew at that time about it.

The mayor of the city at the time was Mayor George Roach. And the city manager was General James R. Townsend. Mayor Roach and General Townsend came over to my office on the campus and we had a conference. In substance, they called attention to the situation, which we acknowledged was a new situation for all of us. They asked, what could the colleges do? My suggestion was that we had rules and regulations printed in the catalog that we sent to students concerning college regulations. I told them that I thought we could handle that all right. I don't believe we would have any problem in handling that situation. I told them that the problem of the students coming down to the Woolworth store was more than the college could do. And they said, "Yes, we recognize that. And so, how can we work this?"

I told them that we'd hold the students to meet all our regulations on the campus. But when they got out in the streets, we'd let the mayor, the city manager, and the police department take over. I think there was a spirit of cooperation between the city government and A&T. The mayor and the city manager did not ask for any more action from the campus administration in preventing the students from going downtown to demonstrate. They handled the police department situation themselves. And I think they handled it as fairly as they could under the circumstances.

## Jibreel Khazan

When Dr. Gibbs refused to interfere with the protests, that was a shock to a lot of people, because they had a preconception that he was "conservative" and an "Uncle Tom," but that was far from being the case. I found out later that Dr. Gibbs went to Harvard and was one of the two living founders of the black ROTC program in the United States. This man was a scholar and what we would call "militant" in his time. He took his stand and that shocked a lot of people, and that built a lot of school pride. It made us feel even greater. Despite Dr. Gibbs' tacit consent, none of us expected any concessions from the faculty. I wouldn't even have thought about saying to an instructor, "Will you please pass me while I am demonstrating?" I would not have thought of asking a professor for that, because we had to live what we were telling the people to do. Between our demonstrations, we got in our homework. Our primary mission remained to go to school, to get an education.

## Franklin McCain

In order to accommodate the enthusiasm of the students, we had to go someplace else, so we elected to go to Kress, which was one or two stores down the street. After going to Kress, our thinking was, "We ought not to just single out these two stores and let everyone else go, as if their garments are clean." Therefore, we went to places like the hamburger drive-ins, where people didn't go in to sit down, but got curb service at one's car, and still couldn't get service. We went to the Hot Shoppe and the Toddle House on Summit Avenue, Eckerd's Drugs, and the O. Henry Hotel, Meyer's Department Store, and the Apple House Restaurants. These were individual attempts later on in the summer, but in the spring of 1960, we kept our efforts focused on Woolworth and Kress downtown.

The four of us received recognition on campus by our fellow students. People knew who we were, what we had done and what we were a part of. There was little relationship between the members of the staff and administration and me, except for Dr. Gibbs and persons like Virgil Stroud and Dr. Robinson, who were very interested in what we were doing and were always eager to talk about it. We also had a special relationship with Dr. Gibbs and, later, with Dr. [Samuel] Proctor [interim president of A&T College]. In retrospect, I think perhaps the greatest contribution we received from the college was when Dr. Gibbs told the administrative officials: "Leave those guys alone," rather than telling us, "You've got to clean up your act or get out of here and go someplace else." Officials at other Southern black universities at that time expelled students for participating in this type of thing. But Dr. Gibbs said on several occasions, "As long as the students maintain responsible grades and don't break laws or embarrass the college, then we have absolutely no control over them."

## James Farmer

CORE had been sitting in since 1942 in many cities, largely northern. The only southern cities in which we had such activities were in Tennessee and Oklahoma. In the Forties and even most of the Fifties, nonviolence was unheard of as a technique in this country. Very few people were aware of it, and when we would speak of it with white and black leaders, they would think that we must be some kind of nuts.

We got no publicity in what we were doing. There was no television to help it spread, so we debated at each convention whether we should invade the South with our technique of nonviolent direct action. Most of the delegates felt that using techniques of non-cooperation and civil disobedience, especially in the Deep South would be suicidal; it would provoke so much massive violence that local blacks would have to face after we had left the area, that it probably would not be worthwhile. The prevailing view within CORE was that there was a distinction between the Upper and Lower South, that the violence encountered would be more severe in Alabama and Mississippi than it would in Kentucky, Virginia or North Carolina.

The student sit-ins that began on February 1, 1960, came as a surprise to us; they were not sponsored by CORE or by any other organization. CORE became involved in it because those students went to Dr. George Simkins in Greensboro, who was the NAACP head there, and asked him to give them some help. Dr. Simkins had read of CORE activities from our brochures and fund appeals, and knew that this was the kind of thing with which CORE had a great deal of experience. We dispatched Gordon Carey, one of our two field secretaries, to Greensboro. On CORE's instructions, Carey moved from city to city in the South, wherever there was a black college and conducted nonviolent training sessions in the technique of nonviolence. So CORE participated in the spread of the Southern student sit-in movement.

There was little competition between CORE, the NAACP and SCLC at the time; there was cooperation more than anything else. Each group wanted to make sure that it had some visibility in what was an autonomous movement. I don't recall any disavowal of nonviolent direct action by the NAACP. It is true that direct action was not the emphasis of the NAACP; its emphasis was in more conventional court actions and lobbying activity. Therefore, the NAACP was more than willing to let such organizations as CORE focus upon direct-action tactics, while it assisted in providing legal assistance.

In Greensboro, the A&T students made it clear that they wanted to maintain control of the sit-ins there through the organization that they had formed [The Student Executive Committee for Justice], and we were perfectly willing to limit our activity to advice if they asked for it. The minutes of the CORE National Action Committee, which was our board of directors, reflect the fact that the members of the NAC were virtually unanimous in believing that this should be student-controlled effort. There was no disagreement between the Greensboro students and CORE on that issue at all. CORE remained in an advisory capacity; we did not want to run it. We just wanted to urge that the technique of nonviolent direct-action was used as the sit-ins spread throughout the South. We recognized that Greensboro served as a symbol of where the sit-in phase of the Civil Rights Movement began, and we wanted to use its reputation in encouraging sit-ins in other cities, and it was effective. Other black college students, watching what was happening in Greensboro on television, became motivated to go out and do likewise. It remains today a symbol of the student sit-in movement.

## Gordon Carey

At that time there were two of us in New York that were field secretaries, James T. McCain and me. We got a postcard from George Simkins that said they were involved with sit-in activity in Greensboro, that members of the American Friends Service Committee had given him literature on CORE's sit-ins in Baltimore in the 1950s. What impressed him about that brochure was that New York CORE at that time had picketed Woolworth in New York to assist the Baltimore project. So, what George was essentially asking us in his postcard and his later telephone conversation was, could we do the same kind of thing now?

I was the one that talked with him on the telephone, after receiving the postcard. At that time, all we knew was from reading little squibs in the *New*

*York Times* that there were sit-ins going on down there. We had no contact with anyone in Greensboro. I think that I must have gotten the postcard about February 7th or 8th. I called George and discussed it with him. I told him, yes, I thought that we could do something like that and, in addition, we could send someone down to talk with them to see if we could be of any help. He said that he thought that would be a good idea. In those days we had a very limited budget and traveled by bus. I arrived about February 13th. But a day or so before I left, all of the lunch counters in Greensboro had closed down, and so there was no activity in Greensboro. They had closed them all down to solve the immediate problem.

I never got to Greensboro. I stopped in Durham instead, and on about the 13th of February, 1960, I got to Durham and was picked up at the bus station by Floyd McKissick, and we went to his house. He told us that the kids in Durham were about to start sit-in demonstrations there, so I never got to Greensboro until later. This was just before the thing took off in many different cities all over North Carolina. I think the Durham sit-ins started almost two weeks to the day from the original one in Greensboro. CORE was surprised when this thing became so widespread, because we had been having sit-ins in places of public accommodation since the early 1940s, and in 1958-1959 had had major sit-ins in Florida. CORE had a long history in this kind of thing, but it had never become a national movement, city by city.

CORE was unique at that time, among civil rights organizations, because in most organizations, the NAACP for example, the local chapters served to support the national chapter, and the national chapter mounted educational and legal programs. In CORE, the whole philosophy was quite different. The national office functioned only to serve local chapters. They set their own policy and initiated their activities, and instead of the chapters supporting the national office, it was quite the opposite. The national organization existed solely to serve them. Our money came from a national mailing list of people. Our chapters didn't send us money; we sent them money. So the delegates at conventions would decide whatever national policy there was. The national organization didn't really exist except at the time of conventions. This same philosophy went over to helping other organizations. Naturally, nobody who works for an organization is going to completely ignore his own organizational interest. Sure, you've have an interest in promoting your own organization, because at that time CORE was the only organization involved in nonviolent direct-action, and it was an interracial organization, it had a long history of nonviolent action and we believed in what we were doing. So, naturally we tried to promote nonviolence.

1960 upset all of that. Greensboro did not negotiate, and a lot of people in CORE thought that was wrong. We should not be responding to this, because they didn't go in and announce what they were going to do, and go through all of the various stages that our discipline required. Most of us felt, however, that we should abort that and proceed, because this was a grassroots movement and we should give them whatever help we could. From the 1940s until the 1960 sit-ins, Jim Robinson, Jim McCain, Marvin Rich and I were the staff. Usually the national office of the CORE throughout all those years was essentially a volunteer organization. At times it had one full-time field secretary. He was a full-time volunteer and got subsistence only. CORE held a national convention each year, to which the local chapters sent delegates, and those delegates ran the convention and set policy.

Typically, before that time, as a field secretary, I would go around and try to organize CORE chapters whenever someone would write us a letter expressing interest in starting a CORE chapter. Initially, many CORE chapters had, maybe, five or six members. There were not big organizations. The only national policy that CORE used to have, until the 1960s, was what was called a "National Discipline," published as a little pamphlet. Every word of that Discipline was voted on by the delegates at the national convention. One of the disciplines was that before direct-action could be initiated, there had to be negotiations. You had to notify people that direct-action would take place. It was very Gandhian. That was the kind of organization that CORE was at that time.

*When news of the sit-ins was reported in the newspaper, three Woman's College students, Ann Dearsley, Eugenia Seamans, and Marilyn Lott, dubbed the "W.C. Three," walked downtown on Thursday, February 4, to join in sympathy with the protest. The next day they were joined independently by Elizabeth Toth, and Claudette Graves Burroughs, an African American W.C. student living as a town student.*

## Ann Dearsley (Vernon)

I remember learning about the sit-ins through a newspaper on the third day, and I happened to be having breakfast with Genie and Marilyn. We just said, "That's the silliest thing we've ever heard, you can't buy a cup of coffee because you're black," and we said, "Well, we figure that needs to change." And so we just marched on downtown. We didn't ask anyone's permission. We wore our class jackets, [but] that wasn't done as a confrontational gesture. We were real proud of those jackets; we wore them everywhere. Wearing those jackets would later become quite a point of contention. They were the flashpoint, because that identified us with the college. This was not calculated; we just decided to just do it. We were pretty naive about what was going to ensue. We thought we would walk up and sit down and say, "Give these people a cup of coffee" We really had no idea what the repercussions were going to be. We didn't sign out; it seemed perfectly innocent, and reasonable, and not breaking any rules. We had no idea it would be such a big deal.

## The Greensboro Sit-ins

I wasn't nervous, not really. It was kind of surprising to see all of these hundreds of people at Woolworth. When we entered the store, the [white] crowd, which was a very rough kind of a crowd, certainly did not dream that three white girls from the college were coming to lend support [to the black students]. We walked in and the crowd gave way for us, because the assumption of all those people was that we were going to be on the white side. Somebody gave us our seats, and then the waitress came up and said to me, "Do you want a cup of coffee?" I was really tense, and I said, "There's somebody here before me." The waitress said to me, "You need to go back to campus." And beyond that, I knew the manager of Woolworth. The family of a friend of mine at Eden Broughton High school in Raleigh [N. C.] moved to Greensboro. Her father was "Curley" Harris, who was the manager of Woolworth. I'm sure it was as much a surprise for Mr. Harris to see me sitting at his counter as it was for me to see him. He also advised me to go back to the campus.

Then the cat was out of the bag, and everybody suddenly realized that the group at the counter had been joined by these white girls in a W.C. jacket, who were supportive. The immediate reaction of the black students sitting near me was one of immense surprise when they realized that we were there to support them. Nothing dramatic happened, just a general acceptance by the black students. "Oh, my gosh. We've got some white girls from W.C. who are here to support us." The sit-ins just quietly continued. Everybody had books; the whole top of the counter was completely covered with books. And we all followed what became known as the "Nashville Code": Look straight ahead; don't make eye contact with the people who are harassing you; stay calm; don't respond in any way.

There was a large white crowd behind us. They were really upset when they realized that they had been tricked into giving up their stools. Our position suddenly became clear, and the crowd became extremely threatening. It was a very scary three hours sitting in that lunch space, because the crowd got closer and closer. There was a man with a knife against my back. If you had had that kind of volatility later on the Civil Rights Movement, I think violence would have erupted. It is a miracle that nobody was knifed or shot or punched out, but they weren't. It was the beginning of the sit-ins, and the passive approach was working well. So, I think that's the reason we were not physically assaulted. I don't remember seeing any policemen, but that doesn't mean they weren't there. It was obvious [to me] that the police would not lend support, and we sat there, feeling really very scared and totally unable to move, because there were hundreds of people in that very narrow store.

We said to each other, "How do we get out of here at five o'clock?" There were hundreds of hostile people filling the store and blocking the exits. We stayed until the store closed at 5:30. We were really naive about what we were walking into and how complicated it was going to be to get out. It was a long way from that counter at the back of the store to the street. And the store was full of angry people who didn't like what we were doing.

The A&T football players linked arms around us and walked up those narrow aisles to the sidewalk, with us in the middle, as members of the crowd taunted us. The football players were standing in the middle of the sidewalk, with us in that circle. Someone must have hailed a taxicab, and when it arrived, that group of students said the Lord's Prayer. I don't think it has ever meant as much to me as it did on that afternoon; it was so heartfelt, so indicative of the emotions that were there. It really did feel like we had protection from a higher power. I don't think I've had another spiritual experience like that. It was one of the most extraordinarily moving moments of my whole life. A cab rolled up, and the guys opened their flying wedge and put the three of us into a cab. That's how we got back to campus. To have walked back would have been dangerous.

I think how difficult things were for Mr. Harris, as one of the segregated business owners. They thought that if they started serving black students, their business would completely collapse. And the black employees were caught in the middle, because it could have cost them their jobs. The whole structure of racial segregation was so incredibly complicated that to challenge it was a threat to lots of people that I think we can't even think of today.

I certainly didn't think about the repercussions, because we had not been questioned by the photographer, although somebody got our names. There were some TV cameras filming and photographers were taking pictures. Our photograph appeared in the paper on the fifth day [February 5th]. But Dean [Katherine] Taylor thought about the repercussions. We were her worst nightmare. I'm sure she did at that moment what she thought was most appropriate for a white, Southern, state-supported girls' school. You have to put the repercussions in the context of another time, another culture, and another set of expectations. There were expectations of how young women would act and how they would represent their school. I basically didn't go off campus for the rest of the year, because we had some threats. But that wasn't much of a concession to the administration; it was necessary for us to sign out for us to get off campus anyway. You had to have permission to go anywhere.

At that point, we thought, "Well, we've done it. Maybe we'll go back tomorrow." We didn't realize that the whole thing was going to blossom such that Dean Taylor was going to be so incensed and was going to throw us out of school. I got thrown out of school, but almost immediately, I was thrown back into school. Dean Taylor called my parents, who were living in London, and said, "Your daughter has done such-and-such, and this is against the rules, and we're going to expel her." My father said, "No, you're not." Maybe there were easier rules for me, being a graduate student than for an undergrad student, but I had a huge scare. Within at least four or five days I knew that I was going to go. They said, "We are going to throw you out." Maybe it was because my parents lived in London, but suddenly, I was back in school, and I was able to finish my MFA here. But I did not participate in my graduation ceremony, because it was still too volatile.

It was frankly in extremely scary time for me. I think in some ways I was less courageous than I have been thought to have been. I didn't do anything great like the people who did through the sustained effort. You have to remember how little this was in the scheme of things, because we did it just one time. And really the repercussions were so dramatic; we did not do it a second time. There were thousands of people who stepped back into the fray over and over again, and really did put their lives on the line. Did I make a difference? I like to think so. I view my participation as just a little drop in the ocean. But I am convinced little drops wear away big stones.

## Eugenia Seamans (Marks)

There was no contact between me and the other women until maybe the day before, and it was in the context of a social conversation. I don't remember whether it was in the dormitory or around campus after classes. I would have been interested in that issue just because of my family's Unitarian background and my sense of what was just, but there was not an organized movement on the part of the Woman's College. Marilyn Lott had a brother at Greensboro College and he had gone to the sit-ins, perhaps on the first day, and it was through Marilyn that I learned of this movement and I was certainly aware of the Montgomery bus boycott. My sense of civil rights dates back to Ralph Bunche in the U.N., and so I was a person who would have been interested in civil rights issues through news media and the Unitarian church, which talked about these issues in its services and in its programs.

I knew Marilyn only as another student living in New Guilford [dorm]. We met in the parlor of New Guilford to touch base about what we were doing, but it wasn't really organized. It's likely that I saw the newspaper article on that day and that I decided that it was the right thing for me to do, especially as a Southern person, to show that not all Southerners were bigoted. And I felt that it was the just thing to do.

I went there with a sense of a need to fulfill a moral obligation. I went to express my religious and ethical beliefs. Quite truthfully, because of the way I was raised, I was in support of what was going on. I walked downtown by myself about 11:00, because I wanted to think about what I was doing. I walked into Woolworth and went to the lunch counter in the back of the store. Marilyn and Ann were already there. Half the seats were occupied by A&T students,

Bennett students, Marilyn and Ann. There was just a sense of who was going to get the next seat if somebody got up, and how to make sure that student activists retained the seats that they had.

Because I was Caucasian, I was given a seat by a gentleman, and the waitress asked what I wanted to order. I said, "The people over there"—meaning the A&T and Bennett students—"were here before I was, and they should be waited on first." And so a stalemate was created. This was on Thursday [February 4]. The other girls may have been there a day before me. I didn't discuss this with them prior to going downtown. No one on campus knew what I was planning to do. I recall wearing my Woman's College blazer because, naive as I was, I thought that I was doing a good thing and that the Woman's College would be pleased with what I was doing. We were supposed to be the New South.

We went out because the store was closing. I recall that we all held hands in a circle and someone from A&T said we were going to fall to our knees and pray, so that's what we did. That first day we all three went back to campus in a taxi. We probably just discussed what had happened and generally what we were going to do next and then we went back to studying for the evening. I don't recall any untoward remarks, and I don't recall any necessarily positive remarks. I recall my [dorm] housemother saying, "Be cautious," but not saying, "Don't do it." I don't recall other students' comments, and I don't think my roommate ever said anything to me about it; we continued to have a relationship throughout the year.

I sat there for two or three days, and the aisles were crowded and the people packed them so it was just this sense of people. And I think there were police there who kept people moving. My memory is that there was a crowd of white people trying to keep the A&T and Bennett College students out of the seats. There was not any physical violence; there was not any pushing that I recall, but certainly, people were aware of [all] the bodies that were there.

I think that went on maybe two or three days. There were meetings with the Bennett and A&T students and the three of us, maybe four of us, talking about picketing outside the store and the issues about whether picketing was legal and creating signs. They were strategizing about how to make the point that black people were permitted to buy food at the counter, but they couldn't sit down, and that is what seemed very unfair to me. That Woolworth could take their money for food but they couldn't sit down, and it just didn't seem like an equitable situation even on the social base of it, without the monetary consideration.

I remember a meeting downtown on Friday in an office [Woolworth store]. I guess it was the A&T students who were trying to negotiate about getting the lunch counter integrated and being pleasantly surprised that it was rational.

I recall attending two or three meetings at Bennett College, where the students who were involved got together to try to strategize, but I was never involved in those strategies. I knew that the men from A&T were the leaders, but I think the students from Bennett had more support from their administration. My recollection is that I participated only two to three days into the next week, because there were restrictions about how many classes you could cut [at W.C.], so I was very careful about not missing classes.

In the beginning, the day that I walked downtown, I was not afraid. I was so convinced that I was doing the right thing. I think that that may be typical of eighteen or nineteen year olds who are very centered on their own view of the world, but there were a couple of nights where cars drove down College Avenue, in front of New Guilford Dormitory, and they were filled with young men who were shouting obscenities. It concerned me, not for myself so much, but that others could be hurt. Marilyn and Ann went through the same sort of thing. We were all subjected to that kind of mail. But again, there were not private telephones [in the dorm rooms], so we were insulated and, rightly or wrongly, I was under the perception that because I was a Southern [white] woman, that there was a certain insulation that there was not for the black people. Also, it was the late 1950s, the end of the McCarthy era, and in that context, that this was communist inspired.

I remember Dr. Bardolph creating a special lecture on the topic, which I attended and took notes, and Dr. Ashby loaned us his car for at least one trip to Bennett for a meeting. As I think back about it, it was remarkable that Dr. Bardolph created this lecture in a very public way, and Dr. Ashby's support, because that put their jobs on the line. Even with academic tenure, I know there are ways to dislodge people. There was a meeting where Dean Taylor met with three or four of us. There was another girl named Ann, Marilyn and me, but there could have been others, and her point was that we were very naive and that we didn't understand how black people really were and that we should stop what we were doing. I don't recall being told not to, but there was always the sense that I could be dismissed from campus.

I don't recall telling my parents what I was doing, but I must have. My mother was supportive, because of work that she had done in Orlando with a group in the mid-1950s who got together to talk about housing and other facilities being integrated. So that kind of work that she had done and her value system led me to believe that she wouldn't be upset. Yet, the *Orlando Sentinel*, which was the local paper, ran a story about a "local girl," and named my name and what was going on and my family received hate phone calls. Many years later, when my father was dying I said to him that I was sorry that I had hurt his business, but I had felt compelled to do this, and he indicated that he was glad I had done what I did. I got notes and letters on both sides.

It was certainly a period of awakening in terms of understanding the politics of issues and understanding life in the context of education and vise-versa. It reinforced my notions about what was right in the context of our society.

## Elizabeth "Betsy" Toth

I had heard what was happening from a black friend named Lilly Wiley. She knew a lot of people at Bennett and A&T. It was also on Channel 2 TV news, and that may have been how Katherine Taylor found out what we had done, and there may have been some mention in the newspapers by reporters at the store. The film footage was right at the end of the day when all the black students gathered in front of the door, out on the sidewalk, as things like eggs were being thrown at them. I was down there at least two, possibly three days. There was a cessation of hostilities. Everybody backed off for about two weeks, to work some stuff out. Then they resumed again.

I knew Lilly, Marilyn, Jeannie, and Ann Dearsley. I knew who Claudette Burroughs was, but I did not know her personally. My compatriots around the theater department, and people I knew in New Guilford [dorm] were positive about what we had done, or they didn't say anything at all. [Those] that we knew personally, if they didn't think we should have done it, weren't coming out and saying so. We got no negative comments from the people that we knew well. Some people did not speak of it, and I was assuming that they were not quite so fond of what we had done. But I mixed in the theater or humanities world, a group of more liberal, leftist radical people.

The first time I went down I just walked downtown, and I walked home. It never occurred to me that there would be a problem. I guess I just sort of wandered away. I walked into Woolworth at the door nearest the corner, where the lunch counter was further over toward the right. I became aware over to my right that there was a whole different thing happening, a whole different feeling. I got that not so much from all of the students who were sitting at the counter, but from the white people who were standing behind the students sitting at the counter, being very loud and vocal and threatening. When I sat down, the waitress came up and said, "Hi, honey, can I get you anything?" I said, "Yeah, I'd like a Coke. But these people were here ahead of me, and I don't think they've been served yet." And she said, "Well, we're not serving them." And I said, "Oh really? Then you're not serving me."

There was a white woman behind me who the guys were trying to instigate to take a two-by-four about three or four feet long and hit me. The police weren't very much in charge of what was going on, believe me. And the crowd was trying to get her to hit me, because it would have been a white woman hitting a white woman. And she was going to do it. They were going to pay her. A couple of them came up with $10 and it probably grew to $25-$35 by the time everything was done. Nobody talked about whether it was legal. The assumption was that she would get arrested, but nobody even addressed that. Although it was extremely frightening, maybe my naivete said, "I'm not going to get hit here, surrounded by dozens of people." Even in a situation like that, there is some safety in numbers. That was the only physical threat I ever felt.

Sitting to my right were a bunch of Bennett ladies who were so much more well-behaved than I was. They were dressed better; their deportment was better. They were the ones who taught me how to do this right. A couple of times I was about to go after the woman who was threatening to hit me. I was sitting there going, "If she even comes close, I'm going to take that right out of her hand." That's when the ladies from Bennett said, "No, you're not." [One Bennett student] said, "Honey, if you even look like you're going to do that, we are quits with you. You're out of here. We do not need that. That will not work." And I said, "Yeah, but she. . . ." And she said, "I don't care if she does hit you. You do nothing. You learn to do nothing. You just sit and be. And you conduct yourself with dignity and quiet." So in one day I learned my civil rights behavior. The ladies from Bennett had it down [pat]. They were the best.

The guys were off to the left, and I was down about the last third of the counter on the right side, where the Bennett girls where. Marilyn was there when I was there, and a couple of people who were from Guilford College or Greensboro College. The white people around us were furious at us. They were angry that they had given up those three seats. They were very hostile. There were a lot of people there, mostly men. We were so convinced we were doing the right thing, we thought nothing could possibly happen to us. As time went on, most of our thoughts turned to how are we going to get out of there. We had to go through a lot of Woolworth to get to the sidewalk.

I was there at least two hours the first day. At W.C., you didn't miss a class. So I was there for about two hours, and I went back to a class. I may have left before the other women got put in a cab. The next two times I went I definitely tried to work it around my class schedule, and make sure I got back in time for the class.

I was not aware of TV and newspaper reporters. I guess I was just naive. I was so surprised to see that footage on Channel 2, because I had not been aware that anybody was there taking that footage. I probably told people that I had participated when I got back to campus; I can't remember a specific conversation. It isn't the kind of thing that I would have kept my mouth shut about, [but] I don't think I would have made a big thing of it. At that time it seemed to me that the students from A&T and Bennett were the driving force. I just felt like I was down there to help. And so, it didn't seem like a big deal to me, as far as talking about it when I got back to campus.

Dean Taylor threatened to expel all of us who took part in the sit-ins. She and I had a good thirty-minute talk in which we did sort of verbal fisticuffs about that. I recall her quoting people like Judge Learned Hand to me: if you broke the law you must suffer the consequences of the law. I looked her straight in the eye and said, "I know that these great jurists had a point, but you tell that to my relatives who were killed in the ovens in Europe about breaking the law." And she said, "Oh, well, that was the Nazis." I said, "No, those were legal laws of the country. You may have a point in what you say, but I think there are times when there is a higher point to be made about what's right and what's not right. It was with that in mind that I did the sit-ins. You have to stand up, because when you don't, things like Nazi Germany happen." She said, "I think this discussion is over," and dismissed me. As far as I knew, I was out of school, but the pink slip never came. I didn't think I won the argument, but it was probably a draw. Chancellor Blackwell and Dean Taylor were very concerned about how many parents were going to pull their kids out of school; they didn't see the bigger picture that the repuation of the college would be enhanced.

The first time I went down I wore my college blazer. And that was one of the things that really ticked off the administration. So any time I went down after that was without a blazer. I think [as a condition] to staying in school, we all agreed not to do the blazer. And then, [Dr. Blackwell, chancellor of Woman's College] gave a speech in Aycock [Auditorium], and you would have known he was definitely pointing a finger at us. It was after that that we were actually threatened with expulsion.

I was there Wednesday, Thursday and Friday, Then both sides agreed not to do anything for about two weeks. While the sit-ins were in hiatus, several of us got together in the Commons Room at New Guilford and decided to lay out a series of newspaper articles that we had written, for publication. Then we went to whoever was the editor of *The Carolinian* [the campus newspaper] and said, "We think we ought to put out one entire issue." Well, they would not do that. So we said, "Okay, we'll go down and have this printed, and we'll pay for the printing ourselves." We contracted with somebody in Greensboro, but he had been contacted and would not touch it.

My parents were liberal Democrats from Pittsburgh, and as a Jew I had a liberal background when it came to being an "other." But when my mother found out that I had done this, she said, "That is not what we sent you to school to do." And I said, "I think it's exactly why I'm supposed to be in school." So, we had some moments about this. My mother felt that what I had done would embarrass her family. She could not see the correlation that if people had done this over in Europe for our family, the Holocaust might not have happened. To me, that was the point of it.

I have no regrets about my participation in the sit-ins. As small as my participation was, I still consider this one of the best things that I've ever done.

I think of it in terms of doing what is right and being true to myself. So, the thing that got me to participate is that [segregation] was wrong, and that this was one of those times in life when you stand up for someone else. For myself, I think it ranks up there with one of the best things I ever did.

## Claudette Graves Burroughs(-White)

On the second or third day, I went by Woolworth after class. As I walked in, one of the white guys there said, "Hey, there goes one of those niggers' girlfriend; let's get her." I had quite a temper back then, and I didn't handle the situation as I should have. At that time I carried a bag big enough to put all of my stuff in, including my books. I turned around and said, "You don't know what I've got in this bag. I want you to come mess with me. Come on." Some of the other students heard me, and they told me to go home. "We don't need that here. Go home," they said. The students were very determined there was not going to be any violence. I felt so bad. That's how easy it would have been for the situation to turn violent. There were all kinds of name-calling and threats. I recall being frightened that something was going to happen to somebody, that we weren't going to be able to maintain our cool.

I had a lot of friends at Bennett and A&T; they were proud of their involvement. I wanted to be proud of W.C., When those three [girls]came that day, I was proud of W.C. I really appreciated their participation. It was truly a student movement. The adults [that] we had looked to for support in the community were sort of riding the fence. You didn't know what the adults would do. I wasn't as noticeable because I was black, and you didn't know if I was from A&T or Bennett or Woman's College. I sort of melted into the crowd. I didn't stand out like the white students did. Oh, I was so proud of them. For W.C. to be a noticeable part of the sit-ins meant a lot to me, personally.

## George Roach

On the morning after it happened, City Manager James Townsend called me and told me what was going on. My reaction was that the students were entitled to use the counter facilities at Woolworth just as much as they were entitled to buy from any other department or counter in the store. We called on the manager of Woolworth and asked him to integrate his counter, and he would not go along with it at all. He said it was a policy of the local community and that the national office left it entirely up to him. At that time it was between the general and me. We sought no publicity, and tried to work it out peacefully. It was purely the merchants' decision.

The city government had taken no action to bring about desegregation in the stores downtown. We thought that race relations were very good. We had no indication of problems existing. The police department was not integrated, but the fire department and the airport had been integrated. With the approval of the Council I appointed a committee to work with the merchants. Ed Zane was chairman of the committee. Not everyone on the Council thought the city government should be involved, and some were unalterably opposed to it. Ed offered to resign, but we wouldn't accept it. I selected leaders of the business and industrial community to serve on the committee. We had two members of the City Council, two members of the Greensboro Merchants Association, and two members of the Chamber of Commerce. Howard Holderness, Arnold Schiffman, Oscar Burnett, Bill York, Jim Doggett were on it, among others. Before then, though, I had met with Dean [William] Gamble and Dr. [Warmouth T.] Gibbs of A&T.

I happened to meet the manager of Woolworth at a function held in the Carolina Theater. He said, "For God's sake, do something. The black boycott is about to ruin me." I said, "My friend, *you* do something. We've begged and pleaded. Now you go see the committee and get them to work something out."

The committee under Ed Zane had worked tremendously hard and it was an outstanding group. While this committee worked, I went to the manager of the O. Henry Hotel and to others, because the merchants were suffering due to the black boycott. I left the daily monitoring of the sit-ins to General Townsend, because in the council-manager form of government, that is the city manager's responsibility. I can't commend the police too much; they did an excellent job of keeping the peace. The city manager worked with Police Chief Paul Calhoun and Detective William Jackson about the situation. They were two of the best police officers in the country.

Governor Luther Hodges offered to send the Highway Patrol and the National Guard to preserve order. But General Townsend and I felt all along that we had the situation well in hand, because we had well-trained policemen. The counter-demonstrators were mostly acting as individuals, although there were some Ku Klux Klansmen under the direction of George Dorsett. I don't remember any serious trouble, other than some pushing incidents in the store. The students conducted themselves well.

And I had help in the black community. Dr. Simkins and Ezell Blair, Sr., were personal friends of mine. I had good meetings with Dean Gamble [Dean of Students, A&T College] and Dr. Gibbs, although they were unwavering in support of the students. The only thing we asked them to do was to try to ensure that the students were law-abiding, and time would take care of the rest. The black community initiated a boycott after the merchants remained intransigent.

I let it be known that it should be done and was on the side of the students. As a result, I received some threatening telephone calls. So Public Safety Director Bill Greene had a police car watching my home at night, although I wasn't concerned about it. I couldn't leave my office without people on the street shaking their fist in my face and saying, "You're not going to let the so-and-so's eat!" I knew that it was an educational process in which people had to get used to the fairness of it. But it would take time, and the effort of many people of goodwill. I had several requests for an interview on television, but I declined; I was concerned about the national image of Greensboro; I wanted it to remain a local incident. I trusted the local newspapers, because the editors were both responsible newsmen. There was cooperation from the black community, which was completely behind the students, and supported their desire to peacefully desegregate the lunch counters.

The City Council appointed the committee on February 6, the same Saturday that a bomb threat was telephoned to the Woolworth store, causing them to close their counter. That was the hottest day at Woolworth for me. That's what got the Council behind the committee and started the ball rolling. Otherwise, I think that it could definitely have been violence, because these young people were serious and ready to fight for what they believed was right. I don't think there would have been any question about it.

## James Townsend

I think that the reason the students picked Greensboro was due to the fact that race relations in Greensboro had always been good, but we were mistaken. And the day finally came when they decided to change things. We hadn't seen anything that disturbed the relations between the races. I did not give any thought to closing the stores during the sit-ins. I thought that things could be worked out, because I couldn't see why, if a black person could buy a comb at a counter, that he shouldn't be allowed to sit down at the lunch counter. Mayor Roach and I went over immediately to talk to Mr. Harris. His reaction was that he'd lose business if he were to desegregate the lunch counter. Some things can be talked over without going to the full Council as to what should be done. I considered it to be a bit of weakness on the mayor's and my part if we had asked the Council what should be done. I instructed the police department to keep order. I also advised them to try to avoid arrests, if possible. We didn't want to go that far.

This kind of situation makes a problem for a city manager, and he has one job: to keep order in the town. I had an able police department, and I had good cooperation from the men that were sitting on the City Council. I think that due credit should go to Ed Zane for having solved that problem, in part because he worked well with Captain William Jackson. I don't think that there were any fisticuffs. There was a tough character that was determined to make trouble, a white man. We kept a pretty close eye on him to be sure that he didn't cause any trouble. [*Note: This may have been George Dorsett or C. J. Webster, of the Ku Klux Klan*] There was one afternoon where we came close to trouble [Saturday, February 6]. The students withdrew quietly, and I appreciated that. The bomb threats were not regular, by any means.

Our talks with Dr. Dowdy and Dean Gamble of A&T were friendly and on a good level. We didn't tell them to keep the students back at the college and to not let them go downtown. We were determined that we wouldn't get Greensboro into the headlines by having a riot where somebody was injured. The police department was doing very well and we didn't give it any particular instructions in that, other than to maintain order. We didn't say anything about the students not coming downtown or to impose a curfew.

I didn't take part in any discussions between the Zane committee and the students. Mr. Zane was a man of great common sense and judgment, and I think he did that on his own. We left that to the Zane committee. We were able to do that because I was under very little pressure from the white community, and none by the city government to maintain segregation. I did receive an anonymous letter one time. It said, "Get the niggers out of those stores, or you will be blown to hell with a stick of dynamite." That was the only threat that I received. I never had any police protection of my residence.

The reason the store owners were so intransigent was simple: money. They could see the white people quitting them if the black people sat at the counter. I enjoy going back there now and seeing the black people drink coffee just like anybody else. My sympathy was with the students. My impression of the students was that they handled themselves very well. I was quite happy when the settlement was announced.

## Edward Zane

Many a time I had sat down at the Woolworth lunch counter and a black person had come in. He could buy a sandwich or a drink, but he couldn't sit down and eat it. Well, that just didn't seem right to me. He's an individual citizen of the United States. He's paying the same price I'm paying. Why should he be told, "You can't eat at the lunch counter?"

When I heard about it through the police report, I went to both the Woolworth and Kress lunch counters between ten and eleven o'clock. The students were sitting at the counters. Whites were calling them all kinds of names and obscenities, and I could tell that all that was needed was a spark, and some serious things were going to occur.

I was on the City Council in 1960. I told the Council and the mayor that something should be done, because if we didn't do something, it was going to develop into rioting, and people were going to get hurt or killed, and we had a duty and responsibility to prevent it if we possibly could. Most of the Council members didn't want desegregation; they wanted the status quo. They said, "Leave it alone. It'll work itself out." I said, "It will not work itself out. We're going to have rioting. We're going to have people killed. We're going to have a lot of bad publicity for the city of Greensboro. There's going to be violence if we don't do something." They said, "What can we do?" I said, "*We* don't do anything." The Council said: "Well, what do you want to do?" I replied, "Tell the segregated businesses that their license will be taken away, because if you operate on a basis which impairs the security of the community, the license shouldn't be granted."

They didn't want to do that. Well, that went on for close to a week, and the situation was getting more tense. I decided I would act on my own. I wrote a resignation to the City Council and presented it to the mayor, and gave my reasons: that we had a duty to perform, but we were not doing it, and if the City Council was not doing it, then I was going to act on my own by resigning. The mayor then refused to accept my resignation and agreed to appoint a committee. That was the beginning of the Human Relations Committee.

## McNeill Smith

I remember when the crowds were on the street outside of Woolworth and Kress stores and a member of the Guilford County Board of Commissioners stood on the street with me. He shook his head and said, "I just can't understand those students from A&T. We gave them new band uniforms and helped them get new buildings. Why would they want to upset things and upset everybody?"

## David Morehead

There were some people that were reluctant to support the black youths when the civil rights movement came in the Sixties. They thought they were crazy and they wouldn't be able to accomplish what they sought. But there were individuals and organizations that were receptive. Mrs. Frances Herbin, of the American Friends Service Committee, began to have [interracial] meetings. And they had a lot of their meetings at Hayes-Taylor Y; they would meet there, because we were both bold enough to invite mixed groups there. So if we wanted to do it, that was up to us.

## Otis Hairston, Sr.

In 1960 the four young men who went downtown to the lunch counter at Woolworth were not the first; you had folk to do that through the years, sit at the counter and ask for a hamburger and when refused, they would get up and leave. But 1960 was the first time that folk had the courage to sit and say, "We're going to stay here, we're not going to leave." So, it attracted a lot of attention, and that kind of a demonstration caused the college students throughout the country to think in terms of kinds of things that they could do. When the sit-ins occurred in 1960, Ezell Blair, Jr., who is credited with being the "Daddy" of the Movement, grew up in our church. And his father was chairman of the board of trustees of the church at that time.

The black community, for the most part, supported the idea. Our church supported the idea. We made available the office of our church for the students to mimeograph materials. I think that much of the churches supported it. Most of the blacks supported this, because they were fed up too. The white community should not have been surprised; they should have sensed this, that things were changing, that blacks were becoming more courageous. Whites used to come into black houses with their hats on. Blacks were getting fed up and were demanding respect.

*Although there was some relutctance in the African American community to support the students, a number of the more activist individuals met to form an ad hoc group to assist the students and present violence. Dr. Hobart Jarrett, an English professor at Bennett College, was elected chairman*

## Hobart Jarrett

The day following the one on which the young men had made their original daring appearance at Woolworth, I was called at home by Major High, of the legal firm of Lee and High. He told me that he and [J. Kenneth] Lee were calling a group of black citizens of some prominence, to map out a course of action. I went to their offices on Benbow Road. Dr. Miller was there, and William Brown, a minister, John Leary, Vance Chavis, and George Simkins. During the course of the discussions, we immediately saw that what we would have to do was to send wires to the police department in Greensboro, to the mayor and the members of the City Council. When we arrived at that particular point, Lee and I were asked to word the messages, and we withdrew from the group to do so. When we returned, I discovered that the group had decided that I should serve as both the chairman and the liaison between this group that we were establishing and the students. We sent the wires, and things did not explode. As far as organization was concerned, it worked extremely effectively.

After a few days the student group mushroomed, far more than the original four young men, and the Bennett girls were very much involved in the whole process from that point on. Once our group saw that the sit-ins were going to continue, we quickly organized the black community in support of the students. We reactivated the Greensboro Citizens Association that had helped elect William Hampton to the City Council. We contacted trustee boards, flower circles, sewing circles, any organization existing in black life. We brought this group together in a hurry, soliciting the support of ministers and others who were prominent, and things started to hum. We met regularly, when any kind of small crisis came up. We were the source that gave counsel to the students; their representatives always met with us. The A&T students named a liaison who came to my office at Bennett College several times a week

Dr. W. L. T. Miller was my right-hand man. We talked about every possible detail before we brought it to the larger group. After we saw that this thing could drag on forever, I called Dr. Miller and said, "I think that it is time for us to do something that will bring people to the conference table." The person that we decided to talk to was Mose Kiser, president of Guilford Dairy. I called him and he agreed to meet with a select group from our committee. This was the very first step toward bringing white merchants together with the cause of the black students.. We went to Guilford Dairy and in his offices had a really good conversation. Mose Kiser said that he would gladly open his doors to Negro patronage, provided that we could get one of the white business people to go along with the idea.

The committee was exuberant, but as we then began to think about who in Greensboro we could get to agree with Kiser, we lost some of our enthusiasm, because we did not have another place to turn to. I said to Dr. Miller, "I am going to call the manager of Woolworth and tell him that now is the time."

*On Friday evening, February 5, members of the administrative staff of A&T, Bennett and Woman's College of the University of North Carolina, students from A&T, Bennett and Woman's College and representatives of the African American community met with the managers of Woolworth and Kress stores and members of the Greensboro business community at the Woolworth store offices.*

## Hobart Jarrett

I called Mr. Harris and told him that our committee would like to bring several people with me to talk with him about the situation, and Mr. Harris agreed to do that. We actually met in his office after the store had closed on a particular night, and we were surprised to find that Mr. Harris had invited a large number of people. It didn't bother us. He was absolutely correct in invitng these other men; he simply had not told us that he had invited the manager of Kress, City Council members and other businessmen. Waldo Faulkner, who was the second Negro person to become a member of the City Council, was there, and Ed Zane, another very effective person in Greensboro politics.

I said, "Mr. Harris, I didn't know that we would see others than you." He replied, "Did you think that I was going to meet with you people alone?" And I said, "Yes, that's what you had said." It turned out to be a very important meeting. Harris took us to task over the fact that he wasn't doing any business with black people, and by this time, students from Woman's College the Bennett girls were doing. Further, there was an air of tension downtown and people, either ruled by their conscience or their fears, stayed away from downtown We knew that we had the opposition in a difficult spot. Mr. Harris was quite flustered, and made emotional comments. I was very pleased to see that all of us— George Evans, John Leary, W. L. T. Miller, Vance Chavis and I—were very calm. The result of that meeting was that our group decided that the counters must be opened.

Harris wanted to hold out until the end of time. As a matter of fact, we were trying to get anyone other than Woolworth management to agree to desegregate, because the word was out in our community, that Harris was going to keep that place lily-white until death came. So, there was no suggestion on anybody's part that we begin to integrate, until we ourselves said, "Mr. Harris, all we can tell you is that things are not going to get any better financially for Woolworth, and they may get worse, because of the conscience of the community. We can assure you that Negro people are not going to be coming here at all." This was the tone, and the effect.

## Clarence Harris

I had a meeting in the store with Ed Zane, at which representatives of twelve restaurants were there; the operators of the two cafeterias [S&W and the Mayfair] were present. I said that I would desegregate if one other restaurant would desegregate, but they refused to go along with it. Guilford Dairy said it would desegregate, but I wanted one of the major restaurants to agree. The Kress management took the same position.

## Jibreel Khazan

Dr. Hobart Jarrett was one of the most distinguished men in the black community. His support had a significant influence on us. He would come to the A&T campus to drop me notes of encouragement. He was very articulate, a scholar, and a person who was well-disciplined and had much self-control.

He was our Ralph Bunche.

There was also Dr. Willa B. Player at Bennett College. She was always feminine, but she was also liberated. And she was not afraid to take a stand. She told the managers of Woolworth and Kress and the city officials, when we met Friday night, February 5, that she was backing the students to the hilt. She said, "These students are only fulfilling the rights spoken of in the Constitution of the United States, and also being good religious people, what was in the Bible. You should have seen the smiles that we broke into when we looked at each other and said, "That's telling them."

We dealt in the spirit of compromise. We knew we had to give some, but we wanted the other side to give some as well. Many people figured we were just four naive black freshman students out on some kind of prank. But we kept trying to tell people, "No, this is not the case. We have been prepared for this by our teachers, by our community, and by the organizations that we have been in," and we were not just coming out with some wild idea. Leadership does not start all at once. You can be put in a situation, but all of the things that we were doing in school, our communities, our families, gradually came out, and this is one of the reasons why the civil rights movement was successful in Greensboro.

## Willa Player

I first learned about it when I saw a couple of Bennett girls' pictures on the front page of the *New York Times Magazine* sitting in at a counter. At first, I thought: "What do you do in a situation like this?" I certainly wasn't going to keep the girls from participating. So, my reaction was to let it ride until I could sense from the most reliable members of the faculty how they viewed the whole thing. Mrs. Louise Street, Dr. George Burthett, Dr. Chauncey Winston, Dr. J. Henry Sales, Dr. Francis Grantison, all members of the Bennett faculty, had been living in the community for some time.

I learned of the sit-ins when we were called downtown to a meeting on Friday evening, February 5, 1960, between students, the Woolworth manager and his representative, and members of the business and political community, to hear the A&T students present their case. We, as members of the black community, were trying to get a hold on what was really happening. At the meeting in the offices of Woolworth on Friday night, Ezell Blair was asked to defend his actions, which he did admirably. Then we were asked whether or not we could support the students in what they were doing. At that time, Greensboro College did not express any positive thrust of participation, nor did Dr. Gordon Blackwell, Chancellor of Woman's College. My comments at that time were pretty much what I said to the faculty. Here were students who were realizing that as citizens and as students of a liberal arts college, they were being denied their equal rights, both under the law and under their constitutional beliefs, and freedom of expression, and I defended what they were doing as being consistent with this, and that I supported it. I think that we all were just expressing ourselves about how we reacted to the situation.

My first reaction was to see how the students felt about it. When I returned to campus, I called a meeting and told them what was happening. We discussed the purposes of a liberal arts college, and decided that the students were carrying out the tenets of what a liberal education was all about, so they should be allowed to continue. They were expressing freedom of expression, living up to one's ideals, building a quality of life in the community that was acceptable to all, and respect for human dignity. It was recognition of values that applied to all persons who deserved a chance in a democratic society to express their beliefs. We spoke to the president of the Student Senate, and we told that body how the faculty felt, and that we were planning to cooperate with the girls. All that we requested of them was that they give us a daily report of what they intended to do on a particular day, which they did.

*Following the meeting at the Woolworth store, Clarence Harris hired Armistad Sapp, a local attorney, to represent the Woolworth Company. Sapp advised him on legal matters and conducted a public relations campaign in the media to create the impression that the students were irresponsible law-breakers under the influence of Communists and other agitators from outside the state. Meanwhile the Zane committee continued in its attempt to negotiate a settlement of the demonstrations.*

*On Saturday, February 6, thousands of people were drawn to the downtown area by the sit-ins, either as student demonstrators, white counter-demonstrators or as curious spectators. The Woolworth and Kress stores were crowded, as young blacks and whites sought to occupy counter seats. People roamed the aisles, watching as white hecklers yelled racial epithets, spilled condiments or crushed cigarettes on the demonstrators. When a bomb threat was telephoned to the store, Harris closed the lunch counter; it remained closed for six months. Unable to sit at the counter, demonstrators changed their tactic to one of picketing outside the store.*

*After the bomb threat and closing of the Woolworth lunch counter, the Zane committee convinced the Student Executive Committee for Justice to suspend picketing for two weeks, in order for tensions to ease and for the Zane committee to attempt a solution. The hiatus lasted for six weeks, but picketing resumed in April, when there was no progress in negotiations. The Jarrett committee, in turn, served as a liaison between the SECJ, the Zane committee, and the managements of the Kress and Woolworth stores.*

## Edward Zane

After the bomb threat to the Woolworth store, I met with the leaders of the students who were doing the sit-ins. I asked them to stop all demonstrations for a period of two weeks. I felt confident that within those two weeks I'd be able to work out a solution. They hesitated, then agreed to do it. I said, "I'll report to you daily." So the sit-ins terminated. I met with the students reguolarly and told them what I planned on doing, and spoke to them on nonviolence as being the basis to accomplish their goals, and that if they were seeking their rights under law, you build resentment by violating the law. You get the support of people in standing by your rights and living nonviolently.

The youngsters were impatient. But they agreed to go along with me. We started our negotiations with the Woolworth and Kress [stores]. Mr. Harris of Woolworth was willing to desegregate the lunch counter, if the Kress manager would. He was not willing to desegregate, because it would destroy his business. I believe that the Kress management shut down the lunch counter. So two weeks later I had to report back to the youngsters that I had failed to secure the desegregation of the two places. I was sure that ultimately it would come. I said, "In fairness to you, I'll have to tell you that I wasn't successful. But I'm still going to go on dealing with this. You're now free to do whatever you must do. And whatever it is, please do it without violence."

The students began picketing— no crowd, probably seven, or eight, or nine of them. They didn't attempt to take over and control the eating places. As a precaution, the city added three police detectives to walk around in the crowd. The police were there for everyone's protection, trying to prevent any violence. But with only three detectives, you can't keep the peace, if anything broke out..

Although I urged the students to be patient, I understood their point of view. They were looking at the thing as: "It's wrong. Why should we be differentiated from the whites?" We're both citizens of the United States. We both live under one law." I didn't blame them, so I told them, "Stick with it."

## Arnold Schiffman

I think we were all aware of the disturbance amongst the students at A&T College some three months before the sit-ins actually took place. They were not quite the bombshell that one might think it was in the community, but they did engender a lot of publicity. There were demonstrations on the street, and there were many comments in the newspapers and other modes of publicity to the effect that the blacks were unhappy with their situation, and they felt that it was the duty of the whites to rectify wrongs made over the centuries

I was appointed to the committee chaired by Ed Zane.He did a masterful job in helping to solve the problem by consulting with the blacks in bringing the matter to a conclusion that was happy and successful. Our first meeting was held upstairs over the Woolworth building at the corner of Sycamore and Elm Street. The problem was presented by Mr. Zane, and we discussed ways and means to solve the problem peacefully. We did not assign tasks to individual committee members. Subcommittee investigated various angles and talked to the owners of the operators of the [Woolworth and Kress] stores, where the problem had come to a head. We met possibly every week or ten days over the given period of time. [Six months.] We met chiefly in the same place downtown; it was central and was close to the problem.

There was little cooperation with the students. I think as much as anything else they wanted to make a loud noise and be heard. There was flexibility in the position of the managers of Woolworth and Kress. And I would say, complete cooperation with the committee to work out the problem. They felt that they should express by their action the feeling of the community. And they wanted to do what was best for the people of the community. After all, the stores were part of national chains, and their business life here depended on how well they were regarded in the community.

Mr. Harris was very serious, and quite a religious fellow. He meant to do the best that he could for everybody. He had some hard choices to make, and he cooperated one hundred percent with us. To argue that the decision was up to the offices in New York was a defensive gesture by the local executive at the moment, and he knew that it was unwise to make a hasty and unpopular decision. It needed to be tempered with time and in a thoroughly considerate way.

Among the questions poised was that if blacks were allowed to sit at the lunch counter, would Woolworth and Kress lose their white customers? And if so, how important would it be to the life in the community? But we did not make any decision. We preferred to continue discussions in order to find the best way to solve the issue. Hogate and Harris brought up the point that it was unfair to put them at this business risk, whereas the other eating establishments were not being singled out. And I can see, today, that it would have been unfair. But at the moment the pressure was on those two businesses. It was not on the other eating establishments, and that question had been raised by the blacks of the community. There were not any representatives of other eating establishments on the committee. I don't think that any of them expected that it would seriously affect them in a hurry. But, I did keep in mind that the cafeterias would be next.

There was no physical violence that I recall. There were people who were unwilling to consider the problem rationally and who simply voiced their personal feelings, whether they were whites or blacks. But those who sat down were well behaved, brought books and just occupied seats. Opponents taunted them at times. The polite behavior of the demonstrators made an impression on the public, and I think that it gave us the key that we needed to solve the problem in the long run.

I believe that the national media was looking for a sensational event. I don't think it made any real difference. I think that we were calm enough in our considerations not to be influenced by national coverage or really by anything from the outside. I don't think that the national media attention had any effect on us. I think that it was the fault of the media blowing up what was happening here, so that it came to national attention. In so doing, they probably defeated their own purpose. If they didn't believe this kind of thing should take place elsewhere, then they were causing it to take place elsewhere. Who knows what the media really wants to do when they write up something and expand it beyond a reasonable report?

Ed Zane, as chairman of the committee, was instrumental in arranging a truce after the first week of sit-ins, punctuated by a bomb threat on Saturday, February 6, 1960. It was discussed by the committee, but we never had any real conflict in the committee. We were all working for the same end, and as a reult, we had a pretty solid attendance of committee members. There were a few who always drop away, but by and large, most of the committee stayed on it. I served on one of the small committees, but I did not have a personal conversation with the students. I recall a meeting at the Woolworth offices on the evening of February 5, with Dr. Gordon Blackwell, chancellor of Woman's College, the president of Greensboro College, and Dr. Gibbs of A&T College and Dr. Player of Bennett College. This was before the committee was officially formed. Dr. Blackwell was concerned for the safety of the W.C. students who were participating. I knew him well, and I knew that he had a broad mind. The committee made no effort for the presidents and Chancellor Blackwell to prevent the students from coming downtown. Upon reflection, I'm surprised that none of the religious leaders of the community had any active part, but I may be wrong. I believe Murphy Williams did; he was the pastor of the Presbyterian Church of the Covenant on Walker Avenue. I recall no efforts by Mayor Roach and City Manager Townsend, other than appointing a committee and turning it over to us. I think George Roach met with us several times, but I don't remember Jim Townsend.

We met often during the period of the truce from February 1 to April 25, 1960. Basically, our meetings consisted of an exchange of ideas about what could and could not be done. I am sure that Mr. Zane's passion was not for immediate desegregation. I know that he saw the value of waiting until tempers had cooled down, and people could meet together with more equitability. When you're angry, you don't think straight.

There was usually a gathering of blacks in front of both the Woolworth and Kress stores, who were backing up those who were inside. And there were some whites who would gather to taunt them. It's amazing that there was no real violence. The city administration's attitude, and police presence had a calming influence. By and large, we all wanted peace, and most of us felt that it wasn't right for a person to work or shop downtown and not be able to buy something to eat.

The position that I took from beginning to end was, "We have the power to open the door, but the blacks cannot enjoy this privilege until they earn it by their behavior." There was little discussion on what would constitute blacks earning this privilege or right. We did not try to define a level of behavior or appearance or cleanliness. But we were conscious of the fact that if they came into an eating establisment or a store and were as loud and vociferous as they were on the streets, that it would be deleterious to them. And the citizens raised here, not influenced by rabble rousers, were well-behaved. We believed that we could open the door, but the blacks, could not enjoy it until they earned it. I did not want to judge whether this would be at the discretion of the individual businessman or the customers. I didn't think that it had to be an agreement between the commission, the City Council and the participants. As it finally worked out, after the rabble-rousers had gone home, our own local people could control [the situation]both in the colleges and in the city, and it could work out peacefully, as it did.

## Lewis Brandon

I met the men now known as the "Greensboro Four" by participating in the demonstrations on the second or third day, and I became a member of the Student Executive Committee for Justice [SECJ], along with Pat Patterson. I attended the negotiating sessions of Ed Zane's committee, on which Oscar Burnett and Dr. George Evans served; they met at the Red Cross building. There was a genuine concern among the members of that committee about what was happening in Greensboro. They wanted to get the thing over with and get back to some sort of normalcy. Mr. Burnett was very sincere in trying to change things. I was very impressed by him. At the meetings of the Zane committee there was a dialogue and cooperation between the Greensboro Citizens Association and the student group.

People try to give W.C. students a bigger role than they played in this thing, particularly in 1960. There were three students from Greensboro College who came up before the women from W.C. came. And the women from W.C came only one day in 1960.

My roommate, Donald Lyons, was arrested for assaulting a heckler, but it was thrown out of court. What it amounted to was that white people bumped against him and then accused him of attacking them, so a warrant was issued on him. I think there was one other attempt to arrest someone for indecent exposure; it was a tactic of harassment. Once the picketing started, it was all day on the picket lines. Donald was burned with lighted cigarettes being put in his pockets, and there was some jostling and shoving. I can remember it because there was a lot of that going on in the first two or three days.

Saturday morning, February 6, 1960, the Woolworth manager closed the counters; things were very tense that day. We were in Kress, and I looked up and all I could see were blue and gold football jerseys. Some white bullies began to move out of the way. The football team had come down, and at that time we had some guys weighing as much as three hundred pounds. Then we left there, me and one of my home boys, Wilbur Matt, the center of the team. We went up to Woolworth, and as we went in there, there was jostling for position. When they announced that the counters were closed, we marched back to campus. As we walked past the King Cotton Hotel, people threw bags of water and other things out of the windows. There was a tremendous amount of stuff going on.

I think that the police did a good job of separating the two groups. One police officer essentially played the role of Captain Jackson in 1963; he had rank but when we got back from summer break, he had lost it. I don't know if he was too friendly and cooperative with the students, or what. I can remember seeing him on the Square directing traffic. I can't remember his name, but he was very cooperative, and his attitude was very good, very positive.

## Hobart Jarrett

On Saturday [February 6], Woolworth closed due to a telephoned bomb threat, and there were other threats that bicycle chains would be used on the students sitting-in. In those days Saturday was when many people congregated downtown. It was this sort of potential for violence that caused the powers of the city to recognize that things would have to be taken care of, and protection was very necessary for all persons involved.

Once we [the committee] was actually in business, the students asked questions of us, and turned to us whenever they needed money—they needed very little money, by the way. We furnished money for the posters they made. The bond money for the arrested students did not come from us, but it did come from the black community. Our organization did not have the kind of capital necessary to raise bond, but Mr. Hargett, a funeral director, and the late Dr. Barnes [a dentist], was quite active in providing bond money.

The black community became unified, and we began going to churches. Reverend Otis Hairston was the vice-president of the organization, and it was to his church [Mt. Zion Baptist] that we went first of all. Our purpose was to bring people in to explain to the community why they should stay out of the five-and-ten stores. On this occasion, several speakers, including Dr. George

Evans and Ezell Blair, Jr., spoke. There were other, similar meetings later on, but this was the beginning of this kind of community education.

## Geneva Tisdale

After that first day, it continued on and as they kept coming back. It was tense to me, because I didn't know what would happen, and it scared me. The store didn't serve blacks. I was used to that, so it didn't bother me until after all of that started. Then I got to thinking about it. It wasn't no more than right that we could be served, because we ourselves worked there. We fixed all the food that went down, and then we couldn't sit and be served ourselves. Each day more and more came.

I remember the day when all the seats at the counter was taken. When they took the whole counter, that's when [the manager] closed it down. But the snack bar was still open out there on the floor.

Mr. Harris [Clarence L. Harris], the manager, was always nice to me. All of them was nice to me. I had no problem with the people or any of the bosses when I worked with there.

I was expecting my third child. Rachel Holt, who was in charge of the lunch counter, would always send me upstairs, because she said it was too much tension for me. She was a good boss to me. Some of the black employees there talked about it some, because we were nervous. We thought there would be a change, but we didn't know. The store lost money when the [lunch] counter closed, but they kept the rest of the store open. Ms. Holt told me to go home and stay there until things got to normal, and she would call me back. After I left, I had my baby.

## Ralph Johns

Within days, hundreds of college students throughout the country joined in boycotting Woolworth, and Kress. A committee was formed at A&T College, and I knew what was going on, because I listened in on a few meetings. Now and then I would advise the students, and I would make sure that the NAACP was in close contact in case of an emergency. Participation nationally soon numbered in the thousands all over America. In Greensboro, it reached as high as three or four thousand.

Violence from white hecklers was kept to a minimum, due to the Greensboro police. Whites were always trying to grab seats before blacks could sit down, and there was some scuffling and arrests. Whites took turns giving one another seats. Blacks would scuffle now and then to beat the white hecklers to seats. Black students would bring books and homework while sitting and studying, as one white dumped sugar on a black student's head.

Tension was very high. A fake bomb phone call was made on Saturday, February 6, and the evacuation was ordered of the Woolworth store. Each day I'd go to Woolworth or Kress, and I would see people like George Dorsett of the KKK and other white segregationists. I neglected my business to be in touch with what was happening. There were many times of tensions and flare-ups. A white heckler threw acid on the clothes of one black student. A white person chased the heckler and the police took him into custody. The NAACP had nightly executive meetings which I attended. Private citizens who helped were few. The committee appointed by Mayor George Roach, was made up of timid persons who patronized the black community and the students. Mr. Zane was the only white I knew who was sincere and tried to resolve this problem.

White girls who joined the movement in Greensboro were insulted and threatened. Most white churches in Greensboro were silent. Whites in general were fearful of violence. The KKK became more active in marching downtown. Some stood in front of my store and walked in and stared at me, and then they walked out. Moods were very bad. One night Dr. [George] Simkins and I walked to Jefferson Square, where crowds were milling about. A couple of whites insulted a black, and I told them that this young black's father had died in the war for democracy.

The newspapers and television helped us a lot in creating moral support in the community and nationwide. The news media was very liberal and honest in its reporting. I kept in touch with Jo Spivey to let her know what would happen next. The local press sent out news releases, and national press and television gave it the push to grow as fast as it did. The sit-ins would not have been successful had it not been for the coverage of national radio, television, and newspaper representation. They told it with no holds barred.

There was little money from outside sources. Poor blacks in Greensboro contributed money for bail bonds as individuals or through collections at church. The decision to include Kress in the movement was discussed by the original four sit-inners, George Simkins and me. I felt that we should go into Kress as well as Woolworth, since Kress had the same set-up for eating. The original plan was Woolworth, but a day or so later included Kress.

The police did a good job of keeping law and order. Although some of the police sympathies may have been with the blacks, but in my opinion, most didn't like this movement and were sometimes overly-protective of the white hate groups. Chief Calhoun was very diplomatic, and I worked with him behind the scenes, reporting any police brutality. Detective William Jackson had a tough job, with feelings at a high pitch, keeping things under control. But he did a good job, in spite of Ku Klux Klan and young segregationist agitation, which came in the form of threats, taunts, and insults. Day after day, the crowds became bigger, and more tension built up.

I called Woolworth's New York office and sent them letters signed by the original four sit-inners, and I used the fictitious name of David Price, an A&T student who I had asked to go to Woolworth in the Fifties. I had many second thoughts about me, my family and students being hurt or killed. When the first few days of the movement passed by, I had told the original four that no matter what, repeat the Lord's Prayer, turn your cheeks, don't fight back. Let the public see that we are nonviolent. Let the publicity be good for us and bad for the hoodlums, and then we would win public sympathy and the press to our side. Our good behavior started winning us friends to the Movement.

Intimidation by hostile whites was becoming unbearable at Kress and Woolworth. Members of white hate groups pushed and punched students sitting at the counter, dumped catsup or mustard on some of the students; taunted black students with racial slurs; and called white students "nigger-lovers," and saying, "We'll get you tonight." Members of the White Citizens Council and the KKK started a "reverse sit-in" by sitting in the stools and chairs. As the students marched back to the A&T campus on Saturday [February 6], hecklers dumped water and debris on them as they passed the King Cotton Hotel.

I was afraid that there would be violence. Blacks were afraid to come downtown at night because of white gangs who might attack them. Each day of the sit-ins, tension grew. There was a big march downtown from A&T College, that came by my store. Many of the students acknowledged me, and I urged them to turn their cheeks and say the Lord's Prayer if anyone provoked them. Each day I faced antagonism from people who had shops near me, and once six segregationists shouted, "Niggers, go back to Africa," or "You black baboon bastards." I yelled out to them, "They are turning their cheeks, but I won't. Come on, I'll take on any one of you." I walked out in the middle of the street, and they started running away, yelling, "Nigger-lovin' son-of-a-bitch." Eggs were thrown at the window of my store. Rocks were thrown at me as whites drove by my store. Every day the Duke Power truck drove by and insults poured out at me. Across the street from my store was a KKK hangout, where they watched my store daily.

The head of the KKK, Reverend George Dorsett, called me up and insulted and threatened me. I kept saying to him, "Man was made in God's image and not his color. I forgive you." One time, at the height of the march, a man stood in the middle of the street, yelling, "Ralph Johns, you nigger-lovin' bastard," and made threatening gestures. The blacks who were marching stopped and passed the word to each other, "Ralph Johns is in trouble." George Simkins, and dozens of other blacks came by my side and asked me if I was all right. I told them not to worry, I could handle this guy. Finally, police and friends persuaded him to leave. Later this man apologized, saying he was drunk.

I met with James Farmer and members of CORE. I told them, "Let's make a large cross and get one of our big football players to carry the cross, leading the march, and put a sign on the cross saying, 'Jesus Christ, crucified daily.'" I never carried a gun; I didn't want to, although my friends said I was crazy not to carry one. I told them, "Violence breeds violence" I had been personally confronted and attacked numerous times. I never knew if I'd be jumped.

One day as I walked by the Gridiron Cafe, a voice inside yelled at me, "Hey, Ralph Johns, you nigger-lover." I went in and told him, "Jesus was a nigger-lover, too." Then he swung at me, and I hit him a few times. Others started jumping me. The man behind the bar brandished a butcher knife as I left the bar. A few minutes later, some white friends who were in the Gridiron Cafe, came to my store and shook my hand and said they were glad I hit the guy. Over a period of years I had about twenty-seven bomb threats, one attempted cross-burning, and obscene letters, which I gave to the FBI. I was ostracized in the Veterans of Foreign Wars, where I finally was forced to resign as commander. I was not allowed to play golf any more at the two golf courses in the city. In the cafeterias, I would be subject to snide and insulting remarks. Racist hecklers would insult me, and I wouldn't turn my cheek. George Simkins would pull me away, and he'd say, "Cool it, man."

The blacks behaved with restraint, but the whites who reviled them were embarrassing the many decent whites who started speaking favorably about the behavior of the demonstrators. Many businesses were hurt economically, and they wanted an end to segregation; others feared race riots. Mayor Roach tried to not antagonize the white elements. Other than Ed Zane and Mack Arnold, there were few white leaders who stuck their necks out. Many Greensboro citizens' consciences bothered them, but a "do-nothing" attitude prevailed. They were afraid supporting integration would hurt them socially or financially.

## Jibreel Khazan

The thing I noticed immediately about Edward R. Zane was that he had finesse. I knew that when he came to A&T's campus in the black community to talk with us. He was quite willing to be an intermediary between the powers-that-be in Greensboro and the black community. I really began to appreciate the type of person that he was, because he was adept at bargaining, and he was also willing to negotiate. He told me in a letter: "I happen to be a Christian person," and I said, "He is a darn good one." That's how I remember him. But as the negotiations progressed, I thought about them as "BS"—"Bull Speech." [Laughs] What I observed was that it was a sort of feeling-out period. We would talk about an hour, but there was really no resolution made. The representatives of the [segregated] businesses said, "We resolve to meet next week and talk about the same subject again." I found it kind of boring, but I learned to understand diplomacy in these discussions: just getting together and looking at each other. Sometimes we would sit for ten minutes before someone made a statement, just looking back and forth at each other.

Armistad Sapp, the attorney representing the Woolworth store, presented an offer for us to be able to sit down at a counter in the basement. We said, "We think that we can get better." But we understood his role as a representative of his client. There's going to be opposition when you strive for social change, so we recognized that he was the opposition. We used him as reverse motivation. We said to our fellow students, "We can go around him; we can get more than what he is giving us. Now, are we going to listen to what he said, or are we going to keep pushing?"

McNeill Smith was a lawyer who was very meticulous in his understanding of law. He didn't speak too much; he did a lot of listening. He would say, "I'll take this report back to the committee." He would come back and say, "We don't like this." We would repeat our position, and he would say, "All right, I'll take your comments back to the committee, and I'll give you their report." Sometimes we'd say, "Let us talk to the committee ourselves," and our advisors would say, "That might not be advantageous." Over a period of time, though, I had a feeling that the students were out of the whole process of negotiation. Sometimes I felt that we had so many intermediaries, and we wanted to talk to people face-to-face. But I guess patience has its virtue.

CORE first came on the scene during the spring of 1960, when we were demonstrating as the Student Executive Committee for Justice. We wanted to keep this movement basically a student-led movement. Even though they may have been positive in their outlook toward helping us, we did not want outside groups to come in and to take over leadership of the Movement. We were very careful about was dealing with the arguments from the "antagonists" point of view, as we called it, the greater community of Greensboro, from some store owners that claimed that the Movement was inspired by outside agitators. We wanted to make sure that that was not true. So, we thanked CORE for their suggested assistance, but we preferred to keep it a student-led movement.

## Joseph McNeil

Quite frankly, we did not anticipate any disciplinary action by the A&T administration. We felt that [segregation] was wrong, and it gets back to the philosophy that even seventeen and eighteen year olds back in that time could understand: When it becomes prudent to disobey a law which you feel was morally wrong, where are you going to make your stand and what is it worth? A&T was certainly not the only school where we could obtain an education. But those possible consequences had to be in our minds, as I look back now, when we made these decisions, that we were putting an awful lot on the line. If we had been expelled or jailed, there goes our education. These things had to be thought out, and we resolved them so that we were prepared to take whatever came our way. It wasn't something that we blindly went into, with no sense of expectation.

We considered the possibility of the state legislature cutting off funds for A&T. That was the old dilemma that other black leaders had: If they took a provocative action, they risked being squeezed financially, unable to extend education to the masses of blacks who needed it. So that was a fragile line, and looking back, those in the administration probably walked it very well.

We were freshmen. What made sense to us at that time was to try to get campus leaders in various elements: the student government, the ROTC program; the athletic program, the fraternities. Get these people involved in this thing and have them get their membership out and see if we can get something going. I think that the average student and the student leaders that we contacted were very receptive. The issue was: "We should have done it sooner. Let's go." There may have been some oblique criticism of what we had done, but I can't recall any that terribly upset me.

We also had a lot of interaction with the adult black community. It was essential; we needed all of the help that they gave us. There were hundreds of people behind the scenes whose names never made a newspaper or stood in front of an audience, which was necessary for this thing, particularly in the early stages. They gave us a solid commitment after this thing got going. We knew that if we put ourselves out there, that we had a lot more behind us than that first day. They're going to stay; they're going to stick behind us. They arranged, through George Simkins and others, to give us legal protection through the NAACP's Legal Defense Fund.

Typically, it was a small-based group, and we'd go out and solicit strategies and ideas from various elements of the community: the NAACP, local people on campus, people in the community. "What do you think we should do?" We'd get all of these ideas and we'd go back and sit down and say, "Here are the options." We had to figure it out in that way, instead of saying, "Okay, we're calling the shots," because it was really a community effort.

When the time came when we needed money for bail, it was there. The community was there. It wasn't a case were we had to put up hard dollars. Many members of the community pledged personal property as bail collateral for unknown students: Dr. Barnes, Dr. Simkins, Reverend Hairston. It's so unfair to name names. The real soldiers were the unnamed people involved.

Thirty-one students spontaneously went to Woolworth the next day [February 2]. But we were not all that surprised by this response. Once people saw what we were doing, we thought that others would join us. But it wasn't any planned thing; you couldn't predict who was going to join us. However, we were pleased and encouraged by the momentum and spontaneity.

We did not speak personally or in a representative way to the administration of the college. We had obviously had an on-going dialogue with various members of the administration. It was important to have this type of dialogue, because the administration was subjected to various types of pressure to keep us in line, to cool it down, or maybe stop the sit-ins altogether. But it made no attempt to stop us. We were allowed to do pretty much as we saw fit. We saw a need to continue going to class, and once we did that, it was not really a question of the administration taking any action against us. We were acting in our own spare time. The administration, if anything, was cooperative in our efforts.

The four of us continued in leadership roles in various ways. But we knew that the Movement was not going to be a one-man effort for a number of reasons. One, we still felt responsibilities as students to try to get an education, and involvement in the demonstrations was extremely time-consuming. Two, we felt that we didn't want to have one person isolated so that he could be subjected to various pressures. We had a lot of talent, and there was really no reason for one person to try to hog the show. We sent someone when there was a speaking engagement or to talk to Woolworth or participate in some activity there. Another person would go to a SNCC meeting. I went to some of these activities, as did Ezell Blair, and a number of people who were not the original "four." The idea was to get as much involvement as possible.

It was not a movement with our identity; it is important to understand that. After the initiation of the sit-ins, the "four freshmen" were more or less symbolic, because it became a community movement. Dudley High School students, under Bill Thomas, were very active. They carried the Movement during the summer, when the college students were not there. The black community supported us; the local NAACP with George Simkins, were extremely important in sustaining the Movement. Local attorneys, McKissick and Person, offered their services. "Junior" Blair [Ezell Blair, Jr.] was elected to go to the meeting at Shaw University, where SNCC was formed, and he participated in the formation of that, so we tried to spread things around. There were many leaders of the Student Executive Committee for Justice. Freddie Jones, Lewis Brandon, who has always been so very active; student government was Charles Benbow; in the ROTC, you had Clint Talley, who went up to New York on one occasion to participate with some labor support in that area. There are just so many names that I feel badly because I am forgetting some. Although we met people from all over the South, we stayed a local movement, but we were getting responses on a nationwide basis. Woolworth was a national company, and it was receiving pressure nationally. There were selective buying campaigns in New York and Detroit and in other places, and we were called on from time to time to send representatives to these areas, to explain what we were doing. It was the students and the local black community that kept the Movement from being taken over by outside organizations. One of the favorite suggestions of those that were opposed to our efforts was that the sit-ins and other forms of protest were organized by "outsiders." That was totally untrue.

The NAACP gave us legal assistance; Floyd McKissick and Conrad Pearson were very active in civil rights during that period of time. The local NAACP, George Simkins; CORE came in and offered to help us with organization, and we thanked them, but indicated to them that we could pretty much do things locally. We needed a couple of signs for pickets, and that was about it. We had the legal support.

There are conflicting views as to whether or not the nonviolent and Christian overtones of the Movement were tactics or genuine beliefs. Certainly, there were those that embraced it as a Christian belief, but there were also many who saw it as an extremely practical tactic, a means by which we could approach the problem. I don't think that the great majority of us were nonviolent by nature; we were not in the mode of turning the other cheek. That was not a part of our upbringing, per se, so it took a lot of self-restraint to participate in the Movement and do that.

We chose Woolworth initially because we thought that it was more vulnerable as a national chain; that we could arouse public sympathy and get a favorable national response. Also, after our numbers grew, it became more practical to think about spreading it in some other area. We had more than enough people to handle a protest movement at Woolworth, so we sent some people to Kress, down the street, and to other places that we eventually branched out into. It was both a small number of regular decision-makers and a broad-based total participation by the entire committee, and it varied at times. The other targets of our sit-ins and picketing were certainly successful in the sense that it communicated what we were trying to do. It was not our goal to get one business to open the counter; we wanted the whole community to respond.

The mayor's committee was the type of committee that Greensboro created because it wanted to be thought of as a progressive community, an "All-American city." I believe that the power structure thought: "There's a problem here that we all recognize. This has come about, and it's highlighting this problem. Let's see if we can get the wheels rolling to get it resolved and not tarnish the image of the city." That's one way of looking at it. I can only speculate.

There were two people who were selected for the negotiations with the Zane committee. One was Clint Talley, and a girl at Bennett College, Gloria Brown. She was president of the Bennett College student body. Franklin McCain and Ezell Blair may have been in on the negotiation sessions. I was not one of the negotiators, but I continued to be involved. I was picketing; formulating strategy, meeting with various members of the community.

In the initial stages, things were rough. I think we had instances where people were burned with cigarettes. We were concerned about remaining nonviolent, but we didn't want to get wiped out by hostile hecklers, so we asked the football team for assistance, a nonviolent show of strength, if things did get out of hand. And I think the football players were effective in that. The police did an adequate job at times, but I guess there were times when things broke down, like once when we were picketing. I don't know if they were Klansmen or what, but there were people making lewd gestures at some of the girls. McCain and I were there, and four or five girls, and there were about twenty of these people harassing us. Things got out of hand, and we had to call for assistance from the campus. But by and large, we communicated with the police; we tried to inform them of what we were going to do and when.

Although Frank, Ezell, Joe and I were recognized on campus as those who had initiated the sit-ins, I don't think that we enjoyed "celebrity status." On the contrary, there was always an element of strain in being involved in the Movement. At times I was often spread very thin. I was not under strain by being identified as one of "The Greensboro Four." Maybe it was with one of the other guys. I think, for example it may have had an effect on Junior Blair, his physical condition, to some degree. But I was never asked to be a "living monument," or a role model of any sort. We were convinced that we didn't want the Movement to fail in any way, and there were a lot of people who felt that way, so to that extent, there was a constant pressure to make this thing work, and we endeavored to do that.

It seems very valid that the black community could only gain a voice by going outside the traditional forms of communication, because the white power structure controlled the means of protest. The television news broadcasts dramatically affected our movement. People throughout America knew that it was wrong all along, but they never did anything about it. But television brought the sit-ins right into their living room, and I think that provoked a reaction, so I think to a very large extent, the media played a role in our success.

We were aware of the potential for personal injury, jail, or expulsion from school. I don't think we had any martyrs in that group, but certainly that idea was a reality, because it could have happened. On day one, we could have been in jail for a long time. When we started the sit-ins; we had no idea what would happen, but we were willing to pay the dues. We were aware that by being civilly disobedient, that we were violating certain laws that we felt were unjust, that we might have to go to jail, that certain people had made a commitment to keep us out of jail, but we were going to go.

I believe that the Student Executive Committee for Justice was very skillful in the way that we used the media to publicize the sit-ins. The ideas were symbolic of the times, in the sense that we were young people who wanted to achieve something. Our strategy was experimental from one day to the next, and some errors of judgment were made. But it's interesting that a group of teenagers could coordinate press releases, national speaking engagements, demonstrations on a day-to-day basis, legal efforts, solicit aid, show up each day to man picket lines, and keep violent people out of the movement, all the things necessary to make the Movement grow.

The thing that probably disturbs me most is the fact that enough people don't get credit for what they did, particularly the females, who were the spirit of this movement. There were black females from A&T and Bennett Colleges, and white male and female students from Greensboro and Guilford colleges. All of these people have never been given the credit they deserve.

## Lewis Brandon

I participated in the sit-ins on the second or third day, and began attending the meetings of the Student Executive Committee for Justice. I wasn't an officer, but I was a member of the Committee. I think that Pat Patterson and I joined about the same time, and that is how I met Dave, Ezell and the others. I was asked to attend the negotiating sessions held by the Zane committee. There was genuine concern about what was happening. A lot of people had different concerns. They wanted to get the thing over with and get back to some sort of normalcy. Mr. [Oscar] Burnett was very sincere in trying to change things. I was very impressed by him. At the meetings held at the Red Cross building, the students were an important part of the negotiating process, and there was some dialogue and cooperation between the Citizens Association and the student group. I think that is one of the differences between the demonstrations in 1960 and the ones in 1962-1963; those held in 1960 were more student-oriented. The ones in 1962-63 were more community-oriented, because we had more people in the community involved in all aspects of the demonstrations. But I don't recall a lot of meetings, and it was because of the few meetings that we had that the picketing began, which was long and drawn out.

*Within days of the beginning of the sit-ins, individual faculty members of the Woman's College of the University of North Carolina (W.C.), Greensboro College and Guilford College expressed sympathy for the A&T and Bennett students*

## Ben Wilson

I'd been here two years before any kind of stirring towards civil rights became apparent to me in town and on campuses. It came through an organization called the Inter-Faculty Forum, which was a group of faculty members from the campuses in the city—the Woman's College, Bennett College, A&T, Greensboro and Guilford College. Occasionally, we had visitors from Elon College and High Point College.

The idea of the Inter-Faculty Forum grew out of a group of people who met for a luncheon at the central YMCA, the only place where people could have an integrated meal. Then they decided, "Why not meet on the campuses and meet in dining rooms or in various department places?" At W.C. we met at the Philosophy Department, and the dining rooms of Greensboro College and Guilford College. A&T and Bennett were also open to us. I think the biggest problem was W.C. [Woman's College], where there was a very strict division of white and black in the city at that time, although you had some little pockets of integration going on at W.C.

We usually met about once a month. And then when the students began sitting in down at Woolworth, a group of us, being from all the campuses in the city, had a good way of being in touch with our students and with the city people. The group of us met quite frequently as this was going on; we had a meeting then at the YWCA where members of all campuses were represented. It was a very tense, very vocal meeting. Some members of the group wanted to rally behind the students in a march and to show solidarity from the campuses.

I can't remember the militants, but the moderates were: Samuel J. Shaw, from A&T; L. H. Robinson and A. F. Jackson from A&T; George Burthet, John F. Hatchett, and Rose Karpula from Bennett; Taylor Scott, Ken Taylor, and I from Greensboro College; Ed Burrows and Carroll Feagins from Guilford College; and Warren Ashby and Jordan Kurland, Robert C. Hudson, and Franklin Parker from W.C.

We didn't keep formal notes other than generally what was said. We were not fools. [Laughter.] We didn't know what our administrations might do; we didn't know what lawyers might do; and we didn't know what newspaper people might do if we had anything written down. Most of what we assigned to individual members, after this meeting at the YW where there was talk of militancy going on, was by telephone, in sort of a round-robin. When things cooled down, we communicated by written correspondence, but most of the time we talked by telephone.

We decided not directly confront the authorities, but go behind the scenes and talk with city government officials and offer our help as mediators between city government and the students. Franklin Parker and Warren Ashby were very effective in making contacts of this sort. Their diplomacy was crucial in setting up these meetings.

The rest of us were new to the scene. We hadn't been on our campuses long, so we didn't know many people. But each of us elected a representative from the campus to go to the meeting at the YWCA with Mayor George Roach. He didn't give us a great deal of hope. But he said to us, in effect, that he would like to keep the channels open and call on us, if necessary. I think it was more to help him than it was us. But at the same time, we were glad to have that interchange going on. Mayor Roach was a strong person, but he was not dynamic. I think it helped the students, and the whole situation to have the city government aware of this and helping out. I think the city government expressed a willingness to allow the thing to move along without either pushing or suppressing it, and at the same time trying to keep the hotheads on both sides from taking over. In other words, they acted like most North Carolina politicians. They like to sit in the middle.

But I think it was helpful. And I do not discredit or denigrate anything that the city government did, because they were facing a terrible dilemma. They had not just the politics, but public safety to think about. Those meetings bore fruit. We had just one meeting with the mayor, and he never called us back again. I think the students then took it into their own hands and worked it out; our role was a very modest one. But I think it was important that the city was made aware that the faculties on those college campuses were solidly behind the students, and committed to a more liberal interpretation of the laws, without coming right out and saying we were radical civil rights advocates.

## Lois Lucas (Williams)

At Bennett, I heard the talk about segregated conditions in Greensboro and I started to get a deeper sense of what was going on. I never really had any idea of what my role was supposed to be in it until I met a man named John Hatchett, who was on staff at Bennett College and who was the faculty advisor to the students involved in the sit-ins from both Bennett and A&T. He taught philosophy and religion, and was a very dynamic speaker; the logic of what he was saying made a lot of sense. He had a charisma that was hard to resist. His lectures about race relations in the country motivated students to become involved in the struggle against segregation. He would say, "Until every black person in this country is free, nobody is really free. Until we can all be able to hold our heads up, then none of us can." It was a lost easier for teachers form Bennett to be involved in the sit-ins, because we were a private school, we were not dependent on state aid for our existence, as was A&T. Therefore, I think that made a lot of teachers who wanted to participate from A&T a little wary from doing so because their jobs were at stake.

It's my understanding that the original concept of the sit-ins began with a group of Bennett girls. They approached Dr. Player about it in December of 1959, but she advised us that it was almost the end of the fall semester and we would be going home, that they should postpone it until the next semester, after the Bennett students had returned to campus. But she did not forbid us to do it. When the spring semester started, we began talking about it some more, but before we could do anything, Ezell and the other three A&T students had gone down to Woolworth on February 1[1960]. Probably because the guys on A&T's campus felt that the girls at Bennett would be hurt, they sort of pre-empted it, because it was planned at one time on Bennett campus, and the four guys at A&T went down and sat in anyway.

## Frances Herbin (Lewis)

I attended Dudley High School, where I graduated in 1959 with Ezell Blair and David Richmond. All three of us had been members of the Greensboro Youth Chapter of the NAACP and attended A&T College. As news came back to campus that they had actually taken the first step and were seeking support from other students, I felt obligated to support them, being originally from Greensboro, and what I had experienced here.

David, Ezell and I, along with other Greensboro students at A&T had close contact with each other during our breaks and sharing classes with each other. I went down to sit-in at Woolworth within the next day or so. Sometimes it was done with only one or two others, but as it picked up momentum, I made plans around when others would go, and we would try to work it around other students' schedules, knowing that some of the them would be due back at campus for classes. We would go down and fill in for them

By then the Bennett students had heard about it and had joined the A&T students. The female students from A&T and Bennett were very active from the beginning. There was Lois Lucas, Gloria Jean Blair, Antoinette Thomas, Ann Staples Shelton, and a couple of white girls from Bennett.I think they received support from most of the officials in and around Bennett. Dr. Hobart Jarrett and Reverend Knighton Stanley were particularly supportive.

Nonviolence was stressed from the very beginning, and those unable to control their tempers were discouraged from participating. Initially, Ezell, David, Frank and Joe were considered leaders, but here was no set individual who made decisions; we all handled the planning sessions and discussed different ideas and tactics as a group and acted upon consensus.

In the very early instances, they would close the lunch counter as soon as a couple of students came down. In a lot of instances when you would go in, they would have closed the lunch counter. If we were to leave totally, the counters would open again. So there was someone there during the operating hours at all times. Sometimes it was really crowded, and some of the students were harassed. I never was, personally, other than verbal abuse. Some other students had things thrown at them and things said as they sat at the counter, but there was nothing I would really consider major.

I don't recall ever hearing negative comments from female students about the male students having the leadership roles. I think it was more an idea of the job and the support, more so than bickering back and forth about who was doing what. I think that it was just the big thing that was being done. It did not matter whether it was a male or a female. I don't recall any instances where any reference was made to that.

I think most of us spent about as much time as we possibly could downtown, any given day or weekend. I guess we probably spent as much time picketing as we actually spent inside. The majority of the abuse came from passers-by, and they were basically from the uneducated segment of the population. After a while, you could tell from comments, as to what intellectual level these people were on, and their background.

I don't think the A&T administration particularly supported its students, certainly not the way Dr. Player supported her students. On our campus, I think that CORE received support from individuals. We did not have the active support, but we had the moral support of many staff and faculty members. Some of the faculty members would formally mention the demonstrations in class. Others were a little reluctant. They did not use class time to discuss it. Most of the instructors adhered to policies of class time subject matter, but there were instances for a few minutes, where it was discussed. It probably should have been more time spent on it, but, again, being a part of the institution, a person is not at liberty to use class time, because this in itself could have been an adverse thing, as far as the Administration was concerned.

The police were present; Captain Jackson made his appearance very well known. In a lot of instances, they had plainclothes detectives, but after a while we learned who they were. I think that they did an effective job of preventing violence. I don't think there were any major outbreaks. Although they were there to prevent violence, most of the students saw the police as part of the power structure. They [police] had not been thrust into this sort of situation before, and I think they were in a position that they didn't have any choice at that time but to carry out orders. I felt that the police reacted in surprise, initially. They really didn't know how to handle the situation, but beyond that point, I think they reacted out of a sense of order, what was expected from their associates and the general public. I think that they did what they were forced to do. I feel like they turned their backs to a lot of things, they allowed things to happen or certain conditions were allowed to exist. The hecklers were allowed to remain in places that the students were told to leave. When the fire marshal ordered the aisles cleared, the students would have to leave or move about. And outside, pickets were not allowed to stand, they had to constantly move. The hecklers could stand around, however. You had some people that would just stand around and watch out of curiosity, and some that would never say anything, but you had others that would come back to heckle.

We were instructed to ignore the hecklers, and generally, that was followed. I had seen some students that looked like they were pushed to the point that they may have physically retaliated, but generally, in a situation like that there was another one close by that could bridge the gap there and maybe calm that particular student down. Or if he felt that he was not in a position to remain, he or she could be taken back to the campus.

## Jo Spivey

The policy of the newspaper was to try not to influence public opinion, but no one at the paper tried to stop me from doing anything. There may have been editors who were segregationists, but I think that they were professionals who believed that every side should be represented. If a Ku Klux Klansman came to me and wanted me to write a story, I wrote it straight down the middle for him, just as I did anything else. I would get threatening telephone calls practically every night. Dorothy Benjamin, who covered the schools, was known to these people as the "nigger-lovin' slut" and I was the "nigger-lovin' bitch." I would get these calls, and the person would hiss "nigger-lovin' bitch" into the phone and hang up. Sometimes they would just call and breathe into the telephone.

One time they got my little girl on the phone and scared her so badly that she wouldn't sleep by herself for a week. The breathing on the telephone went on for about three months, and we couldn't take the phone off the hook, because my husband was a forester and was on call. I didn't tell my husband what was going on, but he finally caught on and got a gun and put it on the chest of drawers in the foyer. This scared me worse than anything, because there were a bunch of little kids in and out of the house. There was a car that would pull up into our driveway, turn around, go down the hill, come back up, turn around in our driveway go back down the hill. It was just at night; they never did anything in the daytime.

The students demonstrated during the lunch hour. The demonstrations were very quiet and peaceful, although there were occasional incidents of violence. Once Bill Jackson swung a man around who was brandishing a knife and arrested him. I think the police did pretty well in protecting the demonstrators and in maintaining law and order, particularly in view of many of their backgrounds. I sat with a number of those police officers at the sit-ins at Woolworth in 1960, and I never really observed them do anything that they should not have. Now, that may have been because I was watching, I don't know. I think there was a good deal of strain on the police officers, because I think that they, basically, were probably segregationists.

The spectators were more militant than the marchers. Sometimes they were hecklers, sometimes they were passive observers. As I said earlier, some of them brought their kids to see it, which I couldn't understand. I saw some violence in the store, mostly pushing, jostling by some of the counter-demonstrators. They didn't physically hurt these people, but there were some white men, probably KKK members, who heckled the Bennett College girls studying at the counter, saying such things as, "Look at that nigger, she thinks she can read," and such things as that. I recall there was a woman who every day would come up, take a seat at the counter and would get up and let a white person have a seat, and when the white person would leave, she would sit back down. Saturday, February 6, was a very tense day. A girl got her teeth knocked in from a thrown rock, and some other people were injured. Some people dropped bags of water off the top of the King Cotton onto the demonstrators as they marched past below.

Both students and hecklers filled the streets. They weren't concentrated just at Woolworth and Kress; they were all over Jefferson Square and down the block. The whole street was just a mass of humanity crowded in that small area. The tension eased when the students agreed to a cooling off period that lasted for several weeks.

## Hobart Jarrett

Negotiations began as a result of the effectiveness that the students had wielded in a community that was intelligent enough to respond to what was taking place in a revolutionary way, and as a result of our calling the shots as far as timing was concerned. No negotiations took place, to my knowledge, until I got with those people.

Negotiations occurred very infrequently. There were only three major negotiations: the meeting with Kiser, the meeting with the manager of the Woolworth store, and the one with the manger of Meyer's. Our committee dealt directly with the store managers, then the students were told what had happened. The only advice that the committee ever gave the students was to be calm and certain about their positions, so that they would take the best care of themselves possible. I also urged them not to incite any violence, if they could keep from doing so, but remain on the dignified level that they themselves had initiated. I don't recall that we gave them any specific advice on strategy. The students told us what they were going to do, and we reacted to it. We never put any strings on the students; we buttressed them. The only thing that we could do was to advise them to be cautious, because their lives, and a whole new era in human relations was at stake. Whenever we had a meeting of the Association, the students were apprised and came. The students knew from the very outset that any advice or help we could give to them, they had but to let us know, and anything that we thought that they should be aware of, we would contact them to tell them about it. They would send over the young man who served as my liaison with the A&T students. He would come to my office on the Bennett campus several times a week, or on a daily basis as the sit-ins continued, and we had many conversations. He would then return to the A&T campus and report to the students the gist of our conversation.

In addition to the Greensboro Citizens Association, the NAACP and the Greensboro Men's Club, there may have been organizations in the white community that were supportive of our efforts. The YWCA was always quite liberal in the city, but we were not aware of these activities, if they occurred. I simply knew that a lot of good people in Greensboro were conscientious in wanting the problems in our city to be solved amicably for the benefit of mankind.

As far as the white business community working on the problem, I can't remember anybody other than Ed Zane and Mose Kiser. Jo Spivey was extremely reliable, and it was good to know that there was such a person as she reporting the events. There was Warren Ashby, a member of the faculty of Woman's College; he was certainly a strong moral influence in the city, and he worked with us at Bennett College in many different ways.The women at W.C. were supporting the group, but there was no organized relationship.

## Franklin McCain

I thought at the time that the negotiations were strained, but now I would say that the people were cordial and probably exercising diplomacy. But then, it sounded like people not really wanting to discuss the issue. We had one negotiating session, which is still demeaning. The Woolworth Company hired Armistad Sapp, an attorney, who proposed that Woolworth build within that store a comparable facility downstairs, where blacks could eat. He said, "We're going to build you a restaurant to eat in right in the store that's as nice as—in fact, a little better—than what white people have there now. You ought to jump at that, because we're going to do something for you that we don't even do for white folks." That was the biggest insult that we ever had throughout the negotiations. We rejected it outright. I recall his saying, "You need to jump at this offer, because I don't have the time to fool around." He meant, "This is the best that you're going to get." Our resentment over that was a good way to keep ourselves psyched up.

We had sessions with McNeil Smith, who had a different kind of approach altogether; not so much with a propsal, but as an individual to clear the air, and to find out what the options really were in terms of our thinking. We told him that the only option that we wanted to exercise was to have the same privileges as anyone else. We didn't want to be treated special. We knew what "special" meant: it meant that you're going to get screwed, and we had had a bellyful of that. But McNeil Smith came on very differently, very polished, very diplomatically, and appeared to be somewhat more open. Sapp's mind was made up before he came to the negotiating table, but McNeil Smith led us to believe that he was willing to hear some of the things that we might say.

That's the reason that both black and white adults sensed that it might be more productive to ease the students out a little bit. The students were initially suspicious about that kind of attitude. We didn't participate in every one of the sessions; we usually had black adults acting as intermediaries. But we did not feel left out, because the Meyer's Tea Room was integrated by Hobart Jarrett and two or three pesons of that committee, one representative from A&T and me, so I really didn't feel left out. In fact, our feeling was that there was enough success, trauma, tragedy, weariness to pass around to everybody. No one was going to have a corner on it, and no one should feel as though he ought to. Success to us was: "Whatever good comes because of the Movement is good for everyone." I think that is probably one key to the success of the Movement. It wasn't a personal thing. We didn't look at it on a personal level; we were bigger than that.

In my case, I was quite relieved when my parents said to me, "It's fine, it's quite all right," because I had a strong sense of family. I cared what my parents thought about the things that I did and the kind of person I was. Once I passed that potential hurdle, there weren't a lot of things that gave me much difficulty in terms of pressures.

All this time, we never forgot our central mission, which was to get an education. I'm sure that none of us put as much time into our studies as we should have. My schoolwork suffered, but all four of us graduated with honors. From a personal standpoint, I had a strong sense of commitment to the Movement, although my involvement in terms of picketing and sitting-in were becoming less and less. But there were some pressures. I continually reminded myself why I was there and that my future could depend on what I did or did not do here. The pressures, also, of doing things gave me a kind of "avalanche syndrome." Sometimes I wanted to curl up in a corner and read a good book, but because there were people downtown picekting, when we were five months into the Movement, and we couldn't find enough people to do a good job of picketing, the resulting pressures said to me: "You were instrumental in getting people down here; you've got an obligation to support the Movement." So, those are some of the pressures that I felt, not that I was pressured each time that I went down to picket, but there were times that I wanted to do something else. However, I felt I had a special obligation, and I couldn't do that something else that I would have liked to do at that time.

We often felt the need, from time to time, for some source of comfort, some place to lighten our burden. But there was an element in the white community that wanted to see the Movement discredited, and the people who wee part of it. So I felt a special sense of duty to keep my skirts clean in terms of my behavior and to support the Movement.

*Through Ezell Blair, Sr., a woodworking teacher at Dudley, the SECJ enlisted the aid of the Dudley students under senior Bill Thomas to assist A&T and Bennett town students in continuing to picket during the summer, after most Bennett and A&T students had gone home at the end of the spring semester.*

## Lewis Brandon

As school was closing, we had a meeting to discuss what would happen after we went home and who would be there to carry on the Movement. The "Greensboro Four", Pat Patterson and I went to Dudley and had a meeting in Ezell Blair's father's woodworking shop with some others—Bill Thomas, his sister Antoinette, Billy Joe Foster, Paula Jewell and others—to discuss their taking over the Movement after we left Greensboro. I liked Bill Thomas, because he had been very active in the community. His father had been very active in the NAACP. So there was some carry-over there. He was highly intelligent, and we became the best of friends. In fact, I spent most of my time over at his mother's. She sort of took us in after the sit-ins began.

## Gloria Jean Blair (Howard)

During the summer of 1960 members of the SECJ tried to enlist the aid of Dudley students to continue the sit-ins after the college term ended in the spring. Bill Thomas, Lewis Brandon and other students would come over to my father's drafting shop at Dudley to talk with him. My father supported the students. He went downtown and watched to see if the students were being hassled in any way by the law enforcement officers. The parents in the town worried about the safety of the A&T and Bennett students, because many of them were not from Greensboro. So the black people in town were concerned about their safety, because they were away from their homes and families.

When I went downtown with my father, I saw the students sitting there. They were not being served; they were basically being ignored. There was never the violence in Greensboro, the overt hatred that was seen in a lot of Southern cities. I never felt that way when I was there, and in talking with a lot of other students, Greensboro was, at that time, a very unique city, because blacks and whites in Greensboro had always interfaced in a very kind and pleasant way. Of course, there was always the name-calling by people who wee insecure as far as their status. But there was a lot of hard staring. I can't remember witnessing physical violence, as far as a peson pushing someone off of a counter seat. I think that people were just shocked, because it was something totally different that was happening in town.

When I was at Dudley, I wasn't that interested in getting involved in it, because I saw it as an A&T-Bennett event at that time, so I watched and observed as a member of the Youth Group of the NAACP. We did other things to support the group: we did a lot of telephone calling, we did paper work during the summer because there was a need for a lot of support when the students were not there. So in 1960 the high school students were not very involved until then.

I don't think that the Bennett students have received the recognition that they deserve for participating in the Greensboro Movement. Rosalyn Cheagle and Jean Franklin. Yvonne Macklin was the president of the Student Government. Bennett had a variety of students from all over the country. A&T did, also, but being a college for women; there was quite a focus on what we women could do as a group of people than anyone else could do. I can remember when I first entered Bennett; there were women who were entering unique professions. Bennett had, at that time a lot of women who were going to become doctors and attorneys in a world where women were not supposed to be doctors and attorneys. There was a focus on doing a lot of unique things. Bennett had a very active student government, and in my freshman year; they were active in the sit-ins, and wantd to be more active in the community

## Franklin McCain

Most people wonder what happened to the Movement after the college students went home for the summer. We were fortunate to have some high school students involved, under Bill Thomas, a senior at Dudley High School, during the summer. He was instrumental in organizing continued picketing and being in on the strategy planning. They carried on some semblance of picketing and protesting, so we didn't lose our momentum. It carried on until we returned in the fall.

## Sarah Jones (Outterbridge)

During the summer, after most of the students were at home, and the students at Dudley became involved, we all handled the planning sessions as a group. There was no set individual who made decisions, but more or less, the groups were called together and they discussed the different ideas, the different tactics. They were told how they would like the things to be carried out, why they were doing certain things, and it was a consensus of the group that they would support that type of thing.

## Frances Herbin (Lewis)

That summer we did a lot of testing of other restaurants, to see if they would voluntarily desegregate, but none did. We had certain people assigned to certain areas. They would take the northeast or the southeast, or whatever. It would be determined by the number of people available at a given time.

*As part of its diverse approach to resolving the issue, the Zane committee held periodic meetings at the Red Cross building, where the various parties—members of the SECJ, representatives of Woolworth and Kress, the Jarrett committee and interested individuals—could exchange demands and opinions.*

*At the same time, behind-the-scenes, individual members of the Zane committee unofficially exerted their influence with the regional office of Woolworth & Co. in Atlanta and the corporate headquarters in New York. Howard Holderness, president of the Jefferson-Pilot Insurance Company, the largest insurance company in North Carolina, met with corporate officers in the late spring of 1960. Shortly thereafter, C. L. Harris obtained permission from the New York office to desegregate the lunch counter at his discretion. He informed the Zane committee that he would do so quietly on July 25, so as to not appear to be intimidated by the college students in the spring. Mr. Hogate, the manager of Kress, agreed to do the same at his store. On July 25, 1960, Harris instructed several of his African American female employees to dress as customers and eat at the lunch counter, then return to work. The desegregation went without fanfare and the lunch counter continued to serve African American customers without incident from that point on.*

## Howard Holderness

During the trouble at Woolworth I, as an individual member of the [Zane] committee, went to    New York to see Mr. Kirland, who was head of Woolworth. I said, "Mr. Kirland, I'm from Greensboro, and you've got real problems down there. You all ought to let the Negroes eat at that counter. You sell them everything you can, so they are entitled to eat there, to get that food service, too." He said, "Mr. Holderness, that is a local matter." I said, "Mr. Kirland, don't kid me. As important as this is to you, you'd better get somebody down there other than your manager." The local manager was dead set against integration. I said, "You'd better get somebody down there."

Then he said, "Well, Mr. Holderness, what do you do?" And I said, "I'm the head of Jefferson-Pilot, which is one of the largest insurance companies in

North Caroliona, and I am the head of public relations of the life insurance industry. I know what this is going to mean to you, not just in Greensboro, but everywhere. You're in trouble."

He called the public relations man in there and said, "Call the manager." He called the manager that was in charge of the territory in Atlanta and told him, "You meet with Mr. Hoderness and the members of his committee." We had a meeting in my home. Now, I'm not saying that we did it, but this was really the key that stopped the manager [C.L. Harris] from blocking it.

## Clarence Harris

The New York office left it to me to decide when to desegregate. I wanted to do it before Labor Day, because we made more profit in the third quarter [Labor Day until Christmas] than the rest of the year combined. But I did not want to appear to be doing it under pressure from the students, so I waited until they went home for the summer. I did not want to wait until the fall, because things would be rougher in the fall; I'd already lost one-third of my business.

So, we waited until 2:00 [on July 26, 1960] when we served our own [black] employees at the lunch counter. People came in immediately, and we never had any further trouble. The story was on the back page of the newspaper. That was the end of the sit-ins.

I regret that I did not talk with the four boys and work something out. I would have said that I would integrate, but that it would have to be on my terms. I would slip into it quietly, without any advertising. I think they would have gone along with it. It would have been within a month and I would have done it on my own. I didn't think it was right to not serve them. I was on their side.

## Arnold Schiffman

Mr. Harris discussed with the committee that he would desegregate after the students went home for the summer, and that the initial desegregation would be by his own employees. I can't say that the stores would have given in to student demands without the wish of the community, represented by the committee. The procedure was worked out between Mr. Zane and the leaders in the black community, and Mr. Harris and the Kress management. I did not have any discussions with the older adult members of the black community. But it was their more mature calming influence that facilitated the eventual desegregation. We've always had excellent relations with the upper echelon of the black community, who really govern the area.

## Keep on Walkin', Keep on Talkin'

## Hobart Jarrett

The decision was that a specific hour and a specific day would be named, and the students would be told what day and how many students would come to Woolworth and Kress at these specific hours. It was explained to us that there would be a few students at first, and they were not to come duing the lunch period, when the normal big flow of traffic would be present at the lunch counter. So far as I know, the manager and the waitresses were the only people who knew the exact hour when the store would be desegregated. My group did know the exact day, but we did not communicate this to anybody. The plan was, and it was followed, that my group would only apprise the black community of the fact that integration would take place at the counters during a specific week.

We invited the black ministers to Hayes-Taylor YMCA to tell them what was going to take place the next week. We also invited Horace Kornegay, the District Attorney, to meet with us. We met with him because the students who had been arrested were to be summoned back to Greensboro during the summer for trial, and we had no idea how this could possibly work. Students were scattered all over the country, and we didn't have the money to bring them back. And we thought that Kornegay was a very hard nut to crack.

Mr. Kornegay agreed to meet with us on the same night that the ministers were to meet with us. Miller, Leary, Chavis and Evans went to hold Kornegay while I went to talk with the ministers. The only real disheartening experience that I had in this was that when I went to this meeting with the ministers. I joyfully explained to them all that we had done in the committee and the imminent solution, the ministers agreed that they would explain to their congregations the following Sunday that during the week integration would take place, and they would explain to the congregation the significance of what these students had contributed to life in Greensboro and the world.

Mr. Kornegay agreed to meet with us on the same night that the ministers were to meet with us, and at about the same time. Miller, Leary, Chavis and Evans went to hold Kornegay while I went to talk with the ministers. The only disheartening experience that I had in this was when I went to the meeting with the ministers. One minister, whom I thought highly of, said, "Brother Jarrett, although these things are what we should be getting, we want you to know that the committee went about this whole matter in the wrong way." I was flabbergasted. It turned out that what he meant was that there had been no minister in the process, in the negotiating group. He did not know that Otis Hairston was extremely involved, but Reverend Hairston was involved in activities in this little city, and that little hamlet, and we were here, and we had to be here to talk; the iron was put on the handle, and that is the only reason that Hairston was not there. We had not thought in terms of the fact that there was not a school teacher and a dentist [on the committee]; we were thinking about the fact that there were black people who had come to respond to what four black boys had dared to say to the world.

I was very much put aback by that. I think that the ministers were a little put out that they had not spearheaded this movement, and I regretted that. That really hurt me. I left that meeting, knowing that the ministers were going to tell their congregations what was going to happen, but sick at heart at their criticism of our group. I got to Kornegay's office, where the other members of my group were waiting. We talked to Kornegay, who had not heard that it would be difficult for the students to get back, and he immediately agreed to postpone the trials until after school began in the fall. We had assumed that he would be a man of no feeling. It was a victory for us, but it was an easy one

## Jo Spivey

The negotiating committee named by Mayor Roach was doing its best to resolve the situation. It was headed by Ed Zane, and among its members was Dr. George Evans and Oscar Burnett. The city administration seemed to be playing a passive role, waiting for a compromise to be worked out privately by the committee and the various segregated businesses. But I am sure that they were kept abreast of what was going on; I guess like a good many of them, they didn't want to be involved. I went out to Oscar Burnett's office, and they gave me an exclusive story on how the negotiations were going.

Then the Tuesday or Wednesday night before the target date of July 25th, I attended a meeting at the Woolworth store. Hobart Jarrett, Ed Zane, C.L. Harris, and George Aull, the Assistant City Manager, were all at the meeting. I had found out three or four days before, when they were going to be integrated and had written my story. So we had a streamer simultaneously with the desegregation of the counters, and I went to Woolworth and one of the other reporters went Kress. There were several nicely-dressed black women seated at the counter. I found out later that they were employees of Woolworth, who worked in the kitchen. They were the first blacks to eat at the Woolworth counter after it reopened.

When the counters were reopened in 1960, I talked to City Manager General Townsend, who was a very dear man, and told him that I needed some protection that night, because these people [Klan] had the idea that if I wrote it, then I had something to do with it. I told him that I didn't think that I needed police protection on a regular basis. I talked with George Dorsett of the Ku Klux Klan. I'm sure that he hated me, but he was very evasive. He had one personality face-to-face, and another personality underneath. I didn't know it at the time. The harassment wasn't constant, and stopped about the mid-Sixties. Many years later, I found out that somebody in an off-shoot klavern headed by Dorsett, had told them to lay off of me.

## Arnold Schiffman

Mr. Harris discussed with the committee that he would desegregate after the students went home for the summer, and that the initial desegregation would be by his own employees. I can't say that the stores would have given in to student demands without the wish of the community, which was represented by the committee. The procedure was worked out between Mr. Zane and the leaders in the black community, and Mr. Harris and the Kress management. I had no discussions with the older adult members of the black community. But it was their more mature calming influence that facilitated the eventual desegregation. We've always had excellent relations with the upper echelon of the black community, who really govern the area.

## Geneva Tisdale

When Mr. Harris reopened the lunch counter Ms. Holt called me and told me I could come back to work. And they had a decision to make. So she called all four of her girls—she called us her girls—out that was working behind behind the counter who were black: Susie Morrison [Kemball] at that time, a girl named Anita Jones and me. She told us that they was going to open the counter to everybody. She said, "But when we open the counter, I want my girls to be the first to sit at the counter. You might be called all kinds of names, people might say something to you. I'm just trying to prepare you for what to expect." So we were the three that were served first when they reopened the counter. And she told us, "The day we open up, I want you girls to bring some dress clothes when you come in to work. I'm going to give you a signal when I want you to go upstairs and dress as customers. Walk around in the store like you're a customer, then come over to the counter." She told each one of us where she wanted us to sit, because she wanted us to spread out, one on the front, one middle ways, and one, you know, someplace else. She says, "I want you to order your food." And she had certain waitresses to wait on us. She said, "Let me know if you don't want to have your pictures taken," she said, "because I got a feeling when this gets out, the cameramen will be in. I want you girls to eat real quick, and when you have finished, get up from the counter, and go back upstair. Get in your uniform, come back on the counter, and go to work."

It was aroud twelve o'clock, I think, when we served the public, and the customers hadn't started coming in too much then. So I sat there kind of near where the sandwich board was. Nobody said anything to me. I ordered an egg salad sandwich and a soda., and I ate it in a hurry. None of us got yelled at or insulted. We all went down and ordered our lunch, something that we could eat real quick. And we went and put our uniforms on, and we came back to the counter and started working. And sure enough, soon as we got back down there, the news had gotten out. Here come the men with the [TV] camera. And people began crowding in, because somebody had seen the blacks, I guess, sitting at the counter. So then they started coming in. And we were standing back there looking at them. They never knew that it was Woolworth girls that was the first to sit at the counter to be served after they opened it up. Later that same afternoon, a black customer came in and took a seat. I don't remember if it was a student or not. We all were kind of nervous, because we didn't know what was going to happen. But that next day, I remember people started coming in, blacks and all.

I don't know how long it was, but I don't think it took too long. Because like I said, whites had been eating there all the time, so I guess they would try to get in there before anybody else would start coming in. But I do recall some of the white customers got up and moved when a black person would sit near beside them.

I was proud of it. I want people to know that it was three of Woolworth's girls that were the first.

## Ima Edwards

Once the counters were reopened, it was just a normal day. We opened, everything went smooth. Nobody bothered anybody. Four of our employees were the first blacks served at the lunch counter: Geneva, Susan, Anita, and Florence. After two or three weeks, if a black person came in and asked to be served, they were served. I've wondered if we had went ahead and served them the first day. The time that it was, I don't think it was best to serve them that day. I think it would have been a bad situation for the company, because it would have been breaking tradition with what was going on in the rest of the South. The company didn't want to do that without the whole city opened up.

Mr. Harris was a good boss He always treated the black employees with respect. And as for me, I'm proud to be a part of history. I tell my grandchildren about it.

## Hobart Jarrett

At the end of the school year, I had left Greensboro to teach at a school in Missouri. I called Dr. Miller to see how things were going in Greensboro.

He said that the high school students had turned their attention to Meyer's Department Store, and that the store had agreed to open their lunch counter. The store understood that there would be no demand that the dining room would be opened, and the black leadership had agreed to that. My wife and I returned to Greensboro. I saw that there was a great deal of tension among the blacks because members of our group had agreed that Meyer's dining room would not become a target. We were already under criticism, because Ezell Blair, Sr., and others felt very strongly that we had made a mistake in accepting the "no contest" pleas for the students. I called a meeting to hear what anyone wanted to say.

Students were always present at every meeting, except the negotiations. We decided to visit the manager of Meyer's. At this meeting, I was very pleased to see my dearest friend in Greensboro, Vance Chavis. I was so happy to see and hear the way that he put things. As the leader of our team, I announced to the gentleman that we were there because of dissatisfactions, and he explained, "I did exactly what your group had asked that I do, and I was told by Mr. Chavis here that this would be satisfactory." Then Vance Chavis said, "I did say that, but I was wrong. You will have to recognize that the course of action that we're taking is an unchartered one, and what appeared to us to be what we were really looking for when we talked to you was not what we were really looking for, and we are now saying that your dining room should be opened." This man knew that what we were saying was something that we had to live with, so he said. "Yes, we can integrate." Franklin McCain, Mrs. Susie Jones [widow of Dr. David Jones], Vance Chavis and I integrated the Meyer's Tea Room, and this was a joyous experience. The black waiters seemed thrilled to see what was happening.

I had several meetings with Edward Zane; I think we met once at A&T and two or three times at the Hayes-Taylor YMCA. There was some sort of altercation at the last meeting, but I don't recall what it was. [*Note: In* Civilities and Civil Rights *by William H. Chafe, Zane is quoted as being upset that the committee representing the black community demanded desegregation of restaurants other than the "five and dime" store lunch counters.*]

## Jibreel Khazan

I was working with the group that was doing the negotiations. There were several meetings headed up by the committee under Mr. Zanek and included Dr. Miller, Mr. Chavis, Dr. Evans, Dr. Jarrett, Dr. Simkins and one or two others. They had taken it out of our hands, so to speak. We met with them and they told us what was going on, and they woudl talk with us, but they were between us and Mr. Zane. We were somewhat upset by that. We felt that we were gradually being edged outof direct negotiations with Mr. Zane.

Most of the college studentshad gone home for the summer, but the A&T

and Bennett students who were the remnants of the SECJ remained in Greensboro during the summer, and students from Dudley under Bill Thomas were still actively meeting. I don't think we would have been very succesful without them, because when we returned in the fall of 1960, we had lost a lot of momentum. Therefore, more pressure and responsibility fell upon a few students at A&T and Bennett Colleges and Dudley High School

CORE representatives came down during the summer in 1960. A white man named Gordon Carey; a black fellow named Rudy Lombard, and several CORE members who came up from Louisiana. Marion Dansby was very active with us during the summer of 1960, with people like Paula Jewell, and Evander Gilmer. This is how CORE came to get more influence in Greensboro, because as students we felt that the NAACP was basically an adult group and was kind of slow in terms of what we called demonstrating and carrying picket signs. CORE was more suited for many of us in the area of strategy tactics; they were more experienced at that. CORE came back down in the spring of 1961, to help us deal with voter registration and organizing.

Our focus had been limited mainly to the Woolworth and Kress stores, but the initial outlook or objective was eventually to desegregate all places of public accommodation in Greensboro. We didn't know exactly how successful that we would be on it. When Woolworth and Kress finally agreed to our objectives in July 1960, we planned to test other places of public accommodation. We went to other restaurants: the S&W, then McDonald's, Howard Johnson's, the Hot Shoppes and the Toddle House.

I received word that Woolworth and Kress had agreed to desegregate in a meeting with Dr. Miller, Dr. Evans, Dr. Jarrett, Mr. Chavis and others who were representing the adult black community of Greensboro in the negotiating group between the students and Mr. Zane's group. We were very happy about it, but the way the plan was supposed to proceed was that the adult citizens, like Dr. Miller and the others of the committee would go in and sit down on the first day, along with persons of the European-American community in Greensboro, as a testing group. We agreed to not rush down there all at one time. In fact, I didn't go down until two years later. I didn't normally go into Woolworth everyday anyway, but that was the whole gist of the thing that people didn't understand. It wasn't the idea of rushing into the restaurant just to prove that we could eat there; it was to do it in a normal way. If I was hungry, I would stop there and get something to eat. That was the way that it was supposed to be, and that was the way that we planned it.

Although CORE acted as unofficial advisors to the SECJ, we were doing this on our own; we were not officially CORE members. What happened was, when the Movement started at A&T in 1960, many of us were NAACP card members. We belonged to the NAACP Youth Group, even though we were members of the Student Executive Committee for Justice, and I became president of the NAACP on campus in the fall of 1960, but as I became involved in other activities, Lewis Brandon, Donald Potts, and others on campus, became more active in the NAACP leadership roles, so that I could relinquish it and do other activities on campus and still be a part of the Movement.

## Arnold Schiffman

After the desegregation of Woolworth and Kress, it seemed to be of public notice for some few weeks and then just died away when nobody thought anymore about it. The public got used to it, and it worked beautifully. Crowds did not gather after the announcement. Black patrons came into the stores from time to time, but there was no picketing; it just died away, and the blacks just walked in. I don't recall any other eating establishments desegregated at that time. I think that I continued on the committee of the Chamber of Commerce for community betterment, I've forgotten the exact title; I was interested in the human side of it. We only met as a crisis developed or as someone had a theory of something that would be beneficial.

I thought that the sit-ins were a radical approach and not in the best interests of the blacks or the community. I thought a quiet approach would accomplished more, with less acrimony. We knew that more aggressive or violent tactics could happen, and we wanted to make sure that it didn't happen. We thought calm consideration on all scores would help prevent it for the benefit of all in the community. I don't think that an economic boycott of the downtown area by black patrons was in effect, other than as a temporary pressure, or that it was the cause of the solution. I think we realized by that time that the solu-tion had to come; the question was how to bring it about with the least stress on all concerned. The trend of civil rights legislation indicated what was in the offing. We realized that they were trying to accomplish in one great jump what should take years of progressive thinking and progress to bring about. All of these factors combined together wwere storeng indicators of what had to come, and that was coming. It was coming to a head fast, which those of us more temperate felt that it should be slow and come progressively.

## Franklin McCain

All places did not open their facilities at the same time. The agreement didn't say that on July 25, all restaurants or places of public accommoda-tions in Greensboro were going to integrate their facilities; it didn't happen that way. It was in a piecemeal fashion. Only sixty percent of places in Greensboro agreed to integrate. In the early days, the Chamber of Commerce made a survey of all the places of public accommodation in Greensboro, particularly eating places. Approximately seventy-three who took part in this survey said that they had no problems with integrating their facilities if their fellow businessmen would. A few were undecided, and something like twenty percent said no. That was a source of strength to me, anyway. There were almost seventy-five percent who were saying, "I'm only doing that which is unjust because my neighbor is doing it." By English common law, the old innkeeper's laws said that you must take in a traveler or anybody who is on the road, if he has money, and put him up for his lodgings and feed him. You must do that. My goodness, that was three hundred years old, at least.

## J. Kenneth Lee

The real heroes of the sit-ins have never been mentioned. Ralph Johns was the backbone of the thing. You had some young black people defying many years of custom, and they'd take them and put them in jail. They were serious about those first few, and they had some real high bonds. The only reason they didn't stay in jail was because those old black people put their homes up and signed their bonds. I was the one recruiting the ones willing to go, when they were just calling in volunteers, andthey did not know whether the students were coming back. There were very substantial bonds, and they didn't know what was going to happen. They could have broken that thing just like that if they had jailed the first five hundred and kept them in jail,. But as fast as they would jail them, they'd sign them out and they'd come right back and sit down. some of those kids had fifteen charges against them, all growing out of a two-or-three-day involvement.

# Chapter 3

## Greensboro CORE

*When the A&T and Bennett students returned in the fall of 1960 and found that the lunch counters had been desegregated, many believed that the purposes of the spring demonstrations had been accomplished, and returned to their studies. But a small group of black college and high school students continued to meet at Reverend Marion Jones' house throughout 1960-1962, to discuss how they could create an on-going campaign to desegregate all places of public accommodation in Greensboro. These meetings resulted in the formation of the Intercollegiate Committee for Equality, an ad hoc organization to pursue their goals. Discussions included such issues as improving economic opportunities for African Americans and voter registration drives, but the focus remained on desegregating places of public accommodation.*

*The group conducted sporadic protests, such as picketing local movie theaters, but these lacked the coordination of the lunch counter campaign. One such effort was to join SNCC's Southwide picketing of segregated theaters showing the film, "Porgy and Bess" in the fall of 1960.*

## Marion Jones

At meetings held at my house from 1960 to 1962, some students discussed ways to break down the barriers of segregation in eating establishments, movie houses, hotels, and other places of public accommodations. I helped direct their thinking to broader economic conditions in the black community, such as employment. There were my three daughters, Sarah and Betty and Marion; Ezell Blair; David Richmond; Bill Thomas; my nephew Wendell Scott; Lewis Brandon; Pat Patterson; Lois Lucas; Paula Jewell; Tony Stanley; Elizabeth Laizner; James Busch; and John Hatchett. Our group initially called itself the Intercollegiate Committee for Equality, because it was made up primarily of college students and faculty from the surrounding colleges. Our group met at least twice a week, and later on, when we were formally organized, we met about once a month.

Whenever the need arose, we would meet more frequently

George Simkins, Ezell Blair, Sr., and I were members of the NAACP and we shared attitudes on improving black voting privileges, job opportunities and public accommodation segregation, among other things. As a result of contacts made during the sit-ins, we called James Farmer to see if we could get advice on moving against these issues. Gordon Carey and Floyd McKissick came to Greensboro from Durham to talk to us about the Freedom Highways project that CORE was planning in North Carolina for the summer of 1962.

## Gloria Jean Blair (Howard)

After Woolworth and Kress desegregated in July of 1960, there were meetings and discussion groups, because the morale and the spirit were there to "Let's see if we can continue to open things up." My brother would go to Reverend Jones' house; he lived just around the corner. They used to talk about what to do when they were testing places. He was very much of an activist, a quiet man, but kids in college really liked going to his home during that time. My brother almost saw him as a surrogate father. Ezell was in his late teens at that time, and I think that he enjoyed just getting away from home and talking with his friends. Reverend Jones had the kind of home where people sat around talking about things. It was that kind of environment, and he was very much into organizing groups. They called themselves the Intercollegiate Committee for Equality.

Occasionally, some adults provided valuable advice as to organization and structure, calling upon local support groups, because the students needed community support, people like Sarah Herbin, Otis Hairston, my dad [Ezell Blair, Sr.], David Morehead and Reverend Jones. Greensboro had a professional black community from the colleges here; very active members of church groups were supporting the students, assisting the students in the area of organization skills. They talked with the students about what was necessary to do. The students were doing the things necessary to keep the Movement going: recruiting people, testing and picketing by college town students and high school students of various local businesses to see if they would desegregate, and forming picket lines.

In 1962, my sophomore year at Bennett, I attended meetings in the basement of St. Stephens Church during the summer months, where people came to speak. Initially only a small number of students were very involved. They were the ones that actually put their bodies there out there: go and march on the picket lines, but there was a lot of machinery that was necessary to keep the Movement going, calling people in, getting funding. I picketed the businesses downtown, and other locations in Greensboro. I also telephoned a lot and taking care of guests who were coming to town.

Our reputation as the site of the first sit-ins was one primary reason that other people started coming into Greensboro. That summer, Ivanhoe Donaldson and Hank Thomas from SNCC stayed in our house while they assisted with the picketing and the sit-ins. But they didn't try to organize a SNCC chapter here; they just had an interest in what was going on in Greensboro. They talked with groups at local churches, giving us advice. They'd tell us, "You should get lawyers to support you, in case you have to go to jail. There are certain things you need to do, if you want this thing to pick up momentum."

## Lewis Brandon

When we got back to Greensboro in the fall of 1960, there wasn't anything going on. Then there was a movie starring Pearl Bailey, "Porgy and Bess," which played at the Cinema Theater on Tate Street. Bill Thomas, Donald Lyons and I went to see it at the Cinema Theater on Tate Street, and were refused tickets. So we picketed it for about two months, and then we moved to the downtown theaters. Some guys from my home town, including my brother and some students from A&T and Bennett, Guilford and Greensboro colleges picketed the National and the Carolina theaters until January of 1961. It was on a nightly basis. Initially, there was some activity from the Klan on Tate Street, but we didn't have any trouble once we got downtown. We would walk beside each other, laugh and talk. The only thing that they [Klan] did that might be provocative was writing down our license plate numbers to try to intimidate us. But on the line, everybody thought they were just one big joke.

Donald headed up the group, and there was a counterpart on Bennett's campus, so we just kind of went along with it, because most of the meetings were held on the Bennett campus. The focus at that point was just the theaters. The lunch counters had already opened up, so the focal point was nothing broader than the theaters at that point.

We would meet with the Greensboro Community Fellowship, and some of us would occasionally test the restaurants. Warren Ashby and I were asked out of the King Cotton restaurant when we went in there and asked for service. I attended some of the Fellowship meetings that were being held out at the Holiday Inn South, and on occasion we would use the pond out at John Taylor's house for a retreat and get-togethers. I really met him through Dick Ramsey when we were picketing on Tate Street. Dick was working with the American Friends Service Committee. He was very active when we were picketing against the theaters, and he was very instrumental in recruiting some of the students from Guilford and Greensboro colleges, because he was the Secretary of the College Committee for the Friends.

*The students were stymied in their efforts to find a more significant direct action opportunity, but that abruptly changed in the summer of 1962.*

*The Congress of Racial Equality established headquarters in Durham to initiate its Freedom Highways campaign to desegregate Howard Johnson restaurants along interstate highways. The number of black colleges and universities in central North Carolina was a fertile source of participants. George Simkins put Gordon Carey in contact with the A&T and Bennett College students meeting at Reverend Jones' house.*

## James Farmer

The Freedom Highways project was an outgrowth of the combination of the sit-ins at restaurants and the Freedom Rides which attacked segregation in bus terminal facilities. Some of us in the national office wanted to attack discrimination in restaurants that were not connected with interstate bus terminals. So we thought of desegregating the facilities along U.S. highways. The perception at that time was that restaurants were private property, and they had a legal right to pick and choose their customers. Therefore, you were guilty of trespassing if you did not leave when asked to do so.

After the Freedom Rides in 1961, CORE began to grow in reputation, and every day we received requests to create new chapters. CORE had only a small staff in 1962, so we had to be highly selective in the campaigns to which we could devote our limited staff and financial resources. We created the Freedom Highways campaign, because the Howard Johnson's restaurant chain on interstate highways was a highly visible target. We could apply economic pressure on the chain to desegregate, based on the national publicity that such an effort would generate. We thought that if the chain desegregated its restaurants in one state, it would do so throughout the interstate highway system. We chose North Carolina because of the many black colleges in the state. With our small budget, we decided to use student volunteers, paying their expenses and a small stipend. Many of those volunteers were students from A&T and Bennett Colleges, and they suggested that we conduct training sessions at Bennett. We contacted President Dr. Willa Player, who invited us on campus. It was ideal because it was a private institution that would not be subject to pressure from the state legislature, and we could benefit from the participation of its students. They became the "Freedom Highways Task Force" that sustained the campaign.

We considered placing our headquarters in Greensboro because of its reputation as the site of the first sustained sit-in movement. But we chose Durham because Floyd McKissick lived there. He was state NAACP Youth Advisor and he was also the leading proponent of CORE activities in the state. He was willing to divide his time between the NAACP and CORE, so our activities were drawn to where he was.

CORE considered the Freedom Highways campaign to be very successful as our primary activity in 1962. The one thing that caused us concern was that it did not receive the kind of publicity that it should have nationally. We were unable to get any news stories outside of the state of North Carolina. We held press conferences with representatives of the wire services and the TV networks present. They told us that the information did go onto the wires, but still was not picked up. I was informed by a reporter of one of the New York newspapers that a memorandum was passed down to the news department from the office of the managing editor saying, "When items come on the wires about the Freedom Highways campaign of CORE in North Carolina, refer it up here to me." There was a blackout outside of North Carolina. I suspect that it was the combined pressure of state and local government officials. Terry Sanford was a moderately progressive governor, but he had to do what he had to do, and we did not consider him hostile. He was trying to get northern industry into his state, and racial turmoil would discourage industry from moving into the state. Thus, the governor is able to make certain calls, and to limit the publicity.

But, we were able to apply enough pressure on the Howard Johnson's chain to convince them to quickly desegregate all their restaurants in North Carolina, and eventually in other states. It was a significant victory for CORE, and its success was due in large part to the participation of students from Greensboro.

## Gordon Carey

As Director of Field Secretaries, I sent B. Elton Cox to Greensboro from High Point. He was a very dynamic individual and we were not very bureaucratic in those days. Field secretaries had flexibility to initiate projects on their own. In theory, a field secretary was not supposed to be an independent agent; he was supposed to work through the local chapter. His job was to organize and support local organizations. But Reverend Elton Cox was not very amenable to discipline, and did pretty much whatever he wanted to do. So, he caused a lot of problems for the national office, in the sense that he was off doing things that we may not have known about in advance, but because of his popularity and his dynamism he was well-liked, but he did not fit into the typical mode of field secretary.

We were very Gandhian, and Gandhi was interested in symbols, so we became interested in symbols. Greensboro was selected simply because it was the historical spawning ground of the national sit-in movement. Another factor was that Bennett College was an independent institution, not subject to the pressure of the state legislature. But the project was initiated in Durham because the dominant CORE person in North Carolina was Floyd McKissick; he was active in both the NAACP and CORE, and this gave the NAACP some problems, because NAACP youth groups became NAACP and CORE chapters simultaneously. This didn't bother us, but I think that the NAACP was more conservative and bureaucratic than we were. We also moved our operations to Durham on the basis of economics. It was too expensive in Greensboro for food and lodging, and we didn't have the money.

I think that the Freedom Highways Project was very successful. As a result of that project, we made major strides in integrating public facilities. Those people that opposed integration were not very clever; it seems to me. Most of the successes of the civil rights movement organizations at the time, whether it was CORE or SNCC or SCLC were based on the illusion of strength. We were not nearly as effective or powerful as people gave us credit for being, but the idea of an assault frightened people to death, and caused them to do very dumb things. Either they overreacted and used violence, which played into our hands, or they capitulated. There was never any community-wide or industry-wide consciousness or thoughtful planning on the part of the opposition; there was none. We were organized, they were not.

Those associated with the Freedom Highways project were Rudy Lombard, Ike Reynolds, Jerome Smith, Tom Gaither, Hank Thomas, and a woman named Geraldine. CORE took the position that we had to go great lengths to protect our image. Back in the old days, in the Forties and Fifties, we wouldn't let people on picket lines with beards, men had to go in coats, ties and dress shirts. Our picket lines were exemplary. Likewise, we felt that we wanted to keep as far away from politics as possible, therefore, we would not permit CORE members to associate with, let's say, the Stalinist movement, or communism, and so on. A part of this was that some of the early people in CORE were really Democratic Socialists, and Socialists traditionally have had no use for Stalinists or Trotskyites or more radical Communists. Carl and Anne Braden were the primary leaders of the Southern Conference Education Fund at that time, and in our estimation that organization was too closely aligned with Stalinist organizations or individuals. CORE, as a policy, did not cooperate with them. We discouraged cooperating with Reverend Fulgham in Hickory and Reginald Hawkins in Charlotte, but not for political reasons.

There was quite a bit of resistance within the hierarchy of the national office of CORE in working in the South at all. CORE traditionally utilized a very disciplined form of nonviolent direct-action, and there was doubt whether the South was amenable to and ready for the kinds of direct-action that CORE initiated. There was a certain amount of fear that we were going to have people hurt. In those days, CORE was made up of hard-core pacifists who, as a matter of principle, would die before they would commit violence, but at that time few in the movement were that dedicated to the concept. You had good discipline, because I think some of the old CORE pacifist leaders misread history. Gandhi may have been dedicated to nonviolence, but he did not require his followers to believe in nonviolence except as a tactic. In fact, he was very conscious of the fact that you couldn't get enough followers if you did it that way. So, he used common ordinary people, and what you did was you got them to accept nonviolence as a tactic toward achieving a limited goal, and we did the same thing.

The NAACP, for many years, was almost opposed to direct action, believing that it might incite violence. It thought that the proper way to conduct social change in this arena was through the courts. I like to think that we were a little more generous in our thinking than they were, because we recognized that it was good that you had moderate organizations like the Urban League, and that you had legally-oriented organizations like the NAACP. We felt that there should be a plurality of different types of civil rights organizations. People should have a fringe, a cutting edge, but the NAACP was a little bit stodgy and a little bit too involved its own bureaucracy. The young people felt that, although they had come through the youth chapters of the NAACP, if they listened to these "old fogeys" then nothing would get done, and that's how they should have thought. But at the same time, we tried, through Floyd McKissick, to make clear to kids that, "We wouldn't be here if not for the NAACP."

Historically, the NAACP has been the most important organization in the black community, outside of the churches. So that needed to be recognized. Although George Simkins was head of NAACP in Greensboro, he was very much in tune with the wishes of the kids. After all, he was the one that was responsible for bringing CORE into North Carolina. CORE did not get involved in law suits. We felt that the Legal Defense Fund of the NAACP was much better qualified to do it, because they knew what they were doing. They had funds, and attorneys, and a rich history of litigation. We had none; we limited our legal activities to bailing out people that were in jail. We preferred that the demonstrators get legal counsel through the NAACP or the ACLU [American Civil Liberties Union]. As a matter of fact, I'm not sure that we ever had a full-time lawyer on our staff.

## Jibreel Khazan

We helped picket the Howard Johnson's on the highway in Durham, but we were anxious to use the techniques that we learned from that experience in our campaign against the Hot Shoppes on Summit Avenue in Greensboro from July 23-27, 1962. The Hot Shoppes management wanted to desegregate, but it wanted to see what it would be like for the other stores. Manager Clyde Irwin delayed by telling us that he would have to talk with corporate headquarters about its reaction to black patronage. They didn't want to come around, but we were out there picketing every day during the summer. They decided that after negations that they didn't want the scene of picketers in front of their restaurant. So they got together with the committee from the black community representing CORE and their leadership, as well as Mr. Zane's group. They would serve us, but they didn't want any publicity. It was planned in advance with Mr. Irwin and his legal representative Armistad Sapp about what would happen. On the first day, a couple of us would drive in and order our food through a speaker; someone would come out to serve us and we would leave. That's how it came off and it was very successful for everyone involved. The management made a statement that they served everyone on an equal first come, first served basis, as long as they were peaceful and did not create any violence. It was understood that we would not go back in there in mass numbers.

I had many conversations with Mr. Sapp, beginning in the spring of 1960 and continuing through 1962. When the Woolworth and Kress stores decided to integrate, Mr. Sapp became the legal representative of other businesses that we targeted for picketing, like the Hot Shoppes and the Cinema Theater. He told us at that time in no way could the stores serve us at the time, and I remember that my response was, "I will go back and talk with our Executive Committee." The first time was when we were demonstrating in 1960, and he came to talk to us. I told him that, "As a lawyer, you should know that the Constitution guarantees us our rights." He said, "No way, you just cannot be served. I'm a lawyer, I know what I am taking about." We told him politely, "Yes, but we know that we are right in our efforts." He would get hot and say, "I'm going to do this" and "I'm going to do that. I'm a lawyer." We would go to his office and talk with him. His line was: "No way will these stores integrate at all," and he took the job and told several businesses that he would represent them in keeping us out, keeping the places segregated. He made statements in the newspaper that made the stores take the same hardline stand in which he approached the Student Executive Committee for Justice or later the representatives from CORE. It was like matching wits with each other [Laughs]. I wasn't a lawyer, but I enjoyed talking with him. Attorney McNeill Smith from the Human Relations Commission would meet with us, and we would get together and talk with Mr. Sapp. McNeill Smith did a good job handling the situation.

## John Hatchett

At that point [1962] Lois Lucas became involved. Reverend [James] Busch was very definitely involved at this time. In fact, from the outset he played a very prominent and active role. But neither Reverend Busch nor I, attempted to function as leaders. We were never considered to be leaders; that designation was never, to my knowledge, applied to us, although I think some of the local black establishments may have viewed us in that light, or as coming in from the outside to stir up difficulties. There was a fair amount of resentment, especially among the ministerial establishment. Reverend Busch had more encounters with them than I did, but enough to know that there was a certain amount of resentment, which we tried to allay by saying that we were not leaders of anything, that we were at best advisors, at the least active participants. Otis Hairston, Lorenzo Lynch, Richard Hicks were sympathetic to us. Given the number of ministers in the area, there weren't that many. But, thank goodness, there were some. The others were more opposed by their silence, by their not opening up their churches, by their not encouraging their membership to take an active role in what was taking place. It was more a posture of silence than it was of open and active opposition.

There was a young man who was sent down—I'm not sure whether he was sent down from New York City or from elsewhere— who was instrumental in helping to form the CORE chapter. [B. Elton Cox from High Point.] I don't know who made the initial contact. I got the impression that what took place was that the young man in particular was on his way somewhere else, because CORE had initiated a series of Freedom Rides at that time. And he was simply stopping off in Greensboro, and somehow was asked to stay around for a while and to assist us in our fight, and assist us in what we were attempting to do.

I get the feeling that somehow CORE sort of drifted, but not accidentally, into this and managed to place themselves as an organization in a very favorable light and to impress the persons involved in our own demonstrations that this would be the best possible organization to handle what was taking place in Greensboro at that time. I recall sitting down with the gentleman sent to us, with Bill Thomas, Lois Lucas, and perhaps a few other people. And we discussed certain things about how CORE would be beneficial to us.

I was not favorably impressed at that time. And I think that subsequent events proved me to be correct in terms of my not being favorably impressed. Having come out of an environment where I knew certain people connected with CORE, I didn't like the whole approach that they took to the Freedom Rides. I felt that large numbers of people were being asked to have all manner of violent physical assault heaped on them and not to resort to any defense whatsoever. And although, to be sure, there was no physical altercation between myself and anyone else during the sit-ins that started in Greensboro, I was not then, and am not now, an advocate of what people have come to call nonviolence. I believed then and now in self-defense.

And I was a bit uneasy that if an organization like CORE became the leading organization for what we were doing in Greensboro, that this was going to mean that a lot of people, including a lot of young black women, could possibly be very badly beaten and otherwise brutalized, because they would have to pledge allegiance to the principle of nonviolence. That's part of why I felt that way. Reverend Busch shared my concern, and I believe that Lois Lucas at that time understood. Even at the time that she was a student at Bennett, she was a very perceptive and a very aware black woman. And I think that she understood what I was attempting to articulate at that time. There may have been some others, but I was, in a sense, out-voted, or reassured that this was not going to take place, that my fears would not be realized, and that CORE could be a very effective force for change in Greensboro.

I participated in the picketing of the Hot Shoppes. I'm not sure why that particular target was chosen, but as I said, we had decided to step up our activities, to open up a number of places. And that was one of the places targeted, in part, because it was a national chain. And the feeling was that if we could put pressure on restaurants that had affiliations elsewhere, then perhaps we could do the same with them that was done with Woolworth and Kress. The attorney for the Hot Shoppes [Armistad Sapp] was adamant in urging the Hot Shoppe management to not capitulate to our wishes. He claimed this on both legal and other grounds, and suggested that we were picking on the wrong people in the first place, and that that particular kind of target was not important. In other words, he attempted to belittle our negotiations. Why he did not succeed, I cannot say. But I think that part of it was because the Hot Shoppes was either a regional or a national chain. I think that they feared pressures outside as much as they feared the fact that we were concentrating on them in terms of trying to open them up.

## Marion Jones

CORE contacted B. Elton Cox, a minister and CORE field secretary in High Point, to come over and speak to us. We went over to High Point to assist in his picketing against McDonald's there. We basically restricted our activities to Greensboro and High Point, although we decided to assist CORE in its Freedom Highways project in the summer of 1962. We attended the Freedom Highways project workshops held at churches and on Bennett College campus. While we were picketing the Howard Johnson's restaurant on the highway, we picketed the Hot Shoppes in Greensboro at the same time. Seldom would they attempt to put on any demonstrations without having workshops so that the thing could be carried out smoothly as possible. James Farmer insisted on that, as well as the Program Director [Gordon Carey]. They discussed negotiation techniques, methods of demonstrating, marches, things to say and what not to say, things to do and what not to do. We also communicated with other groups, particularly SNCC, although we had no interest in organizing a chapter. In the early fall of 1960 we picketed the Cinema Theater in Greensboro, which featured the film "Porgy and Bess," after SNCC announced that it was starting a campaign to picket segregated theaters that were showing this movie.

From those experiences, the group decided to become an official CORE chapter. We adult advisers did not necessarily influence the students to choose CORE. We knew that CORE was a very active organization and felt that it could be very effective in direct action activities. Eventually, they dropped the earlier name, and formed a CORE chapter. The reason for the delay in forming a CORE chapter in Greensboro was our concern about getting a larger, more supportive membership. Things were beginning to fall into place. We never reached a point of becoming complacent or satisfied with what had taken place so far, but it was a matter of regrouping, sorting out things to see where you are, because CORE was young in this area and we had to feel our way.

Due to my support of the group and the fact that my nephew Wendell Scott, the first president of CORE, lived with me, my house became the headquarters of the chapter. But as the chapter grew, we met at various churches, Elizabeth Laizner's apartment, and the Thomas or Blair residences. Bill Thomas was a very sensible young man with a very good, analytical mind, and solid as a dollar. He eventually became president, after my nephew left Greensboro to go to school, and following Ezell Blair's resignation upon being elected student body president at A&T. Lewis Brandon and Pat Patterson were of the same kind of temperament, and any heated conversations would remain among us. We made any decisions as democratic as possible, where everybody could have an input. Things were put to a vote and the membership abided by the vote. Having taken a consensus of whatever the project was, we all picked at the pieces and we would weigh the advantages against the disadvantages. If a certain thing was expedient, then we would do it immediately; if not, we would do it later. The members were all calm and sensible, fully discussing and analyzing situations before attempting to do or say anything. As a matter of fact, I was pleasantly surprised at the attitude of those younger men and women; nobody lost their heads and our meetings served as an example of maturity, even among the teenagers.

## Gloria Jean Blair (Howard)

In the summer of 1962, my sophomore year at Bennett, I attended meetings in the basement of St. Stephens Church during the summer months, where CORE people came to speak. I joined town college and high school students who picketed the Hot Shoppes as part of the Freedom Highways project. I also did a lot of telephoning and taking care of guests who came to town. Although we would contact the press and the television station, they would only cover our activities when members of the CORE national office would come down, and when the Hot Shoppes announced that it was going to desegregate. I enjoyed talking to CORE field representatives, and especially Jim Farmer, whenever they stayed at our house.

## Lois Lucas (Williams)

There was really not very much activity going on until we participated in CORE's Freedom Highway project. I guess we were a little young as far as taking the initiative. Several CORE field secretaries—Isaac Reynolds, Hunter Morey and George Raymond—came down; they took their meals at Bennett College and held workshops at St. Stephens Church. When we picketed the Hot Shoppes in Greensboro, the hecklers passed by in their cars and parked under that roof where the restaurant served the outdoor food, but I don't remember any kind of physical harassment. I got the feeling that the policemen wanted to keep as much peace as possible. The students sensed this and, hence, were not afraid of the policemen, as a whole. I don't remember any students who were billy-clubbed.

Although we became an official CORE chapter, we continued to be very informal; everyone did a variety of tasks. I never held an office in CORE or attended Executive Committee meetings. I would not consider myself an organizer, as much as just an active participant. I just did whatever there was to be done: providing transportation to and from demonstration sites, making placards and picket signs, canvassing black neighborhoods to encourage people to register to vote and distribute literature about aidng our boycott of downtown businesses that had begun during the sit-ins.

The chapter soon became too large to meet in private homes, so we often met at the Church of the Redeemer and Providence Baptist Church. Very little was done on the campuses, although the leaders were very good students who had the ability to communicate effectively, which helped to draw the support of other students, who respected their abilities. But, we remained student-oriented. I don't remember much input the adult black community, other than participation from the Greensboro Citizens Association and the NAACP through Dr. Jarrett at Bennett and Dr. Simkins. They would attend our meetings and give advice. Later on, we developed a great deal more rapport with the adult community.

## Robert "Pat" Patterson

The Freedom Rides had an effect on us, because I think that's when CORE started making its presence felt nationally. CORE was an organization that believed in action rather than sitting around talking about things. So it went a long way to influence the Movement here in Greensboro. I saw CORE as a group that I could identify with, in terms of their tactics. I felt at the time that the NAACP wasn't doing the kinds of things that it was going to take in order to change the status quo. CORE wasn't an on-campus kind of thing. CORE sent a field person into town, and I can't even remember the guy's name. CORE sent in some folks to organize the Freedom Highway project, and those of us that had leanings towards CORE moved in that direction—Bill Thomas, Lewis Brandon, and Reverend A. Knighton Stanley.

I can't take claim for being one of the founders of Greensboro CORE, because they had either already formed it, or it was in the developmental process. However, I did serve as vice-chairman of the chapter. Reverend Hatchett and Tony Stanley were two of our advisers. Bennett College girls played an important role, especially Regina Carpenter and Patricia Murray. Oddly enough, the Bennett College girls got involved a whole lot earlier and were more actively involved in the Civil Rights Movement in Greensboro than the fellows and the girls at A&T. There were only about fifteen or twenty of us at first; basically a few fellows from A&T and a lot of girls from Bennett College, and a few people from the community.

The Executive Committee served more as an advisory group than in an administrative capacity, and most of these people were much older than the average age of the members. It planned what things we would involve ourselves in, but usually the whole chapter made decisions about the choice of tactics, targets or methods of demonstration. There was disagreement among us as to what we should be doing and how we should be doing it. There weren't any real radicals, to the extent that someone wanted to be violent. But there were some of us who thought that there were groups that were making promises to us that they weren't keeping. I remember meeting with several groups of people out at the Red Cross building to resolve these problems. Nothing ever came out of those meetings. One individual that stands out in my mind was Ed Zane, who was on the committee formed at the time of the sit-ins. We got quite a bit of guidance from the national CORE office, because they had a field man here [Gordon Carey], and on several occasions Jim Farmer came down and spoke to the group. And there was Floyd McKissick in Durham, who was actively involved with CORE.

Reverend Tony Hatchett, Reverend Busch, Dr. Laizner and Bill Thomas were a part of the group that could be called activists; they wanted a more dynamic form of demonstrations. They pushed to move faster on some things that others didn't want to move on. Reverend Hatchett, Dr. Laizner and Reverend Busch from Bennett particularly wanted to push hard. All of us wanted to push, but there was a difference of opinion as to how you go about it. Reverend Busch was among those that said, "Let's go, let's go. We need to do something." There were other people that said, "No, we need to think this thing out, to do it this way." Lewis Brandon would have fallen into that category. Tony was a very good adviser and a person who did a lot of thinking about some of the problems that we could run into, and was a stabilizing effect upon the group. I was somewhere in the middle. Some of the things that Reverend Hatchett and Dr. Laizner and some of the others advocated I couldn't agree with, but I would say that there were more things that I agreed on with them than I disagreed. I would have to say that I was one of the moderates.

## Floyd McKissick

The period of the sit-ins in February 1960 was the beginning of CORE's activities in North Carolina. But there were a number of people who were very familiar with its ideas, aims and objectives, but had never formed chapters. There were two very important campaigns: the sit-ins and the Freedom Highways project. Gordon Carey, Douglas Moore, a minister in Durham, David Steth and I went out on sit-ins on various Sundays, not under the name of any organization. We were not particularly concerned about organizational structure at that point. There was just an organization of young people here, and I was a part of it. We were disturbed about the reluctance of anyone to do anything in Durham, and we were moving in that direction. George Simkins knew about our group and encouraged us to work with those active in Greensboro.

Greensboro was a symbol, but Durham was the headquarters of CORE activity in North Carolina. We only had five thousand dollars and the question was, "How can we carry on this struggle against Howard Johnson's in North Carolina with only five thousand dollars?" I said, "We can do it," but skeptics said, "How you can do it, the way that you're spending money in Greensboro, but if we were in Durham, we believe that you could do it." Gordon and I met and he said, "Okay, we're coming to Durham." Using Durham as a base, we eventually organized CORE chapters in Goldsboro, New Bern, Statesville, Greensboro, and High Point. But we didn't have highly-structured chapters like the NAACP. Although we wanted local community structures, we'd take an organization that could become a CORE affiliate without changing its local name.

But I think that Greensboro was certainly a very important city for CORE activity. The two towns in North Carolina to really emphasize the Movement and to push it on were Durham and Greensboro, where there was the leadership and financial ability to support a youth movement. They needed each other; when things slowed in Greensboro, then we'd move to Durham. Greensboro's significance was in large part because of the support of the adult black community, and being a strong college community, it developed good leadership.

Many in the NAACP regarded CORE field secretaries as "outsiders." We were not trying to co-opt the NAACP in any sense, but I think the State Conference of the NAACP feared us, because we were attracting so many young people. The NAACP at one time was against the sit-in movement, then later joined us. George Simkins sought help from CORE because he could not generate interest in the sit-ins within the national headquarters of the NAACP. I was an '"insider" in Durham, and CORE, therefore, was part of the "in-group" in Durham, whereas I was considered an "outsider" to some of the NAACP leadership in Greensboro. But George Simkins provided excellent progressive leadership throughout the years there, and so we worked well together. By the time that we went to the NAACP Convention in Minneapolis, the NAACP had come around, and the North Carolina kids were the center of attraction. The prevailing opinion was that they realized the strength and extent of the nonviolent direct-action movement was so strong with the young people that they would be left behind if they did not support it.

The field secretaries that CORE sent to North Carolina were very effective: Isaac Reynolds, Hunter Morey, and George Raymond. I think that they were good community organizers. The great thing about CORE was that it had a versatility of people that could both blend in and do a thing. But they were loose about prerogatives. While the NAACP was concentrated on structure, we were concentrating on objectives; we were the "shock troops." We knew that we were going to do some things that were not going to meet with everybody's approval, but it was our desire to bring about some changes in society. We had classes, teachings, and commitment to nonviolent demonstrations. That was the difference between us. We carried out nonviolent direct-action, rather than sit down and create structure.

The Reverend B. Elton Cox was a very likable, outgoing personality, and was an excellent minister. He was what you would call a "creative minister"; he would set an example. He would never ask anyone else to do what he himself would not do, and the man had no fear. He was the subject of much criticism from blacks and whites for his comments. He wasn't a typical minister, or else he would never have been in the Movement. He believed that Christianity was to be practically applied, and that Christians should set an example. He attracted public and media attention because he was articulate and he took pride in his appearance and in what he said and did. He appealed to young people because he could make an important point, and yet he also knew how to make a joke. But he always let you know that he was a minister and if something was going on that he disapproved of, he'd say, "Wait a minute. I don't think that God would like that." He was also an efficient field secretary. The national office often talked about asking Cox to conduct activities outside North Carolina. They'd say, "Since things are well under way here, we need him in Louisiana." I used to say, "Look, if we are going to set up some chapters, we'd better keep Cox here." Because Cox could go anywhere and everywhere that he went in a short period of time, he was like the Pied Piper; the young people would just be drawn to him.

In addition to some friction with the NAACP over tactics, there was some tension within CORE as to organization. There was resistance in the national office of CORE to our loose structure in the field. The national office had certain ideas about how CORE should be run locally, which was not realistic, and I think that field offices and the national office had conflicts at times. There were those in New York who felt that there was too much autonomy in the field and wanted more central control. I believe that many of the kids in the local chapters didn't like the national office, because it would say, "Come to New York and do this." Kids would go up there and help raise money and tell their stories, but then the national office could be insensitive to the wishes of the local chapters. But this did not affect the feeling that the students had for the field secretaries. I think they recognized that Gordon Carey was a very effective field man, and enthusiastically supported local chapters. I think the national office was often operating at an incommunicable distance from the field structure. They failed to understand how crucial North Carolina became, in terms of our effectiveness. I felt that it would have been to CORE's advantage to set up a Southern-based office in North Carolina. I suggested to Farmer that that be done. We ended up having a convention here, but I would have prefered having a permanent office of CORE. It was an important testing area, where CORE principles were really taught and trained.

## B. Elton Cox

I headed the CORE chapter in High Point; I think we eventually had nine in the state. When the students sat down in Greensboro, I led the first high school group to sit-in in High Point. I also conducted a demonstration at the county courthouse in Greensboro to protest the segregated tax books and segregated restrooms there. I said we should be able to buy in any neighborhood that we had the money to buy a house. We decided one day to go into Greensboro and protest signs designating "colored" restrooms in the courthouse by walking into the restroom and flushing the toilets—a "flush-in"— and came out to drink from the "white" drinking fountains.

I didn't start the CORE chapter in Greensboro, but I was involved in it; it was entirely a local decision. Some of the students wrote the national office and said that they were interested in finding out about CORE. So the national office sent the nearest field secretary, which was me. The reason for the delay between May and the official submission of forms for Greensboro CORE in November was just the idea of paying a membership fee or something. We weren't well organized at fund-raising; most of that came out of New York City and from national and international appeals.

George Simkins was quite active and bolder than most black leaders, and we worked well with him; our relationship initiated with the sit-in movement. But there was some friction with other state NAACP chapters, because they were losing members from their youth chapters to CORE. The young people were interested in becoming involved in direct-action demonstrations. We made some suggestions to the group that later became the Greensboro CORE chapter, such as asking community organizations to urge businesses to desegregate; pressuring the newspaper to end the separate "colored" section of the newspaper; maintaining a dialogue with members the Ministerial Alliance to integrate their churches; and soliciting publicity through the press. If that didn't work, the last thing we considered was picketing. Most efforts failed, but we were effective in getting the tax list desegregated.

I did not consult closely with the officers of the Greensboro CORE, unless they invited me to offer advice. I maintained a neutral position between opposing factions in the group. Tony Stanley and Pat Patterson were quite conservative, but Bill Thomas and Lewis Brandon were more aggressive. Some members of the Executive Committee would call me and discuss who was conservative and didn't want us to move too fast, to take one step at a time and all that. I told them what actions I thought would take a long time and those that seemed possible to do more quickly.

Some of my actions caused a great deal of controversy for the Greensboro chapter. One of the more dramatic episodes of adverse publicity concerned a speech that I made in regard to interracial marriage, in which I said, "We should be able to find our mates in whatever race we choose." I made it at a white Seventh Day Adventist church in Greensboro, and the next day they said they didn't believe in intermarriage and they refused to let CORE use the church. Apparently, the meeting that CORE held there was arranged by Reverend Marion Jones. I was discouraged from even mentioning marriage, because it raised the specter of miscegenation. I said, "Well, you can look at me and see something has been going wrong for three hundred years, because I happen to be brown in color and have black wavy hair." So I used to use that as an example. People would laugh, you know. One of the campaigns that I was involved in that made the papers in Greensboro was when I advocated that maids boycott employers that wouldn't let them use the bathrooms in the house. It was not a very widespread campaign, because it was difficult for a maid to tell you the truth, whether she had a private restroom or not, for fear of being fired. And the courts took the position that a private residence was different from a public business.

Jerome Smith, George Raymond and Isaac Reynolds stayed pretty much in Greensboro; Hunter Morey was with me in High Point. We would take care of volunteers' expenses and local people would help house and feed them. The field secretaries frequently suggested changes in focus or tactics, because they felt that the national office had spread them a little too thin, had taken on too many cities at once, and were moving the task force members around too frequently. We often pulled back and re-evaluated and re-planned, mainly because of personnel and money. And we still wanted to stay in states where we had some liberal support. Among the most important cities in North Carolina in terms of demonstrations were Durham and Greensboro. High Point and Charlotte and

Winston-Salem become more important later on. Because of the sit-in movement, Greensboro remained as a symbol for the Civil Rights Movement. They started something that involved more people across racial lines to fight for the Amercan Dream than any other one incident. Because of the liberal administration of Governor Terry Sanford, North Carolina was looked upon as the most liberal Southern state, before the Civil Rights Act of 1964. The principal CORE individuals in North Carolina were Floyd McKissick, me and Reginald Hawkins down in Charlotte. We were the trinity of the more aggressive of civil rights activists in the state.

There was one memo written by Gordon Carey in October 1962 in which he referred to friction "with certain members of the national staff of another organization." It was the NAACP. We were having some conflict because it was raising money on CORE activities, even on the Freedom Highways project. I made it clear that they may be raising money in the name of CORE or for the freedom struggle, and they were getting the benefit. But we were definitely planning to get them to foot the legal bill, because we did not have a staff of lawyers like they did. And I thought that was pretty good. CORE was chronically financially-strapped. ACORE-generated memo said that there was some antagonism between the youth that wanted to leave the NAACP and join CORE. And Carey went so far as to suggest that maybe they should first form a neutral organization that could later be formed into a CORE chapter. So we had those little conflicts every now and then.

## A. Knighton "Tony" Stanley

In 1962 I came to Greensboro to work at A&T College as Director of the United Southern Christian Fellowship Foundation, which was a campus ministry program, but in 1964 I joined the philosophy faculty of Bennett College. The CORE chapter had been formed before I came to Greensboro. I became acquainted with it through a young lady, Beatrice Terry, whom I eventually married. She was very active in CORE, and frequently asked me to speak about the Civil Rights Movement to groups, especially white groups. I attended CORE meetings, although I was not terribly active in it. But in the fall of 1962 my fiance and several others were arrested. That stirred me into more activity, because I really had a sense of guilt over not being there with them, especially Lois Lucas, one of my students, who was the vice-chairman at one time. I came there under Bill Thomas' presidency. I was somewhat marginal to the whole movement, because CORE had been active prior to my coming to Greensboro. I was more amenable to talking to the white community and negotiating than were some of the other advisers to the chapter. I discovered that I had a knack for strategy in demonstrations. Consequently, I was not only an adviser to CORE, but a personal counselor to the leadership, which made me very close to them.

The Bennett girls, particularly, were quite militant in 1962, far more distrusting of the system and the people who claimed that they could make it work, than in 1960. To them, the proof of one's commitment was in what they accomplished. As a result, they became totally disillusioned with Ed Zane, because he had not done more to further desegregation in 1960. They were pretty convinced that he couldn't deliver what he said. Plus the fact that simply to write a report and to do research was not very helpful. They were supported by more militant Bennett faculty members who were advisers to the chapter: Elizabeth Laizner, John Hatchett, and Reverend James Busch. Though I considered myself a revolutionary in the goals I sought, I would not call myself a militant in terms of actions to be taken.

I don't think that there was a master strategy within the Executive Committee of CORE, because we had learned not to trust going more than a day at a time. Usually what would happen is that there was an Executive Committee meeting which included adult advisers, then they would present it to the whole CORE chapter, and after long debate and some change of details, the chapter usually went along with what the Executive Committee had proposed. I was entrusted with an informal responsibility to listen to the debates and to develop the sense of the Executive Committee. It was almost a summary of the positions that were stated, sometimes after quite long discussion. But I was never formally assigned that task.

## Jibreel Khazan

The sit-ins had quieted down, but there was a handful of activists, at least thirty-five or forty, composed of summer students at A&T and the students from Dudley High, who wanted to keep the Movement going. Bill Thomas' role was important in the Movement, because he was the leader of the group from Dudley High School.

We picketed the Hot Shoppes on a regular basis during the summer of 1962; it was once every day or every other day for about two hours. We would go over to a place, maybe like McDonald's or the Hot Shoppes. We would choose different places as targets. We would take picket signs and have Reverend Marion Jones, Reverend Busch and Mr. Hatchett from Bennett College as regulars who supported us. And local ministers such as Reverend Brown and Reverend Otis Hairston would occasionally join us.

CORE sent representatives to Greensboro and other cities in North Carolina during this time. They did not press us to become members of CORE, but we eventually decided to form a CORE chapter. We needed an experienced national group that could advise us, rather than the old ad hoc SECJ. CORE quickly offered us people from the national office, like Gordon Carey,

Hank Thomas and Jerome Smith. They would come for a couple of weeks. They were like roving representatives of CORE who would come to Greensboro, High Point, Durham, Winston-Salem, and Chapel Hill. Elections were held only in the case of a new officer, or if we lost a person through other activities or duties. It was not like an annual election; this always depended on the situation that arose. For instance, Bill Thomas was regarded the CORE chairman until he chose to step down.

A reason that there were more Bennett students as members than A&T was because Bennett girls had as their model Dr. Player. She was a very independent person in her capacity as president. Bennett College was a private college, and these young women were leaders in their own right before they even joined the Movement. During that time, in 1960 and all through the decade, they were more organized than the students at A&T. They were a small group, but they came from various parts of the country; north and south, rural and urban, and they had been told that they were the elite among the female black students. The only other school like that in the South was Spelman College in Georgia, and the young women at Bennett had a banner to carry. They were involved from the first week of the Movement. In fact, if it had not been for those students at Bennett College, we probably would not have had a movement like we did in 1963, because they were steadfast all of the time.

In the spring of 1962 we had a big meeting in Durham when we demonstrated against the Howard Johnson restaurant. There must have been at least two thousand people that marched down the highway in Durham. There was a big rally of CORE and the combination of the CORE groups and the NAACP, and the Movement groups that were here in North Carolina. I think that the Freedom Highways project workshop was held at Bennett because of the leadership Dr. Player. She was a nationally-known educator and she was respected throughout the nation by other educators, as well as those in the Greensboro business and political leadership. Her attitude was: As long as you obeyed the Administration rules and respected all involved, she had nothing against having a CORE meeting there. However, it was important that you not do anything to bring a negative image upon Bennett campus.

There were workshops in nonviolent tactics: How to protect your body if someone attacked you; shock therapy sessions in which people had to act out various situations, say, for instance, some of us acted as the protagonists and some of us acted as antagonists at a picket line, and then we would change positions. We were also learning how to conduct negotiation sessions; everyone had to learn how to be an effective negotiator by learning techniques of give and take. There were sessions where we sang songs. There were people from different parts of the country, but more important, there were a lot of people there from different North Carolina cities.

Our Executive Committee consisted of: Elizabeth Laizner, James McMillan, James Busch, John Hatchett, Knighton Stanley, Bill Thomas and Betty Wall. In the summer of 1962 you would have had Wendell Scott, Bill Thomas, Dr. Laizner, Reverend Busch, Mr. Hatchett, and Reverend Marion Jones and me. People were asked to serve or volunteer on the Executive Committee, because sometimes those on the Executive Committee were also on other committees. It was related to their having been on the Student Executive Committee for Justice. Mr. Hatchett, James McMillan, Elizabeth Laizner, and Reverend Busch were on Bennett's campus; they represented the people who were advisers to the female students there.

Bill replaced me as chairman of the local CORE chapter. As a young man in junior high school and high school, Bill had a severe blood disease which affected his skin to the point where it was not certain whether he would be able to walk again. He had to have a series of operations and have many skin grafts, but he never let that inhibit him. At that time, Elizabeth Laizner and James McMillan came onto the Executive Committee. Other advisors that I remember were Reverend Marion Jones and Dr. Elizabeth Laizner. She had been criticized by some people in the community as being what they called a "troublemaker." But she was gifted with a very astute political mind and she was very analytical in decision-making and planning strategy. I considered Mr. Hatchett to be a warrior; if he believed in a principle, nothing could move him. He was willing to put his life on the line for his beliefs. He, Dr. Laizner and Reverend Busch were controversial figures in Greensboro because of their activism. I think that Dr. Player received complaints about him from members of the Methodist Church about his participation in these activities.

Lewis Brandon was kind of quiet and soft spoken, with an easy-going manner about him, but he was a tenacious worker. He was about the same age as most of us. Lewis and his brother were part of a group of guys from Asheville who went to A&T. One was Charles Bates; he was a year behind us. Donald Potts was from Washington, D.C. Bill's brother Alvin was in high school and his sister Antoinette, Marion Dansby, Frances Herbin [Lewis] and Ann Saunders [Staples] at Bennett were all very active from 1960 to 1963. Over a period of time we all evolved into an effective group.

The CORE group in 1962 was almost entirely different from the group of people that had been active with us during the spring of 1960. They came more into play during the summer of 1961 and 1962. Mr. Hatchett, Reverend Busch, and Liz Laizner became stronger personalities during that time. We welcomed them, because Joe, David, Frank and I knew that we couldn't continue being in the leadership role. We were never real leaders, we just happened to be people that the group respected enough to allow us to be spokesmen. But every day a new leader could be appointed, or every week, because the rest of us may have been in school or working.

I had resigned the chairmanship to become president of the A&T student body in the fall of 1962, understanding certain legalities about being part of a group outside of the college. I never disassociated myself from CORE, but you have to learn to wear different hats. So while I was president of A&T Student Government, I was not officially a CORE member. But everyone knew within the CORE group that I maintained a connection with the chapter. If I was called upon to support any CORE effort, I would speak to the student body through the Student Government, but at the same time, I knew that if I was an official member of CORE, it might jeopardize the college. I was asked a couple of times by CORE officers to speak to the A&T students to try to get them to support the picketing in the fall of 1962. Sometimes I did, like on a Saturday, after the movie on A&T's campus, or I would allow a representative from the group that was in charge of a particular project to come forward to speak to the student body to ask the students for help. I just made a way open to them to reach the students. Generally, the students at A&T and Bennett campuses respected me, and I respected them. If they didn't like something, they would come and tell me right off the bat; it was that type of a relationship. I don't consider myself to be a leader, but the students at A&T's campus felt that I could be a representative for them, but at any time I knew that I could lose that position or I could be criticized just like everybody else.

I continued to sit in on Executive Committee meetings and general membership meetings when I could, but that year, 1962-63, I was busy on A&T's campus. Sometimes, if the CORE group was planning a particular project and they needed help from A&T's student body in any capacity, Bill would come and talk with me about it, but as time went on, I was only contacted in case the CORE group needed help on a mass level from the student body. Otherwise, Bill Thomas and the Executive Committee that took over in the fall of 1962, planned CORE activities. So they only contacted me when something really big was getting ready to come down.

All of the members of the Executive Committee were activists; it was just a matter of who was more forceful. The group that Dr. Laizner classified herself with were more forceful. Bill was an organizer, but he would stand up to everyone if he didn't agree with them. Lewis could be as hard as Hatchett or Busch if he had to. Pat Patterson, who was quiet, could do the same thing if it was necessary; if he had to take a hard stand, he could to it. If it came down to the issue whether or not to demonstrate at a particular time, and if the group would say, "We are going down and demonstrate at such-and-such a time," Pat would sit back and listen, but if he didn't agree with them, he would say, "I don't agree with this." They may argue about it for hours until they finally resolved it, but everyone had respect for each other. Even though Bill may have been the president, he did not just have his way. Although Liz

Laizner may have been very strong, she could talk all day, but she might not get past the rest of the group.

"Operation Doorknock" was an intermittent, on-going local CORE project, where we went around neighborhoods talking to people about voter registration and asking them to participate in a boycott, or "selective buying campaign." We were asking people not to trade at certain places that served blacks as a means to put pressure on the segregated. It was never our aim to cause economic disruption to the businesses in Greensboro, only the places that we felt that we had a grievance against. The adult members of the black community cooperated with us in this, because they had influence on the business community through their charge accounts. The adults would report back to us the results of their request to local businesses to desegregate. If the response was unfavorable, then we would reinforce the "selective buying" campaigns by picketing in front of a particular establishment.

## Sarah Jones (Outterbridge)

There were nominal dues in the chapter, but if someone couldn't pay them, we didn't turn a person back. A portion was sent to the national office of CORE, and then there was a portion that stayed within the local group. This was basically for gas for transportation, buying material for signs when we picketed, or anything that might come up. Occasionally, there were some special fund-raising activities, such as the James Baldwin lecture tour, that was held at the Hayes-Taylor YMCA

We would also have workshops conducted by several CORE field secretaries on nonviolence and passively protecting yourself if attacked. Reverend Cox and Mr. McKissick would go through these procedures with us. Initially, we went through these processes, and later, during the mass demonstrations, we tried to do it at every mass meeting that we had where the public was invited to join or to come and be a part of it. Usually they would go over these things before we hit the streets.

## Lois Lucas (Williams)

We had a loose-knit group and there was a period of time where no one knew whether or not we were going to set up a chapter of CORE. At the beginning, we were not backed by any national organization, and their involvement came during the summer of 1962. Bill Thomas and Evander Gilmer were very active then, as far as leadership. James Farmer visited Greensboro earlier. There had been contact with them, but I don't remember the actual date when we affiliated themselves with CORE.

Initially there was Pat Patterson, Ezell Blair and the other three guys that participated in the original sit-ins. There was a small group of Bennett young women who constitued the group where the concept of the sit-ins originated, and eventually, faculty members, such as Elizabeth Laizner and Reverend Busch.

I wasn't quite as close to Bill as I had been with the others, having attended school with them and having known Ezell from elementary school, we were a lot closer. Bill was several years behind us, but we got to know him. He was a very sensitive person and a hard worker. I think the most outstanding thing about Bill was that he was a high school student at that time. He showed a great deal of maturity and responsibility. He was aware of the Movement and he wanted to keep it alive and I think that this was good; it showed some leadership ability, and I think he did a very good job.

Evander was a little ahead of Bill. He was more in our age group, and he was more or less involved at the same time that we were, from the very start. He did not quite have Bill's leadership ability; I guess Evander would probably be a good right-hand man. We did not have conflicts with officers as such. I don't think that students even discussed who held what position. I don't think that was important to them. I don't think there would have been any conflicting personalities between the so-called leaders.

I did not paticipate in much activity at that time, because having just graduated from high school in 1959, we were inexperienced in terms of devising strategy. That's one thing about Bill: he was more creative than most of us, as to things we could realistically do to achieve our goals. I did not participate in the picketing of the Hot Shoppes. I just took part in the "Operation Doorknock" voter registration, and distributed literature designed to solicit support from the black community for the boycott, and picketing segregated businesses

I think that the Greensboro Four were considered students that you could rely on during Bill's year as president. When Bill was President of CORE, I think that he felt that whatever the need was, that he could go to them for support, that they would persuade others to support his ideas. It wasn't that the students would automatically follow Ezell, Frank, David, or Joe's endorsement, particularly Ezell's as president of the student body. As far as making decisions as to what strategies would be used by CORE, I would say that David, Ezell, Frank and Joe continued to influence the younger leaders in CORE, because of their reputation and their ability to rationalize certain strategies.

I just really think that they were concerned about the Movement. I don't know whether they gave him their endorsement as such, but generally a lot of their ideas were similar.

We decided to officially form a CORE chapter in the summer of 1962, because it was a moderate, middle-of-the-road type of organization. It was not as passive as some of us felt the NAACP was at that time, but not quite as radical as SNCC. James Farmer came to talk to us several times, and he was a magnetic, charismatic type of person. CORE was a nationally recognized organization that actively recruited on black college campuses. And at that time we were being advised by attorneys hired by CORE, like Floyd McKissick and Clarence Malone. B. Elton Cox was a very dynamic CORE field secretary; all of them were only an hour or less away, if we needed them. At that time we didn't get a lot of support from the NAACP and the older established black adults in this city, not like we did later on.

The question that we discussed most frequently was, how do you make these stores cease their discriminatory practices? Do we continue to picket? That takes a lot of time and people to go around to each one of these establishments and to picket them every day. Or do you initiate a boycott, which is difficult to convince people to maintain? What do you do that's legal and still do something to attack the problem?

## Frances Herbin (Lewis)

I would say that over the next two years, much of the support of the Movement shifted to Bennett College, due to the quiet encouragement from Dr. Willa Player, and the student body there. I don't think that the Movement received all that much support from the A&T administration, although we received support from individuals on the A&T staff. We did not have the active support, but we had the moral support. Faculty members such as Reverend Knighton Stanley would speak to us and endorse what we were doing. This was usually in informal conversation; they rarely used class time to discuss it. Most of the instructors adhered to the policy of using class time to discuss subject course matter, but there were instances of a few members discussing it in class. More time probably should have been spent on it, but being a part of the institution, a teacher was not at liberty to use class time, because this could have been an adverse thing as far as the administration was concerned.

## William Thomas

CORE was formed as a result of the national philosophy of the NAACP not really embracing nonviolent direct action. What I mean by "nonviolent direct-action" is the tactic of physically demonstrating at particular businesses in order to focus attention on the inequities that existed at the time. The NAACP's basic tactic was through the courts, and we felt as a result of the sit-ins that more was needed.

At the time that CORE was started in Greensboro, I was president of the youth chapter of the NAACP. The president of the adult branch, Dr. George Simkins, contacted James Farmer, who was Executive Director of CORE at the time, asking about the possibilities of forming a CORE chapter in Greensboro. Through those efforts a CORE chapter was initiated in 1962. I was elected chairman of CORE at the time, because Wendell Scott, the first chairman, resigned to attend school outside the state. Ezell Blair served as interim chairman, but had to resign when he was elected president of the A&T student government. Reverend A. Knighton Stanley was on the executive board. There were several students from Bennett College. Regina Carpenter was secretary. Dr. Laizner at Bennett College was on the Executive Board, and at one time she held an office. Lewis Brandon was also on the Executive Board and held an office. Robert ["Pat"] Patterson was vice-chairman and on the Executive Committee.

## Evander Gilmer

I was born in Greensboro and graduated from Dudley High School in 1961. I did not participate in the sit-ins in 1960. I did not become involved in demonstrations and picketing until the summer of 1962, when I began attending meetings at Reverend Marion Jones' house and at the YMCA on Market Street. I don't recall any discussion as to whether we should form a CORE or SNCC chapter. CORE became the active group and the first group that I became involved with and knew a little about it in 1962. Bill Thomas was the organizer and catalyst of the group, as far as the students were concerned. He was the person who was the most involved student, to me, of any of the other persons who were negotiating. Ezell's involvement diminished when he became Student Government President at A&T. Most of us were at A&T, but there were some Bennett students also. I didn't associate it with A&T or Bennett; it was more just a Greensboro chapter. The adult advisers were from Bennett College; there were no A&T advisers.

The formation of the Greensboro CORE chapter and election of officers, including mine as treasurer, was informal. We all knew each other; it was kind of an extension of high school friendships; Lois Lucas was the only outsider. We had elections only when someone had to resign due to conflicting pressures. As far as being treasurer, my duties were insignificant; we rarely used money. It seemed that everything that we did was either stuff that we made or that we paid for ourselves. When we became a larger, more organized chapter, we participated in fund-raising events with the national office. I recall James Baldwin coming to A&T as part of a CORE-sponsored tour. There was an album recorded by the A&T choir called "Freedom Songs" and the music was coordinated by the A&T choir director. I think that it was locally produced or at Charlotte.

One of the most active members that joined at that time was Betty Wall, who was elected Secretary. She and I had been through school together, and I always saw her as the one that was willing to go and do something that the rest of us weren't sure that we wanted to do. She wasn't a part of the planning sessions, but she was one of the people that did demonstrate in the second phase of the Greensboro Movement in 1962.

After we became a CORE chapter, we began testing various restaurants and hamburger places in an informal way to see if we would be served. We went to Biff-Burger on Lee Street and other places several times in 1962, but they refused us, and we didn't get much publicity in the newspaper. We would test by someone going to the counter, asking for service and be denied. A lot of times we would have to do that just to find out if anything had changed. Other times we would picket out on the sidewalk. When any picketing was going on, it was simply to bring attention to it being one of the places that was close to where blacks lived, and they could not go. We just talked about them and we went to them. I don't know who actually decided on the selection of targets. In our meetings we became aware that these places were going to be tested. The managers of these places didn't say anything offensive; we were just refused service and ignored. There was always at least one heckler, or a car that would pass and blow its horn and people would holler out of a window. I don't recall any violence or a confrontation or any arrests. I always thought I saw a policeman somewhere, perhaps not on the premises, but close by. One of the other places that we went to, was a McDonald's on High Point Road, and we went to one on Summit Avenue.

In the summer of '62, we joined CORE's Freedom Highways project, but we were frustrated that nothing was going on in Greensboro. As a result, we decided to picket the Hot Shoppes on Summit Avenue. Gordon Carey, Hunter Morey and Isaac Reynolds from CORE's national office advised us as to how to act during demonstrations, but not much on negotiating techniques. People would go with books and the intention was to fill it, and if they didn't serve us, they would lose business. I recall one particular time Ezell [Blair] and I and someone else were about to enter, and they met us at the door. There was a manager and it seemed to be some policemen that were not in uniform who would not let us in. They had sports coats and trousers, but they appeared big and they appeared to me to be police or some people with authority. Maybe they were hired private police or guards They turned us away, told us to get off of the property and marched us back to my car. There were others of us inside and we thought, "Since there are other people in there, why concentrate on not letting us in there?" I was about to drive off, and it was kind of scary. As I was leaving there, my car rolled forward against a concrete abutment. They stopped me and acted as if they were going to charge me for damaging property, but there were no arrests. We left the property, but we subsequently came back on another day.

As news of our activities spread, some Bennett College professors became involved—Elizabeth Laizner, James Busch, John Hatchett, and James McMillan. Dr. Laizner invited us to meet in her apartment. Initially, the adults' role was simply to provide advice; later, they were the few that also marched with the students in 1962-63. They occasionally provided suggestions as to targets and tactics, but I don't recall them being a part of the decision-making process as to where we would go. What I vividly recall is the discussion of numbers, of getting enough people to go, to make sure that we were orderly, that we remained nonviolent, which was a thing that we talked about a lot, and to not spread ourselves too thinly at too many places, and to work at getting somebody to open up a place in Greensboro, to actually integrate so that we would have an example of some place having been opened.

The Hot Shoppes desegregated fairly quickly, and I recall that being able to be served there was one of the most pleasant things that we could do. Up until then, I had never experienced being able to go into a clean place that served hamburgers and French fries and sodas, other than one on East Market Street, across from the [Hayes-Taylor] YMCA. That was the only place that we had to go that was a respectable place in the community, and it was only a small shop. Now we were able to go to a very modern-looking facility and they had a drive in. I recall that we went out there many times after it opened. We could always expect someone to say something unpleasant, but nobody particularly did anything. We had to get our nerve up to actually drive in and park, to learn how to use the speakers and that kind of thing.

As the chapter grew, we began meeting at the Providence Baptist Church in the fall of 1962, discussing the involvement of the ministers, because the ministers were pretty much the catalyst in the black community; if they supported it, maybe their congregations would support it. Reverend Otis Hairston and Cecil Bishop, but it was difficult in the beginning to get involvement by the ministers. It seemed to me that the adults at that time weren't supportive, because they were not sure what we were doing was right. They didn't want to rock the boat, and they may have feared losing jobs. I don't know what the reason was, but there was not support by the adult Greensboro community, other than George Simkins. I think it was more toward late 1963; I don't recall any involvement during the summer of 1962. It was more like CORE and the NAACP were working against each other. There always had been a NAACP, always would be an NAACP, but they weren't the people who were involved at all. They just didn't seem to support what was being done, and a lot of times it looked as if "outside agitators" had come in and gotten the students riled up, and it was students from outside who were causing the trouble in Greensboro. It was not an accurate assessment, because the students who were initially involved were Greensboro people. Lewis Brandon, Pat Patterson, and Lois Lucas were the only ones from the outside. All of us knew each other and had come through the public school together.

I met with Gordon Carey and James Farmer when they came to Greensboro. Gordon Carey was impressive because all the rest of us were black and he wasn't—of course, Dr. Laizner was not black, either—but there were few whites that were involved with the planning. Another impressive thing to us at the time was that here was an organization called the Congress of Racial Equality and it involved blacks and whites, which is what we were striving for. In the beginning, there was no resentment of white participation, or that they would attempt to dominate the organization. I don't ever remember the group being particularly dominated by whites, [although] Gordon Carey had quite a bit of involvement.

Dick Ramsay, of the American Friends Service Committee, was active in 1962-1963, although I don't think he officially represented the AFSC. He was supportive in coming to our meetings and we would occasionally gather at his apartment, but I don't recall him picketing. I don't know if he actually joined CORE, but he was a familiar face and became a person that we all came to know. Any white person who came into the group would have to be known or would not be allowed in, because some members were suspicious that a new person would leak our plans to the press before we wanted them known. But at other times we were receptive to the news media, because we wanted things to be known early enough for everybody to know what was going to happen and participate in picketing or demonstrations.

Dr. Laizner was also a white supporter, and we held meetings at her house. Dr. Laizner was also very active, being an adult and a member of the Bennett faculty seemed to lend support to the organization, and at the time, the students seemed like they wanted and needed some adults involved, and we wanted to have not just blacks demonstrating; if we could have blacks and whites, it would be even better, because it seemed that everybody wanted to show blacks against whites. She was an interesting contradiction to us. She was older, more serious and emotional, but there wasn't anybody else her age or had her level of education that still acted like a student. She was willing to go, she was willing to serve in any way, and she was full of supportive energy. She was someone we could count on. I don't think she was influential in CORE, but she was respected in that she was obviously a supporter and willing to be a part of the group. None of us was used to being around any whites at all, and to be around a few who seemed to want to be a part of the group, wanted to work and share in the responsibility to awaken the community to what we were doing, was encouraging.

John Hatchett and James Busch were activist and aggressive also. They were very effective in channeling our anger and frustration into positive, nonviolent activity. We had a dilemma when A&T and Bennett opened; we had to make sure that the students understood the importance of nonviolent protest. We had rallies beforehand to make sure that they knew that they were not to be violent in anyway, and we dwelt on that, but I am sure that we didn't feel that sometimes it was to be just nonviolent when there were people who would call you every conceivable name, hoping that you would do something. We knew that if we were to do anything, probably would be arrested, and of course, it would not something that we could not get out of; we would definitely have committed a crime had we entered into a fight.

## Pat Patterson

Our goals at that time were, primarily, integration. We hadn't given much thought, at least when I was involved, to jobs or anything like this. I remember that some time after Woolworth and Kress opened up. I said to myself, "We've opened these places up, now we can't even go in and buy a hamburger, because we don't have any jobs." I think that's when the jobs part of the thing began to surface. That was a goal that came later, because I don't remember us discussing it. The thrust of what we were doing was primarily to go into these places and be able to eat. It wasn't until then that we discovered, "Wait a minute, we've got these places open, but we don't have the money in our pocket to afford to eat there.

## Alvin Thomas

I became involved with the CORE chapter right after the sit-ins in 1960. There was a group of people from Dudley, Bennett and A&T from the SECJ, which met between the summer of 1960 and the fall of 1962. I led the group that came from Dudley. In the CORE chapter, it was Bennett students from the beginning; they were stronger in the Movement at that time than A&T. The women had more guts than we give them credit for, and they really took the first move. Dr. Willa B. Player, whom most would consider quite conservative, supported the students, and they joined CORE. They were centered around intellectualizing, although they partipated in direct-action, and how the Movement was spreading and what we must do to prepare ourselves, that type of conversation took place. The fact that we were not just talking about desegregating places of public accommodation; we were dealing with the whole question of equal rights and what it means, especially economically.

I was involved in the two week training workshop sponsored by CORE for the Freedom Highways project held at St. Stephens Church in July 1962. Jerome Smith, from the national office of CORE, was quite a dynamic individual with a lot of substance and, really understood nonviolence. He was a good teacher and trainer, quite committed. The CORE field secretaries were a little older than the college crowd; they were in their early or mid-twenties The workshops they conducted focused on nonviolence and what it meant and how important it was to remain nonviolent. They were conducted by people who came in from the national office. Isaac Reynolds was a very dynamic gentleman, quite outspoken. But his whole approach to nonviolence was a bit conservative. It was necessary to be dealing with that question, because at that time, people were still about violence in certain areas of the country. The training sessions emphasized demonstration behavior; we didn't get instruction in negotiating techniques. We were trying to persuade people to get more people involved at a grassroots level.

We had numerous conferences in Durham. I recall one very large demonstration at the Holiday Inn in Durham, where Jim Farmer and Roy Wilkins came to speak. Five hundred people walked to one of the targets on the highway. It was a very peaceful demonstration. I spent more time in Greensboro than Durham, and when I went to Durham it was for a specific occasion, such as that demonstration or for the workshops that took place there, but because Greensboro had several colleges participating, plus the community people starting to come out, the demonstrations grew on a constant level.

During the four days of the picketing of the Hot Shoppes someone went in to be served and they were turned down. There were some threats of violence at the Hot Shoppes. Things started to get rough. People started to throw eggs. We dispersed shortly after that, because our purpose had been reached, and nothing serious took place in terms of anyone getting hurt. We were not intimidated by the police. We were turned away by private guards hired by the Hot Shoppes management. They would state the policy and say, "You're not welcome in this establishment." There were some attempts made to get past them. But there was no shoving or altercation, because, being nonviolent, once we tried and were refused, we went back outside to picket. Since there was consultation with management going on simultaneously, that was the best thing to do at the time. I participated in negotiations, mostly through their attorney, Armistad Sapp. He stated the two positions and mediated the situation. I think that he was trying to work out some sort of way for them to desegregate, because he knew that they could not win at the time.

Because my brother Bill was chairman of the chapter, Jim Farmer would often stay at our house. He was quite an interesting man, very humorous, and he was relaxed. He read all of the time; he was always abreast of current events. It was a real pleasure to talk to him; never a dull moment. He would discuss strategy and tactics with us, informally. And the field secretaries also stayed at our house; Mama fed them all. Some would leave to go to other cities and states, but others would remain with us.

## John Hatchett

All of us discussed the possibility of doing other things. I think that what may have taken place was that certain priorities were seen at that particular time. I think that everyone involved, to my knowledge, did see the need for doing many other things in that area. I think it was primarily a matter of priorities rather than any basic disagreements or even basic differences in terms of philosophy.

A different kind of leadership was emerging,. I don't think that our not being able to press for a particular direction had anything to do with our not continuing as spokesmen. I think one reason was a need for exposing other people to positions of responsibility and giving them the kinds of experiences that would enable them to function as we had functioned. Because I think that in the case of both Reverend Bush and myself, I think he was going to leave to take a job elsewhere, and I was contemplating going to graduate school. So in order not to create any sort of vacuum that would not be filled, we felt that other people should be given that kind of exposure. There was no sort of precipitous removal from that position. It was a willingness on my part to step down and to get myself ready to do certain other things.

There were bound to have been differences that would emerge, I think primarily because of background and temperment.. As with most of the organizations at that time, we attempted to be as unified as possible in terms of the greater goals that we were attempting to achieve. But as with any organization, differences of opinion would crop up from time to time. But I think that these were resolved within the framework of the organization. It was not a matter of their having to degenerate into personality clashes.

I never came directly in contact with the people who would have comprised that. These were people outside of CORE. They were beginning to see the need to do certain things themselves. Certain of the ministers were becoming more active and they had taken a not too kindly look at what we were doing, because Reverend Busch and I had been termed outsiders. But that leadership was not a part of CORE.

There were other groups that were coming to the forefront by that time. We were talking about 1962. Whether CORE itself, in terms of its own executive committee, had any direct dealings with these particular persons, I'm not sure of. I recall one instance in which Reverend Busch was invited to a meeting called by a group of ministers. Whether it was in connection with his involvement with CORE, or if it was simply because he was a minister and they were trying to bridge some gaps that had been established, I'm not sure. But he did attend such a meeting.

I was part of the formation process [of the chapter] in the sense that we talked about establishing such a group in Greensboro. We felt there was a need for an organizational structure that had some national stature to it, and we, we didn't view our struggle as being an isolated one confined to persons who either were living in Greensboro at that time, or who were native to Greensboro. We viewed our struggle in connection with the larger struggles that were taking place across the country at that time.

[My wife and I] left Greensboro in either July or August of '63. I had to come to New York City to look into housing and other situations here in preparation for graduate school. So I would say that for a good seven or eight months or so, I was not that active. I kept up with what was going on. After the massive demonstrations of the spring and summer of '63, activities sort of slowed down somewhat. So there was not that much going on in terms of direct demonstrations. I think a period of assessment had begun to take place. But most of my energies were involved, as I said before, in preparation for graduate school.

There was nothing mystical or dramatic in terms of the manner in which decisions were made. They were made in an atmosphere of discussion. Although an Executive Committee existed, it was undertood that whatever ideas were discussed within the committee, before any sort of definitive action could be taken, those ideas would have to be taken back to a larger group. And there, more discussion would ensue, and then some final decisions would be reached. During the entire time that I was actively involved in both the Executive Committee and the organization as a whole, I don't recall anyone, or any group, unilaterally making decisions and taking them to the main body and saying, "This is it, and this is what we're going to do." I think that was one of the things that I admired about the committee at that time, that we were not into making precipitous decisions and then saying to the entire group, "Okay, we're the Executive Committee. We've made these decisions, and you're just going to have to follow them." It didn't work that way. There was a great deal of discussion. The larger meetings were quite open, and there were no hidden agendas involved.

I can't recall any out and out rejection [of Executive Committee decisions]. There would always be some people who would not want to do a particular thing. But once there was a majority vote, then a refreshing kind of solidarity emerged. Very few people, to my knowedge, became so disgruntled or disenchanted with what was going on that they actually pulled out completely and refused to participate.

We met where we felt it was convenient for us to meet. I'm sure some of the meetings took place on Bennett's campus. I can recall some meetings taking place in someone's home at some point. Some of the meetings could have taken place either at Bill Thomas's home or a relative of his.

I don't remember anyone outside of the Executive Committee who wielded or exerted a great amount of influence. The Executive Committee was approved by the general body. And there was a great deal of cooperative interaction between the Executive Committee and the general membership. Many of us who served on the Executive Committee served by virtue of the fact that we were part of the original group of persons who had sat-in initially in 1960. I suppose that in the eyes of the membership, we had demonstrated the ability to get things done. And therefore, it was not a matter of having to compete with someone in order to get on the Executive Committee. We were quite willing to work. That's what it took to be a part of that committee—the willingness to work, and to do things, and to be involved, to give one's time freely, and to be committed to the ideals of the organization. These series of things probably led to the consideration for the executive committee.

In the case of Reverend Busch, Lois Lucas and I, we were listened to initially because we were a part of Bennett's campus, and the Bennett girls were influential in our group. We had all participated from the very beginning. And we were very well known. And therefore, there was no basic opposition to our serving on that committee. They [the Executive Committee] met fairly regularly. We felt that in order to keep the momentum of things going, it was imperative to meet as often as possible. I would say roughly maybe once a week.

Our discussions were basically above board. I don't recall any person who stood out for one particular thing over another. There was also a lot of work that went on in that committee in terms of formulating plans for the future. We drew up a series of documents which we had planned to use after the protests had achieved their purpose. We were then going to move in the direction of economic concerns in terms of employment and gaining a better and more equitable life for black people in Greensboro. There may have been minor differences of opinion, but there were no major differences in terms of a future focus. It was a matter of timing and how we could best implement that. We spent a great deal of time doing research, pinpointing places that we felt would be targets that we could deal with.

At times there was somewhat of a disenchantment with how things were reported [in the news media]. But I would say that overall there was a basic kind of rapport between CORE and the press. We would phone in information that we felt needed to be publicized, and generally it was. And the general coverage was good. I think that some instances, as with any newspaper, organization, there were the inevitable distortions of what may have been said or a slanting in terms of interpretations of what may have been going on. But I think that the overall sense of rapport was there, because we were news at that time. And the press was involved in reporting news.

One of the reasons that Bill's [Thomas] name stands out is because he was very active, very effective in terms of what had to be done at that time. And in spite of his views, I think there were many very good, very positive things that he achieved. I worked very closely with him; I did not do so with anyone else. Not out of any ill feelings or anything. The pressures of getting ready for school, starting a family, and my work at the college, which had suffered a little bit, all led to a lessening of my active involvement. My interest was always there, but I don't think I was as actively involved in the months that led up to my leaving to go away to graduate school at Columbia University. The Bennett College administration, particularly Dr. Player, was very positive. If any animosity manifested itself at all, it would have been within the ranks of some of the faculty. I think that even though Bennett was a very small institution in terms of faculty, Reverend Busch and I were surprised that so few of the faculty got involved. In fact, other than Dr. Laizner, no other faculty person or persons were involved directly in the Movement.

There were some changes that took place[ in the Executive Committee]. That was inevitable as other people came in and became involved in what was going on. I think that this called for certain other perspectives, certain kinds of leadership qualities.

## James McMillan

My activities with CORE began just before the major picketing in the summer of 1962. I met with the students in St. Stephen's Church about the picketing of the Hot Shoppes on Summit Avenue. There was usually a meeting with the students and with those of us with any liaison responsibilities, to ascertain the practicality of making a concerted attempt to desegregate a particular institution. Once that meeting took place, there were usually pros and cons that were raised in terms of the number of people available, whether it would be worthwhile to affect the policies of that particular service, whether it would be more effective on a broader basis. It was that kind of general discussion that preceded any of those activities. We discussed the logistics involved: the cars that would be available, whether it would be students' cars or other cars to drive the students to that particular locale, the kinds of posters that had to be made. I worked directly with the students who made the posters, because it obviously was most directly related to my own area [art instruction]. That was the general approach to most of the activities that took place.

As things became more critical, where there were more students at Bennett who were directly involved, my role became much more immediate in the sense that keeping in touch with students who had been arrested was much more important in order for the college to function properly in the situation. I would say that this was much more a developed role that I helped to create more than anything else. But I knew I had to play a role, because of my particular concern to help change those conditions that all who were black at that time had to endure. And I saw this as the most practical way that I could operate in that frame of reference. I knew, too, that the president of Bennett, Dr. Player, was at least sympathetic to what we were doing, [but she] had to maintain her position as a non-committed person in those particular activities; she had to maintain her role as president. I think that she did that very well, but to function as president and for the students to function as individuals, we all saw there was a definite need for an intermediary role, and I agreed to accept that role.

The meetings centered upon the kinds of establishments that would be most vulnerable to the kinds of activities that we could assert. We listened to the kinds of things that had gone on prior to some of the CORE field secretaries coming to Greensboro. Based on the information that we could gather and the kinds of situations we knew in Greensboro we tended to make those decisions based on that awareness; it was primarily the local CORE group that made those decisions. Because of the small numbers within CORE, we focused on picketing, but we always hoped that we could conduct the same kind of marches led by Dr. [Martin L.] King, because we recognized that they had been very effective in producing many of the ends that we were seeking. It remained a possibility in our minds, because the national publicity of Greensboro as the site of the sit-ins [in the spring of 1960] had strong publicity potential.

The adult black community was, to a large degree, in a position of onlooking at that stage. As a matter of fact, there were some who were a little skeptical about it [picketing]. I gained a glimpse of that through some of my colleagues at the college and high school level, and at my church, the Presbyterian church. There was the same kind of schism in the church that existed in the black community. Reverend Julian Douglas, was a fervent civil rights leader, but there was a reluctance on the part of many adult blacks. It was not so much a disagreement in principle with what the civil rights actions were striking at. Many of them took this reluctant attitude because, first, they had carved out a little bit in the Greensboro situation that was better than nothing, and there was a feeling that whatever we did now might jeopardize any gains, economic and otherwise. Those who had jobs knew that their jobs depended on a sympathetic [white] community, and to maintain that bit of effectiveness that they had, I think they felt that this was just going to rock the boat too much. I think, though, as time went on they saw that this was the best way that any kind of action could take place, because the students did not have that kind of an investment, that kind of economic status, and, therefore, were not vulnerable to the kind of reprisals that could have occurred, and in some instances did take place, where there was too much overt adult participation. I heard of people who voiced a sympathy for the students, who were working class people, who were either spoken to in a very violent way or who may have had to change jobs because of their expressed sympathies.

## A. Knighton Stanley

Once the Hot Shoppes desegregated, carloads of blacks would park outside to order food at the speakers under a shelter. Occasionally, there would be some harassment from whites at the drive-in shelter. When blacks would pull in, a line of cars with whites would circle the drive-in shelter, and continue to circle, which meant that the black patrons could not get out after they had finished eating, until the whites decided to leave.

## Evander Gilmer

CORE sent Isaac Reynolds, Hunter Morey, and George Raymond to Greensboro to advise us about picketing the Hot Shoppes as a part of the Freedom Highways project. I was never arrested at the Hot Shoppes. I never tried to enter it; I was a part of the group that picketed outside. The hecklers would pass by us on Summit Avenue or park under the roof where the food was served outdoors, but I don'trecall any physical harassment. The whole time I participated in the Movement in Greensboro I had the feeling that the policemen wanted to keep as much peace as possible. [For] all of the encounters that we had during the sit-ins and picketing the restaurants, the policemen tried as hard as possible to keep the peace. Therefore, there was never the fear of the police that there was in the Deep South. They didn't have the dogs; they didn't pull their guns out; and I don't remember any students who were billy-clubbed.

I wasn't involved in the demonstrations and picketing until the summer of 1962. We met at Reverend Marion Jones' house and the Hayes-Taylor Y on Market Street. Most of us were classmates from Dudley High School and were Greensboro residents. The meetings at Reverend Jones' house were not part of any formal civil rights organization; it was just meeting and talking about what we could do to change the racial situation in Greensboro. The main student participants were Wendell Scott [Marion Jones' nephew], his daughter Betty, and Bill Thomas. The only adult that I recall was Tony Stanley; I thought of him more like us, but older. Even in our CORE meetings, there weren't droves of people, perhaps thirty; it tended to be the same people. Reverend B. Elton Cox came over from High Point, and convinced us to form a CORE chapter. There wasn't a group in Greensboro that was doing anything at all, and once the students from A&T had gone home, there wasn't really anyone to carry on. Ezell was one of the few students still in Greensboro. There was no involvement by the NAACP. In fact, it worried us that they didn't seem interested in doing anything at that time.

In the summer of 1962, we were frustrated that in other places in the South, black students were actively protesting segregation, and nothing was going on in Greensboro. So we joined CORE's Freedom Highways project in the summer of 1962. We attended training sessions at Bennett College and picketed the Howard Johnson's restaurant on the highway outside Durham. During that time we also decided to picket the Hot Shoppes on Summit Avenue. This time we received publicity in the news media when CORE's national office sent field secretaries to us. I remember Gordon Carey, Hunter Morey and Isaac Reynolds. Their role was primarily to conduct the workshops and to advise us as to what places might be most productive to concentrate our efforts and how to act during demonstrations, but not much on negotiating techniques.

I don't recall any discussion as to whether we should form a CORE or SNCC chapter. CORE became the active group and the first group that I became involved with and knew about in 1962. Bill Thomas was the organizer and catalyst of the group as far as the students were concerned. Ezell's involvement diminished when he became Student Government president. Although there were A&T and Bennett students, I saw it as more of a "Greensboro" chapter than that of a particular college campus. The adult advisers were from Bennett College; there were no A&T advisors.

I recall James Baldwin coming to A&T, but I was not aware that it was part of a CORE-sponsored tour. There was an album recorded by the A&T choir called "Freedom Songs." I think that it was locally produced or at Charlotte.

But we knew that sometimes it was hard to maintain self-discipline when there were people who would call you every conceivable name, hoping that you could be provoked into violence. We knew that if we reacted physically or verbally, we definitely would have been arrested.

Most of the adult members of the black community were hesitant to actively support what we were doing. On one hand, they were sympathetic to our demands for service at the segregated businesses. But I had the feeling that most of the black adults of Greensboro during that time still felt that we were wrong. The students were very active, doing things necessary to keep the Movement going: calling people in, testing local businesses to see if they would desegregate, and forming picket lines when you would go downtown and into places that you were not supposed to go in. I felt that something needed to be done, but for a long time I was skeptical about going to jail. It sounded so bad to go to jail. But as the testing, the picketing and the boycott seemed to not be producing more than token results, we were becoming increasingly frustrated.

## Lewis Brandon

In the summer of 1962 we participated in demonstrations against Howard Johnson between Durham and Chapel Hill on Highway 15-501, as part of CORE's Freedom Highways project. At that time we decided to form a CORE chapter, and B. Elton Cox came over from High Point as a field secretary to help organize us. Although we focused on the situation as it existed in Greensboro, we did not consider ourselves autonomous from the national office of CORE in New York. No organization is completely autonomous, because you really have to adhere to the guidelines of the parent organization. And a lot of the decisions that you make are made within the framework and guidelines of the organization. We had been meeting at the home of Marion Jones, who was a United Church of Christ minister. His nephew Wendell Scott served as the first chairman; Evander Gilmer became Treasurer; I was Vice-Chairman; and Betty Wall, who was the daughter of Marion Jones, was the Secretary. After Wendell left Greensboro that summer, Bill Thomas was elected Chairman. Those were the initial officers; we had just two elections, and all of us were re-elected through 1963.

During the time that we picketed the Hot Shoppes in Greensboro, we challenged Armistad Sapp, who was the legal representative of the Hot Shoppes, to a debate held in the library on the A&T, because he had made some statement about the mental level of black students or something like that. Bill Thomas, Jesse Jackson, Rodney Davis, Carl Stanford and I participated. Don Addison, a professor of sociology, prepared us. A lot of people said that Sapp didn't really believe all that he said, that he was sort of a devil's advocate. I'm not sure whether or not that was true, or what his motives were. If you read his public statements, he really pushed the line of his clients. One would just have to assume that he really believed a lot of what he said.

# Chapter 4

## Direct Action Begins

*The dual success of the Freedom Highways project and the picketing of the Hot Shoppes inspired the Greensboro group to form itself into a CORE chapter in the summer of 1962, which was recognized by the national office that fall. But the chapter seemed undecided about its next action; no other easy victories appeared likely. As the Executive Committee debated courses of action, the chapter co-operated with the NAACP in voter registration and selective buying drives during the early fall of 1962. Small groups of CORE members would test individual restaurants, theaters and cafeterias and picket when they were not served, but these generated little media or public attention.*

*Impatient with the failure of the adult African American community to achieve results through traditional behind-the-scenes negotiations, the CORE chapter chose a more dramatic action. Thanksgiving Day was an ideal business opportunity for the S&W Cafeteria. As the holiday approached, a demonstration there had the advantage of focusing their efforts on a single target, applying pressure on a financially lucrative holiday, and attracting media attention. The pressure was also on CORE to appear viable to potential student recruits, if the Movement were to survive*

### Leonard Guyes

The mayor's committee met from December 1962 until March of 1963 with representatives of CORE, the NAACP and the Greensboro Citizens Association. I would say that it was an ad hoc group, but it probably did emanate from the Merchants Association. Many of us were members of the Board. So, I guess you could say because of the fact that we were a close-knit group. We did have some organizational structure, because of the Merchants Association, we were able to have a more solidified group of business people. I think that the Merchants Association was very fearful of taking any political action that might not meet with the overall approval of its members. We never polled the membership, but the Board of Directors did not feel that it could speak for the total membership, so, as a result, a lot of us who were involved in the Merchants Association also were involved in trying to see what we could do to better help our community in race relations.

## Floyd McKissick

CORE's strategy was to try to suggest demonstration techniques to the Greensboro chapter that had proven successful in the past, and to allocate limited funds for possible legal costs. I had frequent meetings with Gordon Carey and James Farmer from New York, and B. Elton Cox in High Point. Carey and Farmer would come down periodically, but as to what was happening in North Carolina, most of the time, B. Elton Cox and I were a one-two team. We always functioned together. Negotiations were left up to the local chapters.

## Marion Jones

We communicated quite a bit with the national CORE office in New York to get feedback from the national office as to the advisability and the expediency of any action, but it left our day-to-day activities to Reverend Cox. They were favorable, for the most part, but we were always advised to search out a thing very carefully first. The national office very seldom tried to directly influence our decisions. CORE field secretaries Isaac Reynolds, Jerome Smith, Moon Eng, and George Raymond came down from time to time from the national headquarters. They would share with us their experiences as a means for us to make the right approaches in Greensboro.

We often took their advice, but we did not do so automatically; we sought to adapt their suggestions to what we believed would work in the Greensboro situation. We took the psychological approach, the philosophical approach, and the approach extending from our past experience. All of the field secretaries were very effective and influential. They would often stay with me. James Farmer was down several times, and used to spend the night with me on occasion. We did not discuss anything in detail, just summarized what had transpired in the course of the South in general. We would always wait until we met with the officers of the local chapter before we discussed anything pertaining to Greensboro.

We met with white or interracial groups: the Greensboro Community Fellowship, the Greensboro Ministerial Fellowship, and the YWCA. They were all sympathetic and encouraging; some of them endorsed us, while others were very quiet about it. The black groups were more vocal and participated more openly. We had less communication with white ministers in the area, but they did not ignore the race question. Dr. John Redhead, Pastor of the First Presbyterian Church at the time, spoke of brotherhood, fellowship and integration. I don't know if any of them took steps to integrate their churches, but I don't recall any protest to black attendance, there was no problem in Greensboro then. Dr.[Charles]Bowles of West Market Street Methodist Church wrote an open letter to the press, urging the S&W and the Mayfair Cafeterias to desegregate, and Amistad Sapp held a press conference and accused him of hypocrisy. That was about the only instance of any resistance to the support of the ministers in Greensboro.

My advice was the same things that we stressed time and time again. There was always the spiritual side that we would never want them to forget. After all, much of our work was being done out of the churches, and we would do nothing that would infringe on the good name of the church and the good name of Christ. This is how we felt, and for the most part, this was the kind of advice that was sought. Behavior patterns were stressed. No beer drinking, cigarette smoking or any negative public behavior that would cause the slightest blight on anything that we were attempting to do. In other words, we stressed decency, so that the proprietors would appreciate and respect this. Prior to that time, some whites had always felt that blacks were just dirty, so we had to stress cleanliness; they were always well dressed.

## Robert "Pat" Patterson

After Kress and Woolworth desegregated their lunch counters, we expanded our picketing to other places of public accommodation, particularly the Carolina and the Center theaters. One night we went to the movie houses, and we were arrested because we were considered a fire hazard, or something having to do with the fire codes. One time that we picketed the Carolina Theater, I remember there was some heckling going on from what looked to be high school kids. It was the first time that I felt any uneven-handedness by the police department. We were told that we could not sing because they were afraid that we were going to incite a riot, but at the same time these hecklers were coming by saying, "Two, four, six, eight, we don't want to integrate." I specifically remember going to one of the policemen and saying, "Wait a miute; we can't sing, but you're letting them sing." He gave me a very short remark and I went on back about my business, because I saw right then that I wasn't going to get any kind of positive action from him. I thought it was more important to try to achieve our larger goals, instead of trying to argue who was being favored.

I went back in a silent way, because we weren't interested in causing any riots that would get people hurt; we had resolved to be totally nonviolent. I thought that the group was more important in that situation. We had agreed that it was going to be a silent march, but I thought that it was a little bit unfair that they would allow them to do all of that singing if we were going to incite a riot by singing.

# John Hatchett

The scurrilous detective work of Mr. Sapp revealed that a woman on the Bennett College faculty [Alice Jerome], had connections with the Communist party. Whether those connections were as intimate as he sugested, I don't know. The entire country has always had a very hysterical and paranoid point of view about communism. I think Mr. Sapp understood this quite well, and so he used this as a potential means for destroying the entire movement. That was really his aim. It was not to remove Mrs. Jerome from her position at Bennett College or to prevent her from participating in the Movement, which he was able to do. His aim was to destroy the Movement by suggesting that we were very actively controlled by the Communists. He never said "Communist party"; he said "the Communists."

Because of that kind of attention, Lois Lucas and I had to go on the local television news broadcast and say to the city of Greensboro and to whatever media would have been involved, that historically, black social protest movements have not resorted to affiliation with any agent or agencies of powers outside the country. I recall that Mrs. Jerome's husband, who apparently was a very high official in the New York chapter of the Communist party, had come down to Greensboro to visit her and to do some lecturing. Somehow, Mr. Sapp was able to find this information out. At that time, he had no information on Mrs. Jerome herself, but because of Mr. Jerome's prominence in the party, he was able to make the connection. Once making this connection, he was able to use it as a very effective leverage. He put us in a bad position, in terms of forcing us to compromise, and in some sense, apologize, when neither was needed. But we did it at that time, ostensibly to preserve the Movement and to let people know that we did not need "outsiders" guiding us.

But because of the scare tactics employed, the Bennett College administration was put on the spot. They had to call a special meeting of the Board of Trustees, which said that her presence at the college would not be in its best interests, that this kind of publicity would adversely affect the college. And that because of that, and since she did not have tenure, she would have to be dismissed. I was friends with Mrs. Jerome, and the saddest role that I had to play at that time, was when I had to say to a meeting at the Providence Baptist Church, that because of the pressures that were being brought against us by forces over which we had no control, we could no longer allow Mrs. Jerome to be actively involved in the demonstrations. She was keenly disappointed, but to her credit, she understood and agreed basically with what we were attempting to do. She understood the mass hysteria that can be generated when someone shouts "communism" in the United States. So as gracefully as possible, she removed herself from an active involvement in the Movement.

That was his [Sapp's] swan song in terms of that. It was somewhat sporadic, because, after that particular incident, I don't recall ever having any more encounters with him after that. I think that what Mr. Sapp was after was publicity and an attempt to get himself well known. He succeeded in part in that. I think that this governed his decision to meet with us as much as possible.

## A. Knighton Stanley

The more radical element within CORE, the element that had advocated more direct-action [John Hatchett and James Busch] months before, disappeared from the Movement and from leadership roles once it started, and were replaced by those who wanted to escalate demonstrations, but at no time was I aware of anyone who called for violence. Some within CORE did not trust negotiations and wanted demonstrations to begin in the fall of 1962. They were pressing for picketing, and we had not developed at that point the techniques of mass demonstrations, which turned out to be the most successful thing that we did. But they wanted persistent picketing, and attempted entry to places that were segregated, like the S&W and Mayfair Cafeterias and the theaters.

We wanted to be very careful in selecting strategies, because it becomes difficult to maintain picket lines without success; you can picket the S&W to death and people just become very accustomed to it. Plus, you demoralize picketers if you don't change targets from time to time. Although we occasionally picketed the theaters and the Mayfair, the S&W remained our primary target.

We also had to be very careful in our statements to the press. One of the basic tenants of CORE was that spokespersons were appointed and no one was to speak unless they were so authorized. Bill Thomas and I did the speaking on behalf of CORE. The USIA [United States Information Agency] sent a film crew throughout the South to film civil rights demonstrations, and they filmed the one at the S&W on Thanksgiving Day. That was fortunate for us, but neither the national office nor the Greensboro CORE arranged it.

## John Hatchett

There was a hierarchy within the chapter, and I didn't consider myself to have been a part of that leadership hierarchy. I was involved, but not an integral part of it. My active participation stopped some time early in 1963. Lois Lucas and myself, because we knew how to write effective press releases and memos regarding what we wanted to do and where we were going, were designated as spokespersons. Any news release and any other information pertaining to CORE had to pass through us. But ultimately, it had to be approved by the leadership hierarchy. This situation, for a period of time, was very amicable. There were no major problems. But I think at some point, the role played by Miss Lucas and myself came to be resented by some of the persons involved. They became perturbed that we were assuming too much power. But leadership was the farthest thing from our minds, and I apprised them of that fact. They wanted to eclipse that kind of power, and I think that happened.

No one was opposed to direct action demonstrations. I think that you must keep in mind that the mood of the Sixties was for black people a very optimistic one. And at that time we were not that politically sophisticated. We were content to do certain things that would open up certain doors for us. The political sophistication didn't set in until we realized that we had to go beyond the mere opening of lunch counters, movies, bowling alleys, et cetera. It came late, and it came at a time when the voices of those who could best articulate that position were virtually silent.

Later, we addressed more economic goals. Miss Lucas, Reverend Busch and I were attempting to push those goals, but I don't think we pushed it too hard. If anything, we didn't push hard enough. The leadership was very ambivalent about this issue. I think that's one of the reasons why, to a large extent, they failed in this area. This is not by any means to take credit away from anyone. But I think that the record stands for itself. The gain in employment opportunities in Greensboro for black people came about much later; it did not come about as a direct result of CORE's involvement. We talked about it. We drew up plans and proposals, but it did not get beyond that talking stage. I think one of the reasons is because of this ambivalence. The feeling was that, CORE was not this kind of organization. When I speak of leadership, I'm not talking just about local leadership. I was very disgusted with the national leadership and how it was able, at the height of the massive demonstrations that led to the massive arrests, to cool people off and take away the fervor and the actual focus of those particular demonstrations. The upshot of that was that a lot of people were arrested, then very little happened. And then the national leadership, withdrew and left the local leadership to cope with all of this. CORE didn't really provide the comprehensive leadership to translate the immediate gains from the demonstrations into realizable economic and broad social accomplishments.

Local autonomy was not pushed. And I think that is part of what may have transpired here. At that time all of us—students, Reverend Busch, myself—were relatively young, and we had certain ideals and certain beliefs. It was not due to a lack of trying, but I think that one of the things that happens to you when you're young and caught up in having to deal directly with very powerful economic power structures in this country, then you have to realize what may be going on. At that time, we were naive enough that we could not convey our sense of alarm to those who were in "positions of leadership" at that time within CORE.

What I'm trying to suggest here is that if you're not used to certain things, then your head can be turned. I'm not talking about myself, Reverend Busch or Lois Lucas. But when you dangle certain carrots before the eyes of the people, and they've never had a carrot before, they may want to take a bite. And I think once you've bitten the carrot, your appetite increases, and you lose sight of the time when you may have been hungry and anxious to do certain things because they were right, not because they were convenient or expedient.

The quality of advice made available at that point was very poor. There is no comparison between that kind of advising and the advice that they got from Reverend Busch, Lois Lucas and myself. The positions that they assumed came about at the time because our positions had been reduced to a state of nothingness. In other words, we weren't directly drummed out of CORE. What happened [is], the position of spokesperson was temporarily suspended and placed in the hands, I believe, of the head of the local CORE chapter. And we were told that our function would be to assist and no longer to directly speak for CORE. Reverend Busch was not a spokesperson, but a very active participant. And he saw what was happening.

We became rather disgusted and felt that our effectiveness was so severely hampered that it would not be even in our best interests to continue in a very active role. So our roles faded into the background, it was then that Elizabeth Laizner and Tony Stanley came to the forefront. And the quality of advisement that they offered was that they sided with the leadership. And they tried to suggest that some of the rather far-reaching programs that we had talked about previously were not important.

I thought that if they were going to continue to demonstrate in order to make certain gains that were primarily in the social field, that they should at least attempt, along with those demonstrations, to negotiate with the economic power structure in the city to try and determine if jobs could be made available to black people in the certain areas that previously had been closed to them. This was tentatively agreed to. But it was tabled in the sense that the insistence was that it needed more study, it needed more discussion, that people—students especially—were not in a mood to do anything except to demonstrate. And that to talk about issues, which they agreed were vital but not very sensational, would be to also downplay the momentum of the Movement. I also disagreed with this. But it was to no avail.

I would have to put Tony Stanley in the camp that advocated more immediate, sensational things, because I would not include myself, but I would say that his treatment of Miss Lucas and Reverend Busch was not the kindest. I think that, to a large extent, he abused his position at Bennett College in terms of how he treated both persons. I'm not talking about anything that was verbally negative. It was just the attitude that, "You two have played your part. Now it's time to move over and let those of us who have other ideas come in and play our part." That's the kind of attitude that emerged. They exhibited much too much immaturity in terms of what was being dealt with, and that by that exhibition, they played into the hands of the power structure. And the events that we have had reference to took place as a result of that.

I don't recall who were displaced. Some people may have just dropped out because of what they observed taking place at that particular time. People drop out of movements for various reasons. Some get tired. Some become disenchanted with what may be going on at that time. Reverend Busch, Lois Lucas and I were not heavily disenchanted. I think our disenchantment—if I could use that word—was due to a very conservative posture put forth by certain people in the city of Greensboro. Many of the ministers, for example, just would not support us on anything that we did. I would have to say that they were either imitating the wishes of the white power structure, or they were simply not willing to live in a period of time that was in ceaseless ferment and change, because they kept using terms that I would have expected the white power structure in Greensboro to use against us.

They called us outsiders, although that could not have been the case with Lois Lucas. They called Reverend Busch and me outsiders. And although I really can't name these particular persons, because I don't know who they are, they kept insisting that we did not have the best interests of the city at heart, that we were essentially troublemakers, and that we would never be able to establish a firm foothold in the black power structure of Greensboro. We had some disenchantment with the direction in which the leadership was going, but not as greatly. I was disappointed with CORE in terms of the local chapter and the national office being unwilling or hesitant about focusing on issues that we felt were very important. And I think the national office did have a very heavy degree of influence over the local office that was not easily broken, if it was broken at all.

I would have to say that Bill Thomas was put in the middle. It was a situation akin to having to choose the lesser of two evils. Because I believe that the national leadership, far more than local leadership, wanted Reverend Busch and myself displaced. I have no concrete proof of this, but there were conversations in which this was intimated, because, among other things, we were quite critical of the national leadership of CORE. We did not make any secret about it. And I'm sure that got back to them, and I'm sure they didn't like it. So I think that they put pressure on Mr. Thomas.

## Elizabeth Laizner

We discussed continuing to do the occasional picketing of the cafeterias and the theaters at night, as we had been doing that fall. But the suggestion was made to do a dramatic daytime picketing of the S&W during the lunch hour on Thanksgiving Day. Some doubted we'd have much of a response, because students would want to spend that day with their families; others thought we'd get the publicity we had not had when we picketed earlier in the fall.

We debated it back and forth for quite some time. Our meetings were very democratic. When the Executive Committee had come up with something, sometimes with two possibilities, we'd put it before the membership, which was about eighty or one hundred members, and they would vote on it, and we would do what the membership decided. The others would then go with us, and if they didn't want to, then that was too bad, let them not. The membership overwhelmingly chose to go to the S&W on Thanksgiving Day.

## Sarah Jones (Outterbridge)

All of my activity was done after school hours. Basically, when the demonstrations were infrequent, only the CORE officers would meet. We would go over tactics or the procedures for nonviolence. We always tried to keep the people informed, even if nothing was going on in our city, if something was going on in a neighboring city we thought they would like to be enlightened about it in our group, and we'd discuss that, or some group in High Point was doing something and they'd want us to come over there; something like that.

I remember Floyd McKissick, Isaac Reynolds, George Raymond, Hunter Morey, Moon Eng. They would suggest how we should act during a demonstration, but they were not aggressive. I remember eating dinner with Mr. Farmer at our home. We talked about what was going on nationwide, Martin Luther King; he would ask us about what we were doing in Greensboro, and give Daddy [Reverend Marion Jones] some pointers to take back to the group of things to try or places to go, but it was basically just everything that was going on at the time. He was a hero figure to me; he was very warm, down-to-earth, fatherly-type person. A very easy person to get to know, very easy to talk to, even though he was one of the big guys; he was a real regular person.

## Lewis Brandon

We were planning demonstrations and there was this ad in the newspaper, "Come to the S&W for Thanksgiving dinner and bring your family." So we decided that we would go. We went there, got into the line and were arrested shortly after that for trespassing. Reverend William Brown led a prayer service outside, but that was something separate, on his own. It had nothing to do with CORE. During 1960-1961 there were small meetings between the people in the organization, but from 1962 on, it was planned activity relative to attacking the problem of desegregation. By the time we got to November, the thing was to increase and to apply more pressure on the city and the establishment owners by picketing. Another thing was to cover as much territory was we could with the forces that we had.

## A. Knighton Stanley

The picketing of the S&W Cafeteria was part of a long-term campaign because we felt that the S&W symbolized public accommodations. It was a start, and at that point in time CORE had only 100 very active participants, so we focused attention on the S&W as the target, because we thought that it was the key to opening up public accommodations in Greensboro. It was more easily accessible in terms of its having a long store front, and it was also an interstate chain, which would make it susceptible to negative publicity and significant as a court case. The tone of Greensboro students was more militant in the fall of 1962 than 1960. They were impatient with the lack of significant progress in the integration of public facilities, except of the lunch counters at the five-and-ten cent stores.

## Marion Jones

The strategy planned in the picketing of the S&W in the fall of 1962 was just making an attempt to enter, not to force their way in. Violence was ruled out. If the management prevented us from entering, we did not force our way in, unlike the F. W. Woolworth store, where they just went in and sat down. When someone is standing in the doorway, you don't try to force your way into a man's establishment.

[*Note: Contrary to this tactic, some students entered, sat down and were arrested.*]

## B. Elton Cox

When Greensboro CORE picketed the S&W in November, one of our field secretaries, a young Chinese boy, Moon Eng, was singled out for arrest. He was taking the names of people, and they got him for aiding and abetting. A lot of time we needed witnesses, and it was nice if that person was a Caucasian or of another race to take pictures. But most of the time just to be there, and to be able to retell the story. The main thing you need is someone to stand there to watch and observe and then report in our next training session: how we acted and whether we were nonviolent or what we should have done here, or who to watch there. The task force went around to various cities to help train and to help plan strategy. Sometimes they brought directives from the national office to tell us who in the restaurant national chain offices needed to be contacted to apply a little pressure, or if there had been a change in policy.

I was in several demonstrations in Greensboro, particularly picketing restaurants and talking to people about integrating businesses and industries. I was consulted regarding the picketing of the S&W and Mayfair cafeterias. If I was confronted with a question or a tactic, I would give them the Christian nonviolent approach to the situation. My input into defining CORE goals in regard to the broader goals of the black community was just in general terms.

## Jibreel Khazan

The picketing of the S&W and Mayfair cafeterias and the theaters began in October 1962. There had been something going on all of the time from 1960 on, even though it was only a few of us at times; we made sure that the spirit of the Movement was not lost. There was a group, not exactly CORE members, but always a group of people either on A&T or Bennett campus, or Dudley High School— who were out there weekly after 1960. We didn't take on too much at one time, depending on the number of people that we could count on to participate. We would select the restaurants one time, and then we selected the Center and Carolina theaters later. The theaters were always on our list for 1960, but we couldn't get to them all of the time, so during the fall of 1962 we focused on the S&W Cafeteria.

## Sarah Jones (Outterbridge)

Several CORE members were stopped as we entered the serving line. We were told that they would not be served and to leave. When we didn't leave, the police came and they were arrested and escorted out of the cafeteria. They took us downtown and put us in a big room. Then they fingerprinted us, took a "mug shot," and within so many hours they let us go.

## Lois Lucas (Williams)

One of the most dramatic incidents was in the fall of 1962, when we sought entrance to the S&W Cafeteria, because I spent Thanksgiving Day in jail. It had been two years since the sit-ins. We had thought that the desegregation of the lunch counters would enable us to take advantage of the little gains that we had won, and that other things would open up. But the only places that had opened up were the Holiday Inn and the Hot Shoppes. There were still recalcitrant restaurant and store owners and motel and hotel owners, who were saying, "A few of them gave in, but we're still not going to integrate." We had a number of students on Bennett's and A&T's campus, whose fathers had fought in the war, and we felt that our fathers had risked or sacrificed their lives for this country, and certainly on Thanksgiving Day we had a right to be able to go into any restaurant in this city that we wanted to and be served. Therefore, we were trying to find something that was dramatic yet practical enough to get people to start acting as they should.

There was a Bennett student who spoke fluent French, and she put on an African headband. Since she was speaking French, the S&W management thought that she was an African exchange student and they let her in, but not us. Then she told them who she was and asked, if she could go in, why couldn't the rest of us go in? Once they realized who she was, she was asked to leave. While they were talking to her, some people managed to slip in one way or another, and asked to be served, but the police were summoned to arrest them. There was a pray-in conducted by Reverend [William] Brown at the head of the line outside.

We all were arrested and then the day after that, there was another arrest; we had three or four hundred people in jail, and CORE arranged for our release. I think that probably more than anything committed us to function as a CORE chapter, because it was a national organization that had money and lawyers to get us out of jail, and to provide whatever we needed. We had a line of communication in case we were arrested. But when we went down there, we really thought that, by being Thanksgiving Day and there being so many of us, that the S&W would be so glad to get the money, that they would let us eat, but it didn't turn out that way.

*Although the S&W was to be the focus of the CORE demonstration, a number of Bennett students spontaneously went to the Carolina Theater as well.*

## Lois Lucas (Williams)

While this was going on, the Bennett students and some A&T students marched on their own. A lot of things we did emanated from Bennett's campus, because we were in a better position to do it. We marched down Market Street, which meant that we had to go past certain portions of A&T's campus, where we picked up the lettermen as flankers.

We were trying to get in the S&W, and when we were refused entry, we had a prayer service on the sidewalk. The emphasis on nonviolence and a religious tone was not just a tactic; it was a heartfelt commitment. As a matter of fact, even when the crowd was very large, there was a plea on each day of the march: any fingernail files that one may have were to be left behind. Anything as small as that.

The Carolina movie theater was not far away, so we went by the jail and had a prayer service there, and then on to the Carolina. About two hundred of us were arrested at the Carolina Theater. We were told that we could not go in the main entrance. We refused to leave, and a number of us were arrested. The police officers were mostly young and, by and large, they weren't violent or verbally abusive. They had a job to do and a lot of them seemed embarrassed, because I think that they realized that times had to change and that they had to change with them. The only thing that I thought was insensitive was that the city used some black policemen, and that put those officers in a very uncomfortable position. I was arrested there. We were taken to the city jail in vans to be booked, fingerprinted, but the jail was overcrowded and they took the overload to the armory, where we stayed for three or four days.

There was that arrest on Thanksgiving Day, then the day after that and the day after that, so we had three or four hundred people who were in jail. They tried to put all of the females in the armory so that we would be separate from the males, but it got so filled that eventually they had to open another room of the armory and put some of the guys out there, too. There were people on our campus who would relay the information that we were in jail and we were doing fine. Of course, once the information hit the news, then everybody knew. We had made plans for a communications network, to keep morale up. We wanted to make sure people understood that, even though we were spending Thanksgiving Day in jail, that we were there for a purpose. That purpose was so that our children on some future Thanksgiving Day, would be able to eat at those restaurants.

One of the nastiest results of this demonstration was that a white female Bennett faculty member named Alice Jerome was accused of being a Communist. She and her husband had been involved with the HUAC [House Un-American Activities Committee] in the 1950s, and he had gone to jail on the Smith Act for contempt for not answering the committee's questions. I heard later that the attorney for the S&W [Armistad Sapp] took her picture and sent it to the FBI, and also mentioned her in a letter to the editor of the newspaper. The Board of Trustees at Bennett voted to dismiss her, because they were afraid of the college being linked to a suspected Communist.

Also, Dr. Laizner, who was German and spoke with a heavy accent, was accused of being a Communist. We got a lot of nasty stuff in the press that the Communists had infiltrated the group and that all of us "nice little black children" were being led astray by the Communists working with CORE. The Bennett administration took no action against her, because there was simply no truth to it. We believed that it didn't dignify a response. And of course, if people don't respond to things, then it pretty soon ceased to be worthy of putting it into print. There were a few nasty articles [in the newspaper about] Alice Jerome, Harry Boyte and others, but nobody really believed it. In any case, they had little to do with what happened in Greensboro. Any alleged Communists who may have come to Greensboro had nothing to do with CORE's strategy. They may have come to see what was going on, but they had no input in terms of deciding how we were going to do things, or what strategy we would use. The Communist ruse didn't work very well in Greensboro; it never really got off the ground.

But there were a large rash of articles coming out saying that blacks were inherently inferior to other people; if whites associated with us, then the inferiority would affect them, and that we were prone to commit crimes because it was our nature. My function as Pubic Relations Director was to try and defuse the negative publicity by proofing whatever statements we put out, and writing letters to the editor in the local newspapers. Most of them didn't get printed. The press releases usually were written by Bill Thomas, in which all I did was make sure that it was firmed up and everything was said the way that it was supposed to be said; that it read nice, that it flowed easily, that every thing that you said was the truth.

*The most significant result of the Thanksgiving Day demonstrations was that city officials had been awakened to the importance of seriously responding to Greensboro CORE's demands. Mayor Schenck appointed an ad hoc Human Relations Committee to study the state of race relations and current segregation practices. He asked that CORE allow the committee time to issue a report sometime in early 1963. Adult leaders in the African American community requested that CORE await the release of the report before engaging in additional direct action protests. Reluctantly, the Executive Committee agreed, and its recommendation was accepted by the membership.*

## John Hatchett

I was not in agreement with the suspension of demonstrations after they had begun to be effective. The decision for the suspension of demonstrations did not come from the local body. That was a decision that came from the national office. And I was vehemently opposed to that, as were some of the other members of the executive committee.

I'm almost certain that in '62, James Farmer, who was the national head of CORE, came down to Greensboro ostensibly at that point to give us encouragement, and to be a part of demonstrations, and to reassure us that there was not going to be any interference on the part of the national office in what we were doing.

All of a sudden, Mr. Farmer suggested to us to have a moratorium on the demonstrations. And there were some very subtle threats made that if we did not suspend the demonstrations, we would lose our status as a CORE chapter. I honestly do not know what happened to cause this change of mind. We knew that what we were doing was very effective. I have to say very emphatically that that was not a local decision.

*Greensboro Core had been successful in attracting national and local media attention in its first large-scale independent action. Although CORE field secretaries had provided advice, the Executive Committee was pleased that it had planned and executed the protest on its own. The thoroughness with which the leaders had conveyed the importance of nonviolence, the logistics of large crowd control through parade marshals, and the communications network to maintain contact with those arrested and bailed out had been handled adroitly. Perhaps as important, large numbers of students had displayed a commitment by sacrificing vacation plans for the goals of the Movement.*

*But this had been a short-term, single action. It had garnered CORE vital media coverage, but it had not achieved the greater purpose of desegregating a significant target. Was a sustained campaign against multiple targets possible? The independent action of those that went to the Carolina Theater, contrary to announced plans, presented the difficulty of inadequate crowd control, communications, and centralized authority necessary for larger demonstrations. These problems must be addressed in any future planning sessions.*

*The Executive Committee suspended further demonstrations pending the release of the mayor's committee report. In the interim, it conducted voter registration drives in cooperation with the NAACP. But the Committee made it clear that an unfavorable report would result in a resumption of demonstrations.*

# Chapter 5

## Juggernaut

*The activities of the fall appeared to have achieved the purpose of forcing some sort of positive action by city official through the mayor's ad hoc committee, which everyone referred to as the Human Relations Committee. When the committee's report was released in February, 1963, it recommended that places of public accommodation voluntarily desegregate, but made no provision for mandatory compliance. CORE had given the city an opportunity to act in good faith, and it felt betrayed by the maintenance of the racial status quo disguised as progress in race relations. Frustrated CORE members joined the NAACP to picket City Hall three times in March, but it failed to influence city officials and generated little publicity.*

*The CORE leadership faced a crisis. Desultory student response and the intransigence of theater and restaurant operators presented the chapter with a dilemma. As the spring semester was drawing to a close, the frustration of failure threatened the loss of student support and the dissolution of the chapter. More decisive direct action was necessary. The questions were what type of action and its timing. Should CORE do something to revitalize the flagging Movement through a small, symbolic action, or regroup over the summer and initiate a vigorous campaign in the fall? Whatever its decision, the Executive Committee knew that it must act quickly and decisively.*

## Alvin Thomas

We took Jim Farmer's advice to accept the truce asked for by the Human Relations Committee. Although there was some mixed opinion as to whether or not mass demonstrations and arrests were the best tactic, we had quite a bit of encouragement and moral support from the adult black community. We began participating in voter registration drives at the time; people would loan us their automobiles or participate in taking people to the polls. We were doing things that encouraged the adult black community to come to bat for us.

## Lois Lucas (Williams)

In late 1962, early 1963, things had sort of subsided, and there was really no concerted effort. It was just sort of keeping things alive by continuing to monitor businesses of public accommodation. We had many strategy-planning sessions, in which we discussed the best possible way of our actions having an impact on eradicating further vestiges of segregation in Greensboro. We did not say, "We're going to have a sustained boycott, and we're going to plan it for such-and-such a day." I think the boycott was largely spontaneous. People just made up their minds individually that, "We're not going to buy at that store, because they don't have any black salespersons in there, although there are a great number of qualified people that can work in that position," or "We are going to take our accounts out from Wachovia bank, because there are certainly a lot of people that can qualify to be tellers at Wachovia Bank."

The activist wing of the chapter felt that we should push immediately for the same rights that anyone else in Greensboro had. The moderates, on the other hand, took the position that since we had waited so long, we could wait to give the committee time to make its report. We hoped that it would exert some pressure in the form of good will to convince the city government and the business community that desegregation could occur peacefully and would in fact, be a financial boom for Greensboro. Within CORE, timing was the critical issue. "How long do we wait? We have made our position plain; we are not asking for anything that is not guaranteed by the Constitution. How much time do you want to give them, above the time that they have already had?"

I think that Bill [Thomas] was more of a moderate than an activist. He would say, "Maybe you have a point here, and you have a point there. Let's try to bring all of these things together to the middle and see where we stand." What we finally ended up doing was waiting to see what happened. I was basically an activist; I wanted to do something right away.

The central question was, "What do we do when the business community and the local government are intransigent? Do we picket? It takes a lot of time to go around to each of these businesses. Do we conduct a boycott that causes these businesses hardship?" Our frustration at the "go slow" attitude of the city was the motivating force behind the decision to picket City Hall in March 1963. It was the place where governmental decisions and laws were made. Buildings in this country are very symbolic. I felt that this was a way of dramatizing that we wanted to be law-abiding, yet we wanted the powers-that-be to take notice of us. What came out of it was simply more letters to the mayor's office, stating our position. The mayor sent a spokesman to Bennett College to urge patience, and criticized picketing as making their task more difficult.

We met in Pfeiffer Hall at Bennett, where we voiced our resentment that the picketing of City Hall had led to nothing except more empty promises and the realization that they didn't want to see us back downtown again. The activists and the moderates debated, and the result was that we decided to act. It was just a discussion of what each faction wanted: to wait and see if over the summer the city fathers would come up with something acceptable, weighing that against the fact that when we came back in September we would have to mobilize all over again, and get people up again. The decision was that we needed to do something then. It ended with both groups being completely unsatisfied with what the other had wanted to do.

## William Thomas

I was pretty angry at the slow pace of the negotiations. The powers-that-be were not in tune with what was really needed. The white community had a philosophy of: "Put off doing anything substantive until tomorrow—wait, wait, wait. When you're dealing with such fundamental rights, it's very difficult to accept the pace that they wanted us to follow. There was no reason for any black person not to be angry.

Activities were continuous from the beginning of the sit-ins. There was picketing of the S&W and Mayfair cafeterias in the fall of '62. This was more or less a continuation of the sit-ins. From the five-and-dime stores, it went to other business establishments, not only in the downtown area but those outside of the downtown area. The protests spread not only from a demand to actually sit down and buy a hot dog, but the opportunity to earn the money to buy a hot dog. If we were going to spend money in Woolworth, then we wanted salespeople in there. We wanted the entire work force integrated. The entire thing just snowballed.

The mayor urged the CORE chapter to suspend activities until the report of his committee, which was supposed to come out some time in February. CORE decided to return to overt demonstrations when the committee urged desegregation of public facilities, but said in the last paragraph that they had no power to enforce such a resolution. At that point, we cooperated with the NAACP to picket City Hall three times in protest.

The Greensboro Chamber of Commerce and the Greensboro Merchants Association published in the newspaper that they had passed a resolution advocating desegregation of all public facilities. But the segregated businesses said, "They don't speak for us." CORE's reaction was that we welcomed any support that we could get, but it had no teeth; it had no enforcement power. We recognized that the Merchants Association and the Chamber were trying to say to us, "We made this resolution, now call off your dogs." We said, "We're not going to stop demonstrations until they actually desegregate. The resolution doesn't mean a damn thing until we can actually achieve what we're after. It shows some good faith, but the places are still segregated."

## Elizabeth Laizner

In the spring of 1963 we were asked by an ad hoc Human Relations Committee to stop the constant picketing of the restaurants until they could issue a report. The Commission resolution condemning segregation sounded beautiful, until you came to the last line. It said, "unfortunately, our committee has no power to enforce our suggestions." After this, we got together and picketed City Hall shortly afterwards as a response to this. Bill Thomas called a meeting at Bennett College of as many of the membership as could attend, to ask us what we should do, since we had only a few weeks left before the students would leave at the end of the spring semester. The meeting was rather heated, and we were given a choice: Shall we prepare over the summer and make mass demonstrations in the fall, or shall we have a little demonstration right now? I think Pat suggested McDonald's on Summit Avenue, which was near the A&T campus. A committee was nominated to explore what we should do. They came up with the idea of "Let's do something small now. We can picket McDonald's and be arrested."

## A. Knighton Stanley

We did not engage in mass demonstrations until May 1963, because you do what you have people to do, and you develop that kind of volunteer personnel within the context of the particular conditions. For example, when you picket, you have to picket for a long time to make it effective; we couldn't go on for an hour and then come back like we were able to do in mass demonstrations. One person could picket, but if you are going to have a mass march, you've got to have masses; otherwise, it appears ineffective. Several of the more militant members of CORE were Bennett College students and two of them were on the Bennett faculty; they grew discontented and left the chapter. It may sound ironic that the radicals withdrew from CORE just when the mass demonstrations began, but some people are committed to rhetoric, while others are committed to action.

## William Thomas

McDonald's on Summit Avenue was selected as a target because it was a highly visible national chain, and it was directly across the street from the Hot Shoppes, where we had achieved significant success earlier. There were about forty-some members of CORE that we could call upon. The first four days of demonstration at McDonald's was principally a CORE activity, and then a large number of students became involved. It was really very easy to get large numbers of students involved quickly. You had basically two campuses, A&T and Bennett, and it was easy to get word around through the campuses.

## Lewis Brandon

We had been building, and the S&W demonstrations was the impetus for people to come out and be involved, but we were willing to agree to the suspension of demonstrations in the late fall of 1962. We have always done this. One, it was a part of the nonviolent technique, to give people a way out. So, in the Sixties there was always a moratorium, a period of cooling off and for giving them a time to work things out. You hope, but if it doesn't work, you know that you have to be ready to move beyond that point.

One of the things that we had to try to get people off center was when the Executive Committee decided in a meeting on Sunday morning that Bill and Tony should be arrested. This would draw attention to the picketing, because they were the most visible people in CORE. That's when the decision was made to make a major push and to not let up.

We had been out on campus recruiting to get more students involved. In fact, one of the nights at McDonald's, I had about ten people who were new recruits, and we had people who came on campus and threw rocks and bottles at the dormitories, which helped to motivate people to participate.

## Elizabeth Laizner

On Saturday, May 11, about fifty of us went out Summit Avenue with our signs and walked up to the counter and asked to be served. We were refused by the manager. He informed us that we were trespassing, and if we came back we would be arrested. Bill Thomas, Pat Patterson, and Reverend Busch returned to the window and asked for service, and were arrested by Captain Jackson. Reverend Knighton Stanley was not arrested initially, because he had something to do on the A&T campus, but once he got someone to assume his teaching duties, he returned and was arrested also.

They went to jail and there was a public outcry, because Stanley and Busch were ministers. Mr. McKissick came over from Durham to see them, and they told him that they wanted to stay in jail and not accept bail. Mr. McKissick, seeing the attention that they received in the newspapers said, "Get out, you've got something going."

## Pat Patterson

We had called for several boycotts, where we asked people to abstain from buying, except for basic necessities. For a while that was almost ninety percent effective. We agreed to wait for the report of the committee in February 1963, but when it came out, it was essentially meaningless. We talked about the fact that the Human Relations Committee was holding discussions with other groups in the community, but we felt that we had reached a point where just talking across a table wasn't getting anything done. That is what led to the mass demonstrations. I think that it might have been out of just general frustration that we weren't getting anyplace. We had a meeting and we decided that we were going to have a mass demonstration. We picked out McDonald's because it was a national chain, and highly visible. It was also near the black college campuses, and at that time we were depending primarily on college kids to support us. The manager said that we were going to be arrested, and that was the time that we decided, "Well, we'll go to jail if it takes that to get this place open."

Bill, Knighton Stanley, Reverend Busch and I were along. Dr. Laizner was there, but she wasn't arrested; there weren't too many things that we had where she wasn't arrested. I don't remember much about the hecklers, although I was told later that as I was picketing, a fellow was coming toward me with a knife, and that Captain William Jackson grabbed him. The word got out that there were certain people who were going to commit violence against CORE members. I never paid it much attention, because, for some reason I wasn't afraid. I don't know why. We knew there was a possibility that we might be attacked. We always talked about the possibility of that happening, and what we should do in the event that it should happen. We sort of prepared for whatever happened in that sense. We were arrested and taken downtown, our pictures were taken, we were fingerprinted, and we were put into cells and kept there overnight. I remember that it was Mother's Day. It was about ten o'clock in the morning when we were released on bail.

There were some 800 spectators and hecklers at the McDonald's picketing the next day, and only eight police officers. That was probably the closest to an attack that I had experienced in Greensboro. We had some fear, especially concerning the hecklers that followed us back to campus, throwing rocks and bottles. I don't think that it would be normal to say that there wasn't.

Our goals at that time were, primarily, desegregation. We hadn't given much thought to jobs or anything like that. The issue of jobs came later, because I don't remember us discussing it. The thrust of what we were doing was primarily to go into these places and be able to eat. It wasn't until later that we said, "Wait a minute, we've got these places open, but we don't have the jobs, we don't have the money in our pocket to afford to eat there."

## James McMillan

I drove my car carrying some of the pickets, and on the last trip, I had to park my car away from the McDonald area as a group of us were carrying signs and we were proceeding to picket, moving toward the picketing area. There had been quite a bit of activity and there was concern that there would be some violence because of some of the anti-picketing group who had begun to gather among the whites. I recall that there was great concern among those of us who were the older members, wondering if someone would be hurt if there would be violence, and just what would take place.

## Sarah Jones (Outterbridge)

I picketed at the McDonald's in May 1963; I was on the first march on May 11, 1963. Only about twenty-five to thirty people took part. We didn't plan on arrests, but every time that we went out into the street, we knew that we might get arrested, or we might get hurt. So, we were basically geared up for whatever might occur. We went out and the first four people went up and asked to be waited on and then were denied service, so they just continued to stand up there and they were arrested. Then those of us that were left began to picket; I don't remember if we were escorted away or not. We had arrived by cars in a caravan; we always tried to stay together. A lot of times we would even have the "buddy system," where you would walk two abreast so that you knew who was with you, and we could very easily tell if somebody was missing, and could keep up with people. There was not a very large crowd the first day. We picketed all evening. It was a long, hot evening. [Laughs]

We did not work in shifts. We usually had a spokesperson with each group, and they would always say, "Okay, we're going to wrap it up now." It was always frightening, because you knew that it was a nonviolent thing. You knew that if someone approached you, you would just stand there; other than try to block a blow, we were instructed not to fight back, so there was always this fear in the back of your mind. I don't remember seeing anyone attacked or hit. They only had a few policemen; police protection was terrible. It was obvious that if something broke out, they might come out or they might just stand there. We were not sure that they would protect us.

As we were passing the Hayes-Taylor YMCA, we decided to go into the downtown area and march to the Carolina Theater and hold a prayer service. It was a very spontaneous thing. We always tried to keep God in the forefront of our minds, so when someone said, "Let's stop and have a moment of meditation," we knelt down in prayer. We stayed on the sidewalk. We knew that if we hit the street, that we would definitely be arrested. They didn't want us there, so we tried to conform to the law as much as we possibly could, without deviating too far from it. The group was not that large. We were just on the sidewalk and knelt down; I don't think that we surrounded the ticket area. We were followed by hecklers from McDonald's and downtown. Generally, they were close to us. A lot of times, they would be on the opposite side of the street, but sometimes they would come very close. After the prayer we marched back to the church or Hayes-Taylor YMCA.

*The picketing of McDonald's was the catalyst that CORE had been hoping for to generate large-scale student support. In an open meeting at Providence Baptist Church, Reverend Cecil Bishop and other activists urged CORE Executive Committee members to keep the protest going until the ministers could enlist the support of the adult black community. The picketing continued for the next three days, which expanded to spontaneous marches downtown to the cafeterias and the theaters, where demonstrators prayed, sang Movement songs and some were arrested for trespassing. On May 15, corporate representatives of McDonald's asked for a meeting at Providence Baptist Church, where they agreed to desegregate all of its restaurants.*

*Now the logjam broke. Responding to overwhelming student demand, CORE began an intense campaign against the restaurants and theaters downtown through nightly marches and demonstrations. The question was how to manage it. In the past, CORE had a small, well-disciplined membership, trained in nonviolent tactics. The leadership was suddenly faced with the responsibility of controlling a crowd of hundreds of enthusiastic students, without provoking a violent response of the authorities or disillusioning their new recruits.*

*The first task was to organize this mass and educate them in CORE's goals and tactics. Instructions were given in mass meetings at the various churches, followed by a march of between one and two thousand A&T and Bennett students. As the column entered the business district, groups would converge on previously-assigned targets: the S&W and Mayfair Cafeterias, and the Center and Carolina Theaters. Arrests of hundreds occurred nightly as students either gained entry and sat down, or refused to move from entranceways.*

*Faced with the sudden tactic of marches in large numbers and mass arrests, Mayor Schenck called a meeting of the Chamber of Commerce and Merchants Association members to discuss the situation on May 16, then issued a statement recommending desegregation of private businesses. As a conciliatory gesture, CORE marched through the downtown area that night, without seeking arrests. But when the managements of the targeted businesses publicly rejected the mayor's statement, demonstrations and ar-*

*rests resumed. Over the next four days 940 were arrested.*

The mass arrests galvanized the activist members of the adult black community. On the evening of May 15, members of the Greensboro Men's Club, the Citizens Association and other organizations formed the Coordinating Committee of Pro-Integration Groups, led by Father Richard Hicks, pastor of the Church of the Redeemer, to support CORE, arrange bail for those arrested, and to act as a liaison between CORE and city officials.

## A. Knighton Stanley

After we were released from jail, we discovered that as the cafeterias and theaters were targeted, the number of people that began to demonstrate with us increased. The leadership did not anticipate this; there was a great rise, just a great rise. There were no flyers. We very seldom circulated anything. We weren't equipped to do it. The mass meetings that were held immediately after the McDonald's arrest drew large numbers, and here again, the *Greensboro Daily News* and *The Greensboro Record* did a great deal to stimulate that. We didn't need a leaflet as far as strategy.

## William Thomas

CORE had a definite policy concerning the patronizing of establishments that did desegregate. For instance, after McDonald's announced that it would desegregate, I was quoted in the newspapers as saying, "We're not going to come down in large numbers. We will wait until this ceases to become an emotional issue, and then we'll come." What I was trying to say to the powers-that-be was, "Let this thing occur naturally and gradually. You're not going to have four thousand black people standing in line to get a hamburger." Once they opened their doors and we knew that we had the right to eat there, then we would patronize that establishment the same way we would any other place. It wouldn't be an onslaught of people going there just for the sake of going. We weren't looking to create either economic problems or violent confrontations with anyone; we just wanted the right to utilize those facilities.

Frequently there were mass meetings at one of the churches beforehand. The meetings before and after demonstrations offered a place where people could gather. We had to have some central place where instructions could be given as to exactly what tactics would be used that particular evening, where we were going, and so forth. The mass meeting afterwards was emotional. It was religious and also strategic. And it afforded us an opportunity to assess where we were and what we had to do, and to make plans for the next day. So each day our activities were, in fact, planned, and with some degree of flexibility to be able to adjust again to the situation once we arrived at our target area. Most of the churches in the black community were used: the Church of the Redeemer, Providence Baptist Church, Trinity AME Zion. But Providence was centrally located, in that it was in the direct path of going to the downtown area, so it was used most often for meetings.

The tactics were adopted according to what we thought were most appropriate for the particular circumstance. For example, in attempting to assess the situation, at times we may have felt that a silent demonstration would be more effective than singing or a more vocal demonstration. It may have depended upon the type of people that we had participating. It may have depended upon the type of negotiations that were going on at the time. Any number of factors would go into making a decision as to what was needed. It may depend upon the type of emotionalism or the climate that we were attempting to create; it did not just happen. There were these types of factors considered and analyzed before it was decided upon exactly what would occur.

To a certain extent, the tactics were based on the classes that CORE held in Greensboro and Durham, particularly during the Freedom Highways campaign. But in another sense, they were not. We were taught how to respond to different situations, but we were able to adapt to our own particular local situations. I think we were quite fortunate that we were some of the forerunners in that entire thing. So in that sense, you might say that we helped other communities that were looking at us to learn from the experiences that we had in Greensboro. I believe that contemporary events—the desegregation of the University of Mississippi by James Meredith in 1962, and the Birmingham demonstrations in 1963,—had an influence on us. And through media and other forms of communication, I'm sure that all of those things had something to do in creating a climate where what happened in Greensboro could occur.

Once students knew what was going on, it had a dynamic effect. But we also utilized the media and distributed leaflets. The local ministers were very cooperative in permitting us to use their churches for mass meetings. We had smaller meetings where we discussed what we were about and what we were trying to do. And through basic community organizational type of techniques, we were able to get people out, especially students. People respond to crisis; sometimes we had to create crisis in order to get the community response that was needed. At times we created a situation, to force the police to make arrests and then utilize it through the media to create the type of sensationalism that we wanted, in order to get more people involved. So to a certain extent, some of it was spontaneous. We would use the spontaneity of it to achieve the goal that we sought. After some of the emotionalism wore off, we had meetings in churches, community centers, and people's homes. And we would go out into the community, explain to them what was going on, request that they boycott certain stores until our demands were met, and encourage them to get involved.

## Lewis Brandon

When the demonstrations expanded to the downtown area, we selected the two cafeterias and the theaters because of their central location. It was easy to get people down there. Downtown was very viable at that point, because people were used to coming downtown. We had more visibility there than we would in an isolated area. And we had to think of transportation to the demonstration site, so high visibility and proximity to the campuses were considerations in selecting targets.

One of the things that we were concerned with was being able to draw upon all of the resources of the community. So all of the organizations that were involved with civil rights and the problems of the black community were called upon and came together to try to facilitate the demonstrations, and there was a loose-knit kind of thing, which was formed into the Coordinating Committee of Pro-Integration Groups. Father Hicks of the Church of the Redeemer became chairman of that organization. I think that we needed the support of the community because when you have the backing of the ministerial group, there is a certain amount of legitimacy that you don't have if you are outside of their group.

I don't think that the adult community was using us to push for their separate goals; the people were very concerned about eradicating segregation, and all black people would have a vested interest in that goal. CORE participated in that organization as an autonomous organization, as did all of the other member groups. But there was a concerted effort to work within the group; as a matter of fact, the Coordinating Committee came about at the insistence of CORE, and it never attempted to control us. We still had our own meetings. In fact, after the Coordinating Committee was formed, we moved from Providence Baptist Church to the Church of the Redeemer and had an ongoing operation there, which was manned almost twenty-four hours a day. We maintained full control of the demonstrations and took chief responsibility for planning them. But we did touch base and did inform people of what we were going to do, and when the Coordinating Committee suggested that we have a moratorium, we agreed to that. The marches were not strictly separated into student and adult marches; we had a large march down from the Trinity Church of both students and adults, and all of the other marches were both student and adult. CORE was not all students; McMillan was not a student, Laizner was not a student, Charles Davis, Julian Douglas, Busch, Hatchett, all of these people were members of the organization. There were a number of people who were in CORE and participated in the demonstrations.

One thing that we had decided was that all of the leadership would not be arrested. Some people would be left out in order to run the operation. And essentially, that is what I did; I laid back and did the leg work. People did not all go to the designated targets simultaneously, because of how things were situated. People would leave, and then they would go to where they were assigned. So basically, you were going at the same time, but you would probably arrive at different times, because of the way that things were situated downtown. The number of people to be arrested at each site was basically left up to the individual, because if they were asked to get out of line, they could get out, and a number of people that were asked to move away from the doors, moved And that was a conscious decision on the part of the person involved. We did not try to say that people had to go or to force people to be arrested; that was their decision.

## Pat Patterson

We would sit down and have strategy meetings on what we would do. We wanted our presence to be felt, but not where people would get hurt. That would have an adverse effect on what we wanted to accomplish. So, we would try to assess what the overall feelings were in the community. We wanted to do enough to keep it on the conscience of everybody, but at the same time, we didn't want any riots. We did a lot of singing and carrying on, and the police department came to us and said, "Wait a minute, this could cause a lot of problems." At other times we agreed that it was going to be a silent march, and we weren't going to do a lot of singing and chanting.

Groups of hostile whites came by singing and chanting, but we would not respond; that was a part of our strategy of not causing any violence. That was our biggest concern. Our songs were an expression of what we really felt and were a way to keep us all together. Even when we weren't successful in doing some of the things that we were attempting to do, these songs and things helped to keep the group together. The songs helped to build our morale, reflect our dedication and alleviate tension. We had no difficulty in maintaining a nonviolent stance in dealing with this large number of people.

In some of those marches we might have had three or four thousand people. We talked about it so much that there was little doubt in anybody's mind as to what we were all about, and that we would not tolerate any other way. We didn't think that violence would get us anything. The students and the adults marched together; when they were involved, it was a together kind of thing. You just sort of got in line and got wherever you wanted to get. We always had monitors all down the line, and we tried to keep communications open. For example, we would have a person that we had confidence in to maintain control, to go out with a group of people. I might end up at the end of the line one time, or somewhere in the middle or down the side. We didn't want to get any of the girls hurt. We were trying to take care of our troops, and to a great extent, our troops were young ladies.

I honestly felt that Captain Jackson tried to be as fair as he could. I don't know what his personal feelings were, but he projected a kind of attitude of, "Fellows, as long as you are within the law, we're out here to protect you. But if you get out of line, we're going to have to arrest you." Therefore, we tried to cooperate with him by notifying him whenever we were coming downtown. Most of us in CORE knew Captain Jackson, and he knew the CORE leadership. I don't remember any incidents where anybody got hurt, because the police didn't do something, although I do remember some isolated negative remarks from individual policemen. Under the circumstances, I think you're going to have some occasional incidents like that.

## Ralph Lee

Everything was detailed to students. Certainly, nobody would be allowed to participate in any marches if they weren't dressed properly and schooled in nonviolent philosophy. And when I say dressed properly for purposes of the demonstration, male students were required to wear shirt and ties and jackets. Female students were required to wear either skirts and blouses or dresses. That was optional with them. But we just didn't want to create a bad image in terms of appearance.

We felt that would be a psychological thing in terms of getting our message across through the news media to people in North Carolina, and for that matter, people of the country or whoever was reading about us or watching us. We instructed students that, in all probability, they would be arrested. None of us were lawyers, so we weren't in a position to realize what the outcome would be. But the major concern was not getting arrested. The major concern with us, and through all of our sessions, was avoiding, at whatever cost, any type of confrontation with white onlookers who might try to harass us or physically assault us. There were a couple of incidents where eggs were thrown. But that was the major emphasis, to avoid at all costs any kind of physical confrontation between students and onlookers who were opposed to us.

## Lois Lucas (Williams)

I don't know if there was a conscious shift from small numbers picketing to mass street demonstrations, but I think the experience of the Freedom Riders, and the marches like those Martin Luther King was involved in during the Birmingham demonstrations that were going on at that time, with the dogs and the fire hoses, led to our sense of frustration of trying to do things in a gentle way, to try to wait and mark our time and say, "Please, if we just stand out here with our picket signs, you'll notice us and you'll finally come around to doing what is right." The frustration of what was happening around us in other places in the South penetrated our way of working through the problems in the kind of gentle fashion that we had become used to. Now people were more passionate in their appeals and tended to make people want to see things happen in Greensboro, because, even we had suffered some of the abuse from the people in the stores and the restaurants, of people who would pour hot coffee on you or stick you with a lighted cigarette.

The news media reports provided information to students who wanted to contact CORE, and of course, by word-of-mouth, telephone calls, leaflets and posters on campus was helpful. As a CORE member, I attended meetings more frequently than the non-members. They were generally held in areas that were very convenient to the campus. The marches were prearranged, but also fairly spontaneous. We would say, "We will march down to City Hall," or "We will march down to one of the restaurants or theaters." Generally, the marches started out from one of the churches. We would start out from a given location, one of the churches or Dudley and go up Market Street; they were good landmarks near the campus. We were not usually assigned specific targets, until we focused on the S&W and the Mayfair. On some occasions, we would just march downtown.

When the mass demonstrations escalated in the spring of 1963, the mass meetings that we had were not to develop demonstration strategy. Those were pep rallies and also to remind the students of the discipline of CORE. The plays were actually called by a very small group of people. It would have been a subset of the Executive Committee, because we lost some of the Executive Committee to jail and fatigue. The Executive Committee met all day, every day, and every minute. In the mass demonstrations, what we sought was to get the people up to a feverish pitch, and then we called the game plan: Follow the leaders, stay in line, sing or don't sing, and so forth. The CORE leadership was usually on hand, and a demonstration was organized so that it was one unit; there were no splinter groups and very few people who could call decisions on the spot. We usually informed the police through Captain Jackson, as to demonstration routes and as much of our strategy as we wanted him to know in order to protect the demonstrators, which he did a most adequate job of. We would go to targets simultaneously, with groups breaking off to go to different targets. That was a part of strategy from time to time. There was no point, of course, in having a demonstration if it was totally predictable.

I incorporated my role as Public Relations Director into part of my life as a college student. It didn't supersede or take over the fact that my primary purpose was that I was in college to get an education. I remained focused on my studies, although I tried to conscientiously perform my duties as a CORE officer. Despite my title, I was not the official contact with the press, because the press chose to do whatever it chose to do. The press was looking for in-house bickering, a lot of fighting, "Was there friction with this group and that group? Was someone trying to take over from this person? Was there animosity in this group?"

If they couldn't get this from you, they would go to someone totally and completely different, or a reporter would just be walking on campus and single someone out and say, "What do you know about what is going on?" The press had ingenious ways of trying to get the information that they want or taking no information and printing it as information, if it suited its purposes. In the beginning, the members of the press were just as frightened as all the rest of the Establishment in Greensboro. They didn't understand what had happened to these nice, quiet black people of Greensboro. Why, all of a sudden, going to the back door and getting something out wasn't good enough; why were people suddenly becoming dissatisfied with our role? Here you were getting a good education, or at least an education that was better than a lot of people in the South were getting, and what had they done to deserve all that we were supposedly giving them."

## James McMillan

The marches were pretty much on a nightly basis, because we felt that there was an extreme urgency that this issue be resolved. It was quite obvious that it was not an easy thing because, with the students being in school, these activities had to be a secondary thing with regard to what our main activities were. So it really extended our days and nights tremendously. It was mainly in the evening when these activities took place and, of course, it took place with great fervor. The students were giving and doing their thing with a great excitement. As a matter of fact, I think that the students became more involved in their school because of these activities. I think that they could see a very close relationship. There were all kinds of secondary positive things that came out of that effort.

It was kind of a word-of-mouth passing of information on campus during the day as colleagues—those of us who were involved—would meet for lunch. We'd say, "Such-and-such took place last night, and such-and-such a thing should take place. What would you do if such-and-such a thing were to follow? Have you heard that so-and-so person was arrested? Have you seen the paper today, and what were the comments about it in the paper?" But it was the leadership among the students who were the ones who kept the main issues on a circulating basis through a word-of-mouth form of communication.

I think that Captain Jackson was a very professional policeman, in every regard. I think that it was with those who were under him that we had our greatest concern. There were several occasions when there was the old status attitude of referring to black men as "boys" and to the women as "girls," and a kind of general disrespect to ethnic origin was very clear. However, I saw no overt violent racism on the part of the police. During the time of the marches, there was a respectful rapport between the marchers and the police. There were no ugly verbal interchanges between the demonstrators and the police in my experience, although I heard about incidents of such exchanges at some of the points of incarceration. And I did not witness any physical attacks on the part of the jeering whites.

## Pattie Banks

At that time we met at Providence Baptist Church, which was in an area between Bennett and A&T campuses. We were told to march in an orderly fashion, always have books, newspapers, magazines or something when we went into restaurants or whatever area that we were covering at that time, to take a seat and read our material until somebody came to wait on us or told us to leave. CORE instructed us in nonviolence and appropriate behavior during marches, usually just guidelines from the leaders, such as Bill Thomas and others, and ministers who reminded us of the nonviolent tactics that we were to adhere to. We were prepared for or told about it, but there were no specific classes as such. We would go into these establishments and sit down. We received verbal abuse from those who were inside until the proprietor would call the police and have us arrested for trespassing. I was arrested and taken downtown to the city jail. We were released, fingerprinted, pictures taken, and released until our court date. Basically, the police were fairly courteous. Of course, there were always those who were ill-tempered. Captain Jackson functioned in a rather courteous manner. I don't really remember any harassment or mistreatment, considering the circumstances.

I was a junior at Bennett College in the spring of 1963. The Bennett students got together with the A&T students from A&T in the peaceful marches downtown. It was not difficult to get a group together to march, because information was widespread on campus and on the TV news. The students of Bennett and A&T got together in the peaceful marches downtown. We each had different areas that we were to cover on a particular night, and mine usually was the Mayfair Cafeteria. We hoped that if we focused on specific targets, then general desegregation would follow.

Dr. Laizner, Reverend Busch, and Mr. Hatchett were Bennett instructors involved in CORE and who sought to drum up enthusiasm among the students. Communication came from these individuals, CORE members and the campus newspaper. The CORE chapter met at local churches. It was usually on a nightly basis or every other night. It seems that the bulk of the support or input came from the students from Bennett and A&T. So, of course, when the students were gone, we had problems publicizing what our stand was, what we felt needed to be done, and what changes needed to be made regarding desegregation. I think the informed awareness was as important as anything else. For instance, there were rumors that some A&T officials may have been a little reluctant for some of their students to participate, and were even acting as informants for the administration, but they proved to be unfounded.

It was a volunteer thing; I don't remember anyone saying, "You ought to participate," or "This is what we need to do." But there were some students who did not want to get involved, particularly students from the Deep South, for fear that their pictures may be on television. One young lady from Tupelo, Mississippi, whose mother was a teacher, was afraid to become involved, saying that if she should be recognized on television, then her mother would no longer have a job. I had difficulty dealing with that, but it made sense to her. I remember hearing that local parents also might be subject to harassment or lose their jobs. You have to keep in mind, most Bennett students at that time were pretty much removed from the outside community, and we sort of had our own little world. There were certain places that we didn't go, not only because of segregation, but because Bennett forbade its students from going there, even though they may have been black establishments, because we were instructed in what was correct behavior and what wasn't correct.

CORE instructed us in guidelines on nonviolence and appropriate behavior during marches, usually from Bill Thomas and various ministers. Many of us only knew the officers of CORE as respected leaders, in a detached sort of way. We attended open mass meetings, where instructions for that night's march were passed on to the marchers. We were told about maintaining a nonviolent behavior, but there were no specific classes.

The procedure on the marches varied. Sometimes we would go into these establishments and sit down and read our books until someone came to wait on us, which they never did. We received verbal abuse from those who were inside until the proprietor would call the police and arrest us for trespassing. The police would come up to you and tell you that "We are going to arrest you." I think at that point you could move back if you did not want to be arrested, and those that wanted to be arrested took a stand. Once you took a stand you were automatically arrested. I wasn't worried, because that wasn't the first time that I was arrested. [Laughs] I was arrested and taken downtown to the city jail. We were fingerprinted, had our pictures taken, and released on bail provided by CORE, until our court date. Basically, the police were fairly courteous. I was apprehesive as to the kind of treatment we might get from the police, but there wasn't any harassment or strong abuse.

There were no problems of maintaining order during a march. We all knew what our specific purpose was; we knew that we could achieve our goals better in an orderly manner, and we were all of the same accord. In my march to the Mayfair, we lined up on the side of the sidewalks, so as to move toward the entrance. Once, when the word got out that we were coming, the doors were locked. There was concern by the male students at A&T as to the safety of the female students, but not to the point that we were discouraged from participating in the demonstrations. There were large numbers of hecklers and spectators on the street. I was frightened, as were a lot of other people, because we never knew what might happen. Rocks and racial epithets were hurled at us, but the police kept the hecklers on the other side of the street. And there were people, mostly black, who offered encouragement.

There were some members of the adult black community at the mass meetings, although the majority consisted of students. We would get in groups after the marches, at various churches or the Hayes-Taylor YMCA, and discuss what the events of the night had been or what we hoped things would be like the following night, but it was almost a ritualistic kind of thing. People were tense, but somewhat reverent. Although there were large groups of people involved, it was kind of a personal thing.

I don't think we placed so much emphasis on the word "movement" at that time. Rather, we used words like "demonstrations" or "achievement." We were aware of what was going on in the rest of the South, but our primary concern was in this area, more so than saying, "This is a part of what's going on in Mississippi or Alabama." It was part of the overall Movement, but it was like the other part was the outer rim.

## Lois Lucas (Williams)

The demonstrators were schooled in nonviolence. That was one of the main purposes of the meetings that were held at the old Trinity Church. I remember several times when we were marching we were verbally harassed, but there was never any retaliation for it; it was just ignored. Some of the white hecklers were close. Normally, we always marched on the street and they were on the sidewalk, but there were a few that wanted to get physically involved with the marchers that would get a little closer. I remember some demonstrators being struck and also some being spit on. I think that the first time that I marched I was a little scared, but after that I just felt a part of it and there was really no fear involved. I think the police did a good job of protecting us. I guess I just considered them as a part of the system and that's what they were there for, primarily for our protection. Nobody in the march got into any type of discussion or confrontation with the hecklers. Normally, if there was some type of confrontation with the police, there was a spokesman in the march who calmed things down.

I marched pretty much on a daily basis. Most of the pre-march meetings were held at Trinity; sometimes the march was followed by a meeting. They were mainly inspirational-type meetings to keep everybody attuned to what was going on, and to inspire everybody to just what the purpose was. On some occasions James Farmer and Floyd McKissick spoke to us. At first I was naive, not knowing that much about what the purpose of it all was until I got involved. Then it made me feel proud being black and being able to contribute to what was being done. Before then, the only accomplishment that I could see was a short-range one, the integration of the theaters and the cafeterias. I didn't see the long-range goals that the other activists did.

Although the Executive Committee monitored the marches with marshals, it did not exercise coercive control; it kept its focus on the well being of the marchers. If someone went downtown and decided on their own that, "We're not going to leave; we are going to get arrested." There was no "We'll run back and call an Executive Committee meeting and see how we can use this." There was concern about "What's happening to the kids that have been arrested? Are the police going to be brutal this time? What is their attitude going to be?" There was no saying "How can we capitalize on this?"

## Marion Jones

We were quiet in the marches. The only thing that we would do was to sing "We Shall Overcome" or some hymns and prayers. There were never any altercations. My daughter was narrowly missed by a knife that someone threw at her. That was the biggest thing that I recall. There were never any other instances like that; we didn't give them any reasons to do anything violent because we were not violent. Naturally, there were catcalls and epithets. But the police did a very good job of keeping order.

We usually contacted the police as a committee prior to a march. [William] Thomas often went, because he was well known. He would generally take someone with him as a witness that we did contact the police. We never used the telephone; we spoke personally with Captain Jackson. He was a very nice fellow. He would ask where we would be demonstrating, what time would the demonstration take place, and where it would end. We never had any trouble obtaining a permit to march. We had to; it was a requirement. But he never tried to discourage us from demonstrating, because he knew that we were going to demonstrate anyway. We did not speak with any other city official, other than just casually or when we went to secure our permits. There was never any long, drawn-out discussions; they knew what our objectives and motives were, so there wasn't any difficulty. Nothing really happened when the students would stand in a circle and come on the mat of the door of the place where we were demonstrating; they would go quietly, without resistance.

## Boyd Morris

The law of the land was that businesses operated segregated. I had some [demonstrators] removed from the premises. I only brought charges against the ones that came into the business and sat and wouldn't leave. And we did the same with whites that were with the blacks. There was a female teacher at Bennett [Elizabeth Laizner]. She wouldn't talk. I just said, "Why are you doing this? Why are you here?" She said, "I am with them." I said, "Well, I am not going to serve them, and I would like you to leave with them." She said, "I am not going to leave." End of conversation, and the police took them out.

I was surprised that the demonstrators came in, and then we had a lot of that sort of thing. I believe that this came first before they actually started picketing. We politely asked them to leave, that we were not going to serve them. Most of the time they left, and then as it grew more militant, we had to bring the police in and have them taken out. Captain Jackson deserves an awful lot of credit for a cool head. I thought that he handled the situation with extreme good judgment.

I was never stepped on or spat at or shouted at. I had a great rapport with black people, but I think that a lot for the blacks wanted me to capitulate and get it over with, but I would have lost face with the whites. It was a two-edged sword; whichever way I went, I'd get cut. I talked to several of the black leaders of the community, and I told them that when the law was changed, I would abide by the law. I was never antagonistic toward any black that I talked to. They wanted what they wanted; I wanted what I was doing, so I didn't feel any animosity. I felt that they liked me, didn't approve of me, maybe, but they liked me as a man.

I didn't want any damage. I didn't want my help to be subjected to this type of demonstration and possible violence and injury. We didn't know what to expect. We heard their chanting and marching; we knew that they were militant. CBS [Columbia Broadcasting System], had their cameras on us. I was not grandstanding, and in my heart I just deplored the whole situation. This came about through no fault of mine; I was abiding by the law. I told Abernathy [sic], and I told Mr. Farmer, "When the law is changed, I'll be the first to capitulate."

The demonstrators marched on many nights, and I stood at the door. One night I felt that they would push on through, so I locked the door. Since there wasn't a customer in sight, I sent the help home; I locked up and went home. I did that on three nights, because I didn't want any confrontation. I didn't want me or any of my staff hurt if they pushed the door down, and trampled me. I didn't have the experience of the S&W, where I repeatedly locked and unlocked the door for patrons, because there was only three nights when I closed my business. There was never any violence.

I talked with [Frank] Sherrill, [assistant manager, S&W Cafeteria], Jim Bellows [manager of the Center Theater] & Neil McGill [manager of the Carolina Theater]. We all shared a sense of frustration, of "What are we going to do?" knowing full well that the government was going to capitulate, change the law. It was just a matter of time; we tried to decide whether to carry on the way that we were doing, or go ahead and desegregate. We never sat down and had a formal meeting. If Mr. [Richard] Bentz [assistant manager, S&W Cafeteria] knew about a march, he would warn me. I felt that my phone was tapped. I tried to find out from the FBI, but their answer to me was, "We don't know whether it is or not; it could be." I could hear the clicking in and clicking out.

I met with the Human Relations Committee, and I told them, as I told the business leaders of the city when they wanted me to integrate the Mayfair Cafeteria. I said, "Gentlemen, if each of you will integrate your place of business, the Mayfair Cafeteria will integrate tomorrow morning. You want me to be the fall guy." The Commission just tabled it; they wouldn't go into it. So, in my heart I did what I thought was the right thing. I offered and was rejected. I felt that I turned the Human Relations Committee off. I tried to do what I thought was the best or the right thing. I made the offer publicly in all seriousness, and they hardly even let it get on the table until they changed the subject.

I received obscene phone calls. The people were volatile on both sides, and there was no way to win in a climate like that. You are going to do what you think is best, and then you just have to let the chips fall [where they may], and this is what I did. There are some white people who would say, "Boyd Morris is absolutely wrong in what he is doing." I had the Ministerial Association to come in and say, "We won't eat here any more unless you integrate." And I told them the same thing that I told the Committee. I said, "You integrate your churchs, and I'll integrate tomorrow." They responded, "We're not talking about that." They would not address themselves to the question. I said this to everybody who wanted to chastise me. I would tell them, simply, "Well, what do you do about integration?" And this would stump them, because they well knew that they weren't doing anything about it, but wanted me to do it.

## Neil McGill

They were peaceful demonstrations from the very beginning. My employees weren't interested; they weren't entering the theater, so they didn't care. I had a black projectionist, one of the best in town, but he never mentioned it. My maid at home was frightened to death; she thought there would be violence, but there was never any violence. They didn't actually force their way into the theater, because there was no one to stop them; they just walked in.

It was one of the most frustrating experiences of my life. The blacks would form at A&T College and march downtown, surround the Carolina Theater and sing, "We Shall Overcome." It paralyzed our business. They would march every night for about a month. One night they knelt and prayed. One night part of this black group forced their way into the Carolina and, unfortunately, we had to have them arrested.

There wasn't any movie crowd. The theaters were practically empty. It cut down maybe seventy-five percent of our business. I remember on one occasion a person who appeared to be white walked up to the box office, bought a ticket and started into the theater, and Jesse Jackson said to me, "See, she's a Negro, you sold her a ticket." I said, "Yes, but she appears to be white." She was not stopped from going into the theater. As long as they were marching, it was perfectly legal. We may as well have closed the doors. The police and firemen were working with us one hundred percent. The police would be in certain positions, and came ahead of the marchers. We didn't arrest anyone unless they forced their way into the theater; then we had them arrested. We took pictures of those that forced their way in.

There was no way to stop them, there were too many. Of course, we had to have them arrested. I never suggested desegregation policy to my boss; I left that decision up to him. I couldn't do that as an individual, I couldn't make that decision. The home office was in Charlotte. Mr. Kinsey operated the theaters under contract for ABC [American Broadcast Company]. The only thing that I objected to was the way that they were paralyzing our business, but from a personal standpoint, I didn't have any ill-feeling toward the black race before this happened, except that it was such a trying experience for me.

As far as the fire laws were concerned, the police and the firemen were arresting them on their own. It was sort of a mutual agreement between Captain Jackson and myself to arrest them if they trespassed; it was a cut-and-dried thing. They surrounded the theater and marched. It would start in the early evening around 7:00. They were well-behaved. I didn't have anything like being called names, shoved or spat upon. The police were very well-behaved. It was sort of a trying experience for them. I didn't really expect any violence to erupt, but you can imagine how frustrating it was to me, because I was in charge. I didn't expect a rushing of the door or anything like that, but it was frightening because there were such large numbers, and, of course, all ages. However, there was always the possibility of violence between the hecklers and the demonstrators, but there were always enough police to handle almost anything. There was no violence, even when they made arrests, the blacks would go quietly, and there was no struggling. I recall that there were a few spectators every night. The crowds were not large.

In talking to the press, most of the time I just said, "no comment." This was a policy both on my part and my company's. Armistad Sapp told the press that the Kennedy government had tapped all of the operators' telephones. I know that my telephone was not tapped.

It had no effect on my home life except my maid was worried to death. I went ahead and showed the film anyway. There's an old saying, "The show must go on." Jimmy Barrows and Gene Street and I talked to each other, mostly by telephone. I don't think that I ever communicated personally with the mayor. If we were requested to do certain things, I'd always take it up with my company. McNeill Smith is the only one that I remember calling on me.

## Frank Sherrill, Jr.

I came to Greensboro in October of 1953, and I was Assistant Manager then. Mr. [Richard] Bentz and I were [assistant managers] and were very close in what we were saying and doing. We had to carry out the policy of the company, and the policy was not to feed the colored people at that particular time. At that time we had about sixteen or seventeen cafeterias. There were demonstrations at a lot of them in Raleigh and Charlotte, but nothing as extensive as in Greensboro. I just did whatever the cafeteria management wanted me to do. I felt like we should feed them, but I worked for the S&W and I wanted to do what was best for the S&W, and so I would do what they asked me to do. I'd talk to my father [owner of the S&W Cafeteria], but I felt that what he wanted done was what he wanted done, and I was concerned mainly that we would lose a lot of our business. We had customers that said they wouldn't eat with us if we ever fed one black in the cafeteria. We had been in business a long time, and we had a lot of customers, and practically all of the whites were telling us this, so we didn't know exactly what to do. Most of the reaction we had from the other businessmen downtown was that they didn't want to feed them [blacks]. There were only a few in town that did want to. As for Boyd Morris, we just asked him what he was doing, and he would ask us what we were doing, and we would let him know.

They [demonstrators] were at the theater [Center Theater], right around the corner from us. They had started there, and we were getting worried that they were coming to the cafeterias to try to come in and eat, and it wasn't long until they were there. Right before they came, the S&W Cafeterias organization was having a managers' meeting down in Florida. I called the place where they were meeting, and told them what the situation was. I told them that I would like to talk to all of our help, and they said, "Oh no, not that." They didn't want to do that; they were afraid that it might stir up a lot of stuff.

They finally called me back a couple of hours later and told me that I could talk to [my staff]. So, I did talk to the help. I told them exactly how the company felt, that we couldn't feed [blacks] until the laws were changed, and that we would continue to not feed them until [the laws were changed]. I wanted them to know our position, and to be as honest with them as I possibly could so that they would know the situation. Course, we were telling the pickets the same thing. The reason that I wanted to call them together was because our help looked like they were very nervous, and they didn't know what to do. I felt like if we could talk to them and tell them our situation and how we felt about feeding colored people and tell them our situation and how we felt about feeding colored people at that particular time, that they would be a little bit more at ease.

We had a chef, Isaac Reed, and he had a son at A&T College, who was very much caught up in the demonstrations. I remember that I was at the front door and he came up and said, "Why don't you feed me, because my father works for you?" It was a pretty good question, if you ask me. I just told him our policy, and that was all that I needed to tell him. Isaac said, "Mr. Sherrill, I know that times are changing, and my son is caught up with what is going on now, and this is the way that he feels about it, and I am not so sure that he is not right." I just said, "I understand, Isaac, what you are talking about." That question was often asked of me, and I thought that it was a pretty good question. But the only thing that I knew to tell him was our policy was such-and-such, and if and when it changed we would do what was supposed to be done. We didn't threaten anybody. Of course, we wanted them to work normally. No one was ever fired because of anything like this.

Sometimes I discussed matters of policy with my father, but not all the time. Armistad Sapp was talking with him most of the time. My father communicated with Mr. Bentz and myself through Sapp. On occasion, I would go down to Charlotte to talk with him, so that I would know what his policy was. My father would keep in daily contact with us.

I don't think I was ever interviewed by the news media. Mr. Sapp would tell us not to talk to them, that he would do all the talking. We hired Armistad Sapp as an attorney for the S&W, because we wanted a lawyer that would really fight for us, and we couldn't find one except him. He was also employed by the Center Theater around the corner, and so we talked to him and he sounded like what we really wanted. We hired him and he came and talked to us. He said that there were five things that he could do; I can't remember them all, but he did every one of those five things. He said that he was going to change [influence] public opinion [in our favor]. When he got through telling us that, I said, "Well, you can't do any of those things," but he did. He really fought for us. He was at the cafeteria most of time when things were going on, and he saw what was going on. He would be outside and inside, and he would talk to the pickets. He stood on his own two feet, and would wade in. He would go in and talk to them. He even went down to A&T and talked to them in their own auditorium [library]; he wasn't afraid of anything. And a lot of people here in town were afraid to even go down to that part of the city. I thought that he was terrific. I felt that Sapp was right at that time.

I talked with [James] Farmer when he came here and some of the students of the A&T College, because they were the ringleaders at that particular time. I told him [Farmer] that we couldn't do it [integrate] until the laws were changed, that when we could do that, then the S&W would accept it.

One incident really stands out in my mind. We had a man and his wife and little boy, maybe three or four years old, sitting at a round table in the front of the cafeteria. The students that were demonstrating were very rude to these people, and they sat down at their table. I went up and asked them to leave that particular table and go to another table, because they were upsetting the father, mother and the child; the little boy was crying. And I asked them to leave the cafeteria, too, because they were agitating the customers. We had a reporter there from the newspaper standing four or five feet away and seeing all that was going on. The demonstrators said that they were not going to leave, and they were talking ugly, and they were going to sit there, and they banged on the table. But finally we got them to leave after they had done their little episode. The police were usually around, but not at that particular time. What was so interesting to me was that I began to see a little bit about how the newspapers work. When it came out in the paper, it was nothing like what we saw; the paper had soft-pedaled it. It said that they came in very nicely and they weren't rude, and the people who were there were not upset, and I saw that they were telling a lie. I called the paper and talked to them about it, but they wouldn't do anything about it.

The demonstrators would usually come at lunch time and at the evening meal. We stood in front of the door, but we wouldn't lock the door because the fire laws would not allow us to lock it. We had another door that you could push open; it was sort of a fire door, a swinging door; it wasn't a real thoroughfare, but a lot of people went through there.

The newspaper would usually let us know beforehand that the demonstrators were coming, sometimes not; but we were ready all of the time. The police arrested the demonstrators on their own initiative. If they came in, then we had to swear out a warrant for trespassing. They got in several times, but it was pretty well controlled. The police did an excellent job of keeping things under control. [Captain] Jackson was terrific. I think even the colored folks respected him very much, and we did, too. He would talk to both sides and keep things calm. And when things looked like they were going to blow up, he would walk out into the middle of it, and he would settle it and talk to them. I just can't say enough about the way that Captain Jackson handled that thing. He was a remarkable man to go out there in the situation like it was. I talked to him a lot. He would just say, "Well, Sonny, we are just doing the best that we can." He was friendly with me, but he was also friendly with the demonstrators. I think that he was very friendly about the whole thing. He conveyed that, and I think that he was. He was just unbelievable. And the police department of this city they worked night and day, in both sections, the colored and the white. They did a beautiful job.

It got to be a steady thing. They came at lunchtime, in the afternoon, and every night. It went on and on and on. I spoke to Jesse Jackson several times. As a matter of fact, when I spoke to [James] Farmer, Jesse Jackson came up and I talked to both of them. They asked for us to feed the colored folks, and I told them our policy, and that was the only thing that we needed to do. It was right at the door, and we talked back and forth. They had a crowd up there with them; it lasted maybe five or ten minutes, then they walked on.

They were very orderly; I never felt threatened, but I felt like they might come behind the S&W and tear up some cars. We put lights up to shine down on the parking lot in the back of the cafeteria, but nothing ever happened. As far as I know, we never had any acts of violence, but it was constantly on our minds. We were really concerned about our customers; we were at the door so they couldn't come in and give us trouble. We had the front doors open, but we were guarding the door and letting people in and out. A lot of times I'd would go out there and they were yelling at me and that kind of thing. I'd get off at 2:00 in the afternoon, but when I heard that something was going to happen, I'd go down to the cafeteria to be with Mr. Bentz. As far as I know, the whole thing was very orderly, except for when they came into the cafeteria that first time, banging on the tables. But a lot of times, there would be reporters there and when you read it in the newspapers, it wouldn't be what it was like at all.

The white hecklers were country boys that would come to town. We were afraid that violence might erupt in the confrontation between them and the demonstrators. They were yelling at one another across the street, and that was sort of scary. To my knowledge, they did not come in contact with each other, but there was a lot of verbal stuff going on. There were spectators all around, but wherever they [demonstrators] were marching in long files, the spectators certainly were not in that group [of hecklers]. They'd be on the streets, watching. We didn't have any trouble with the Klan as far as I know. But people would call up and give their opinion; some were anonymous and some were not.

It was something that you didn't know exactly what was going to happen next; we didn't know if we were going to feed them, if we weren't going to feed them. When we were going through all of this, we felt that we weren't going to feed them. Tension was everywhere. I would go to a party and people would talk about it and ask me questions, and it was very much on the minds of everybody at that time. I never said anything about my personal feelings. I just didn't feel that it was right not to feed them, but if I had come out and said that, then, my goodness, that would have been something else.

The managers or owners of the other targeted businesses would come by the cafeteria and we would talk. Sapp may have talked to all of those men, because he was working on that almost full time. He would tell us what he thought and what he was going to do about it. He didn't tell us everything, I'm sure, but he kept us right on the line. He'd be in contact with my father. Sapp felt that his telephone was tapped, but I never felt that I was under observation by the government. I think that the FBI was talking to him, too. I don't think that they would tell him anything, but if he asked the question, they would answer the question, and they would let him know what was going on, but only if he would ask the question.

The demonstrations were all outside. We wouldn't let any colored folks in; we'd try to let our [white] patrons in, and business went on as usual. It was kind of surprising, all this activity going on outside and people coming in and eating as usual. We all lost a lot of money, but we still had large crowds.

*Police Chief Paul Calhoun appointed Detective William H. Jackson to control the situation. Calhoun had confidence in Jackson, because he had handled the sit-ins in 1960 and the demonstrations in the fall of 1962 with intelligent restraint. Given full authority to make decisions about crowd control, Jackson selected a squad of trusted officers as an elite force to direct the other policemen assigned to the downtown area. Jackson's low-key, even-handed determination to maintain the peace and enforce the law earned him the respect of both the white and black communities.*

## William Jackson

The demonstrations were anticipated to a degree, but we did not think there would be as many involved as there were. We began to get intelligence to the fact that they were planning this, but not in any great numbers. Officers in their basic training were taught how to handle crowds, but nothing specific for this particular thing.

At the time, I was in charge of the detective division. I had contact with a number of the individuals that were involved in these things, and, I think, my ability to deal with individuals helped keep the situation under control. The first demonstration that I monitored involved a group in front of the S&W Cafeteria that was holding a prayer service [November 29, 1962] and at that time, there was a permit required for that type of thing, and they sent me up there to take care of that. I was able to handle it without any incidents and arrests being made, and from then on out, I took it over.

My instructions were to see that the laws were not violated, to keep peace as much as we possibly could. The city authorities—the City Council, the Chief of Police [Paul Calhoun]—never once dictated to me in what manner we should handle these things. We were committed to enforce the law, and handle it as best as we knew how, under the existing circumstances, and this is the way that it was carried out. I chose the officers of my special squad because of their ability to follow instructions and their ability to handle people. I always like to surround myself with people that I did not have to worry about, and that's why they were selected. My instructions to them were to handle all things with as much diplomacy as possible, to not use any force unless it was necessary, and to discuss it and see what we could work out with them. At times, there were as many as one hundred officers assigned, but normally, thirty-five or forty; my own special squad consisted of sixteen men that I had personally selected to work closely with me. The majority of the officers came from my division; people that I had worked with and I knew what to expect from them. You couldn't have asked for them to have been any better. Those people were gentlemen; they were officers, they did their job, and I had no criticism whatsoever of them.

The majority of the routine of the demonstration was normal, everyday behavior, but I feel certain that some of my officers had to control themselves to some extent, because lots of them did take abuse that they normally wouldn't have. I don't think that an officer is put out there to be abused. I think that some of these officers actually restrained themselves under the circumstances, to try to handle this in a manner that would be acceptable by all and not leave a black eye for the city.

In 1963, the first night that we made arrests, they [demonstrators] flopped down and had to be dragged or toted. About three o'clock in the morning of the first night [May 15], I had a meeting with Ezell Blair, Sr., and two others in my office, and they brought up the fact that we had mistreated some of the people that we had arrested, because we had dragged them. I told Mr. Blair and the others at that time, when those people deliberately fell to the ground when they were arrested, they were mistreating the officers, too, and if they didn't want to be dragged when they were placed under arrest, to walk with the officers and they would not be mistreated. After that, we had no trouble with that type of thing. We got it across to the Blair group and they got it to the people in the demonstrations, and as a result, it was very smooth from there on out.

There were white spectators on the side heckling, but they, too, respected the police department. There was a group of them in the Ku Klux Klan, and some of the people were actually national officers in the Klan, but as far as the main hecklers, very few white people participated in it. And this is another reason that we were able to handle it in as quiet a manner as we did, because the people of the city of Greensboro didn't come down, and they didn't show up, and they didn't antagonize those people.

You would have people along Elm Street and Greene Street, and you take five hundred people and you spread them out over six or seven blocks, they are not going to be too many large crowds in one area. At no time did the demonstrators have any trouble in marching up and down the sidewalk; so therefore, you couldn't say that there were people there that were interfering with them. Normally, the people that were there observing it were standing across the street. There might have been four or five hundred uptown on occasions, but they were very few, and they didn't bother the demonstrators. We had a group of sixteen officers that circulated among the spectators and marched along the line with the demonstrators, being as inconspicuous as they could, and if we saw someone there that was giving trouble, we let them know that we didn't want it, and as a result they got gone.

Normally, prior to each demonstration, we knew what to expect. I had met with some of the CORE members. Other information came in through other people. We got together and usually knew what they planned to do, and we would discuss it before we went out. We had a room ready at the Fire Training Center, where we let the officers know what to expect. It was through a combination of intelligence gathering, and talking with the demonstrators..

The press was not bad at all; most of them were pretty cooperative. A group of reporters came from out of town. They were told that I was in charge of it. I would get together with these people, and give them what I had, and I'd tell the newcomers to town what they could expect of us, and what I expected of their conduct. For instance, in front of the Center Theater one night, we had to make several arrests there, and some of those people came in there and put these floodlights in my eyes and in my men's eyes, and I called their hand on it right quick, and that happened no more. This should not be done by a newsperson. I like for them to get their pictures, but don't interfere with the operation of that officer. We had a good understanding. The news people got along pretty good, I'd say they did.

## Furman Melton

I was a Detective in 1963, but I was reassigned back into patrol to work the demonstrations. At that particular time, I was an investigator in the vice squad. Sixteen police officers were assigned to Captain William H. Jackson, who was in charge of all the demonstrations and marching activities.

We were assigned to this special unit, and we followed all of the marches and demonstrations that occurred in the city. Wherever they may be, we were sent to that location and we worked these demonstrations, sit-ins, marches, or whatever, until they ended. I think a part of the decision in our selection was our size; all sixteen of us were over six feet tall. The main purpose was that this particular unit was unassigned in any other area. In other words, for three months we were assigned to that specific detail, and we didn't have any other assignment.

The demonstrators first got a permit to march, so we knew when they were going to march, the streets they were going to cover, and if they were going to have any speeches and gatherings at any location. The leaders of CORE coordinated with us. They were very cooperative as far as their organized marches and demonstrations were concerned. This was in an attempt to allow the marches and demonstrations in an orderly manner.

We had some unorganized groups that were trying to hassle the CORE. We were thrown in the middle, because they heckled us and harassed us along with the demonstrators and the marchers. They would cut the police officers down, and the demonstrators down. Most of the time there were more blacks downtown than there were whites, because the blacks were organized and they had more numbers than the whites. The whites weren't that organized and I think a lot of them didn't know whenever these things were going to happen. They didn't have time to organize, because the marches would be at night. The police kept the area that the marchers were in cordoned off, to prevent the two groups from clashing. It was a little more difficult when they were marching, because, occasionally, you would get vehicles that would pass and be throwing things, and harassing and heckling the demonstrators. But in the uptown area, there were enough uniformed and reserved officers that we could seal off the area, or march along with them. There would be an officer about every ten or fifteen feet, so that if there was something that happened in any specific area, there were enough officers within sight of each other that they could close off anything that was going to happen.

There were not too many incidents of violence. One night at the Carolina Theater, a group of hecklers were throwing things and shouting, but whenever the officers approached them, they ran. There was a group of whites that chased a group of blacks down East Washington Street, but we headed them off down at the train depot and moved them back downtown. We were just trying to protect both groups from each other. If they had gotten together, I'm sure there would have been some people hurt.

The KKK was involved, but they weren't organized to any degree, and the people that were siding with the KKK weren't that aggressive or organized. They would mostly just holler out obscenities; they would never show any degree of violence. There were a lot of sympathizers with the KKK, but they *only* sympathized. They may have shouted and carried on for a while, but there never was a force movement from them, not when the demonstrators were having their marches.

Our instructions were to march along with the demonstrators, just to keep a surveillance of all the marchers and the hecklers, and never speak to either group unless spoken to directly. As long as the demonstrators were in the formation that they were supposed to be in and the route they were supposed to take, then we did not force any issue either way. We were instructed to take the verbal abuse and only defend ourselves if we were attacked personally.

There were a few incidents where we were subject to a lot of harassment and a lot of abusive language. We were a nose-to-nose confrontation with the demonstrators. We had blocked off the entrance of the S&W and the demonstrators wanted to go inside. We were instructed to keep the demonstrators out. Any time we faced a confrontation of that nature, then we got a lot of verbal abuse. Sometimes pushing and shoving occurred, but I think that six hundred people crowded into an area, through sheer physical force, there's going to be some pushing and shoving. But I think, for the most part, it wasn't intentional on their part.

The demonstrators would line up in large numbers, which would block anyone else from getting in. People that really wanted to get in would walk past them, but most of the people that were trying to go to the cafeteria or the theater just backed away. The smaller group of demonstrators would circle and try to enter to try to purchase a ticket, and they would be refused. The manager would ask them to leave the premises and, if they didn't leave, the officers would instruct them that they would be charged with trespassing.

Most of the time there was no resistance. There were a few instances where there was resistance, but I think that was *not* the design of the CORE. It was a situation where an individual would be placed under arrest, and he would try to resist because of his own individual feelings. The students of the CORE *never* resisted. The only thing that they came out with was verbal abuse. There were some of the people living in the community that were not members of the CORE, but joined for the cause; *these* were the people that usually caused the resistance.

Captain Jackson did an outstanding job communicating with the leaders. There were a lot of times when there were confrontations and things were discussed between Captain Jackson and the leaders of the demonstrations, and the store managers, theater managers and, sometimes, the press and the TV personnel. I felt he had control of the situation every time we had a march or a confrontation. In the normal routine of things, he could create a lot of steam, but under these conditions, the man was under control and had more patience and control then [than] I'd ever observed from him before that. He briefed us daily on every situation, and we understood exactly what we were to do. By his actions, he reflected this idea back to us, and we followed suit. We were as cool as he was about it. If he had gotten out of control, there's no doubt in my mind that the officers probably would have gotten out of control.

The police department here handled our situation better than anything I'd seen on TV or read in the paper. I think that our officers were determined, if possible, to keep the sort of thing that occurred in Birmingham from happening. We *didn't* want to have to use fire hoses; we *didn't* want violence, we *didn't* want to have to use any force at all. We certainly didn't want to injure anyone.

We were under a lot of stress and strain. We didn't like the situation; we didn't like the idea that these marches and demonstrations were forced on us and on the people of Greensboro. We felt like they were in violation of the law, and that integration should be handled through the courts. We strongly resented the fact that they were allowed to deliberately violate the law. But, even though we felt this way, we still upheld our position as being a police officer. We were asked to go along with the program. If there was an arrest that was necessary, we'd make the arrest as quietly and quickly as possible without any back talk, or any verbal disputes with the persons that were being arrested. We took pride in the fact that we were not going to do anything that would create more problems, and I think we carried it off real well.

We never had much training in crowd control. We knew the basic fundamentals in using the nightstick.. I feel that we were chosen for our high tolerance, for not losing our temper and could operate coolly and calmly, without doing anything that would create a problem for the department, or a particular officer.

We started out arresting them and taking them out to the regular jail on the fourth floor at City Hall. All of the male and female prisoners were transported to the county jail. But after the numbers got so large, they set up a temporary restraining place at the Greensboro War Memorial Coliseum. We transported them by city buses and any kind of vehicle that we could get. All of the demonstrators were booked and processed out there. There was a certain number of officers that were sent with each bus, and they had officers set up to there that would bring the groups in from the bus. There were no incidents out there; they were real quiet. Most of the time, they would be singing those freedom songs that they sang all during the marches. Any time that we arrested them in a group, they'd start singing those freedom songs.

They tore up some of the seats on the buses. I don't think they were frisked well when they first started putting them on the buses. A lot of damage could have been done without any kind of a weapon, but there were some seats cut and they were ripped up and torn.

The hours that I worked would depend on the marches and demonstrations. If they lasted sixteen hours, then we worked sixteen hours; if they lasted four hours, we worked four hours. There were sixteen officers in my group, and we set up headquarters at the Fire Training Center. When we weren't marching with the demonstrators, we were out there. We had to remain there and be available on the spur of the moment, along with a lot of other officers.

Sometimes we made arrests at the cafeteria or the theater, where there weren't that many people involved, and there wasn't that many officers, then we booked and processed them, and signed the warrant ourselves.If it was an individual situation, then there would be just a few arrested, and we as individual officers, would book the ones that we arrested and process them. The booking officers always made out the arrest sheets, the paperwork, and took the pictures of the prisoners as they came in. Because of the large number arrested, quite a few officers had to assume those responsibilities. When there were large groups, the officers would just assist in getting those prisoners to those locations, and regular booking officers were assigned to process them. When you have five hundred to nine hundred people to book, you can only do it in so much time. On occasion, the booking officers were up all night.

The normal procedure for a demonstration was that there would be a group of twenty to forty people; I think they would assign certain numbers to go to certain locations. When they would get there, they would start their demonstrations, and they would try to enter the cafeteria or the theater. Each one, individually, would attempt to go in, and the manager was there to refuse them entrance or refuse to sell them a ticket. They would get on the premises of the property, and after all of these attempts had been made to gain entrance and refused, they would move into the property, and the manager would ask them to leave. The officer in charge would say, "If you don't leave, then you are subject to arrest for trespassing, and if they didn't leave, they were arrested.

All of the officers that could be assigned to the area were assigned. There were a certain number of officers that would carry on the regular duties. I don't mean to imply that there were sixteen officers that took care of everything; there's no way that they could handle it. There were many officers and reserve officers, and in some instances, State Highway Patrolmen, FBI agents and State Bureau of Investigation agents present at all of the locations. The FBI and the SBI were assigned for observation and surveillance. A lot of information was gained by their contacts that supplied them with information on what the demonstrators' plans were, what they would do, along with some of the officers that had that assignment.

Captain Jackson and our group of sixteen were in charge of going to wherever the problem areas were. On one occasion, the S&W Cafeteria was the target for a particular evening. We knew this from the CORE and our own sources of information, so we would be there at that location. One night it was the Carolina Theater; one night it was the Center Theater. Sometimes the demonstrators would just move from one location to another, and you never knew exactly which one they would try to approach. It was a kind of continuous thing. We followed the ones that were more subject to violate the law.

Acting with restraint was stressed more than anything else in the briefings. We went over a lot of the riot control exercises at the Fire Training Center while we were waiting for things to happen, because we *didn't* want anything to happen. The police officers that were assigned squads and the squad leaders were instructed on what to do in case they had to move a group of people out of one block into another block. All of these things were practiced and gone over daily. The whole police department went through quite an extensive training program because they have to know what the other officers were going to do in a particular situation.

There were certain officers assigned to certain locations just for observation purposes, because they would just have small groups that would try to go to restaurants and theaters. All of these instances were handled by a smaller group of police officers. It was only whenever the demonstrators formed together in large numbers that all of the officers were involved. But that took up a lot of their time being assigned to all of these different areas. We had those kinds of assignments, then we'd fall back on other assignments.

The demonstrations ran from May to July. It was the first part of August when I was reassigned back to my regular duties. All of the officers resented having to work long hours, subject to call-back on a minute's notice. I'm sure all of the police officers' families were really upset and under a lot of stress and strain at that particular time. I know my family was. They were disturbed because I had to work those long hours, and we couldn't do anything together during that period of time. After it was all over, and we were allowed to take vacation, I took my family to the coast and relaxed and took it easy for a week.

*As arrests depleted the numbers available for demonstrations, William Thomas and Tony Stanley came up with an idea that revitalized the Movement. They asked Jesse Jackson to join the demonstrations. Handsome, popular and charismatic, he was the quarterback of the A&T football team and president-elect of the Student Government. At first reluctant to participate, Jackson was persuaded to lead the nightly marches, but he was never a member of the Executive Committee. Although compliant with the directions of the Committee, he proved to be a "loose cannon" capable of impromptu decisions that were counter to CORE plans and unpredictable in his statements to the press.*

## William Thomas

It was my decision to get Jesse Jackson involved in the demonstrations, based on his popularity at school. He was an athlete, and at that time we had very few athletes involved. He was also involved in student government. It proved to be a very good move. At first, Jesse's main contribution was who Jesse was. In terms of actually sitting down and taking care of the details in planning, Jesse was not initially involved. Later on he did become quite actively involved. We never had a problem cooperating with each other. I believe in utilizing the talents of people around me. And even at a very early age, Jesse demonstrated a great deal of what I would call charisma. He was an excellent public speaker. He could create the type of emotionalism that was needed. And I am not that type of person; I never wanted to be a preacher or a professional civil righter. I was responding to a cause. I looked at myself as more of a tactician, as a detail person, someone that can get a job done.

## A. Knighton Stanley

Jesse Jackson was a reluctant participant. He was the president of the student body, a very popular young man. He was reluctant to participate, because he was somewhat enamored by the administration, but it had more to do with it than that. He wanted to see who was going to win this thing; he didn't want to be on the losing side. That is my assessment of it. Plus, the leadership was pretty much intact; how do you break into something and become a leader if the leadership is intact? I believe that I converted him.

We talked in terms of needing a fresh face. We needed a person who was articulate, we needed A&T College students, and we were counting on the women. You see, the ranks were shrinking because the Bennett College students had just about gone down the tube by then, because all of them had been arrested. Jesse being an articulate, handsome guy could bring out additional troops. Jesse came on board. He did not participate in strategy sessions and decisions; that was the responsibility of the Executive Committee. He was dynamic, which means that he could be unpredictable, but he didn't necessarily go off on his own. What became apparent was that he was a fresh face. Jesse was a media person from day one. When he led demonstrations; he always managed to get his picture taken, and I don't think that it was deliberate on his part; he's just a media person. His statements were spontaneous, and some of the best statements in the whole Movement during that time, including Martin Luther King, were made by Jesse Jackson. He was fantastic.

## Jibreel Khazan

Jesse had been preparing himself for getting involved for three years, but the thing that kept holding him back was that he knew that the four of us were on A&T's campus, and during that time, it did not seem feasible for him to become involved in the Civil Rights Movement, because we had asked him personally around March, 1963, if he would help, and at that time he turned it down, because we were "wasting our time"—those were his exact words. I said, "Well, Jesse, I know that you are preparing yourself for something," because he would be up late at night studying all of Dr. King's speeches, and other people at this time who came to the campus, like Robert Weaver, and every time a national speaker would come to the campus, he would ask for a copy of the speech, and he would memorize it. And he would be practicing on his tape recorder at night with King's speeches.

So this is why I approached him, because I knew that he was a very influential person and that he could do a lot to help the Movement, because we were graduating in the spring, and we would need someone who had a very strong personality to continue, and we knew that he had the ability, but he would not help at the time. It could have been also that at this time he was preparing to marry his wife, Jackie, and he had a lot of pressure on him. I don't know all of the ramifications, but I can tell you what he told me when he became active in the Movement. Still, there were a lot of students at Bennett and A&T who couldn't understand how he became involved in the leadership of the Movement, because he was not active in CORE or the NAACP, and the Bennett women who were active leaders did not like the idea of him coming in and taking over a leadership position. There was some discussion about that by the women of Bennett College and some members of the CORE group, because Jesse had never been in on any planning sessions.

Jesse came out of nowhere in the spring of 1963 when daily speeches were being made at the Providence Baptist Church at the time, which was on Market Street. One day he came up while the students of Bennett and CORE were speaking—I don't know if he was asked to speak—but he was prepared and he made a speech about freedom, and that's what began his involvement in the Movement in Greensboro.

## Alvin Thomas

Jesse did very little of sitting in on strategy sessions and meetings of substance. The Executive Committee would inform him of what he was to do. He was kind of a maverick. On occasion, we were not sure that he would do what we told him to do, but he never really pulled a surprise on us. I knew Jesse quite well. He was captain of the football team and also involved in campus politics. He had just been elected President of the student body for the 1963-1964 academic year. He stayed quite busy. He had very little to do with CORE before the massive demonstrations of the spring of 1963.

## William Jackson

Several CORE members met with me, William Thomas, Jesse Jackson and others. I'd contact them and ask them what we could expect, and what did they want in the march. They'd tell me what they planned to do, and I'd say, "This is all right, but this is a violation of the law, and if you do this, I'm going to have to arrest you. I'd rather not do it; let's don't do this." And they would tell me, "Well, we're going to do that," and I said "If you do, then we will have to arrest you." We had an understanding with each other. There was never any animosity between myself and my men and the demonstrators. We realized that they were doing something for themselves, so we had no objections to this, as long as they did it in a lawful manner.

National leaders were in here on several occasions. I talked with James Farmer many times. One meeting was in William Thomas' mother's home. I worked with him, talked with him; I met with them anywhere they wanted to meet. At the campus of A&T they had a meeting down there one night, and they called me that afternoon and asked me if I would come, and I said "I certainly will." Some of the city officials didn't want me to go; they thought that it was dangerous for me to go by myself, but it didn't make any difference. I parked my car and got out and walked into the Student Union Building. They wanted to know what they could do that wouldn't violate the law. At this particular meeting, they wanted to know what they could do to bring this thing down to where our community would become peaceful again.

William Thomas, his brother Alvin, and his sister, Antoinette, were three people that were leaders. William Thomas had sense and wasn't rattle-headed. His brother, sister, and their mother were the same way. I never met their father. That family was all right. And Jesse Jackson wasn't rattle-headed. It was my opinion that he was being prepped for his leadership into this thing [the Civil Rights Movement], and being directed by some of the members of the faculty of A&T; I don't think that it was all on his own initiative. Don't misunderstand me; he had a lot on the ball, too, but I think he had advisers. I never discussed my personal feelings. Back then when we met, it was purely on a business manner. I was a representative of the city, and they were representatives of their organizations that were trying to achieve something.

We had very little interference with the outside world. The whites were more against the white participants in the demonstrations than they were against the black ones. There was a group over in High Point, the Quaker organization [American Friends Service Committee], and there was one young man from over there [Richard Ramsey], and there were several white people involved in it, one that actually proved to be a Communist. They were given a harder time by the white hecklers than the blacks were, the taunts that were directed at them.

We had quite an active Klan in Greensboro. George Dorsett, C. J. Webster, Frey, and several big people in the Klan. Some of them held national offices in the Klan, and they were demonstrating on the side, but they knew that if they started something in Greensboro, they'd be arrested. I did arrest some of them, and we treated them just exactly as we did anybody else. They would never tell you that they were part of an organization, but they were organized. Part of the job of that special squad was to keep them under surveillance.

We did not want our city to become known as a place of hell as far as these people were concerned. We wanted to handle it in a way such that we would say that we had done it in a rightful manner, and we did this and kept up with these people as much as possible, to know what was going on so that we could handle them. Some of the national news media came here—CBS, ABC television crews—and I never will forget that we put one of them in jail one night. It started at the Carolina Theater, and the City of Greensboro had an ordinance that gave a police officer authority to establish a police line. This police line can be an imaginary line or it can be a physical line. We were having a little bit of noise at the Carolina Theater, and some officer left his radio up high and over the radio it was announced that there was some trouble at the Washington and Davie Street intersection two blocks away. It turned out that it was not even related to the demonstrations, but everybody made a break to get down there and we saw what was happening. The way that you get in trouble is by letting your people get out of control. So I established a police line and said, "Nobody cross this line." We drew out a rope and stretched it out across Washington Street, and one of those newsmen had to get over there, and I told him, "You can't go." He went under that line, and when he did, I grabbed him by the seat of his britches and gave him to one of my people and said, "Lock him up," and he did. The next morning he went into court and pled guilty and got fined and came back out. He paid the City of Greensboro and the police department a compliment. He said, "You people are the toughest I have ever encountered, yet the fairest." That's the way that we tried to operate.

We as a city would not permit a Birmingham situation. We kept a lid on it; we knew what was going to happen, we knew about gangs of people that were hecklers, we knew what to expect of them. If something came up, we put people in jail, if they needed to go to jail, whether they were black or white. We would not nitpick with the law. If it was a flagrant violation, we would arrest them. If we could get around it on either side by warning them, "Let's don't do this, let's stay away from this," and if they did, then that was all there was to it. But if they insisted, then we made the arrest.

Normally, they would march from the campus, up East Market Street, and as they crossed what is now Church Street, we would try to count them. If we didn't have any idea of how many they had prior to this, we'd take a head count to see how many they had and try to know how to handle it. We might have six or seven hundred, or it might be under fifty. They came up the south side of East Market Street by the S&W Cafeteria, then turn at Belk's, come back and occasionally go down to the Mayfair Cafeteria, or down to the O. Henry Hotel. Normally, it was around the Square, Market Street, the theaters, down to Greene Street, and down to the Carolina Theater.

I usually picked up the leaders about Davie Street and Greene and Market Street, and I would be right in front with the leaders. We would have a conversation during the march, find out if anything had changed or had happened. Sometime I would pick them up at Forbis Street; it would depend on how many they would have. Later on, they began to get a little more secretive about what they were doing, and the information began to get a little more tight, but not a great deal.

The information began to get a little thin, and the tensions were beginning to grow a little bit, but that is where our meetings each evening and afternoon helped. We had cots set up at the Fire Training Center, and all the rest that we got was right there. It wasn't anything unusual for me to spend the night there, two or three nights at the time. The city brought a bunch of army folding cots to be set up there where the men could get some rest, and we fed the men out there. You take a man from his home and his people and dealing with other people that are doing something, of that sort, it could get to be a personal situation, and tension did begin to mount, but not a great deal. I want to pat our men on the back for their restraint. They were able to control themselves. They exercised brilliant restraint.

I would say between ten and eighteen hours a day were divided up between demonstrations and planning sessions. I tried to run my other division business, too. I had conference with the professors from A&T College, conferences with the ministers, lawyers and students and I always made myself available, if they wanted to talk. I think that this is how we were able to best handle it, by making ourselves available to these people. They'd ask if I'd go to their homes and talk with them. Sure, I'd go, if they wanted to go to the church, I'd go; if they wanted to go to the school, I'd go.

## William Thomas

There were no alternative strategies that we considered, other than what we employed. In terms of action, things went pretty much according to plan. The basic form of action was through demonstrations and boycotting; those were the two main types of direct action that were involved. Very little litigation went on at that time, other than defending those people that were arrested. And we were eventually able to get all of those cases thrown out. Basically, there was nothing that was planned that really did not go off.

The tactics were adopted according to what we thought were most appropriate for the particular circumstance. For example, in attempting to feel the pulse of the city, at times we may have felt that a silent demonstration would be more effective than singing or a more vocal demonstration. It may have depended upon the type of people that we had participating. It may have depended upon the type of negotiations that were going on at the time. Any number of factors would go into making a decision as to what was needed. It may depend upon the type of emotionalism or the climate that we were attempting to create; it did not just happen. These types of factors considered and analyzed before it was decided upon exactly what would occur.

To a certain extent, the tactics were based on classes that CORE held in Greensboro and Durham, particularly during the Freedom Highways campaign. But to a certain extent, they were not. We were taught how to respond to different situations, but we were able to adapt to our own particular local situations. I think we were quite fortunate that we were some of the forerunners in that entire thing. So in that sense, you might say that we helped other communities that were looking at us to learn from the experiences that we had in Greensboro.

I believe other contemporary events—the desegregation of the University of Mississippi by James Meredith in 1962 and the Birmingham demonstrations in 1963—had an influence on us. And through media and other forms of communication, I'm sure that all of those things had something to do in creating a climate where what happened in Greensboro could occur.

We had no difficulty in maintaining a nonviolent stance, even though we were dealing with literally thousands of people, and no trouble controlling the adult members of the black community, as well as the students. I think what was happening was really the way that the police in Greensboro responded. The confrontations that occurred in the South, in most instances, I think you would find that the police probably provoked eighty-five percent of the violent confrontations. This could have happened in Greensboro if the police had used excessive force or attempted to actually have physically broken up those demonstrations the way they did in other areas. But this didn't occur, so we really had no reason to become violent. I would say probably two-thirds of the people did not believe in nonviolence as a theory, as a way of life. But they were disciplined enough to use it as a tactic. But if the police or the citizenry of Greensboro had reacted violently, we would have had pure hell on our hands. I don't think we could have controlled the people. I don't think that we would have stood by and permitted to happen to us what happened to people in other areas of the South. I had little contact with Sheriff Jones and Police Chief Calhoun. Captain Jackson was a field person. I'm sure that the police chief had some influence in giving direction and understanding bureaucracy. But Captain Jackson was the person that I dealt with.

Frequently there were mass meetings at one of the churches beforehand. The marchers came up from East Market Street with parade marshals along to inform people of where they were going. Upon reaching the downtown area, they went to their separate assigned targets for that evening. The meetings before and after demonstrations offered a place where people could gather. We had to have some central place where instructions could be given as to exactly what tactics would be used that particular evening, where we were going, and so forth. The mass meetings afterwards were emotional. It was religious and also strategy. And it afforded us an opportunity to assess where we were and what we had to do, and to make plans for the next day. So each day our activities were, in fact, planned, and with some degree of flexibility to be able to adjust again to the situation once we arrived at our target area. Most of the churches in the black community were used: Church of the Redeemer, Providence Baptist Church, Trinity AME Zion were all used quite a bit. But Providence was centrally located, in that it was in the direct path of going to the downtown area. For the initial meetings that church was used most often for meetings.

Most of the white people on the sidewalks were there just as observers. We didn't have many hecklers. No rock throwing, no eggs. There were a few remarks made, but I think we were fortunate that most white citizens just stayed home. I didn't witness any violence or police excesses.

I had an argument that went through the press, with Armistad Sapp, who was the attorney for the S&W and other segregated businesses that we had targeted. In effect, I said that "Greensboro could be another Birmingham." He interpreted that as a threat. I responded that that was false, that what I said was that members of the community, white and black, would have to work together to prevent another Birmingham. I recall Mr. Sapp as being a reactionary-type of individual. I made the statement because, if we had not had the conciliatory-type of attitude by the powers-that-be, the police, the students and the black community, we very well could have had an explosive situation.

I communicated with Sapp and other representatives of the targeted businesses only through committee meetings. Not too many individual discussions, but through the committee meetings, in terms of trying to negotiate, to actually bring about the desegregation of those facilities. Mr. Sapp also alleged that the Justice Department had first asked for the names of people who had chain businesses in the South, including Greensboro. And that they sent two people from the Justice Department or the Internal Revenue Service, and that they were in the O. Henry Hotel, and that once their cover was exposed, they left. I doubt very seriously that it happened. Why would they come under cover? They wouldn't have to come to Greensboro to get that kind of information. I'm sure they had dossiers on whatever and whoever they wanted. So I think Mr. Sapp was dealing in scare tactics, attempting to show the citizenry of Greensboro that even the federal government was against them. He was reacting more like a Bull Connor than someone from Greensboro.

## Boyd Morris

There were two or three times when Jesse Jackson and Ralph Abernathy [sic] were leading the marches. They went from the O. Henry Hotel to Kress and Market Street from the King Cotton Hotel to the county courthouse. They were reputedly two thousand of them. I was warned by a reliable source that they were coming that time, so I stood at the door. I was told that they were going to throw acid on me, and the caller suggested that I wear the largest glasses that I could find, which I did on two nights.

One confrontation was with Jesse [Jackson]. He put his nose against mine and said, "I'm coming in." And I said, "You're not." And he says "I'm coming in." And I said, "Over my dead body you're coming in." He said, "Why don't you let me come in?" I replied, "Jesse, I'm not going to serve demonstrators." He said, "Well, I love you." And I said, "Jesse, I love you, but you're not coming in." [Laughs] I look back, and it seems childish and funny now, but it certainly was not then. The police thought that there was going to be a confrontation because he put his nose against my nose, breathing in my face, and I felt that he was trying to intimidate me, but I was never really afraid. There I was, nose to nose with Jesse, wondering, "Why is this happening to me?"

## William Thomas

The newspapers sometimes characterized the arrests as having almost a comic effect. For instance, not taking away from the seriousness of the situation, but there was one episode where Captain Jackson asked if the students would be willing to walk the block-and-a-half to the police station. They said, "No, we'd rather ride." And so the buses and police vehicles were called up. At another time, the students waited in an orderly manner at the curbside until the buses came. They climbed on very willingly and then sang as they drove off.

A newspaper editorial characterized the demonstrations as having almost the formality of a Japanese dance. The newspaper accounts tended to portray the demonstrations as if they were a student prank. I think it showed the lack of sensitivity on the part of the reporters. What was actually occurring there was that people were serious. Sure, they were angry, but they understood what was happening. And if people had been going around so uptight the way they were in other parts of the country, you would have had a violent situation. I think what was going on was an emotional outlet on the part of the people that were involved. The singing and smiles did not necessarily indicate joy but, rather, an emotional outlet. Sometimes it was a funny situation, because the demonstrators were able to look at just how silly that whole thing was, as far as arresting a person for attempting to exercise his or her rights. In many ways the powers-that-be made fools of themselves. And I think that's how many of the people that were demonstrating looked at it. "See, we have been able to force these people to make jackasses out of themselves." Some circumstances were funny, in a way, but it was sad in another way. That was the reaction of many people. But it was not a joyous occasion overall.

## Otis Hairston, Jr.

The demonstrators were schooled in nonviolence. That was one of the main purposes of the meetings that were held at the old Trinity Church. I remember several times when we were marching we were harassed, and several times people were spit on, but there was never any retaliation for it; it was just ignored, as though it never happened. Some of the white hecklers were close. Normally, we always marched on the street and they were on the sidewalk, but there were a few that wanted to get physically involved with the marchers that would get a little close. I remember some demonstrators being struck and also some being spit on. I think that the first time that I marched I was a little scared, but after that I just felt a part of it and there was really no fear involved. I think the police did a good job of protecting us. I guess I just considered them as a part of the system and they were there primarily for our protection. I never got into an altercation with any of the officers or the hecklers. There was nobody in the march that would get into any type of discussion with the hecklers. If there was some type of confrontation with the police, there was a spokesman in the march that would normally calm them down.

I think that every time that I marched, Jesse Jackson led the march, and he was normally the spokesman. I marched pretty much on a daily basis. Most of the pre-march meetings were held at Trinity. And sometimes the march was followed by a meeting. They were mainly inspirational-type meetings, I guess, to keep everybody attuned to what was going on, and to more or less inspire everybody to just what the purpose was. I think most of the meetings that I attended, Jesse Jackson spoke at a majority of them, and he had the same type of rhetoric now that he had then, so it was very easy to get the crowd really going. On some occasions, James Farmer and Floyd McKissick spoke to us. I guess it sort of made me feel proud being black and being able to contribute to what was trying to be done, I just felt like right then and there, I had no idea, I guess, with me being a high school student, not knowing that much about what the purpose was when I first got involved in it. I guess that I was sort of narrow in my thinking. The only accomplishment that I could see was a short-range one, the integration of the theaters and the cafeterias, these types of things. I guess I didn't see anything long-range, as far as what the other activists talked about.

The demonstrations were not the central focus of attention at Dudley High School. I don't think students really got involved initially, as far as their thinking was involved. It was probably a week or two after the marches had really started and arrests were being made before the students saw any real purpose in it, or really got involved in it. I wouldn't say that there was a lot of high school student participation. I think that the black community in general was sort of responsive to it, and was really behind the marches, but I guess the really big difference between the high school students and the A&T students was that the A&T students were here on their own, whereas the high school students had a responsibility to their home and parents, and I guess a lot of parents didn't want their children involved in marching and being arrested. So I would think that is why a lot of high school students didn't get involved in the marches. My father, I would say, was an activist and was very much involved in it, but I think that my mother was just the opposite at first. But once I was arrested, she started marching, too. I don't think they were worried that I would be harmed; they never expressed it to me.

## Marion Jones

When the adults got the message, they began participating in the demonstrations. There was a wave of fear among blacks, having been subservient for a number of years, the feeling of reprisals, a loss of jobs, but it wasn't very long before they put that behind them and took the chance. They were contacted at church meetings, primarily. Sermons were preached and prayers said about justice and equality, and this really had more effect than any formal meetings. The mass adult march on May 23, in which there were from 200 to 500 people, was the first significant adult participation. It came about as a result of people being convinced, being inspired that they could help bring about a change; that it would take all of us to get the heart, the ear, and the eye of the community. I would say that the ministers, primarily, were responsible for bringing that about, and the NAACP and CORE depended on us. They counted on us to use the church facilities to get the message over.

The objectives of the demonstration would be presented at the meeting, and the methods of approaches would be presented, and always the discouragement of resorting to violence, name-calling, rock-throwing, all of this was done repeatedly. We would always map out the places that we would frequent, what time element we were talking about, the approach, and this kind of thing.

There was no serious division in the adult community between those that thought that this was not the right approach and those that supported it. Seldom did you have a negative attitude about the whole thing. There were those who were reluctant to get involved in the very beginning, but that soon phased out and people found themselves involved. The word that there would be a demonstration on a particular night was communicated through the churches. It was usually a prayer meeting on Sunday and people attended church regularly; we would send out flyers and pass them out, telephone calls. We used every form of communication that we could possibly use to alert the people. I would consider the most active leaders of the black community to be Reverend Hairston, Dr. Evans, Dr. Simkins and Dr. Tarpley. They became very active.

*The demonstrations had been going on nightly for a week, but the situation seemed no closer to resolution. CORE was conducting the kind of dynamic movement that it had always sought, with hundreds of troops at its disposal; the police had devised effective measures to handle the massive number of demonstrators in this unprecedented predicament; and city officials and segregated business operators remained intransigent. Conditions were too volatile to remain at such an impasse for long. As each side searched for a stratagem for victory, the unstable circumstances presented the increased risk of explosive violence.*

Men arrested for trespassing on Gillespie Park Golf Course on December 7, 1955. Left to right: Phillip Cooke, Samuel Murray, Elijah Herring, Joseph Sturdivant, George Simkins, Jr., and Leonidas Wolfe.

Josephine Boyd, who was the first African American student to attend Greensboro Senior High School, on September 4, 1957.

The Four freshmen who conducted the first sit-in at F. W. Woolworth store in Greensboro, N.C., on February 1, 1960. From left to right: David Richmond, Franklin McCain, Ezell Blair, Jr., and Joseph McNeil.

A&T and Bennett college students sit-in at F.W. Woolworth store, Greensboro, N.C., Spring 1960

Student sit-in at the Kress store, Spring 1960.

Students picketing the Cinema Theater on Tate Street, showing "Porgy and Bess" in February 1961.

CORE members sit-in at the Hot Shoppes, Greensboro, N.C., Summer 1962. William Thomas is seated third from right.

Captain William Jackson arresting Dr. Elizabeth Laizner in downtown Greensboro, May 1963.

CORE picketing of the Mayfair Cafeteria, May 1963.

Sit-in in Jefferson Square, June 6, 1963. Captain William Jackson and detectives making arrests.

Sit-down on Greene Street, June 5, 1963. The man in the foreground is John Marshall Kilimanjaro.

Captain William Jackson arresting Jesse Jackson, at the Church of the Redeemer, June 6, 1963.

Sit-in on Jefferson Square, June 6, 1963.

Mass arrest in downtown Greensboro, May, 1963

# Chapter 6

## Counterstroke

The demonstrations had been continuing nightly, with ever-increasing intensity. Although the hundreds of arrests placed a burden upon the arraignments, the police and the courts were able to process those arrested in a reasonably efficient manner. Students were arraigned photographed, fingerprinted and released until their court date. Frustrated that the segregated businesses owners and city officials refused to negotiate, CORE had to come up with a new tactic that would shut down the judicial process and force the city to act in good faith. The new tactic was "jail, no bail." It had been employed in other parts of the South, but it had often evoked a violent municipal response. Could it work in Greensboro, but not create the type of repression that all sought to avoid?

There was a risk involved, because it required a commitment that few demonstrators had experienced. Most members of Greensboro CORE were unfamiliar with the dynamics of this radical tactic. Of greatest concern was the reaction of the hundreds of new recruits that flocked to the mass demonstrations. They were enthusiastic, but not all had considered what long-term incarceration would mean to their exam schedules and graduation prospects. Serious felony charges could result from their actions. The tactic assumed that they could post bail whenever they grew weary of confinement, but the demonstrators might be held until trial many weeks later, and conviction could mean months in prison. Even if this drastic situation did not occur, CORE faced the possible humiliation of the students not honoring their commitment, thus reinforcing the resolve of the powers-that-be to refuse to negotiate CORE's demands. Following lengthy debate within the Executive Committee, the activists won over the more reluctant moderates. All knew that it was a calculated risk, but given the current impasse in negotiations, no one saw any other option.

Beginning on the evening of May 19, students refused to accept bail and would not be released on their own recognizance. District Court Judge

*Herman Enochs was surprised, as the process of arraignment ground to a standstill. Police officials were suddenly faced with having to find places to incarcerate those arrested until their court appearance. City jails, county cells and prison farms quickly filled. In desperation, the city received permission from county officials to house students at the Central Carolina Rehabilitation Hospital, an abandoned facility known as the "old polio hospital," the National Guard armory, outlying jails and prison farms. Processing was conducted at the Coliseum, after which students were transported to the designated holding centers.*

*CORE now had the media attention and leverage to put pressure on city officials. But it also had the nightmare logistics of maintaining contact with all those arrested and trying to devise new strategy. Nevertheless, CORE's Executive Committee members were heartened to witness the judicial process come to a halt. An added benefit was the arousal of the adult black community, outraged at the appalling conditions in which the students, many of whom were their children, were being held.*

## Lewis Brandon

I think that the "jail, no bail" decision was a pretty unanimous one. I don't remember any big discussion about that. The people that were arrested were expecting it. As a matter of fact, that was the attitude. I think that it might have started someplace else in the South, and people picked up on it. That tactic started before the mass thing, because I think that was the attitude of those of us that got arrested at the S&W in the fall of 1962, and we refused to leave jail. It's just that the judge decided that he wasn't going to lock us up, but we had already decided that if we were locked up, we were going to refuse bail. I was against being arrested just for the sake of being arrested, because there were a lot of people in other areas that were getting arrested and were getting out, putting notches in their belt for the number of times that they were arrested. Those kind of arrests didn't mean anything. My position was to make your arrest mean something. At the time of the mass arrests, there weren't any high school kids; the bulk of those kids were college kids, Bennett and A&T students. I think that the high school kids came with the sit-ins in the streets, as opposed to being arrested on the picket lines.

The meeting with Mayor Pro Tem Trotter took place after the first mass arrest on May 15, when the police first treated the people as criminals. They blocked off the downtown area and treated the students as criminals. That was when Trotter agreed to create the committee that became the Human Relations Committee. We met with him because Mayor Schenck was out of town. They blocked off the whole downtown, brought buses in. Some people that were viewing that came back and said, "We're not going to stand for this."

## Robert "Pat" Patterson

And so it came a time when we had to make the decision that we were going to go to jail and that Greensboro and Guilford County didn't have enough jails to house all of us. I think that was a tremendous turning point, because then I think that the power structure found out that these kids were not afraid to go to jail,. We had so many people they had to put us in the old rest home down on Huffine Mill Road. Some were out at the armory lying on the cement floor and this kind of thing. So that proved to be a very significant tactic in order to get some people to begin

By Friday morning we said, "We'll fill every jail in Greensboro, if it takes that to obtain the goals that we want." I think that it was more like a chain of events than anything else. We just decided that this was something that we had to do. Nobody gave any thought that the semester was just about over. It probably wasn't good timing, but the community seemed to be at the point where they would support the mass effort that we thought necessary in order to get some things done. There had been some criticism from the black community in terms of the way that we were going about doing things. We had some people in the adult community that were marching at that time, so we felt that we had the general support of the community. Consequently, we felt that if we were going to meet with any group results, now was the time to do it, while we had that good support. Therefore, we held a number of meetings at Trinity AME Zion Church, Hayes-Taylor Y and the Providence Baptist Church to encourage this tentatively favorable attitude in the community.

## A. Knighton Stanley

What prevented violence in the Greensboro Movement was the deliberate effort to avoid it on the part of both the police and the demonstrators. Greensboro was a small city, but we had more demonstrators or as many under our command as Martin Luther King had at the same time in Birmingham, because of the colleges, and our strategy became one of creating a problem for the Greensboro and Guilford County officials and the State of North Carolina, by filling up every available jail space in the county. They had to reopen the old polio hospital; some arrested persons were contracted out as far as Gibsonville.

It became a test of nerves; Captain Jackson never understood that the more people that were arrested, the more the Movement swelled. It would increase our numbers. We could have had every student at A&T and Bennett Colleges in jail, and we were getting high school students involved, and some more militant adults in Greensboro. Every time he arrested folk, it increased enthusiasm for the Movement. That became our strategy. One night Captain Jackson thought that he had wiped us out when he brought Duke Power buses in to haul people off to the Coliseum to be processed. But it proved to be more than they could handle, and they let them out wholesale.

## William Jackson

The arrest procedure in 1963 was the same as anytime else; we booked them and wrote out our papers the same as anybody else. This depended on how many that we were arresting. We had to set up a situation at the Coliseum to fingerprint and picture them, process them, and distribute them to a place of keeping. Most of them would go along. They would get on the buses, and some members of a group who were not from the colleges, cut up some of the bus seats.

We made no plans for the vehicles to take the people to the incarceration centers; it developed during the demonstrations, and they were standing by. We commandeered two Duke Power buses at the Square.

At the booking center at the Coliseum, we had one girl spit in an officer's face, and in one case, a capus was issued because one failed to show up in court, and we had a picture to go along with it. I went down to the east side of town to a very nice, well-kept home. A lady came to the door, and I introduced myself. She said, "I know who you are, Captain Jackson, come in." I went in and told her that I had a capus there for her daughter. The daughter came into the room, and she said, "I wasn't up there." I took the picture out, and it was not her, and she told me that it was a girl that had been up here visiting from Mississippi, and had used that child's name. That type of thing happened a lot. We photographed, fingerprinted, and put each one on record. We fulfilled the requirements of the state in our arrests.

## Herman Enochs

Those arrested were charged with minor misdemeanors, things like trespass, violation of fire laws, blocking streets, sidewalks and that sort of thing. They were all minor violations. Most of them were city ordinances. And most of the argument was about the constitutionality of the ordinances.

There were hundreds of defendants in handling bond, those who had to post bond and who didn't. We tried to release everybody. We didn't want anyone locked up. One time we released everyone on condition that if they came back the second time, we'd make them post bond. And some did come back, because this was a continuing thing over several days. They arrested so many that they incarcerated some out at the old polio hospital out in Bessemer, just to process them, to hold them until they got to court. Of course, we released them out as soon as they got to court, most of them.

On May 21, the City Council met in a one- or two-minute session to approve my request as senior jurist for an alternate site to hold court. It was while we were involved with the tremendous number of defendants involved. They were holding some out at the Coliseum and some out at the polio hospital. They didn't have room in all the jails in adjoining counties, but what I and the defense counsel wanted to do, was to process these matters as soon as we could to get these people out, to decide whether or not we're going to hold them under a bond; if we were, how much, and then release everybody we could.

We tried at first to get everybody into the court. We had the regular case docket tried in another courtroom. We improvised a courtroom and put all the regular cases there, and I was hearing all these. But it became painfully obvious that there was no way to expedite the process. Although Mr. Malone and Mr. McKissick represented most all of these people, it was necessary to consider each one on its own merits, because each person had a different background, and some had been involved in these things before, some hadn't. You couldn't just do it in a blanket procedure; you couldn't say, "Everybody post a hundred dollar bond." You couldn't do that. So [that's] the reason I asked that we be allowed to hold court somewhere else. And I suggested the polio hospital.

The idea was to set up a court on government property to hear these arraignments. At that time I had the authority to appoint special judges, in order to hear those bond motions. We could dispose of them a lot quicker by going to where they were, rather than putting everyone on buses and bringing them to where we were. It'd be easier to move four judges than to move five hundred people. The idea was to expedite the procedure.

On the morning of the 22nd, after the Council had approved the third site, I opened court, and it was in session for some forty-five minutes. Mr. Malone made the motion for a continuance, because, arguing that the mayor's committee had been appointed, and it might jeopardize negotiations. I made the stipulation that meetings were going on with black leaders, and members of the committee were trying to resolve the matter. I didn't know what the negotiations were, because I wasn't involved in them. I said that if the meetings were successful, then I would continue to hold court on the arraignments. They were being arraigned to get their pleas, and, of course, the bond hearing came up as part of the arraignment. My second stipulation was that if they were unsuccessful, then court would reconvene under a special court after two o'clock.

It was done to expedite matters, because those arrested were being held in pretty cramped quarters. And the places where they were being held had inadequate facilities to go to bathrooms and it was hard to feed them, because there were no kitchens. It was hard on everybody. The city and the county had responsibility for the prisoners, and it certainly was hard on the prisoners being packed into these places. We were just overwhelmed. It seemed to me the best thing to do would be to get these hearings behind us as quickly as possible, and that's what we were trying to do. I recognized all but the first twenty-five for trials between May 16 and June 3. The first group was called, and almost all refused to be recognized for a later trial date, and so had to be held. When the court was willing to recognize them and let them out without posting bond, I could not understand why anybody would want to stay in jail. I was talking to one group, and I wanted them to promise me if I released them from jail, that they would not engage in any criminal activity. This meant that they wouldn't commit a misdemeanor while they were out without bond, and, of course, they would have to promise to come to court. That's all I was asking them to do. But one group I talked to almost en masse refused to promise that. I stopped asking them if they wanted to be recognized. I think by that point I realized that they were not going to promise not to be involved again.

I never talked to Mayor Schenck, because he was out of town when this happened. I never heard that CORE was trying to fill the jails, and I never had any negotiations with CORE. I talked with the lawyers—Mr. McKissick, Mr. Malone, Mr. High and Mr. Lee—and the District Attorney, Mr. Kornegay. The legal proceedings had slowed down, because each person was claiming the same man as their lawyer, which was Mr. Malone.

What I wanted to do was to split them up and take Malone's clients and arraign them one place and let Major High take his somewhere else. But then they came up with the tactic of saying that they had only one lawyer, so I couldn't do that. That thwarted my plans to hear them in different places. And it did slow it down, because we could only operate in one courtroom. It appeared to me that they wanted to slow the process down for reasons of their own; I don't know why. The people were in jail, and I wanted to get them out. And they wanted to slow the process down, to leave some of them in for some reason. All I was trying to do was to move the cases along, to resolve things. That's what the courts were for. And when you get in a position where you can't go forward, to dispose of the cases and do something with them, you get a little frustrated, but I was not angry. I had the power to appoint special judges. I was senior judge of the Municipal-County Court. There may have been some discussion about appointing more help in the solicitor's office. But I don't recall that there were any judges or solicitors appointed, although the possibility that they would be needed was discussed.

I recall there was some discussion about whether or not it would be possible to join more than one to consolidate cases. If you can consolidate twenty cases and try them, you're a lot better off than you are if you have to try five hundred different cases. We talked about it. I remember talking about the possibility of consolidating and trying several of them at the same time. But, of course, they were several different types of ordinance violations. And they happened at different times, different places. It wasn't as easy as it sounds to do that. This was unprecedented, although the act creating the court provided for that possibility. I didn't have to have any special legislation to do that. I had the power to do it. I just never had even considered it nor had any reason to consider it before that or after.

## Furman Melton

Sheriff's deputies guarded the polio hospital and the National Guard armory because they had jurisdiction over the county home They served our meals out at the polio hospital by shifts. So many officers at a time would go out and eat, because all the law enforcement officers that could be there were there at that time. All leaves, vacations, and time off was cancelled at that time.

I think that the prisoners were quartered real well down there. They had all of the facilities that they needed. The fact that we had hundreds of prisoners meant that they didn't have individual facilities like separate beds, because of the places that we had were overcrowded. They were fed and allowed to use the bathroom facilities. They had all of the opportunities that any prisoner would have, only they were just so crowded that they may have to wait to use these facilities because of the crowd.

## Clarence L. Malone

As a result of my affiliation with the NAACP, I was called by CORE through Floyd McKissick, who was on the CORE general staff of attorneys. The general push, while it had its beginnings in Greensboro and Durham, and all of your major cities across the state, it had a "domino effect." The demonstrations erupted on Friday or Saturday, and it was like putting out fires. There were only three or four black lawyers across the state who were on call. I was young enough to have only a small practice, and I could be out of my office for extended periods of time, and through McKissick and C.O. Pearson, I had experience with civil rights cases. McKissick had his hands full in Durham.

As a tactic, the cohesiveness of the activity made it desirable that there be a united front, a coordination of defense tactics, obviously with consent of the defendants, it was their election to be represented by counsel furnished to CORE by the NAACP. There was little pay involved; it was a duty that we felt that we owed. Therefore, it was a deliberate tactic for me to be designated attorney of record for all of the defendants.

I had the logistical support of the black bar in Guilford County. Parks, in particular, comes to mind, he must have been seventy or seventy-five years old, and Kenneth Lee, Major High, all of the guys practicing there. If I wanted to use their office or their library, their secretaries. My specific role was that of trial lawyer of the person who had been arrested in connection with the demonstrations. I was also legal counsel to CORE from time to time and consulted on the legality of the decision, that were obviously made almost hour-to-hour. For the most part, they relied on the general consensus of the CORE chapter and from the national office of CORE.

By the time I got to Greensboro, there must have been a thousand or fifteen hundred or more persons arrested and in custody. In various places in the county. I couldn't get around to all of the places they were being held, so Judge Enochs permitted me to use the courtroom as a consultation room; he removed himself and the court officials, and the general public, so that I could talk with the defendants. It was unusual, but necessitated by the large number of defendants. As they were brought in I would ask for and was graciously granted, as a matter of logistics, the use of the courtroom as a meeting room to discuss their cases.

They were obviously attested as individuals, but my conference with them was in a group, setting forth the guidelines and the tactics and having explanations of what was done sufficiently to allow me to present their defense. It was during these conferences that anyone who desired to be represented by me or by the attorneys furnished by CORE was permitted to withdraw or to speak then and there. There were no dissents in Greensboro. Most of the students were charged with trespassing after being forbidden entry. I advised them of what the possible punishments were, advising them of their rights to counsel, what a plea of not guilty meant, and in general what their activities meant legally.

It was my contention that the trespass law as it was being applied was unconstitutional, and for that reason we were testing the legality of the trespass law, together with the fact that there was the feeling of mine, and I so advised my clients, that we had a moral duty to assert those rights guaranteed to us by the Constitution, which would override any application in violation there of on the part of the state. My advice to them was that we believed that we were both legally and morally right, and had not violated any law. In fact, the action of the state and the city in enforcing the segregation laws was both morally and legally wrong.

The individual private citizen had a right to refuse service, if he so chose. However, state action in enforcing his whim was invalid under the equal protection clause of the Fourteenth Amendment: when an individual, by applying for a license to serve the public, he therefore made his individual rights subservient to that of the rights of the public. The next thrust was that, while he may hold those views, it is unlawful for the state or municipal government to lend aid and enforce his private whim or right against the rights of other citizens. That was an abuse of the police power on the part of the state.

Historically, this had not been presented before. It had been argued in its various aspects on one or two occasions, but it had not become the law of the land. *Plessy v. Ferguson* was the ruling case law of the time, but this tactic had not been employed prior to the application of trespass law. Ordinarily, it was just the question of an individual going in and requesting service, and the individual business owner tossed him out, but it was only with the beginning of the mass sit-ins that it reached proportions that it was necessary to call in a large amount of state action to enforce the de jure segregation.

To have a concerted single interest point of view, I simply didn't have it. It was a feeling of striking at it in any direction, and hope that it would eliminate the scourge of segregation. Being careful to get into the record those things that will enhance it on appeal to the Supreme Court. I had no illusions about getting relief from the state courts of North Carolina.

As it turned out—this would have to be limited to Greensboro and Guilford County—the blocking of fire entrances came about for lack of any other law to apply. There were many more demonstrators there than the businesses could accommodate in terms of physical facility. They had not trespassed, because they were gathered around the exterior of the building, and had not gone inside the building. But this was a means on the part of the city to apply an ordinance that would permit them to arrest all of the participants. The charge of blocking of the fire exits was placed against persons who conceivably did constitute a fire hazard, but the application of the ordinance itself was not designed to cover this kind of human behavior. It was sort of stretched to apply it to this kind of activity.

I do not think that it was "forcible trespass" at the Carolina Theater, because the public was invited, we were very careful to ask them not to go in without offering to pay. Having offered to pay, and the refusal of pay having been made, represented an activity on the part of the management which we held was morally and legally wrong. There was no overthrowing of his right to collect a fee for his services; there was always an offer to pay the advertised admission on the part of every person there; it was only after the offer to pay had been refused, that they entered what we argued was a place of accommodation, a place that as citizens and members of the public to whom all advertisements had been sent, that they had a right to enter.

It was not the objection on the part of the management of their entry into the theater. The objection on the part of the manager or the owner was the section of the theater that they entered. There were places reserved in balconies for blacks, so that the overall prohibition by the management was not that "you can't come in here with or without admission, you can go up there where you belong up in the balcony." So, that for those reasons I did not feel that it was forcible trespass. Number one, they offered to pay admission, and it was their right, in a place of accommodation for the public, to enter all of the portions of that business open to the public. The whole thing was fraught with inconsistencies; but not studied inconsistencies. We have to look at it in the light of the officials being face with situations not theretofore faced, and therefore, they applied whatever came to mind.

I visited the polio hospital and eventually succeeded in getting into it. I went to the Coliseum and was denied entrance, and after that, we devised tacitly or otherwise, the idea that the defendants would be brought into the court, the court would then permit me to confer with them, and then we would proceed with the trials. I think that it was out of sheer ignorance, for lack of a better explanation. If you recall, as the demonstrations arose, it was close to election day, and the Republicans swept into several local offices. Sheriff Jones had assumed office just before all hell broke loose, and he was trying to cope with an impossible situation with absolutely no experience. I don't know how they chose them, but they had a number of auxiliary police officers and auxiliary sheriff deputies who, apparently without any training, were put in there and told to keep that area clean of blacks, and upon my informing them that I was a lawyer, a uniformed person said that he was an auxiliary sheriff's deputy and that "no parents, no doctors, and no prick lawyers or anybody else" was permitted in the hospital.

I called the Justice Department and told them that I was denied entry. Out of sheer frustration and the fact that I had not been home for a couple of days, I came back to Durham, and by the time that I arrived home, there were calls for me, saying, "Now you have access." The atmosphere that prevailed was almost unimaginable; rationality simply did not apply. The feeling was extreme throughout on what I chose to call both sides. It was a feeling of crisis, the "we's" and the "they's." It turned out to be war, cold or hot. Fortunately, it remained cold, but both sides exercised all of the psychological tactics that they could. It was simply a time of turmoil and upheaval.

There was one hundred percent intransigence on the part of city officials. For instance, one statement would be made in an effort to call off the demonstrations—commitments were made that, before you could get in your car and turn on the radio, were being denied by the officials that had just made the commitment behind closed doors.

All the plumbing broke down at the incarceration centers, under the sheer force of numbers; there were not enough blankets, nor beds, nor food. The black community organized a cadre of people who did nothing but take food to the students. The slowness in providing food was not a punishment by recalcitrant officialdom; they didn't have the facilities for it. I heard many complaints, but as far as I could tell, there was a tremendous effort put forth to avoid circumstances that would permit criticism on the part of the officials involved.

Tactically, the idea of getting students released on their own recognizance was a practical solution to the overcrowded prisoner conditions. The city originally began arresting [them] as a matter of punishment, and a part of the tactic was a mass jail-in on the part of the demonstrators, to clog the facilities, to clog the court system, to force the administration of the city to look at what this foolish practice of segregation has resulted in, so that the tactic resulted in the efforts of the administration through Judge Enochs, to clean out the jails and prisons to relieve the impossible conditions. I was interested in not having these special court sessions set up as a means of keeping the jail system clogged; that was a part of the pressure.

The city did not succeed in getting around CORE's tactic to jam the legal system of the city. In fact, they compounded it. The result was the students on their own recognized what was being done and that it was a pressure relief valve, so that as they were released, they just went to another establishment, sat in and got arrested. First of all, each of the defendants, as they were called to the rail and arraigned, were asked if they desired to be released on their own recognizance. Their response was that they preferred "jail, no bail," and of course, without the acquiescence of the defendants, there was no legal way to keep them in custody if they were ordered released by the court, and put under contempt proceedings if they failed to return to court. Obviously, our overall tactic was to comply one hundred percent procedurally with the law, to test only that law that we felt was illegal for whatever reasons. I think the court knew, based on past behavior, that everyone was going to return to court. So, what they did was, since they could no longer stay in jail, they went out and got rearrested. Before the day was over, they were getting the same defendants back again.

It didn't relieve the incarceration at all. It was an exercise in futility, because [Judge Enochs] would have to arraign each student, and apprise him of his rights and the consequences of failing to return, so that it was a slow process. By the time that he got twenty-five released, there were fifty more coming in. We have since pretty much joked with each other about it; it was like a game of poker. The court officials obviously attempted to act within the law, and, to show complete fairness, bent over backwards to adhere to all procedural standards. We were doing the same thing, and that was understood, and it was a question of who could come up with a maneuver to get around the counter-maneuvers. But there never were any [personal discussions between Judge Enochs and myself], and he acted very fairly, as best he could under the very trying circumstances. I would not say there was collusion between the court and the city, but they were aware of each other's activities, and the court was, as it should, seeking to protect the government.

I had no discussion with either the A&T or Bennett administrations. William Thomas, as president of CORE, called the tunes in conjunction with a steering committee, although it was not designated as such, on the part of the students themselves. They were advised by the more mature black citizenry of Greensboro, and, for a period of time at least, during the actual negations. Some— I would not say most of it—was done under the direction of Jim Farmer. There were various advisory groups, made up of clergy in the city of Greensboro; some of them acted as mediators between the demonstrators and the city administrations, some obviously more partial to the city administration than to the demonstrators than others, and others more partial to the demonstrators than to the City of Greensboro. My personal activities were generally confined to trial tactics, although I was usually reasonably briefed on what was going on in the negotiations.

I sat in on a number of the advisory or strategy meetings of CORE, but not in the actual negotiations themselves. They discussed the cause and effect of tactics and strategy. The overall strategy was to break the back of the segregated politics. There was an absolute distrust of everything the mayor said; anything he said was what he thought was appropriate at the time, with no desire or thought of adhering to any promises or discussion that he made.

The cry of the city appeared to be: "We're ready to negotiate, but not as long as you are in the street." The cry of the blacks was: "We have been waiting three hundred years to negotiate; do something to make a good faith showing that you truly want to negotiate. We have our momentum going, we are not going to stop it until you show something." And he [mayor] would make promises calculated to stop or slow down the demonstrations, and most people concerned felt that he did not intend to live up to any promises he made, because once the momentum of the demonstrations died down, it couldn't be rekindled overnight. So most of the strategy sessions were devoted to trying to determine how best to make him adhere to whatever statements he had made. I don't refer individually to Schenck, but to the powers-that-be. CORE debate centred on which of these were bona fide, what were they trying to accomplish and how best to combat it. That sort of a strategy session.

What he would say in the negotiating sessions, and then what he would publish at his press conference were usually directly opposite. For instance, statements were made generally, "If you stop the demonstrations, I think that I can get the merchants to do this, that or the other." Then he would call a press conference immediately thereafter and say, "We aren't going to do anything at all until you get out of the street."

There were many white ministers that, in my opinion, stuck their necks out with their congregations to restore common sense and produce a spirit of calm. There were a number of police officials, one of whom [Captain Jackson] dealt fairly with everyone and everyone had tremendous respect for him. I know that everybody knew that he was in the middle, but he played fair. He had the complete trust of the [black community]—and merited it. Not once did he try to mislead or go through the devious mechanisms with the leaders of the demonstrations. There were a number of police officials who I think very genuinely were trying to quell the situation. And of course, there were various city officials who made what I call "political hay" out of it by the hue and cry of "Get these outside agitators out of the streets." I am referring to city administrative officials. My impression was that there were very few, if any city officials who indicated in any way, except by means of devious conduct, that they were in any way sympathetic to the grievances and demands of the students.

A general tactic that was not only found in Greensboro, but that we found across the state, was "Give them a bone in the meetings, and if we get them out of the street, we'll take care of business." That was the carrot dangled at the end of the stick: "We are not going to negotiate except in the spirit of calm." The meaning being: "Stop your demonstrations, and we'll talk. We are not going to make any commitments until the demonstrations stop." And with every indication that the only talk that you were going to get was that once the momentum of the demonstrations stopped, they applied the old adage of "law and order"—"order, to hell with the law." So long as it is orderly, and it is only orderly when you are back in your place."

The release of the students began late in the evening. It began after lunch one day, during the court session. And I was surprised when Judge Enochs began to release them on their own recognizance. I think that the release of those from the other places of incarceration evolved from that tactic. Finally, what happened was that—and I don't know, but I am sure that the police officers were acting under orders—when the jails began to fill up and the tactic of releasing the persons who were arraigned on their own recognizance wasn't working, many of the students said that they would haul city buses up to the places of demonstration, arrest everybody, load them up and take them two or three blocks down the street, stop and let them out of the buses rather than attempt to incarcerate them. [Laughs]

Pandemonium reigned. There is hardly anyone who can give an orderly sequence of events because it just didn't happen in order. You come up with this tactic—and apparently the city officials were doing the same thing—and you would try that. If it worked, fine; if it didn't, then try another. I think that the negotiations had begun in a reasonably earnest fashion when the students agreed to come out of jail. It was not wholesale turning them out of jail, as such. There had been negotiations going on all the time— two periods: one in which they started to release them on their own recognizance, and the one that resulted in the students leaving incarceration; generally, they were a week to a week-and-a-half apart.

I talked with some of the individual members of the committee, on occasion, but one of the reasons that I personally was not involved in the actual negotiations was the hue and cry of "outside agitators." I was not from Greensboro, and we didn't want to give the newspapers fodder for that kind of thing. There were so many cross-currents in tactical maneuvers, not to mention the fact that I had my hands full dealing with court proceedings. The newspapers supported wholeheartedly the official position of the city, and that's really a two-fold question; the facts were presented, I think, truthfully, but presented in a light most favorable to the city ninety-nine percent of the time.

My defense was to develop trial strategy based upon the factual circumstances. In a war like that, you utilize anything that you can come up with that is effective. One of the strongest things that we had going for us was the inability of the restauranteurs and theater operators to identify the students. We capitalized on the age-old adage that all blacks look alike to whites.

A large number of the charges were dispensed with in this manner, particularly blocking fire exits and trespass cases. A very large number of those were dismissed for lack of evidence. But now, as to the later street blocking incidents, what we did was selected some typical cases, tried them out to a jury, and the District Attorney agreed not to prosecute or just to hold in abeyance the cases to see what the Supreme Court would do, whether or not we had an effective defense. And it turned out that the Supreme Court ruled that the ordinance under which we were being tried was unconstitutionally applied, resulting dismissal in the remainder of those cases.

Not many of the cases from Greensboro went to the Supreme Court. I think that the thurst case is cited as *The State v. Fox*. It was a consolidation of people. Lonnie Herbin, the District Attorney, selected what were his strongest two cases. He was assisted by Hubert Seymour, who was employed by the city to prosecute these cases. That side chose two of what the considered as their best cases; the defense side chose two of what we considered our best cases, and one was chosen at random, and consolidated them for trial. The lead name was Brenda Fox, but that does not mean that she was any more active than anyone else. Her name was just listed at the top of the pleading, and you then shorten the leading to *The State v. Brenda Fox et al.* On that basis, the District Attorney dismissed the cases because they were substantially factually and legally the same cases.

The first case that came up for trial in the Recorder's Court was dismissed because the warrants citing fire laws violations were defectively worded. The factual circumstances were roughly these: I got there early that morning and I had a conference with the defendants. That was in the very outset of the trials. The demonstrations had then been going on some three or four days, possibly more. But the first case to come to trial, a part of the arraignment procedure, obviously, is a reading of the charges against the defendants, and upon the reading of the warrant, I detected that it was too generally drawn or that there was some element the specifics of which I don't remember at the moment. There was some element that made the warrant improper, and I moved to quash the indictment. The Court allowed my motion to quash.

As a matter of logistics, the warrants had been mimeographed. The mimeographed [copies cited] the language of the charge, and of course, individuals had filled in the names of the complaintants and the defendants, but the specific charge was mimeographed on the warrant form, which I recognized immediately. Upon the allowance of my motion to quash that warrant, I called to the court's attention that all of the warrants were drawn exactly alike and for that reason, I moved to quash them all. The District Attorney then moved to amend the warrants to properly allege a crime, at which juncture I insisted that each of the defendants be served with the new copies of the warrants, because every defendant to be tried in a criminal action has a right to know of the offense whereof he is charged before coming into court. This was a bogging-down tactic for the simple reason that as many people that were in the various centers of incarceration, there were absolutely no ascertainable records where or who anybody was. That was an almost impossible task for the city. On the other hand, it was a requirement of the law, and they were very hard to comply with. This resulted in a stalement within the courts for some two or three days, because it was necessary that every arrested person that was charged with that offense had to be served with a new warrant.

The old Civil Rights Acts of the nineteenth century were specific and adequate; it was just the interpretation of them in the various cases that stripped them of authority. I did not advise CORE in its demands of the city. The demands were pretty much drawn up by what I chose to call these students' Steering Committee, and sort of criticized by the more mature active leaders of the black community. I felt as a lawyer I should not advise what amounts to what I know is going to lead to litigation. I had input; we discussed it, but I specifically let them act of their own free will. The city could have passed an ordinance requiring desegregation. There has never been any law prohibiting such action. The city for its own welfare can pass any provision not inconsistent with the laws of the state or the federal government; certainly there was no law requiring that there be segregation.

I had only informal conversations with Armistad Sapp. I recall his wearing his white suit and a string tie, on the one or two occasions that I [happened] to meet him. The first time that I met him, he walked up and introduced himself to me as "Sapp the sap." He knew his position, and I knew mine, and we joked about it; it became a standing joke between us. Frankly, the legal positions of the segregated businesses were so ludicrous to me, that I didn't take any of them seriously. It was the age-old right of the private citizen to his property rights and that kind of noise. [Laughs]. Sapp's function to these businesses was pretty much advisory to various unincorporated associates for this or for that, sort of a lobbying kind of thing. No litigation arose from any of those organizations.

I witnessed only a few marches, because ordinarily I was in court all day and I was strategizing for the next day. On several occasions I was on the platform at a rally in one of the churches when the marches started, but for the most part, my time was spent in trying to strategize what was going on at the actual sit-ins or jail-ins. I meticulously avoided counseling, on what I personally considered ethical grounds. My official position was: "I am here to represent you and guard your rights if you are arrested." I felt that for me to teach them, so to speak, how to get around the law bordered on unethical or illegal behavior, and I didn't want to get ethically involved. This was, in effect, what the legal counsel of the city and these businesses were doing for their clients, but who was going to file a grievance against them?

## Otis Hairston, Jr.

I didn't experience or witness any harassment or mistreatment by the police the first time that we were arrested at the Carolina Theater. We didn't have any problem. The demonstrators were schooled in nonviolence. That was one of the main purposes of the meetings that were held at the old Trinity Church. I remember several times when we were marching we were harassed and several times people were spit on, but we never retaliated for it.

After being arrested we were taken to the Coliseum for booking. We sat in the bleachers and were called down to the processing area down on the floor. We were asked questions, searched, photographed, fingerprinted, and then taken by bus to the polio hospital. I think that everybody on the bus realized the purpose for which they were there, but it was sort of a jovial mood. I guess everybody realized that it wasn't a confinement that was going to be permanent; it was something temporary and it was for a cause.

There were some that were bailed out. Because I was a high school student, I was bailed out by CORE after two to three days. I was not worried at all about being arrested. I just assumed that there wouldn't be any active sentences, possibly fines. I don't ever remember going to court. I was just under the impression that we were represented by legal counsel, and it was always disposed of that way. As far as I remember, I never made a court appearance.

## Sarah Jones (Outterbridge)

We were told at the meeting that the strategy was to go for mass arrests, but it was left up to the individual. If you did not want to be arrested, there was a point where you could move away from the door and not be arrested. The police were not overly abusive, other than occasional racially derogatory comments. Sometimes that would take out their nightsticks and push you with them or jab you in the ribs, but I never saw anyone hit.

The last time that I was arrested at the S&W cafeteria was a pretty long one, even to the point that they had run out of room at the jail, and had to use the old polio hospital. I was not placed in a cell; it was just a big room, and they went through the procedures of fingerprinting and photos. The CORE officers had told us about the arrest procedure format. And we went in knowing that it would be a fly-by-night thing, that we would be taken downtown and you would be released on your own recognizance. Some of the younger ones, they would have to hold them until their parents came to get them, if you were under sixteen.

At first, I was not aware that the people were being taken to facilities all over Guilford County. I was in the second group. I can't remember exactly which night I was arrested. But at first, we thought that we were going to the police station, and we tried to get as many people involved as possible, because we knew that the police station was small, and they could not hold but so many. I think as far as the police were concerned, it baffled them, because, at one point, the group that I was arrested in was just held in the paddy wagon for a long time, because they didn't know where to take us. I recall them commandeering Duke Power buses at the Square.

Basically, we would sing and try to be as happy as possible because the arrest was what was going to bring it to the people's minds, the television and the radio media and all of this. So the attitude was good, because at that point, we knew that it was working and they were definitely going to arrest us. As soon as one group was arrested, others would come.

## Evander Gilmer

I was arrested five times. The other times, we were just processed. We went through the waiting and wondering what was going to happen, getting fingerprinted and mug shots, then signing something and being released. That usually was five or six hours. When I was arrested at the Carolina the fourth time, the police weren't too pleasant, because this was towards the end. Probably rightfully, the police were irritated; under the circumstances, I think that they were very restrained, but they seemed mean. A man in a coat and hat said something like, "You can't come in" and if anyone walked across a line, they were carted off. The police took us down to the polio hospital by bus. We were joyful; we weren't mad. I remember joyfully going out on the bus to wherever they were taking us. We were singing freedom songs and trying to show the police and anyone else that this is what we wanted, that they weren't hurting us by taking us to jail; they were doing just what we wanted them to do.

We had never expected that we were going to a hospital. It didn't seem to be ready for us, either. On my ward, I was the only member of CORE who had been involved for some period of time. The other people were students, most of whom had never been jailed before, and some of them were very scared. We didn't know when we would be able to talk with somebody like Bill Thomas. We wanted them to come in and know that we were there; in case no one knew where some of us were or who was arrested. We knew that, probably, Bill wasn't arrested. He usually tried to remain out during those times.

Our conversation centered around what we thought was going to happen to us. We didn't think they could keep us there forever, but we weren't sure what they would do. We were encouraged by the additional people that were coming in, because we could see them filing by, going somewhere else, and so we knew that people were continuing to come in.

## Lois Lucas (Williams)

I felt strongly that the people who were sitting up at the altar of the church talking "jail, no bail" ought to have a try at it to see how it felt. As a member of the Executive Committee, I felt obligated to accept arrest without accepting bail. But I had a lot of questions in my mind. Would we be there through exams? If so, could we make up exams? Would seniors miss graduation?

I was arrested on Wednesday night, and I remember that it was a long week. I was hoping that we would not be kept in jail over the weekend. We went to the polio hospital, because the armory was overflowing. That's where I stayed the first night. There were some people who went to the armory. First, we had to go to a holding place [the Coliseum], where we were processed, and I think that they didn't know what to do with us.

I felt like a caged bird that wants to fly and can't. I made a joke of hoping to be in jail during exams, which really wasn't true. A number of us had taken books, because we figured that we were going to be there for a long time. After our first night there, we got assurances from the college that we would be able to take make-up exams when we got out. By that time, I was not that concerned about exams. I was more frustrated that after all of our efforts, that we were reduced to having to go through this again and again. It's like saying that nothing works unless people are forced into dealing with you; that people don't want a peaceful solution to a problem. We believed that unless something drastic happened, they were just going to ignore us, and this would go on, with more and more people being arrested and jailed. By the time they finally realized that they weren't going to be able to release us, and it would involve so much manpower, and the cost of feeding us was getting to be an economic burden on the city, then they probably started to get the sense that this was different. Maybe now the time had come to settle down and start to deal with us.

A lot of us spent a great deal of time trying to keep up the morale of the younger kids, because that incarceration involved many high school kids. Just talking to them, telling them that they had a stake in it, and they had laid claim to that stake by being there. The Sheriff's guards were a lot nastier than the local police, because most of them were older. Nothing physical, just nasty, making comments like, "What do the niggers want now?" and subtle threats like, "Bull Conner really knows how to handle his niggers," and stuff like that. It was supposed to make you be afraid and to make you not want to come back again. We had a certain amount of safety in the fact that there were quite a number of us. I don't know what happened at the other facilities, but there was no taking one person or a few out at a time to try to scare anybody. I think that beyond talking, for the most part, the people that were in charge of our care were just as bewildered by what was going on as everybody else. And there had probably been a statement by the mayor, saying that everything was to be handled with a great deal of restraint. This was probably due to a lot of national reporters and television crews being in town. Greensboro had its reputation as a moderate Southern city to think about.

We studied, wrote letters, waited for CARE packages from home and from school. It was overcrowded, and there weren't adequate lavatory facilities. It was sort of warm; nobody was freezing. We could have used more blankets, but we shared what we had; people doubled up or slept three people to a cot. We would have liked to have taken a bath, and being able to get personal items. Unlike elsewhere in Southern jails, they didn't put terrible things in the food. Later, some of the kids at other facilities talked about the terrible food they got. It couldn't have been hot if it wasn't served on time, because you have hundreds of people to feed, so that by the time that you got to some people, it had to be cold. We were fed breakfast and dinner; I don't recall lunch, because by the time that you got finished with breakfast it was almost through the afternoon. Somebody from Bennett came when we were allowed visitors. We told them what we needed, and they were able to bring it in. Parents brought all kinds of things: food, hair-rollers and shampoo. It was almost like being in a hotel.

After we had been there for four or five days, you can imagine what kind of bathroom facilities they had, and our not being able to take regular showers. The conditions in the barracks where I was held had terrible sanitary conditions, especially the bathrooms. There was no privacy, because we were all overcrowded. You couldn't characterize the experience as pleasant, but there were some that were a little more pleasant than others, and that May arrest was one of the least pleasant ones.

The general feeling was that it was not a tactic by the city to make it deliberately hard on us. We were there about a week, because the whole thing about going back to school under house arrest had to be worked out before we could go back to campus. By the time that we were released, we knew that a compromise was in the making, and out of this something had been done; it wasn't just going to be like the other times. The only thing to think about then was to get back to campus and get exams over with, because by then it was just about time to go home.

*Bennett College students were buoyed by a prompt visit by president Willa B. Player, who assured the students that they had the support of the college. Dr. Player, as president of a private institution, informed Captain Jackson that she could not act* in loco parentis *for the students and did not intend to serve in the role of "jailer." Citing legal advice, she told Jackson that it was illegal to hold the students under the unhealthy conditions of the hospital and recommended their release.*

*That evening, Dr. Player obtained the permission of the Board of Trustees to use her discretion in handling the situation. She then called a faculty meeting in which she made it clear that the students were to receive all possible assistance from the college. The college secretary was instructed to send reassuring telegrams to the parents of the arrested students.*

## Willa Player

I had an anonymous phone call from someone identifying himself as a friend of the college. He said that the Bennett students had been placed in the polio hospital without its inspection, which was against the law. I made a personal visit down to the library and I read this code. I then went to visit Captain Jackson and told him about the danger if he did not remove the girls from the polio hospital, because it had not been properly inspected, and this was the law, and the city could be in trouble. He was very cordial about it; he wondered where I had gotten this information. I didn't tell, but I quoted the book from which I had gotten the information.

Then I told him that unless he agreed to lift the charges against the Bennett girls, that they were going to stay out there while I pursued this issue. Then I went out there, and I told this story to the Bennett girls. I urged them to stay there, because Bennett College was not a jail, and the administration would not accept them being released into our custody until the Chief of Police lifted their sentences. I told them that Bennett was a private institution, and the difference between a public institution and a private institution was that a private institution could not be dictated to by the state, and that if the students came back to the college under arrest, they would be transferring the concept of a jail to the college, and the college was not prepared to be a jail to anyone. I had information that this hospital was not properly equipped to take care of them legally, and they would have to trust that I would do the best for them in terms of this situation. They assured me that they had no intention of leaving.

That very night I met with a group of faculty people and said, "What shall we do for the students tomorrow?" to make clear that the faculty was with me. The faculty agreed to set up something like an army camp; they delivered their [students] assignments and mail every day. We arranged two alternatives concerning exams. One was that a student could go home if she wanted to and come back; or she could accept an incomplete and take the examination when she returned to campus in the fall

## Lois Lucas (Williams)

I can remember Dr. Willa B. Player coming down to make sure that her girls were all right. The guards stood up when this regal-looking woman came in. If she walked into a prison with some of the worst cutthroats in the world, she would command their respect, simply by the way that she carried herself. Bennett College's strength was in being independent with a president and a board of trustees who would stand behind us, and having articulate faculty members like Dr. Laizner and Reverend Busch.

She came in with words of encouragement. She told us not to worry; she gave us the important news that the Board of Trustees had met and they supported our position. For her to give us their support was very good for us. At that time, I think there was a lot of pressure being put on A&T to kick out the students involved in the demonstrations. Dr. Player made a statement to the press about that time, saying that our administration was behind us one hundred percent, and she would not knuckle under to any kind of pressure tactics. You can imagine what that did for our spirits.

## A. Knighton Stanley

Few people knew how much Dr. Willa B. Player supported what the students were doing. She had been out of town, but when she learned that there were at least two hundred of her students incarcerated at the old polio hospital, she called me immediately. She was permitted to go in where they were housed, and she walked through and talked with them in a very personal way, inquiring about their health and so forth. She let the girls know that she was behind them one hundred percent.

When she looked at me I could see that she was deeply moved; she really had compassion for those girls. On returning to campus, she notified her Board of Trustees that the girls were in prison and that they had to have the college's support. Secondly, she called a meeting of the faculty and staff. She said that we should all support the students, because if there were conflicts within the college, the students could not maintain their morale, and that was important, or the Movement would be broken. The other thing she did was to make clear that in order to be fully-committed to Bennett College, the entire student body should support the students being held in jail. In other words, she had 600 students in the school; 400 had not been jailed, and it was a signal to them that they should have been in jail, too.

## William Jackson

The conditions at the incarceration centers were not bad at all. For instance, we set up at the county home, where the polio hospital had been, and if the cooperation of the people that were incarcerated had been half that what the city and the state were trying to do for them, it would have been all right. But as a whole, it wasn't bad. I can't complain with the action of the Sheriff's Department at all. They were treated all right. The same was true at the Guilford County jail and the city jail. We maintained the jail ourselves at that time, and we had some in High Point; we had some as far away as Lexington, and they were fine. I can't say that there was anything that was wrong with it.

They were hoping to flood the police system and the courts, but it didn't happen. We all discussed it to see what would be best to do. The substance of the meetings held with city officials consisted of what I thought might be better to do to handle the situation more easily, what they could do or suggest. Mayor Schenck was a magnificent individual to work with—understanding on both the part of the police department and the individuals who were seeking their rights. He was a man to be admired. I kept my superiors informed as to what was going on, what they could expect and what we were doing along with the city manager, the mayor and the city attorney. It wasn't unusual for all of us to get together to discuss the situation. It was going so well, and we had no confrontation at all among the individuals in this group. Paul Calhoun gave me the authority to run things as I saw fit. He backed me one hundred percent. If he had a suggestion, he came to me with it, and we worked it out together.

## William Thomas

I was incarcerated only twice, and each time I was in the city jail, which had very terrible conditions. I guess the reason why I was not arrested more often was that the mayor's committee felt that I would serve more of a purpose by being outside. In fact, at times I would have welcomed being arrested; I could have gotten some rest. That way I would not have been in meetings twenty-four hours a day. I was able to have access to the polio hospital basically at will to go in and out. I had that type of arrangement with the police. It was overcrowded, but it was almost jovial. No one abused the students. They couldn't get hot baths, and there was really no place where they actually could get hot meals. But the Sheriff's deputies did provide them fruit, milk, juice, sandwiches. And they were not in jail that long. The big thing was that it was overcrowded, and the conditions at the National Guard armory were basically about the same. Whatever negative conditions were more a result of the overcrowding than any planned condition by the police. Greensboro was totally different than any other area of the South, in terms of how the police reacted.

## Alvin Thomas

I was arrested seven or eight times. I refused bail on one occasion; I had to spend a night in the city jail and several days out at the polio hospital. It wasn't the most comfortable setting in the world. You had to adjust to your surroundings and comfort one another. People were coming out every day from the community bringing food, including my mother. I don't think there was ever really a point of total unawareness, although that would be a normal assumption that some people made. Bill and other CORE leaders would not come as a total group, but he and the others would see some of us, and we would communicate with the rest. Most people understood that we intended to stay there until something broke. Jesse Jackson led a mach out to the hospital and conducted a prayer session on Sunday, May 19, where they prayed for those that were in jail, for our movement, and prayed for the country.

## Jibreel Khazan

I was asked by the CORE leadership to go to the polio hospital, because there were 200 or 300 female students from Bennett College there. We adopted that strategy because there was no leader in there with them. The Bennett students knew me, and my sister Gloria Jean was in jail with them. I put on the clothes of a catering service deliveryman and brought them food and personal items supplied by the adult community. When I came in, the guards did not know who I was, and they let me into the hospital.

I found that the girls were put in unsanitary rooms, with fourteen women crowded into each room meant for three or four people. They had no proper toilet or bathing facilities, and their morale was getting low. As they gathered around a table, I began to tell them encouraging things like, "We'll have you out in a little while." If I hadn't gone, Joe would have gone, but he was in jail in the mass arrests, along with Robert Patterson and other students from A&T and Dudley High School.

## Elizabeth Laizner

Nine hundred were arrested that evening [Friday, May 19], and others followed later. A few were transported to the local jail and they overflowed, so some of us were put as far away as High Point. On Saturday we were all put into the polio hospital. What information I could gather was through the "window telegraph" between the young ladies and the young men who were in another of those barracks. These barracks were made for a maximum of about thirty nurses, with about sixteen rooms, give or take one, with a maximum of four nurses in each. They stuffed into this place 135 young ladies from A&T and Bennett and one old teacher. There was one corridor not much wider than this table. I was scared to death that if a fire should break out there, we would all be stone-cold dead.

In the room where I was, there were eleven Bennett ladies and one from A&T. The sleeping arrangements were very simple: five young ladies slept sideways on two beds pushed together. Five more slept sideways on the floor on two large mattresses, and I was the proud possessor of a narrow jail mattress, but no pillow. We had a few blankets, but not enough. The first day, there was little food. We were given sandwiches, but some of the young ladies in the rooms farther off never made it through the crowd in the corridor, and some of them stayed without food until the next day. On Sunday evening they finally decided to get a caterer in, and we got halfway decent food, but up to that point, it was simply frightful.

Our treatment depended upon the individual deputies. The only good thing that Sheriff Jones did was to take those of us who were Catholic to Mass on Sunday morning. I was a member of the Newman Club, a Catholic organization for the two black colleges. Some of my members were in there, and they approached me very worried. "What's going to happen? Can we go to Mass tomorrow? Is it a sin if we don't go?" I told them, "I'll ask the Sheriff. But if not, don't worry; the Lord will forgive you." To my utter astonishment, the Sheriff said yes. The next morning, the Sheriff's car and a bus were there and seventy or so of us were stuffed in and brought to Saint Mary's Church. We came in about twenty minutes before Mass started. Father Jacobs came out with his hands outstretched and let us all in. We didn't have a real rosary, but I made some from malted milk balls that I had for the young people to eat. The congregation at first didn't even know who we were. The Sheriff was a little bit worried. He let us sit in church for a long time, waiting for the people to disperse, which they did not. They made two rows outside, and finally we were brought out.

*To boost the morale of those being held in the polio hospital, and to maximize publicity in the news media, the Executive Committee arranged for Jesse Jackson to lead a march of over a thousand students and an increasing number of black adults to the hospital to conduct a prayer meeting and to sing Movement songs. The situation was tense as police kept dogs ready in case of a riot. But tension eased when Captain Jackson ordered his men to maintain a low-key response in which they respected the prayers of the crowd and the singing of the National Anthem, as long as it was done in a dignified manner.*

## Elizabeth Laizner

When we came back to the polio hospital from church, a large crowd of people were standing outside the wire fence, hailing us. Reverend Bishop had kept his promise to bring out the people in his church and the black community at large, to support us. One thousand people came out to the polio hospital, where they assembled. The police were so scared that they had guard dogs there. It was a tense situation, but do you know what the people did? They started singing the "Star-Spangled Banner" and everyone, including the dog handlers, stood at attention.

## William Jackson

A large group came out to the polio hospital. We respected both the National Anthem and their prayers, unless it appeared that this was a decoy for something else. If it appeared in this manner, we would conduct ourselves as officers, we respected the singing of the National Anthem and their prayers, as long as we did not think that it was sung in a vain sense.

Some of them would have liked to have caused a confrontation. I recall there was around the Bessemer Avenue side of the place there, one girl apparently fainted, and I went to her and tried to assist her. Some man grabbed my hand and objected to me assisting the young lady. I didn't say anything, and we were able to get them away. There was not a whole lot of trouble there, but there was a big bunch around there. In another incident a woman got verbally all over me, but that didn't bother me. As a police officer, I was used to that sort of thing and I didn't take it personally. I saw this man that I knew, and I told him that I thought it would be best to get them to leave, and he led them on out. In cases like that, I have found that you have to be able to select individuals to talk with and to get them to lead the crowd out of a situation like that; this was one of those situations. This thing started early in the morning and ended up way late in the afternoon.

## Evander Gilmer

Things like that rally on Sunday encouraged us. We knew that the black community was involved in full force. Just before that time, the black adults had started coming around, so there were adults in the group. Ezell Blair's father was one of the first ones who started marching down with the students, and helped to get the adults involved.

## Frances Herbin (Lewis)

I was taken directly to the polio hospital. After a period, we were booked. They were large open rooms. Some people were held in smaller rooms, but it was one big recreation area or something. We just lay out there on the floor. We were led into the rooms by the Sheriff's Department. They were much more aggressive. They would bring out a nightstick once in a while and push you on, and say ugly things to us. It was quite some time before we were fed, because I got arrested that night, and I was not fed until the next morning. But we always got three meals a day. It wasn't the best food in the world [Laughs]. Some of the prisoners decided to send it back on their trays—it was horrid. At that point, the YWCA started sending donations of little knick-knacks that the relatives could send in there. I didn't see my father the whole time that I was out there, but CORE representatives came out there. I don't know if any of the officers were arrested; if so, none of them were where I was staying. I did not speak with an attorney, nor did I see any of the adult advisors.

We would just sit around and sing, and some books came in, so we would read and talk, and that was about all. We were just on the concrete floor; no beds were provided. There was a blanket and a pillow. I remember when the people marched out to the polio hospital that Sunday; I heard them singing, but I could not see them. There was little or no communication between the wards, nor do I remember any information coming in. I remember seeing Elizabeth Laizner; I heard later that she was taken to High Point. I did not see Dr. Player, but I heard that she came out and spoke to the Bennett students.

## Elizabeth Laizner

That visit to the hospital boosted our spirits, but we were still in jail, and the conditions were pretty lousy. We had absolutely nothing. The clothes we had were the clothes that we were wearing when we were arrested. We had no soap, no towels, no nothing. There were only a few bathrooms for between twenty and twenty-four young ladies. Some of the young ladies had not eaten for quite some time. But that very afternoon, people were beginning to give us things, in small amounts.

Ezell Blair Jr., came up to where we were, pretending to be a deliveryman; he had borrowed a counterman's jacket and had brought us a box of sandwiches. He told me that I was in charge of the young ladies, and Joseph Warren was in charge of the young men. So I took charge of the young ladies; I was a teacher, and I was determined to protect and counsel them. I told the Sheriff's deputies that if they had anything to do with the young ladies, to channel it through me. But they were extremely slow about doing anything. Sometimes, they didn't even want us to get some things, and what especially upset the young ladies, somebody sent us several cases of Cokes. Now, there is a rule that prisoners should not have glass because they might commit suicide. Well, we were in no mood to commit suicide. The state cops were extremely severe and treated us like criminals. They sat where we could see them, drank those Cokes, while all we had was the brackish water from the faucets. And they threatened to cut off the water if we didn't stop singing Freedom songs, and there wasn't much water to have anyway. They didn't do it, but we didn't get very much. How can you, when twenty-four women have to use the same little spigot in the bathroom?

I remember the trouble that I had to locate a doctor when a young lady had an anemic attack. One of our local physicians, Dr. J. Davis Taylor, apparently saw what was happening on TV, and the next morning he came to treat anyone who needed medical attention. And a nurse also came out from Bennett to assist the students. The place was unheated; it was warm in the day, but very cold at night. A number of students contracted colds.

The county jail matrons were ambivalent in their treatment of us. There were two matrons; one was charming, but the other one, was crude and nasty to the young ladies. It was really bad, and the young ladies suffered. That first day, Sunday afternoon, when the community realized what was going on, the first really bad, and the young ladies suffered. That first day, Sunday afternoon, when the community realized what was going on, the first people came; they brought us a few things. I think that there were about twenty cakes of soap, which wouldn't go very far for 135 people. I organized the young ladies in their rooms; each room had a group. We had a room far away from the desk of the nasty matron; she was afraid of us, and usually she had retreated behind her desk. And when anything was going on, we met there.

That first evening I went in to distribute the soap to look things over. There were about ten young ladies. I said, "We have some soap. I'm sorry, but everybody else has to get some. There are two pieces of soap for you." We were all, excuse me, stinky dirty. We had been arrested Friday, and that was Sunday afternoon. One young lady grabbed some of the soap. I lost my temper and said, "Do you realize that the young men in the other barracks are being kept incommunicado" They cannot even be visited, and they aren't getting anything, and you take some soap from them?" I went into the next room and spoke to the ones in the next room who were nice, only taking two or three pieces of soap. As I was leaving the room, the same young lady came back, with every piece she had grabbed. She said, "I'm sorry, I wasn't thinking about anyone else. Look, the girls want to send some soap to the boys." I gave her back two cakes of soap, and that was that. Despite the terrible conditions, those girls did marvelous things. But the treatment was miserable, absolutely miserable.

*Governor Terry Sanford was widely perceived to be a liberal Southern governor, sympathetic to the Civil Rights Movement. But the threat of violence and an apparent inability to maintain law and order prompted Sanford to call Dr. Dowdy on the evening of Monday, May 22, ordering him to accept the A&T students into the custody of the college. He then informed Mayor Schenck of his action, whereupon the A&T students were released from the polio hospital and the armory. At 10:00 p.m., the Sheriff's Department loaded the A&T students onto buses and transported them back to the A&T campus.*

*Confused and angry, A&T students were taken by bus to the campus, where they met in Harrison Auditorium. Shouting down CORE and community leaders alike, they demanded to seek immediate re-arrest. Finally the students were persuaded to reluctantly accept a temporary suspension of demonstrations until further word from CORE and the adult Coordinating Committee. The next day, the Bennett students were released from the polio hospital and returned to campus.*

## Frances Herbin (Lewis)

We were released at night, and I had no way of contacting my parents to come and get me. They just took us out in buses and let us out. We had A&T and Dudley students out there, separated by male and female. There was no forced removal; the students just went along voluntarily. I went back in a bus. We were let off in front of Harrison Auditorium on A&T's campus. It was after ten o'clock. I was afraid to leave, and I didn't know what I was going to do, because the Sheriff's deputies just said, "We're going to let you go." And they did not tell us where they were taking us. I did not go into the auditorium. By word-of-mouth my father found out that there was a group of people coming out, and he came and picked me up.

## Elizabeth Laizner

Monday was very hot, the day, and the guards threatened to cut off the water, if they [students] danced and sang. We were all finally beginning to calm down a little bit when the rude matron suddenly came to me and said,. "The Governor has ordered the students from A&T out. They have to leave for the campus." I tried to get more details from her; I didn't know if I should believe her or not. She told me that I should announce it to the A&T students in there, and that they had to pack, and they would be taken back to campus. I tried to ask her to see a clergyman; she didn't know that I was a Catholic, and I had the right to ask for my priest. Of course, I instead asked for Tony Stanley, but she re0fused that, too.

So I went to the first room, opened it and made the announcement about the Governor. The girls looked at me as if I had lost my mind. As I said, the matron was a little afraid of us, and when we came to the next room, she was standing a little bit behind, and I was able to mutter to one or two girls, "Tell the room leaders to meet with me in ten minutes in room fourteen." When I came to the third room, she heard me make the announcement loudly, and retreated fast behind her desk.

Well, we got together and they asked me what was going on, and I said, "I don't know if this is true or if that woman is lying." We discussed what we should do. The only thing that I suggested was that we wait until the next morning, when we could find out if this was true. If the Governor had really ordered the hospital emptied, we would leave. Then one girl had a stroke of genius. She said, "They never took the locks off of our doors; let's all go to bed and lock ourselves in. I don't think she will dare get us out."

Well, she didn't. Ten minutes before they had been singing and making that disturbance that had caused her to threaten us. But then it was so silent that you could have heard a feather drop. I did not lock my room, because I had to know what was going on. The next thing I knew, the matron was there, and she said, "What's going on? Aren't they getting ready?" I said, "No, ma'am, they are very tired. They're all asleep." She said, "That's ridiculous, they were just dancing in the hall ten minutes ago." I said, "Yes, that's why they're so tired." She tried the locks and couldn't do anything.

I went back into my room, still with the door open, and the next thing that I knew, the matron and two state cops said that they would take me out to another building, and I had to pack my things and go. That was one of the worst decisions of my life. Every girl in the room, and there must have been close to twenty, had her arm or her hand on me. "Don't leave us," they said to me. If I had been alone, I would have done what I have done in other demonstrations: gone limp and had them drag me out. But I was afraid that if I said, "I'm going to stay," some of the young ladies may have been hurt trying to keep them from dragging me out of there. Or maybe something else might happen. So, I said that I was going, and they took me out as if I were a criminal. The Sheriff was waiting outside in his car. I wasn't going to another building. The Sheriff, the two state cops and the matron brought me down to the county jail in High Point. So from that moment on, I didn't know anymore what happened to the Bennett girls.

## Willa Player

The student leaders from A&T and Bennett used to meet on each other's campuses. It had my complete approval. It was so clear to me that what these people were struggling for was within their rights that I never equivocated on it at all. Because of that, the students were very cooperative. They would always come to me first to tell me what they were going to do or what they were planning, or what it was all about, and they would ask me if I had any suggestions. So it was a communication and a give-and-take that was so open that the students never did anything behind my back or a feeling that it was something that I did not approve of, or holding back what they were going to do.

I did not have any misgivings about faculty members being CORE advisors. I think Dr. Laizner was an illustration of an over-enthusiastic person to bring about change, but I did not think that she had anything vicious about her. I think that Dr. Laizner was put in the High Point city jail. I worked through Mr. McMillan; he was instrumental in bringing about her release. I asked him to tell her not to worry, that we were going to see her through. I just wanted her to know that she had my good will.

The Bennett students were never released into the custody of the college. The A&T students were released into the custody of their college at the request of Governor Sanford, who wrote a letter to Dr. Dowdy. That left the Bennett students there by themselves, and they began to get disturbed.

Dr. Dowdy was, after all, the president of a public institution, and he was under tremendous pressure. In my view, Dr. Dowdy had either to pull the students in or resign his position. Publicly, I think that he did what he was asked to do, and I don't see what more he could have done except resign his position. I saw the letter, and it was a direct order [from the govrnor]. There was no mention about any funds from the state. It was a direct order to pull the students out of the demonstrations. He couldn't attempt to enforce the dictates of the letter; the atmosphere was such that, if he had tried, he wouldn't have been successful. I think that at that point, Dr. Dowdy was just powerless. However, if I had been in Dr. Dowdy's position, my first impulse would have been to resign rather than carry out that order.

## Jibreel Khazan

We had a mass meeting at A&T's Harrison Auditorium later that night, because all of the students were released there. The students demanded that someone speak to them. No one wanted to speak to them. Attorney [Henry] Frye came and he spoke to them; Dr. Darwin Turner, an English professor, was on the stage. Jesse [Jackson] was supposed to speak to them, but he wouldn't go out on the stage. Something happened, he couldn't face them; he had been speaking [publicly], but that particular night, he just froze. The students were yelling and chanting, so they got me and asked if I would speak to them. I wasn't the leader of the Movement, but Attorney Frye and Darwin Turner came to me, maybe one or two other leaders, because, the students didn't recognize Jesse as being their spokesman, even though he had won the election to be president of the Student Government; the Movement was something very different. It's like the difference between being the person who is steadfast constantly and someone who at the moment may have captured the news media. Those of us who had been with the Movement for three years straight, had a rapport with those students who had been with us since 1960. So [they wanted to hear from] the tried and true leadership of the Movement, who had gone through the fire, and not spur-of-the-moment spokesmen.

Everybody was chanting that they wanted to go back. Dr. Dowdy, was there, but the students didn't want to hear what he had to say. The tension was very high, so I told them, "You know we are all brothers in this, and we all want our freedom. You know that I wouldn't lie to you. Nobody wants to go back more than me, but we are in a tight situation here. The president is under pressure from the Governor; he's only trying to do his job. We have an obligation, also, as students. Graduation is coming up, your parents are going to be coming up this weekend, and we have got to get ready. We've proven our point, now, let's put it to a vote: Who wants to stay and who wants to go back?" They put it to a voice and shouted, "We want to go back!" I said, "Okay, let's talk this thing over some more." So, we talked it over some more. Finally, everybody calmed down and reluctantly agreed that they would abide by the order of the president. At the same time, they also agreed to continue to picket.

## Lewis Brandon

The night when they dumped the A&T students out, I was manning the headquarters, and I was called by someone who said that there was a lot of confusion, because they were bringing people back to campus in cars. Darwin Turner, Chairman of the English Department, and I were both there because he had a little newsletter called *The Candlelight*. He was responsible for getting that together, editing it, and circulating it. There was a telephone committee and another one that was responsible for circulating that paper. He and I both left and went to campus. By the time we got there, Ezell was there, Jesse was there, and attorney Major High was there. Dr. Dowdy was there; he had tried to talk to the students, but they didn't listen too much to what anyone had to say. Ezell tried, and Jesse tried, but Turner was the one who took over and talked to them, calmed them down and suggested that they go back to the dormitories, take hot showers and get a good night's sleep. At one o'clock in the morning, there wasn't too much to do.

The next day, people were back on the picket line and getting arrested again. We had massive demonstrations the next day, and most people were back in the lines. We had a revolving picket line, people would get back into line and the police would pull them out. And people would simply come back. At one point, they had gone out and set up facilities out at the Coliseum to process people through the arrests. Then they began to pick people up, put them into patrol cars, take them around the corner and let them out. And those people would simply come back and get into line. We did not see this as a defeat of our mass arrest tactic, because we seized upon the opportunity and, in fact, people were out there the next night. It happened so fast that people really didn't have time to react to it, because when we got the call, it was early, one or two o'clock.

## William Thomas

We were "tricked" out of jail, because negotiations were going on. And in some kind of way, a rumor got started that we—meaning the Executive Committee—had authorized the people that were down at the polio hospital to leave. And most of the A&T students and adults left, based on that rumor. And the Bennett girls refused to leave until we actually arrived—"we" meaning myself and a few other people. We learned afterwards that it was the power structure that started that rumor in order to be able to evacuate the people that they had arrested. The newspapers reported that the City Council had worked out a deal with the governor's office and with the administrative officials of A&T, such that the A&T students were released into the custody of the administration.

I don't believe that Dr. Dowdy was a part of any "deal" with the Governor. There may have been discussions, but I don't think any deal was made. I think that any statement suggesting that Dr. Dowdy threatened to expel any student that continued to demonstrate was taken out of context. I recall that particular incident, but I don't think that those were Dr. Dowdy's words. I think that he probably said that exams would be held on schedule. But again, I don't think that the students were looking to have exams adjourned. We weren't looking for any special treatment. We were committed to a certain cause, and if it meant getting incompletes and taking exams during the summer or the following September, we were prepared to do that.

But at that point, I think that we had basically achieved what we had set out to do. The jails were literally filled; they were overflowing. And I question the fact that a deal was in fact made with either A&T or Bennett. I can recall Dr. Willa Player specifically instructing her girls to do whatever their conscience told them to do, regardless of the effect of examinations or anything else. That she understood their plight and their cause. And as long as they were committed to doing what they were doing, then they should stay there and act out their commitments. I know, for one, she was not a part of any deal.

## Lois Lucas (Williams)

The A&T students had to leave before we did, and we could not go because Dr. Player would not play the role of jailer. You had people that were in one place and people that were in another place, and you had different people being in there and different matrons and people who acted differently.

My feeling about the formation of the Human Relations Committee was that we had been pre-empted, in a way. Suddenly, the city was saying, "We won't deal with you as students or as a CORE group. We are going to go to the larger community and talk with the Establishment and make a deal, although you can sit in if you like." I felt a little bit "sold out," but realized that it wasn't a movement just to get what black college kids wanted; it was a movement to benefit all black people, which included the established black community in Greensboro.

So, even though we had borne the brunt of the struggle, we had been out there on the front lines, so to speak, if now was the time when it came down to saying, "These are the results and if they wanted to give it to somebody else, if they wanted to call in somebody else and let them relay it to us, well, what are you going to do?"

## A. Knighton Stanley

Dr. Dowdy was a committed person, but he was really over a barrel. In personal conversations with me, he did not encourage sit-ins, but at the same time, he let it be known that it was the only possible route that could be taken, and that it was a matter of moral commitment for students to protest in that way, although it made it very difficult for him and the college.

## Lewis Dowdy

By the demonstrations of 1963, I was acting president [of A&T College]. At one time, I believe, there were over twelve hundred students in jail. We took the school physician, nurses, and a minister to take care of those persons who had certain kinds of ailments, such as asthma, and the minister went talked to them. After that, the governor [Terry Sanford] got with the judge, and they had an order which freed all of the students from the jail. They called me and asked me to go out and get them. That was about one o'clock at night. When I went out to the jail to get them, they didn't want to leave. I had to tell them that I wasn't freeing them from the jail; it was an order of the governor and the judge. Finally, we got them to come back.

The students had a meeting in Harrison auditorium while the administration opened the dining hall—it must have been three-thirty in the morning—to fix breakfast for them. Afterward, they went to the dormitories, and then to class. But the demonstrations didn't stop, because they went right on back uptown to gain what they were trying to get in the first place.

*Conditions were in a chaotic state. At this juncture, an aroused adult black community, concerned with the safety of the young people, came forward. After the first mass arrest in May 15, members of the Greensboro Citizens Association, the NAACP, and the Ministers Forum met to create the Coordinating Committee of Pro-Integration Groups under the leadership of Richard Hicks, pastor of the Church of the Redeemer, to act as both a liaison with CORE and to initiate negotiations with city officials.*

*Further, if substantive, long-term gains were to be made by the black community, its representatives had to assume the responsibility of negotiating with the city administration. Black ministers opened their churches to mass meetings. The adults resolved to conduct a silent march, but separately from student marches, and it would have to be carefully monitored. Their first effort was a silent march of over two thousand participants. It proved to be an inspiring act that impressed both the city administration and the general white population.*

## James McMillan

I was booked, fingerprinted, and released under my own recognizance. I had just returned home after being released from jail, about ten-thirty, and Dr. Player called me. She said that she had heard that Dr. Laizner was not with the students who had been arrested, and she wondered if I could find out what had happened to her. I got into the car and drove out to the polio hospital, where they were holding most of our students, to try to get some information about Dr. Laizner. It was not easy, because the policemen were not very cooperative. As I talked to the students about Dr. Laizner's whereabouts, I gathered information about conditions at the hospital. As time went by, there was less a concern about the welfare of the students; perhaps this, too, was a part of the jailing process, but there was very little concern for the care and the comfort of the people there. Many of them had to sleep on the floor, or leaning against the walls. There was hardly any privacy.

I talked to some of the students, and they told me that Dr. Laizner had been removed. I drove to other places of incarceration to try to find her. I knew that some students were being held at city hall, and at the courthouse. eventually discovered that Dr. Laizner had been carried to the High Point jail, very much against her wishes. She had been separated from the group; they had assumed that she was some kind of an instigator, and they didn't want her serving in that capacity. I think that there was a fear on their part that disruptions would occur if there were any further communication between Dr. Laizner and the girls, and that it was an attempt to prevent any resistance to the structure imposed there that took place under Dr. Laizner's direction.

I found Dr. Laizner locked in a basement enclosure with other female prisoners, who were drunk. I think that it was done mainly because Dr. Laizner was white, and the facilities were segregated. The dampness of the area was rather severe, and it gave her a cold at the time; she later came down with some type of flu or respiratory disorder.

After arranging her release, we heard about a meeting at the AME Zion Church where James Farmer and others were addressing members of the community. Despite her ordeal, she insisted on going immediately to the meeting.

## Elizabeth Laizner

We mostly met at Providence Baptist Church, unless we saw that there would be a very large crowd; at those times, we met at the Hayes-Taylor YMCA. Later on, as attendance at the marches grew larger, we would often meet at the Providence Baptist Church, which was Reverend Bishop's church. That was a favorite meeting place for the adult black community.

Mr. Farmer was speaking, and he gave us several options to consider. We could go right back to jail, which was what a lot of us who had just come out wanted, we could just do something little, or we could have one big march, or we could do nothing. We decided after some of us had spoken, on one effective silent march. We went all the way uptown to the Square and then back. When the first group of us was coming back to the old Providence Baptist Church, we saw the last ones leaving the chuch.

## Willa Player

I marched with the people. I believe that it was the march that began at the Student Union Building and went down Elm Street. I don't think that was the first time that the adult members had participated. I think that they had participated pretty much, maybe just a sprinkling but this was more of the adult community than any other time. Somebody said that it was not wise, that it was a mistake for me to march. The president of the Security National Bank called and said that it was a mistake, but it was so orderly that he could not criticize it. It formed from the Student Union Building on the Bennett Campus and into Elm Street where it met all the rest of the group and passed by one of the churches, and then went down Elm Street to Greene Street and terminated at the old post office.

*Both sides remained obdurate as the situation reached a crisis stage. CORE had been successful in filling the jails, but it was running out of troops as the academic year was drawing to a close. City officials were faced with providing for the care of hundreds of arrested students in very overcrowded conditions, and mounting pressures from an aroused adult black community on one hand, and intransigent managers of segregated businesses on the other. If a violently explosive situation were to be avoided, something had to be done quickly.*

*While the A&T students were abruptly released from the polio hospital and the armory on the evening of May 22, Dr. Player's stance forced the retention of the Bennett students in custody. City officials agreed to release the Bennett students and transported them back to campus the next day, without requiring any commitment of custody from the administration. The immediate pressure was temporarily removed, but the tension remained palpable as the antagonists pondered their next move.*

*CORE had been successful in its dramatic change in tactics, which had virtually broken down the judicial system. But the counterstroke of government officials had brought about another stalemate, and the Executive Committee seemed unsure of its next move. Students were anxious to maintain the momentum of the demonstrations, but there was no immediate plan to utilize these restless troops, many of whom wanted to return home, now that the semester was over.*

*CORE, the campuses, the African American community and city government all paused to assess the situation. Students began taking exams, and seniors prepared for graduation. The adult Coordinating Committee took a more assertive role in negotiations, but nothing had been resolved. CORE reserved the right to act independently. As the two sides warily awaited action from its opponent, the tension continued to mount.*

# Chapter 7

## Crescendo

*A week after the mayor's announcement, negotiations had again stalled. Tony Stanley released a statement to the press on June 2, that CORE was losing control of the demonstrations and violence might occur if meaningful results were not forthcoming. Setting a deadline of June 3, he added,. "I'll step back and let others take charge." Without notifying the police, Jesse Jackson then led students and black adults on a silent march through downtown, but did not stop at any designated targets.*

*Armistad Sapp charged in the press that CORE was threatening street riots. At the June 2 City Council meeting, the Coordinating Committee, led by George Simkins, demanded that city employment be based solely on merit and that government facilities be desegregated. Armistad Sapp also presented a petition requiring CORE to pay for damage done to the polio hospital while the students were incarcerated. As in the past, the Council again announced its inability to pass the ordinances requested, tabled Sapp's petition and appointed yet another subcommittee to study the desegregation petition.*

*CORE faced what could have been its most ominous crisis. Students, the mainstay of its troops, were weary after what some considered the failure of the "jail, no bail" strategy, and became concerned that exams and semester's end were fast approaching. The adults had yet to express a commitment to direct action. Although CORE's statements to the press were calculated to maintain pressure on the city government, there was an increasing possibility of violence. At this point, the more militant activists in CORE suggested a radical shift in tactics. They advocated filling downtown streets to block traffic, which might shock the city into meaningful negotiations. The Moderates feared that it would ignite smoldering anger into violence and provoke police brutality. After strenuous debate, the activists prevailed.*

*On June 5, Jesse Jackson announced to the press that demonstrations would resume, citing bad faith by the city. Confusion reigned at the mass* meeting at Providence Baptist Church. Some demonstrators knew that they were to sit down in the street during the march if Jackson gave a pre-arranged signal, others later claimed they did not know what was going to happen. Some CORE leaders thought they were committed to the action, while others thought the decision was to be left up to Jesse Jackson, depending on his take of the mood of the demonstrators. With mixed signals, several hundred demonstrators embarked on the most radical tactic yet of the Movement.

After walking through the downtown area for over an hour, the crowd stopped on Greene Street in front of City Hall. Jesse Jackson told the protesters to kneel while he gave a prayer. Captain Jackson warned Jesse that they would be arrested if they did not disperse, but took no action at the conclusion of the prayer. The demonstrators then marched back to Providence Baptist. Unknowingly, they had initiated what would become the climax of the Movement.

## A. Knighton Stanley

The main reason for the truce from May 25 to June 3 was because the students had to take exams. Jo Spivey was a real friend of ours, and so was Scott Jarrett over at WFMY-TV. We wouldn't tell them the straight-up truth, but even if they saw through our strategy, they would not editorialize on it.

Despite the apparent impasse on June 3, 1963, I never felt that violence was imminent. My comment to the press was a statement of strategy. I had been noted in the press as a somewhat moderate and responsible person with the CORE organization, and by June 6, A&T and Bennett Colleges were both about to close at the end of the school year, which meant that we would not have adequate personnel for demonstrations. What I was indicating by my statement to the press about things getting out of control, which was simply strategic, was that I was going to withdraw, suggesting that the demonstrations would in effect become accelerated. But my chief concern was that we bring closure on the Greensboro situation prior to the closing of school; otherwise we might not have a Movement.

The press interviewed Jesse Jackson after the silent march on June 2, which appeared to break the truce. He said that it was a community march, not one sanctioned by CORE, hinting that CORE could not dictate to the community. That was an intended strategy to imply that CORE might lose control and to say, "We can keep the students calm, but we are not sure that we can keep the community calm." Also, it gave the press the false impression that the march was being conducted by a splinter group of CORE not bound by the truce, which it was not.

## Lois Lucas (Williams)

The Executive Committee vigorously debated the tactic of a mass sit-down at City Hall. Pat Patterson Lewis Brandon, and myself were opposed to it because it bordered on violence. With the college students leaving after exams, more and more of the demonstrators were high school kids not as well disciplined and trained as we were. When people are frustrated and tired, there is the possibility of things getting out of control. I felt a responsibility when there were high school students involved. I believed that those of us who had been a part of the Movement for a long time had a responsibility to those kids who were going to be out there. But that was as far as I was willing to go, at that point. With the tactics that they were advocating, I was against the street sit-down, because the high school kids were not well-disciplined as CORE members and college students,

Both arguments were presented to the membership afterwards. Bill Thomas and Jesse Jackson spoke, and everybody was highly excited about it, with everyone singing "We Shall Overcome" and saying things like, "We shall do this, we're going to go down there, and it's going to be "jail over bail." People got worked up into a frenzy, without thinking through the consequences of what they were going to do, marched downtown and got arrested. I felt that, whereas some of the older ones may have known what they were doing—certainly college students may have known what they were doing—the tenor of the meeting did not allow those kids to think through what they were doing before they went down and were arrested. But I doubt if everyone in the mass meeting heard the announcement, or understood what to do. That is why I did not participate in that demonstration.

## Lewis Brandon

The march led by Jesse on June 3, that the newspaper characterized as a "maverick" march without CORE's sanction, was really a CORE operation; we authorized it. As a matter of fact, in that demonstration there were the students and adults that had been involved in the demonstrations all along. He may have believed that he was doing something without CORE's approval, but we were not about to let any personality run the operation. He had to understand that his role was cosmetic, because he was not a part of the Executive Committee, so he was not a part of the planning activities. He got involved very late, but I insisted. It was the result of my telling him to "put up or shut up. Don't criticize if you're not going to be in on what you are criticizing." That was the kind of conversation that he and I had, so he decided to become involved at that point.

We had been demonstrating and doing things for a long time. His running for president came after his coming out.; it was easier for him to run. Jesse and I had been friends all along. As a matter of fact, I had been his campaign manager for president. One of the things involved was that if he was going to run, he was going to have to get involved with other students, because the other students are out and getting involved in demonstrations. We selected Jesse to lead the march to sit-down on Greene Street in front of City Hall because he had been the person that had been doing all of the leading, all of the praying, and there were a number of instances where he had been at the head of the line.

## James McMillan

The march to City Hall on June 5 was perhaps the most memorable one to me. Despite the downpour the students and the adults followed us in this very quiet procession in twos. As we approached the Square, there were a lot of jeering people, as well as casual onlookers. I recall coming up to the Square just before turning to go south on Elm Street, and noticing this particular group of very angry faces of white men. One of them had a very long, shiny knife held down by his side, but in such a way that we could see the knife. I recall the awful hatred that was etched all across his face. As we approached, I asked Dr. Laizner if she saw what I had seen, and she said that she did. Of course, we were committed at this stage to nonviolence, and there was a kind of a strange feeling that went through me, and that was that this is something that we simply must face. If the person had dared to strike out at that point, there would have been very little that we could have done, other than protecting ourselves by throwing up a hand or something like this, but at least we were committed to that notion. Fortunately, nothing happened as we turned that corner, and marched on down toward the Center Theater, which was, at that point, being picketed.

## William Jackson

The night of June 5 they came around the O. Henry Hotel and down into Greene Street, and this was a little surprise situation. We didn't exactly know that this was going to happen. They sat down in the middle of the street, and we tried to get them out of the street. Jesse Jackson, that time, actually initiated a disturbance by his actions and his words. They came around the hotel, singing, and then Jackson made a speech. I can't recall what was said, but they all flopped into the street. I went to Jackson and asked him to get them out of the street, not to do that, and he went ahead anyhow. We discussed the situation with them, and finally got them to move on out.

That particular night, there was more trouble and more words, tempers were beginning to get short. Things passed between myself and some of the others in the department that ranked above me, but did not have the authority that I had at that time, as far as that demonstration was concerned. In controlling the operation of it, I ranked in authority above some of the lieutenant-colonels. There were State Bureau of Investigation agents there, and one of our people there ranked above me. He and I were real good friends, but I had to tell him to shut his mouth and get out of there. He wanted to prefer charges in the department against me for telling him to shut his mouth. As far as I was concerned, I didn't give a damn whether he did or not.

*For city officials, the die was cast. The demonstrations in May had been orderly, even somewhat ritualized. Now the situation had taken an ominous turn. Instead of well-controlled students, the marchers were largely adults and juveniles who lacked the discipline of the CORE chapter. Although negotiations were being held with members of the Coordinating Committee, CORE officials had made statements to the press suggesting that they were losing control of the demonstrations and did not consider themselves bound by any arrangements made with the Committee. Now they had broken the truce of May 25th with a militant demonstration, involving thousands of unruly participants. The situation was becoming dangerously close to violence. Something had to be done to re-establish control of the situation. The most effective means appeared to be the arrest of Jesse Jackson, a highly-visible symbol of the new militancy, on the serious felony charge of incitement to riot.*

*When Executive Committee members received word of Jackson's imminent arrest, they quickly realized this as a golden opportunity to once again revitalize the Movement. Twice before a dramatic event had given them the means to ratchet up the pressure on the city: the arrests at McDonald's and the mass incarcerations. With the Movement in danger of dissipating once the students were gone, this was their last chance for success. With combined exhilaration and desperation, CORE quickly mobilized to take advantage of this latest development.*

## Furman Melton

We had a few incidents that we considered to be serious. There was the one on Greene Street beside the city administrative building [June 5], and the one where five or six hundred people sat down in the Square at Market and Elm, and the one on Greene Street beside the city administrative building and the police building across the street from the public library [June 6].

On June 5, they started their march from the A&T College campus. They marched up Market Street to Elm Street, up north on Elm Street, and down Greene Street. This was their normal marching pattern. On this occasion, they came to Market and they turned and went north on Elm, and around the old O. Henry Hotel, down Greene Street. Their purpose was to come to the administrative building. I'm not sure what the main issue was, but this is where they were going to specifically stage a sit-in. I think it had something to do with wanting to talk to the city administrators for some reason, and this was where they were going to do it.

They were refused entrance to the building, so they stood there, and Jesse Jackson spoke to them for ten minutes or so. Then, they were ordered to disperse or to proceed with their marching demonstration. They refused, and he ordered all of the people involved to sit down in the street, and they blocked off Greene Street. There was an order directed to Jesse Jackson to tell his group of people to disperse, and, if he refused, then he would be charged with inciting to riot. He was given that order, and he did not order the dispersal, so I placed him under arrest for inciting to riot. He was not taken into custody that night, because of the tension that had been displayed at that time.

That was probably one of the closest instances in all of the demonstrations where, if someone had gotten out of hand, there may have been a lot of people hurt, because both sides—the demonstrators and the police—were truly under a lot of stress. They'd been going on for some time and it had reached a point where everybody was getting edgy, and it was a lot different than when we first started out. The demonstrators were relaxed then, and they would sing their songs. Sometimes I'd see officers sing along with them, because it was just something to do. As the marches proceeded, the day-in, day-out situation saw the tension build up, and there would have been problems that night if we had arrested Jesse Jackson at that time. That particular night it was a very tense, hostile situation. I think that if Jesse Jackson had had a stronger group, if he had of gotten them worked up a little more, or if he had said, "Let's break the police lines, we're not going to be arrested," then it would have been a bad situation.

I know that the charge of incitement to riot against Jesse Jackson was dismissed in court, but the reason it was dismissed was because there wasn't a riot, per se. But the law says there doesn't have to be a riot to be charged with inciting to riot. We had incidents where we had vehicular traffic that we had to block off, and there were a lot of irritated people that were trying to go down Greene Street. All of this grew larger and larger, as a result of him not telling the demonstrators to disperse and move on. So he, being the leader of the group, created that hostile situation. The only reason that there wasn't a riot was because of the patience of the Greensboro Police Department officers. I'd seen in other parts of the country a lot of situations that had reached that stage, then all of a sudden, there were tempers flaring and there was a lot of fighting and injury. I have to credit the Greensboro Police officers that were in these situations; they showed a lot of restraint.

We wanted to charge Jesse Jackson with inciting to riot. The administrative officers, Chief of Police Paul Calhoun, and the city attorney wanted to make sure that the warrant was drawn up properly. So they called the Clerk of Court. They were going to type the warrant up and they wanted it to read sufficient to charge him with inciting to riot. We had never experienced that kind of situation to arise. So they wanted to make sure that everything was right when they served him with the warrant. They knew that the warrant was going to be handled by his lawyers, and it was going to go through the whole process. The decision to arrest him was Captain Jackson, Colonel Birch of the Highway Patrol and mine.

## William Thomas

On my way up to the Church of the Redeemer where we held our offices, I ran into Captain Jackson on East Market Street. He asked me, "Willie, have you seen that Jackson fellow?" I said, "Not since last night, Captain. What can I do for you?" He said, "We have a warrant for his arrest." I said, "For what?" And he said, "Disturbing the peace." So I said, "As a result of his actions last night?" Now, mind you, no riot had occurred. The only thing that happened was Jesse led the group in prayer, and Captain Jackson got on his bullhorn and told us to disperse. And Jesse said, "Not until we have our prayer." Then he told everyone to kneel. He prayed for the Captain and everybody else. And afterwards, everyone rose. They got back in a line, two by two, and we marched back to the church.

So I told Captain Jackson, "Captain, I haven't seen him since last night. But as soon as I see him, I will call you and let you know where you can pick him up." In the interim, we got our leaflets out. We had Jesse to come to the church, where we had photographers, the newspaper and cameramen waiting. We wanted to force the police to literally pick him up and drag him from the altar, but they just waited, waited, waited. And then we said, "Hey, let him go on out." Jesse going to jail for a long time was my least worry. There was no riot; that was a joke.

## William Jackson

We issued a warrant against [Jesse] Jackson the next morning. We were looking for something as a deterrent against any future outbreaks, and if this is what it took, this is what we would do. We did not draw that warrant up just to be drawing a warrant up; we were drawing it up because a law had been violated, and there needed to be something done about it.

After a few telephone calls, I knew that he was at the Church of the Redeemer. When I went to the door, I recognized the fact that he was holding a religious service, so I came back outside and called someone out and said, "When Jackson finishes in there, tell him I want to see him." I waited there on the steps, and when he finished his service, he came out of the door. I placed him under arrest, put him in the car, and he and I came to town. It is probably true that they used it as a way to get publicity, because the news media did not know that I was going there, and the picture was not taken by a *Daily News* or *Record* representative. It was taken by a representative from the college, who was placed there to take this thing. I conducted my business as an officer, and that was it. The photographer snapped his pictures as it was going on, but I had no control over him. I did not pose, and did not cooperate with Jackson. That was a set-up situation.

## Lewis Brandon

Anyone could have been arrested. I remember Captain Jackson coming up to me and saying, "You've got five minutes to get the people out of the way." The city arrested Jesse because he was the most visible person. Once we found out what the police wanted, we staged a media event, which turned out to be newsworthy. We had a good rapport with a Channel 2 reporter whom we could always call and he would be on the spot. But, here again, we used it to get people out and to put more pressure on the city. The plan was to have a rally at the church there and have the people see Jesse go off to jail, and have it so that it would be on the news by 12:00 noon, and the people would see it and would be up for a march.

I called Jesse and told him what was going down, and went and got him and brought him back to the Church of the Redeemer. The leaflets had been prepared and the TV people had been called. Jesse got up and made a statement to the folk who were sitting in the chapel. Captain Jackson and his people had arrived by that time and would not come into the church. The picture that you see of Jesse coming out and shaking Jackson's hand did not show friendship. That's what people suggest, but Captain Jackson was really shocked and he knew that he had been set up, because when he did that a man was on top of him with a camera. You don't see that in the picture; you see Jackson pulling back and Jesse coming out. He wrote "A Letter from a Greensboro Jail" to emulate Martin Luther King's "Letter from a Birmingham Jail," but it was not released to the press. That was his idea; it had nothing to do with us.

## A. Knighton Stanley

It was not planned that Jesse should be arrested. Captain Jackson threw the book at him. But they did not come up with the incitement to riot charge until the day after the sit-down on Greene Street. I think that it had to do with Captain Jackson's provincial suspicions. Here was a new face, an out-of-towner. None of the leadership was downtown that evening, and here rises a person who had apparently assumed leadership, who was unknown to Captain Jackson. He didn't know what was coming down. It was the most radical form of protest that had taken place. What were they going to do with him? I don't think that he did enough to be arrested on the scene; he just made a speech.

He was arrested the next day in a most melodramatic setting. We were over at the Episcopal Church of the Redeemer. Captain Jackson came to arrest Jesse, and we had him in the church. There were not many people in there, but he was making a little speech and we were singing. Captain Jackson came to me and asked for Jesse Jackson. And I said, "Well, he's speaking in the church." Technically, the church was his sanctuary. That's not what I said to Captain Jackson, but that was the symbolism of it all. The press was already there, and I'm sure they were very interested in how the police were going to get this fellow out of there. Captain Jackson looked very much like a puppy dog that day, and he said, "Look, will you go in and tell him to come out?" So I looked to the other leadership, and they said with their eyes, "Yes, there would be nothing wrong with bringing him out to Captain Jackson." We knew that we had really put him [Captain Jackson] on the spot. So Jesse was escorted out of the church by CORE participants with great hoopla, and taken down to the jail.

At that particular time the demonstrations were beginning to be the same old thing. The whole emotional climate had reached its low ebb, and we needed a lift. I can recall the incidents of that very clearly. That's really what created a name for Jesse, and we actually created that whole scene. Once Jesse was arrested, within twenty-four hours we had at least ten thousand leaflets on the street proclaiming Jesse as a great leader. The leaflets basically read, "Your great leader had been arrested," and we called for a mass demonstration that particular night.

Jesse wrote a "Letter from a Greensboro Jail" similar to Martin Luther King's "Letter From a Birmingham Jail", and we passed it out throughout the Greensboro area. And this was read in churches on that particular Sunday. And it was quite dramatic, and it really caused the citizenry of Greensboro to respond. And it brought people out again.

## Alvin Thomas

I think most people knew that we were going to sit down in the Square on the night of June 6. It was discussed in the pre-march meeting. We told them that we would have a sit-down in the Square when a signal was given, and that is exactly what happened. We took the police by surprise. I think that patience on the part of the police and the demonstrators was at an all-time low. The police may have wanted to do something, but Captain Jackson had things very much under control.

When Jesse was arrested at the church on June 6, we hastily arranged for the printing of flyers. We found enough community people to put an effective organization to work on it and get it distributed.

*CORE's strategy worked, as over a thousand members of the African American community marched downtown. But the situation was different from the demonstrations in May. CORE decided that blocking the intersections could be more effective than just marches. The night before, Jesse had led demonstrators through the downtown area, kneeling in the street in front of City Hall as he gave a prayer and then returned the crowd to the Church of the Redeemer. But this time everyone would go to Jefferson Square, sit down and await arrest. The heated debate over this tactic caused several Ecutive Committee members to refuse to participate over concern about possible violence. As instructions were given to the boisterous crowd, some Executive Committee members were confident that all knew what was to occur, but others had deep misgivings as they watched the demonstrators file out of the church and into the street.*

## A. Knighton Stanley

The adults were, by and large, support people. They became involved after mass arrests when emergency needs developed. There was conflict at that time with the adult community because they felt that since the town was really in a state of crisis as a result of the arrests, that the city fathers should negotiate whatever settlements were to be made, and the CORE leadership insisted that they had no control over it; the committee couldn't negotiate anything because they didn't control the troops. Its role was basically support and positive encouragement.

In the Executive Committee debate, I lost control over the strategy. The strategy was to go to the Square where Elm Street crosses Market Street, and they would march orderly and then they would break ranks and sit down in the middle of the street at the intersection. My impression of that decision was that it was the most irresponsible thing in the world, because we were using some adult citizens and teenagers who were not trained in nonviolent passive resistance. I have the feeling that it was done under extreme exhaustion.

I was bothered that no leadership went that evening. Another thing was that the seats of the Duke Power buses that were used to take away the people arrested were slashed. Part of my reluctance to support the sit-down tactic was my basically conservative nature about such things. But in retrospect, it was not bad. It was good strategy because we had gotten a lot of local citizens involved. They were not people with big names in Greensboro or professionals that the city had been used to dealing with, but high school students and laboring kinds of people. If they had not joined us, the demonstrations may well have failed. A&T and Bennett had been almost our total source of troops, but schools were ready to close, and we had nothing else to throw out there. It was very interesting that the news media never picked up the fact that we didn't have anyone to fall back on; we were operating out of a closed closet with very few people. Therefore, that evening gave a signal to the City of Greensboro that there would be an escalation and disorderliness if something did not break very soon.

## Lewis Brandon

There was some discussion about conducting a sit-down in the Square for about two weeks before it occurred. It was inevitable that it was going to take place, but we had been talking about it all along, but there was nothing left but to do it. That was the climax of the demonstrations. It had been building up to the point that we had to do something very dramatic. It was tense, but as to how explosive it was, I'm not sure, because the police had pretty well sealed off the area. There was a meeting about it with McKissick. Something had to be done, something very dramatic that would break this stalemate. There was some discussion about flooding the stores downtown, with the people sitting in them; getting the students to walk out together from the schools. Something very dramatic.

The sit-down on Greene Street probably was more spontaneous, because there had been no real discussion about Greene Street. The discussion was always sitting down at the Square. Some of the people were taken to High Point and others to the city jail, but they weren't put back in the polio hospital. I don't think that people were thinking about violence, but they felt that there was going to be something dramatic, that there had to be a showdown, that we had to force Schenck out and take a stand.

There was legitimate concern within the Executive Committee about the participation of high school students, but this was a community event, and people from all walks of life were participating, and there had been high school students all along who had been very active and were participating and very vocal in the meetings. There was a lot of leadership from the high schools that were participating in CORE and revolving around the Executive Committee, so to me, that was not the point; the point was whether someone else would do something that would hurt anyone.

That was not the only thing that people were considering. One of the things was going to the major stores like Belk's and having a massive sit-in in one of the stores. Another thing was at a given signal, all of the kids would walk out of the schools. There were a lot of different things that were discussed. One of the things with me was, if you did have a mass sit-down in the street, how would you guard against someone just driving through the crowd, not whether the people were high school students. We had to assume that the police would protect them, because you couldn't guard against that. There was always a risk of anything happening whenever you had demonstration.

## Cecil Bishop

The people were, I guess, four or five abreast from just west of the railroad overpass where Old Pearson Street used to be, what is now Murrow Boulevard, from there all the way back up to Hayes-Taylor YMCA. You just had the sidewalk abreast as wide as the sidewalk could take all the way back. And this was largely the adult black community.

The reason that it hadn't happened sooner was that there had not been the synthesizing of leadership and of focus. But now we started to have a focus. And that focus then brought together the black community: students, adult blacks, religious and educational institutions. If you were black, these were your problems. The Coordinating Committee sort of evolved out of people talking about an imperative to coordinate the demands of the students and the needs of the broader black community. I think it came about as a result of the basic initiatives that did emanate from the student community picked up, supported and carried on by people in the adult black community, particularly at that time, leadership in the black clergy, Greensboro Citizens, NAACP, and the Greensboro Men's Club.

We'd have a mass meeting. And then people from these various entities would make statements and suggestions: "The Citizens' Association's going to meet Tuesday night, and we're going to do so and so." There was an obvious need for coordinating this whole movement. And I think a lot of that kind of thing did it, gave rise to the Coordinating Committee. The fact that people were often members of more than one of this organization also facilitated cooperation. Sometimes the students would come to the Committee and inform us what they were going to do and ask for a coordinated effort or just to let us know what would be going on. And at other times, the Coordinating

Committee had decided on a course of action, and we would inform the students of our intentions. The Coordinating Committee would say "X, Y and Z," and that would go back to the member organizations of the Coordinating Committee. So both of these methods of operation were employed.

A goodly number of things arose from the student community. It was just sort of like the student community provided the advance troops and the adult community provided the backup.

## William Jackson

The events on the next night [June 6] were altogether different than it was with Jackson the night before. He was in jail on that particular night, and there were more than fifteen hundred or more marching without a recognized leader. They came up Market Street to Elm Street, turned down by the O. Henry Hotel, came back by the Mayfair Cafeteria, and up to the Square, and somebody said "Sit down." When the marchers heard that, they sat down, and when they did, I stood up on a car bumper there and told them who I was and said, "You will get up and move, and if you do not, you will be arrested." They didn't move, and I said, "You are all under arrest." A cordon of police officers circled them, and we arrested them.

Tempers flared a little bit. One of my men had taken about all that he could, and he was throwing a punch; I happened to get there in time to stop his action. It could have really caused something. I will have to say that the man was justified; he wasn't put out there to be abused, and we weren't abusing them. On that particular night, there was a lot of verbal abuse.

## Furman Melton

We sealed off the area around City Hall and the Administration Building, and from Sternberger Place to Friendly Avenue. The only way to handle them was to take just so many at a time, load them in the bus, and we used cars, three in a car and filled up a bus, eight or ten in the paddy wagon, or whatever vehicles that we could work in there, and move them out, and to be as organized as we could under those circumstances. We had officers that were directing vehicular traffic from citizens that were trying to get through Greene Street. Everything was bottled up. So we had to take care of that traffic, plus we had to move the vehicles in there that we were going to use to transport the prisoners.

It was quite an ordeal to get all of that organized, and to get them out of there as quickly as possible without any trouble. The theory has always been that when you arrest someone, especially in a group, the policy is to arrest them, get them into the vehicle, and move them out of the area. If you start having to struggle with the group, then this is when all your problems start happening. So this is the way we did it that night.

All of them were told by bullhorn that they were under arrest, and told not to break the police line. In this particular situation, they wanted to be arrested. So it was not like a group of riotous people, where there's violence going on and they're not going to abide by what you tell them. We didn't have that kind of situation, thank goodness. It's hard to have crowd control if they're resisting. I'd say it was on up in the wee hours of the morning before we got everything calmed down to where some officers could be relieved.

Those that created problems and resisted were taken to jail. All of those were housed in the jail, separate from the group that wasn't causing any problem, because if we put them in with the other group, then they'd just incite the other group to do more damage. If you have an individual that is resisting, then other people are sympathetic with them, and want to get involved.

## A. Knighton Stanley

I did not concur in the sit-down in the Square when it was discussed in the Executive Committee of CORE, because I felt that if that radical move was taken, that the leadership of CORE should have been present and involved in it, and to have seen to it that the demonstrators were protected. [Jesse] was given the order; the demonstrators themselves did not know that was what they were supposed to do. The notion was advanced by Isaac Reynolds. I did not concur as a part of the strategy committee. Therefore, I did not go. Bill Thomas did not go, nor did Isaac Reynolds. Lewis Brandon did not agree either. I don't think that he went, but he was not with us when we heard the commotion in Jefferson Square from the Church of the Redeemer. I had a deep sense of guilt about demonstrators being there without the kind of controls we usually had for their protection. Pat Patterson, Lewis Brandon and I were against it, but there was not a split in CORE. The leadership remained together as to the strategy of the Jefferson Square.

The next night at the Square the police perception and that of the press was that it was a leaderless mob. But it actually was not. Both evenings, the groups were sent downtown with specific instructions as to what to do; it was not spontaneous. Despite the apparent impasse on June 5, I never felt that violence was imminent.

## Cecil Bishop

The demonstration that I remember most vividly is the one that took place right here in the Square when all those people were arrested. Here was this march on downtown. And it was just a street full of people. And a lot of the adult community, a mix of students, adults, the community was visibly demonstrating its protest. I think people had had it just about up to here and they were read to go to jail. It really seemed spontaneous.

And so Captain Jackson and the police department were there. And they just made mass arrests and took people to jail in buses and took them over to the Coliseum and processed them. That could have erupted into something of a violent nature, because of the numbers of people, but it did not. And it was amazing. I was standing right on the curb, saying, "Well, I'm sure that somebody is going to take me by the hand," but they just went on past me. The interesting thing was that many people who were not sitting down were arrested. The reason I remember it so well was that I had a member of my congregation who had formerly been a member of the police force. He was in the demonstration. He was not seated, but they just herded him right on in. And there were others like him.

The motivation of the ministers was two-fold. One, most of the black clergymen saw their participation as constantly keeping "the white power structure" mindful that the black community is not happy, is not satisfied. "There is great unrest; we want conditions to change." And two, saying to our own constituency, "Do not despair, and do not become so frustrated that you become violent. Stay with the movement, participate. Have no fear of anything happening."

We were counseling nonviolence. That was the whole thrust of what we were trying to say to downtown and the other message to our people. And we would say that to both sides. I remember some meetings where there would be representatives [of the white power structure] present. Mr. Zane, who was with Burlington, was like an unofficial goodwill ambassador, with a lot of clout, both ways. He would bring a lot of things and take a lot of things back, on occasion with some members of the City Council.

We would say to our people, "We're trying to keep the pressure on those folks downtown. We would say to downtown, "We're trying to keep our people informed, and we're urging nonviolence. We hope that we can continue, that, and we would hope that our counsel will be heeded." And we were quick to point out that we got no assurance from city officials that progress was being made. I got the feeling that downtown wanted us to promise, that nothing would happen. But we couldn't make that promise.

## Evander Gilmer

The night of the big sit-in on the Square was the point when my mother was willing to participate, but she didn't want me to go to jail. We had a meeting at Providence Baptist Church, and then we filed downtown. [When we got to the Square] the command was given to sit down, but before everyone could sit down, the police locked in all of those who were in the Square for an arrest. That was not something that we had talked about, or even thought would happen. We didn't go expecting that. We were going, expecting some prayers in the Square area and return to the church, like the night before.

The police were rough with those billy clubs, and they were roping us in. They were trying to contain all of the people in the Square, prodding us and pushing us. My mother and I were just on the inside of the police line, and we broke loose [and went] under their clubs. There was little they could do, because if they opened up to get us, then others would have come out. I did that because my mother was in there. I wasn't sure what they were about to do, whether they were going to arrest us or not, and I felt a little protective. We started filing back, and they started busing these people away. I'm not sure how many people they arrested that night, but there were still a lot of people on the street. Whenever we marched downtown, there were always some of us who were monitors, who walked along to make sure that people stayed in twos and moved along. I was a monitor. When we were going back down to the church, I recall again being roughed up a little by one of the policemen on the street. My mother was upset that this policeman had pushed me and raised his billy as though he were going to hit me, and they got into an argument. From that point on my mother was ready to go and demonstrate.

## Otis Hairston, Jr.

On the night of June 6 we marched to the S&W, and a few people tried to enter, which they couldn't. There were a few small speeches made there by some march leader. After that, I think that things sort of got out of hand, because we were all arrested for blocking the intersection, and everyone sat down in the middle of the intersection of Market and Elm. Things were in danger of getting out of control, and it wasn't like it had been in the past. There was really an "I don't care" attitude by the marchers as to possible vio-lence, and I think that really could have been a big confrontation if there had been a lot of hecklers, or if the police had tried to impose rigid control. Jesse's arrest was upsetting to a lot of the marchers, and their attitude was, "You have arrested our leader, and we want to join him." It was a very tense time. I think that there was a little fear in me that night, too, because I could just sense the tone of the marchers. I was not fearful of anything actually hap-pening to me, but it was just the atmosphere and the tone of the whole situation that things could explode. At that age I probably could have exploded with it. It was not planned from the beginning that the people were to sit down in the Square; in fact, I don't remember receiving any instructions.

I think that the arrests at the Square were a little different than previous ones. I was either taken away in a police car or a paddy wagon, and I was taken to the courthouse to be processed, as opposed to the Coliseum. At that time I was placed in the city jail, and I think that because of the atmosphere there, it was a little harder to deal with than the situation at the polio hospital. Behind bars, I had the feeling of being criminal, rather than a protester. There were a few other prisoners there, but the protesters were primarily the only ones there. I was there two or three days. I believe that we were bailed out again.

## Frances Herbin (Lewis)

I sat down on Greene Street on the night of June 5 and in the Square on the night of June 6. On June 6, the police did not give us a chance to sit down, although that was our intention. When we got there, the police made a circle around us, and everybody that was within the circle was arrested. I felt that there was a possibility of violence, but I never feared that it would happen. I would protect myself, but only if my well-being was in danger; I think that this was the basic attitude that prevailed.

I actually believe that some hecklers would have enjoyed a violent confrontation, but I never saw any violence. The police kept the hecklers away, to an extent, but they allowed them to stay. They got close enough to spit on us and throw things and shove us. It never happened to me, and I did not see it directly. There were reported incidents of hecklers spitting on people. We got our share of shoves and verbal abuse from the hecklers, and the articulations with the police; in the event that they had the opportunity, they took advantage of it. I was roughed up and shoved and hurt.

But of course, it is always the excuse that, "Well, we're in crowded conditions," which can be true. I didn't really notice any change in attitude in the police that night. I think that they were a little anxious. I think that it was before they really had the opportunity to see what was to be done. They had already made up in their minds, or received instructions, to arrest us. They didn't know whether you would sit there for a long time, or you would sit there one minute and leave. They didn't wait to see. Looking back, I'm not angry; I think that it was something that had to be done, and I think that was the opportune time to do it. [The sit-down on June 6] probably wasn't as well planned as the earlier activities. Many of the college students had left town, but their places were taken by town students and high school students. We usually got support from some of the high school students, but as things shifted further into the summer, the high school students constituted a large percent of the marchers. Some of us were taken to the Coliseum, or that we may have been taken directly to the hospital. Unlike before, this time we were not held. We were arrested, processed, released and returned to the campus.

## Marion Jones

My wife and my daughter were both arrested the night that we had the sit-down in the Square. There were no bails. They were incarcerated uptown there at the Square. This is where they were all arrested, including my wife. They all stayed out at the polio hospital. We carried supplies to them that they wanted. As a matter of fact, I didn't visit my daughter and wife; we just carried the stuff out there, but we were allowed to talk with our families. The conditions were all right, just crowded. But they were willing to put up with the conditions rather than be released from prison.

## George Evans

Local groups in the black community— church groups, fraternity groups, sorority groups—wanted to demonstrate support of the CORE marches by establishing contact with the leadership of CORE, while independently trying to effect some sort of compromise with the managers of the various restaurants, theaters and other businesses in desegregating, and to open negotiations with city officials. We named our organization the Coordinating Committee of Pro-Integration Groups. This committee consisted of leaders from CORE, the NAACP, the Greensboro Citizens Association and the Ministers Forum. An increasing number of members of the black community were joining the demonstrations as individuals, and we thought that it would be useful to coordinate our support of the young people with broader concerns of the black community.

We served as a liaison with CORE, but were separate from it. But we thought that CORE served a positive function through its demonstrations, because it was a much more militant organization than the NAACP. And the demonstrations were of such a nature that I think personally that they needed more militancy in the leadership of the demonstrations than any other organization at that time would have given it. The NAACP and various members and leaders of the black community supported the demonstrations, but felt this was not the role of the NAACP.

CORE did not offer any cooperation with my committee at all, regarding the resumption of demonstrations after the May 25 truce, so that it came about without our knowledge. The only contact probably would have been some unofficial contacts. But for the most part, they went on their own in conducting the demonstrations. I should add that most of the members of my committee were not opposed to what the demonstrators were doing. In fact, a number of the members of my committee, including my wife and me, joined the demonstrations in their marches on several occasions. I didn't feel that there was any conflict between our action and my role as a negotiator at all. It was just a matter of different groups, different organizations trying to achieve the same goal, just going about it separately but also agreeing with the ultimate aim of all of the organizations. I was not in the demonstrations in which people were arrested. On a couple of evenings when that did take place, my committee was meeting, so that I couldn't be at both places at the same time. I think had it not been for that, I probably would have been in the march.

As far as I know, there was not any clear form which the demonstrations would take. And, I think, perhaps, if any decision was made about which way to conduct the demonstrations, it was done by the leaders of the demonstrations, and without the knowledge of those who participated in the marches. Those in which my wife and I participated were silent demonstrations. For example, we left the Trinity AME Church on a couple of evenings and marched silently from there right on down Market Street to Elm and so on around the downtown area.

The city officials did not directly enter negotiations as a Council. The mayor himself, I guess, was the main contact that we had with the Council, or with the city fathers. And some of the white members of our committee, including Mr. Zane and Mr. Burnett, had much more contact with members of the Council than I had. I guess largely because they felt that they would be able to get a little further toward some resolution of the problem than I could. So their contact was made with members of the Council, not necessarily on an official basis, but more or less unofficially. Mayor Schenck gave the appearance of wanting some kind of compromise. But at the same time, I think he was a little bit recalcitrant, not because of any desire on his part personally,. I think he was wary of the reaction of the business community and city hierarchy and his own friends and neighbors in his community to his going too far afield in trying to get things opened up. I think if it had been left to him personally, without having to think about the reaction of others in the community, he might have moved a little bit faster.

We felt that the City Council dragged its feet a great deal more than they should have. We thought all along that they could have done a great deal more to facilitate the solution of the problem if they had been willing to do so, by taking an active role in urging some of these businesses that we had talked about to go ahead with the opening of their doors and welcoming anybody in the community into their businesses. But the City Council did not at any time, to my knowledge, take any official position on trying to influence these business people. If they did, it was done without it being made an official act.

I think it was feasible for the Council to have passed an ordinance such as the one that CORE demanded. At the same time, I can appreciate the position of the Council in going very slowly with it because of fear of reaction from the leading businesspeople in the community. But in the light of the unrest that was going on and the threat of violence down the way, I felt that the City Council could have and should have, acted more vigorously in trying to bring things to conclusion, regardless of the reaction of businesses.

For the most part, I think the Police Department was somewhat restrained in its handling [of] situations. Those in which I was involved—the marches, for example—were handled well. Members of the law enforcement agencies were on hand, and they saw to it that the marches were undisturbed. When it came to the matter of the more vigorous demonstrations, such as sitting in the streets, I was not present at any of those. I heard such conflicting reports about the behavior of the police, that I couldn't make a definite judgment. Some people felt that they did a good job of handling it, and there were some others who felt that the police did not do half of what they could have done. So there were conflicting opinions depending on the person's point of view. I didn't hear of any direct police brutality. But I'm thinking of such things as arresting large masses of demonstrators and putting them in the county home [Central Carolina Rehabilitation Hospital], or some place like that and keeping them there sometimes overnight, and the place being cold and without enough sanitary facilities, without enough sleeping facilities, without adequate provision for food, and so forth. So it was felt that that was sort of "insensitivity" there. We thought that those things could have been handled on a better basis.

## Clarence Malone

It was just a fluke that I didn't witness the sit-down on Greene Street. I had not planned or had any idea that I would be involved in the Greensboro demonstrations until about five o'clock in the morning before I was to appear in court in Greensboro, because as far as I know McKissick was supposed to have handled the cases that arose in there. And it just happened that there were mass demonstrations and jail-ins in Durham, and when it broke, I remember that I left the Durham county jail at one or two o'clock in the morning. I finally got home from that, and just as I started to get into bed, McKissick called me and asked me if I could be in Greensboro the next day and hold the fort until he could get there. So I hurried there without closing out my affairs or taking any steps to be away for any extended period of time. Once having gotten there, it was an around-the-clock kind of thing, and that weekend I simply came home. [Laughs] And for that reason, I was not present or did not witness any of it.

Jesse Jackson was president of the student body at A&T, and the least effective of the student leaders at that time, but he represented to the power structure a leader because of his position as president of the student body. He had made a couple of fiery speeches, but the true spirit behind the Movement was Bill Thomas, who was generally unknown. He was quiet, so nobody in the city administration knew where the impetus of the guidance was coming from, and since it was mostly students, it focused on A&T's campus. And he

[Jackson], being the titular head of the student body, I think that he was charged with a very serious felony simply as a tactic of picking off the top: "You cut off the head and the body is bound to die." There was every chance of conviction in his case. The jury selection process at that time was geared so that the the officialdom could rig juries any way that they wanted them. And, for the most part, they would rig it up with Pomona and all of the outlying areas, rednecks to whom the evidence would have made absolutely no difference at all. You had prevailing at that time, a much less serious scale, the atmosphere in which the Wilmington Ten were convicted. His case was simply dismissed.

## Otis Hairston, Sr.

The Coordinating Committee played the role of trying to get the businesses to negotiate. The students thought that they needed some adults to represent them. Dr. W. L. T. Miller, Mr. Vance Chavis, Dr. Barnes, Dr. Simkins, Dr. Player and I were on that committee. I served on that committee. We had one person whom the students wanted to represent them in negotiations with the folk downtown. It may be that the folk downtown did not want to negotiate with the students, and this committee was picked by the students to negotiate with the folk.

## Marion Jones

I served on the Coordinating Committee of Pro-Integration Groups. Actually, we felt that the organization could reach the greatest number of persons, both white and black, who were influential businessmen, and people respected them highly. The Ministerial Alliance, naturally, could reach all of the people, and the objective was to get a listing here of all of Greensboro citizens. We felt that because these businessmen were as well known as they were, we would be getting the ear of the people. We met as regularly as we saw the need to meet. We would always focus on the needs of our people, their hopes and aspirations and work toward those goals. At the same time, we tried to encourage people to attend meetings by publicizing it in our church on Sunday. These are the things that we focused on when we first began to march.

The mass adult march on May 23, in which there were from 200 to 500 people, was the first significant adult participation. It came about as a result of people being convinced that they could help bring about a change; that it would take all of us to get the heart, the ear, and the eye of the city. I would say that the ministers, primarily, were responsible for bringing that about, and the NAACP and CORE depended on us. They counted on us to use the church facilities to get the message over. The objectives of the demonstration would be presented at the meeting, and the methods of approaches would be presented, and always the discouragement of resorting to violence, name-calling, rock-throwing, all of this was done repeatedly.

We would always map out the places that we would frequent, what time element we were talking about, the approach, and this kind of thing. There was no serious division in the adult community between those that thought that this was not the right approach and those that supported it. Seldom did you have a negative attitude about the whole thing. There were those who were reluctant to get involved in the very beginning, but that soon phased out and people found themselves involved. The word that there would be a demonstration on a particular night was communicated through the churches. It was usually at a prayer meeting on Sunday and people attended church regularly; we would pass out flyers and make telephone calls. We used every form of communication that we could to alert the people. I would consider the most active leaders of the black community [in this effort] to be Reverend Hairston, Dr. Evans, Dr. Simkins and Dr. Tarpley. .

## A. Knighton Stanley

There was work behind the scenes, but for the most part, when the demonstrations escalated, the components of the Coordinating Committee of Pro-Integration Groups other than CORE—the NAACP, the Greensboro Citizens Association, and the Ministerial Alliance—served as service units to take care of humanitarian needs of those in jail. There were some negotiations but, by and large, they turned their attention to the health and humanitarian needs of those who were in jail. They did some negotiating, but it was not very serious.

*With the creation of the Coordinating Committee by influential black adult organizations, Mayor Schenck realized that the demonstrations had broadened to a more sophisticated protest that would not end with the students going home at the end of the academic year. The city government would have to take a more decisive role in bringing the increasingly volatile situation to an end. Although harboring reservations about Mayor Pro Tem William Trotter's promise to create a new Human Relations Committee,, he endorsed it and called for a meeting of business leaders in his office, to be followed by a press conference on the morning of June 7.*

## Clarence Malone

The major number of persons that were arrested arose out of one march. They were charged under a construction ordinance, really, for blocking a public street. What happened was, during some of the marches, they marched down to the Elm and Market Streets, the hub of the traffic center, then lay down in the middle of the street and blocked traffic in every direction. There must have been fifteen hundred or two thousand persons arrested at that time and charged with blocking a public street; I don't recall the specific charge. Those cases were subsequently carried to the State Supreme Court, and the State Supreme Court's decision, written by Hunt Parker, threw out the application of the ordinance, in that it was taken out of context and therefore simply did not apply. The thrust of my argument was that the ordinance was originally passed to contemplate inanimate objects, certainly not human beings and, therefore, should not be applied to them.

## James McMillan

The night that everyone sat down in the Square was another memorable night. It represented a frustration out of all the activities we had gone through to shake loose the last vestiges of segregation in the city, and it looked as if just about all of our efforts had gone to naught. But, perhaps, it was at that time that many of the changes did take place, because out of that came the major, final changes.

On June 6 I was not arrested, but I was a part of the march that preceded it. The sit-down in the Square was really a kind of frustrated "fallout" in the black community over the intransigence of the city administration. We saw that there was no other way to solve this concern that we had addressed ourselves to all these months. Perhaps that was the kind of thing that helped to make the change, but it was really the boycott that did the job that we had been trying to do by other means. The combined activities were the main thrust. My father, who was in his seventies, was arrested on June 7. This is an indication of the broad community involvement which had escalated to that point.

We saw that, as many of these changes would not take place, and that some of the resistance was not so much with one particular establishment, that it was the financial power structure that had become the crux of the matter at this stage. The black community began to focus itself more toward businesses and business attitudes, and [decided] to boycott downtown businesses until these changes took place. Several of us in the art department of Bennett made posters and bumper stickers that urged people in the black community to support the boycott, and we had a printer run them off for us. We had quite a time trying to come up with the right catch phrase. So the boycott came only as a last resort, but it made the difference. It seems to me that it lasted right up until changes took place.

# Keep on Walkin', Keep on Talkin'

## David Schenck, Jr.

There was a sense of a boundary between [my father's] private and public life which he attempted to maintain at that time. I remember an air charged with tension. He would disappear on Sunday afternoon, and I wouldn't see him again until Monday or Tuesday or Wednesday, because he would be late at the police station, and my mother seemed very nervous. I remember two evenings in particular when my mother came home very upset and bundled us all into the car, and we all spent the night at my grandfather's house, and at the home of a family friend another night. Later I was told that it was because there had been threats made on us children by white groups of various kinds. My uncle has told me that there were plainclothes policemen sleeping in the house from time to time. There were no threats from the black community, insofar as I was aware. We had a second phone put in with a private line. Because the phone was constantly busy with mostly abusive phone calls, often threats, we didn't answer the public line after six o'clock in the evening. Eventually, my father had the phone disconnected.

We also received hate mail. There was a telegram dated June 13, 1963, which read: "What outside pressure could have made you sell your Greensboro voters down the river in your speech? Don't make us give in. They will only want more. Let's quit giving in and make the Negro earn a place for himself." Another said: "Don't appreciate your discourtesy on a phone call to you to explain to you my personal feelings, plus many others who are chicken. I think that you have thrown Greensboro for a loop because of your so-called 'political aspirations.' You have sold Greensboro down the river." Another said, "Your attitude over integration is shameful and disgusting. You no longer represent the white majority of your city, but are devoted only to dragging them down to the Negro's level. Your support of these savages is inconceivable and your fear unwarranted, since we can whip the Negroes any time that they want to fight." In another, addressed to the City Council asking for [my father's] resignation, was worded: "Is he a Communist, like so many of the NAACP group? I would like to ask you to request his resignation, since he does not represent the true citizens or the majority."

Those were not from people with any significant power in the community. But there were some letters relating to the statement from some more prominent people. Joe Hunt, former Speaker of the House, wrote: "Yielding to blackmail has never paid off in Washington, Greensboro or any other place in the world. You are in a tough spot and I have felt for you, but yielding to the mob will not solve you problem; it will only compound it." Another from an attorney in the Smith, Moore, Smith, Schell & Hunter firm, a very prestigious law firm: "While I agree with you that peace is desirable, how could infer that demonstrations and violations have been the fault of law-abiding businessmen? To deny them protection of the law is unthinkable. Capitulating to threats of violence, lawlessness and vandalism will bring you more headaches in the future than you ever thought possible." A partner of that firm was also very active in representing the theater group and some of the motels that wanted to maintain a segregated policy. [*Note: McNeill Smith, another member of that law firm, was very active independently and behind-the-scenes, seeking to resolve the crisis in such a way as to meet the demonstrators' demands.*]

My father's political philosophy, was fairly conservative, but he was not a racist of any sort. He took Christian principles seriously and combined that with his conservative political philosophy. So, when he said "The government can't resolve this," that was his genuine conservative political philosophy. He believed that, given the kind of economic system and the government that we have, there are limits to what a symbolic statement could do. I think my father overlooked the importance of such a statement, and it was the genius of the CORE strategy to force him to make that statement. So he rejected the idea that the City Council could pass a resolution barring segregation in places of public accommodation. But I don't think CORE was really asking for an endorsement from him. I think that they wanted a statement and a kind of a closed-door persuasion.

If you think about the city government of Greensboro and the economic structure of Greensboro, demanding that city hall put pressure on the business community was backwards. The council-manager form of government is relatively weak in terms of political power. The dominant economic powers in Greensboro were Cone Mills, Burlington Industries, and the life insurance companies. My father was thirty-six in 1963 and was running a small insurance business. He was not in a position economically or socially to muscle around Cone Mills or Burlington Industries. He tried to arrange a crucial meeting before he made his statement [on June 7, 1963]. Howard Holderness [Jefferson-Pilot Insurance Company], Caesar Cone [Cone Mills] and Charles Hayes, Ed Morris [Blue Bell] and W. C. Boren [Boren Brick] all declined to attend.

This was not the kind of support from those with economic power that would have been helpful at that time. I think that he believed the situation had gotten to the point where he had to act, and here the CORE strategy was at its most successful. He could no longer wait to get these people's support; something had to be done immediately. But the stack of letters that he received indicates that the supportive letters were about three to one. They were from all segments of the community. Despite the lack of support from many prominent members of the economic community, slightly more than fifty percent of the people who did attend the meeting agreed to desegregate. Most of the segregated targets were not on the "yes" side of the list: Casey's Barbeque, Apple House Restaurants, the General Greene Motel, Honey's, Irving Park Delicatessen, Lawndale Steak House, the King Cotton Hotel, the Mayfair Cafeteria, the O. Henry Hotel, the Plantation Supper Club, the S&W Cafeteria, Swain's and so on.

I was told that he was on the phone on a daily basis. There are various and sundry memos that say, "Governor holding on line two" and things like that. City Manager Townsend retired and there was a period in which Dad was city manager and mayor, in effect. Hines was hired [as city manager] and soon died of cancer, creating another interim period, and then George Aull was recruited. So there was a long period where my father neglected his insurance business almost completely and worked as city manager and mayor. The mayor's position was a part-time position and paid very poorly. During that period, his senior secretary embezzled about $10,000. To a small businessman, that was a significant amount of money. In other words, the drain of the office was significant.

I think that he regarded the pressure that CORE put on him as unfair. He felt torn in a variety of directions, and I think this was part of CORE's strategy. I think that he felt several ties to the white power structure, although he was very much a junior member of it. On the other hand, he was very much repulsed by Klan-type activity. But he was very upset, as a political conservative, by pressure tactics, and felt they violated the basic rules of order that were necessary for political discourse to come into play. At the same time, he was sympathetic to the cause of desegregation, and not understanding why certain of the downtown businesses could not go ahead and desegregate. So he was being pulled in a variety of directions at once. I have no doubt that there was no deviation from his own conviction and the June 7 statement.

I don't think that my father's role in this needs a defense, but I think that the personal side is very complex. My parents had an apparently mistaken sense of the relationship between my father as mayor and Governor Sanford, which they believed to be warm, cordial, with mutual respect from working closely together in a time of crisis and holding things together. It is clear that Sanford's record on racial matters was more progressive than my father's, but that is not the point. It seems that a part of the complexity and the tragedy of political life comes in having to convey one impression to one audience and another impression to another audience. I think that Terry Sanford subsequently made political hay out of the claim that he essentially wrote the statement that appeared in the newspaper on June 7, [which] was, to a certain degree, justifiable. He had a more astute moral vision than most Southern politicians, but I think that it is clear from the drafts of the letter in my father's papers that he, and not Governor Sanford, wrote the letter.

# Chapter 8

## Resolution

When the demonstrations ceased and the adult members of the African American community took over negotiations with city officials in June 1963, the college students left Greensboro either for summer recess or to pursue post-graduate careers. Once again CORE was reduced to a small cadre of committed activists. Although they participated in small picketing and boycott activities over economic or employment issues, the CORE chapter was frustrated by its inability to formulate a comprehensive program to integrate the Greensboro community on a broad scale.

After the excitement of the demonstrations and initial success in desegregating the cafeterias and theaters, the members experienced a loss of dynamic focus. There were occasional small victories: forcing a local bank to hire a black teller or a retail store to employ a black clerk, but this paled in comparison to the exhilaration of the thousands of enthusiastic supporters that had brought city officials to the negotiating table. Some believed the battle not over and missed the fervor of the struggle. And there were divisive elements that plagued Civil Rights Movement organizations nationally. Increasingly, the members wanted the Movement to be a totally black one, and the few white participants felt unwanted. Militant members still advocated the use of direct action methods, but they were being displaced by those who recognized that period had passed, and it was now time for quiet, behind-the-scenes bargaining with the powers-that-be.

Despite CORE's apparent support of the compromise with city officials, the Executive Committee was in a quandary. The members recognized that they needed the clout of the leaders of the black community to force the city to negotiate in good faith. But they resented being pre-empted by the adults. The students' persistent sit-ins and picketing of segregated businesses, their nightly presence in the streets and their willingness to go to jail had created the Movement that could realize the deferred aspirations of the adult black community. It rankled them to be shunted aside as if *they were children, while city officials and the adult African American community took over the "serious work" of negotiations.*

*But CORE also knew that the volatile dynamic of direct action was passing. With the ending of the academic year they could no longer command the troops that had given it strength. The inevitable "battle fatigue" of intense commitment and the desire to pursue individual careers was causing an increasing number of students to leave the chapter. Many reluctantly recognized that the long-range demands of the adult African American community would be the most important results of the Movement, and that could only come about by patient negotiation. Like revolutionaries of the past, they had been the means of change, but now they must retire into the background, to let others consolidate the gains they had achieved.*

*By now both the Federal Government, through Attorney General Robert Kennedy, and the North Carolina state government under Governor Terry Sanford, were applying increasing pressure on the headquarters of the targeted businesses and Greensboro city officials to desegregate. Informed of these surreptitious activities, Dr. George Evans agreed to accept the chairmanship of a new Human Relations Committee to conduct negotiations with city officials. Although anxious to initiate discussions as soon as possible, Evans made it clear to Mayor Schenck that the black community would not participate in yet another ad hoc committee that would dissolve after a few token achievements. Consequently, Evans agreed to chair the committee only until it would eventually become a permanent part of city government, known as the Human Relations Commission.*

*[Note: Between 1960 and 1963, there were several ad hoc committees created to deal with immediate crises, sometimes overlapping one another and consisting of many of the same members. Mayor George Roach appointed a committee under Edward R. Zane, known as the Zane Committee, during the spring of 1960; although it met occasionally into the fall of 1960, its mandate was achieved with the desegregation of the Woolworth and Kress lunch counters, and was dissolved. As picketing of the cafeterias and the movie theaters resumed in the fall of 1962, a Human Relations Committee was appointed by Mayor David Schenck to make recommendations on race relations in Greensboro, but it failed to achieve integration of places of public accommodation. Leading organizations within the black community formed the Coordinating Committee of Pro-Integration Groups under the chairmanship of Father Richard Hicks, during the marches of May 1963, to support CORE and to negotiate with city officials. The last committee appointed was the Human Relations Committee under Dr. George Evans, which evolved into the permanent Human Relations Commission under W. O. Conrad in the fall of 1964].*

## George Evans

Mayor David Schenck decided, during the height of the demonstrations, that he should appoint a special committee to work on the problem. The result of this announcement was that there were no further mass demonstrations, and the boycott was called off. I think the black community went the extra mile, in that it was willing to give the mayor and the businesses a chance to prove that they were more sincere than the community had believed earlier that they were. Perhaps that was justified, for it was not too long after that before things began to open up on a wider basis. Whether that opening up can be ascribed to his statement or to the work of CORE or to the work of the special committee, or to a combination of all of these things, is hard to judge. It may be that it was a result of an accumulation of work of all of these different groups.

The committee was composed of sixteen people, half white, half black, and I was chosen by the mayor as chairman. It was felt that negotiations between the demonstrating groups and the mayor had not been very productive in solving some of the problems that were being brought out. And the mayor apparently felt, as he stated to us, that a special committee appointed by him to work directly on these problems with the powers-that-be, as well as with the demonstrators, could perhaps get closer to the crux of the problem than the Council itself could. And he felt that a committee designated to do just that job, and that alone, would probably come closer to being the answer to the problem. I was only vaguely aware of the pre-existing Human Relations Committee. I had no relationship with that committee, and I did not really know much about their work. But I think it did not go very far and did not last very long. I think that is one of the reasons for his appointing this special committee. Many people in the black community thought that the committee should be made permanent, rather than just having an ad hoc status. So that, as time went on and the demonstrations cooled and some progress was seen in the manner of opening up facilities, under our urging, the mayor convinced the City Council to form a Human Relations Commission as part of the city government.

I believed that the Coordinating Committee of Pro-Integration Groups had gone about as far as we could go in terms of direct negotiation, and if there was going to be a permanent commission appointed, that it would probably be better handled by a different group of people. I think that was the position that the mayor took after I talked with him about it, and he asked me to be the temporary chairman of the committee until the permanent commission was appointed. During the approximately two months of this interim period, I did very little of my own personal work of practicing medicine; I had to give most of my effort to this work. At the end of this period, I felt that it was time for some new blood, because I believed that we had at least started the ball rolling in the right direction, and that another group of citizens should continue the work which we had started. So I was happy to see the mayor appoint a permanent Human Relations Commission. I think that the present Human Relations Commission is considered a direct outgrowth of the special committee of which I was chairman.

We served as a liaison between CORE and the political and business communities in Greensboro. I would say that ninety-five percent of the work of my committee was done by subcommittees, rather than by the committee as a whole. We had a number of subcommittees which met with the leaders in the restaurant businesses about the city, with the movie houses and with the management of hotels and motels, trying to get some kind of a compromise by which we could get them to open their doors to anybody in the community who wanted to attend their places of business. I believe that ninety-five percent of the work of my committee was done by subcommittees, and their work was responsible for what we like to think of as the success of our efforts than the committee as a whole. I participated in subcommittee discussions by making myself an ex-officio member of several of the committees.

For example, in talking with the representative of the chain that controlled the O. Henry Hotel, I asked him to talk with their board of directors to see if we could get them to open their doors to anybody who wanted to use the hotel. I also was in on some discussions with a S&W Cafeterias representative from Buffalo, New York. These negotiations led directly to a solution of the problem. They wanted to return to their headquarters and acquaint the owners with the problems, and then the decision would be made later at their headquarters rather than here on the spot. I did not have any direct communication with Boyd Morris, but some of the subcommittee work was done with him. I had very pleasant communications with Neil McGill, however. I think Mr. McGill indicated a spirit of cooperation in wanting to do something to quiet things down. He brought a regional representative of his organization here, and I think that helped lead to some of the solution to the problem. I also met with Mr. Eugene Street, the manager of the Cinema Theater on Tate Street, who was rather helpful with carrying on the work that we were attempting to do.

The position of the managers generally took this turn. I recall particularly two people who indicated that as far as they were concerned, segregated businesses should open their doors to black people. Their only reservation was that they were afraid of opening their doors wide open in the beginning, because they said, "Doctor, we would be willing to open the doors, except for the fact that we fear what would happen to our businesses if a whole mass of students from A&T College or Bennett College should demand entrance to the Carolina Theater. They might take up all the spaces so that the regular patrons would not have anywhere to sit down." I don't think it was all a matter of rationalization. I think some of it was a genuine concern that they would be overrun. But the members of my committee hastened to tell them that there was one factor that they were overlooking: not that many students could afford the price of admission to the Carolina Theater, or to rent rooms in motels and hotels, or to buy a decent meal at three, four, five dollars, so that there wouldn't be any great influx of people at one time, to the exclusion of their regular patrons. They were reluctant to believe that at first, but I think we finally convinced them.

There was a joint statement issued by the managers of the National Theater, the Center Theater, the Carolina Theater and the Cinema Theater, that was issued on June second, stating that they were going to desegregate and that the specifics of exactly how this would occur were going to be a subject of on-going negotiations with our committee. After several sessions of negotiating, this group of theater managers agreed finally that they would open their doors on a limited basis to certain small groups of black people to begin with, and then increase the size of the groups if the matter proceeded without any great amount of trouble. To this end, they had issued a number of tickets, which my committee controlled, to be issued to respected persons in the black community: ten tickets to the Carolina Theater, ten tickets to the National Theater, ten passes to enter into the S&W restaurant, and so forth.

As things proceeded, there was no problem with this, and for that reason, some of these management people eventually said to me in private conversations, "Doctor, if we had had any idea that it was going to run this smoothly, we wouldn't have hesitated as long as we did." When we proved to them that it could work without any great amount of difficulty, there was no further problem in those areas. There was a mixture of people who did receive the tickets. Initially, the tickets were given to adult members of the community, then later to some college students. The issuing of tickets did not last very long, though, because as soon as management found out that they were not going to have any severe problems, then the tickets were discontinued and the doors were open to anybody who wanted to come along.

If I had to single out any one subcommittee chairman who I think did more than anybody else on the committee to get things going, it would have to be Oscar Burnett, who was my vice-chairman. He was instrumental in making contacts and negotiating with people that we thought a white member of our committee might be able to begin negotiations with better than a black member could. And then, as things progressed, we had mixed groups to meet with the management of the various places that we were trying to open. And in that way, we think it was rather successful.

We attempted to influence the business people of the community that it was only right that they should serve all members of the community without regard to race, which was the question in everybody's mind at the time. And that, to a large extent, much of the business of the downtown merchants was dependent on the black community for a lot of its business, and that they owed it to everybody in the community to give some of this back by acccommodating anybody who wanted to participate in their businesses. So we felt that our mission was to influence them that this was the thing to do. And that the matter of segregated facilities and refusal to accommodate black people was something that should be outlawed. It was our feeling that the time had come for change, and that there was no better time to make a change than at that period, when so much protesting was being done that it was disrupting everything about the community. And that everybody stood to suffer, including the downtown merchants, if something wasn't done to get things quieted down.

The committee believed that if we could get the leading businesses to open their doors, then smaller businesses would be less recalcitrant. And that they might fall in line more readily if they saw what the leading businesses were doing. Therefore, my committee did not have any confrontations with many of the smaller businesses, because we didn't feel like it was necessary.

Our meetings were held on a call basis, depending on what we felt was the need for holding meetings or to have reports from these committees and to decide what the next step should be in our efforts. In the very beginning, we met more regularly than we did later on, maybe once a week or thereabouts. But after the initial phase of the efforts were being organized, it was felt that it was not necessary to have a meeting every week, but to meet as the need arose for meetings.

We met with the owners and operators of these businesses on a one-to-one basis, largely because we felt like we could deal with them individually better than we could in a group, particularly, since there were different kinds of businesses involved, with different types of management and different programs. There was greater intransigence on the part of the management of the eating establishments. Mr. Morris never really agreed to open the Mayfair Cafeteria, and Mr. Sherrill, the owner of the S&W Cafeteria, was not very amenable to negotiating. There was more success with smaller eating establishments than with the larger ones. I did not detect any "Let's all open together" attitude by the managements of the restaurants; for the most part, I think they were rather adamant in refusing to integrate. As far as I knew, they did not seek any settlement on a gradual basis, as the theaters did. They were much more adamant. To my knowledge, they never explained their point of view as to their stand, unless they said something like that to Mr. Burnett or maybe Mr. Zane or some of the people who did most of the negotiating with them directly. As I look back upon it now, it appears to me that it was just a matter of their being afraid of what would happen to their businesses if they opened their doors. We think that our committee was responsible for the S&W integrating, although I think most of that credit should perhaps go to the demonstrators, because they are the ones who started the process.

There was a sense of frustration in the black community at the apparent pace of the negotiations. That was understandable, because the work on my committee was done in a quiet manner. And for the most part, neither the press nor the business community knew very much about what went on in our committee meetings, because our work was not publicized very much. We held our committee meetings without any public pronouncement that they were going on, because we didn't want any reporters present. So that the only news that came out about the committee meetings was what came from us as a committee. I think that was the proper way to handle it. We believed that if too much publicity was given to what we were attempting to do, that it might sabotage our efforts. So we negotiated quietly, and made few public pronouncements about what we were doing until after some of it was accomplished.

Many of the people in the black community felt that these were things that should have been done immediately. While we thought that it perhaps was difficult, we felt that it certainly should progress more rapidly than it did at times. As a result of this attitude, I, as chairman, received quite a bit of flack because of the fact that we were not working hard enough and fast enough. I received anonymous letters and telephone calls at all hours of the night, where nobody answered on the other end. Because there was no way to satisfy everybody in the community, I didn't let that disturb me too much. I took the position that I was doing what I thought was the right thing to do, and in the right manner. I received no real threats; just indications that they didn't approve of the way my committee was handling things. I made occasional public statements to accelerate the efforts of the city fathers toward getting something more done to advancing the process. I felt that we needed to do a whole lot more than we were doing at the time. Unfortunately, the response of the city officials was not as rapid or as forceful as they might have been. Perhaps they were afraid of creating violence by the demonstrators, or continued intransigence on the part of the segregated business operators.

In a general sense, the efforts from that point on were directed toward not so much opening doors to businesses like theaters and so on, but to opening doors of employment to qualified black people in various capacities where the doors had not been opened to them previously. For example, bank tellers, secretaries in the larger business organizations downtown, white-collar jobs in some industries, rather than just janitorial jobs. So the emphasis was toward economic matters, I think, rather than simply opening doors and businesses to people who wanted to eat something or wanted to see a movie.

When the committee was first organized, the mayor indicated that [it] was expected to take over the task of trying to work out a satisfactory peaceful solution to the problems that the community faced. And once that work was accomplished, the committee was not meant to continue its work. I don't know that Mayor Schenck ever directly decided on a date when the committee could be dissolved. But I think the committee itself, when it felt like it accomplished most of its purposes, sort of faded away. As chairman, I made a final oral report to the City Council on what we had attempted to do. And immediately after that, the permanent commission was appointed.

## A. Knighton Stanley

The statement in the *Greensboro Daily News* on June 8 that the demonstrations were called off by CORE due to "the strong statement by Mayor Schenck" was absolutely untrue [Laughs]. We knew that under the Greensboro system and given the political weakness of Mayor Schenck, whatever he said really didn't amount to much. There just comes a point in time when you become tired. You have to sit up all night to keep the mass demonstrations going, and so there were times when we would call things off, and there were several times I was quoted in the press such as to be gracious for what had been done, whether we believed it to be significant or not. It can be described as "street drama." You fight through the press. They were our ally in all of this. They needed news, so a lot of our statements were a matter of strategy and often what was said was not what was meant, but the intention was either to be gracious in Greensboro society, or to put the pressure on through the press by implying capabilities that we did not have.

And we had to consider our ambiguous relationship with the older black community leadership. There was always a kind of power struggle between the older black and student communities in Greensboro. The students constantly felt undercut by the older black community, and the older black community was very much of the opinion that a transient population was trying to dictate the future of the city and take the responsibilities of leadership. There was not always coordination between the two. Looking back, it might have been different had the students realized their inability to negotiate and articulate goals and objectives for the black community. Sometimes, the established black leadership said, "Where is the Movement going, because I'm supposed to be leading it." I have the feeling that was pretty much the role of the Coordinating Committee for Pro-Integration Groups. It was an opportunity to communicate with the students, so that it would be in charge, or at least maintain a semblance of authority.

There were no students on the committee at all. They saw no point or future in discussions with that group. It was a volunteer organization outside of the public sector. Conrad's best contribution was the establishment of the Human Relations Commission. The initial persons on that from the black community included Kenneth Lee, George Simkins, Gladys Royall and me. I can't remember any whites who were there. A formal vote was not taken; no formal votes were taken in most of these commissions because it was basically for discussion. The students didn't think that it would do very much, but it at least had their toleration. They liked Dr. Evans; he was a solid citizen, open person, but there was little that he could do. Most of the hard negotiating on the matter was with the Governor's office, the powers-that-be, in control of the S&W and so forth.

We knew there were behind-the-scenes negotiations and promises going on at the time of Schenck's June 7 statement, but nobody would say what was forthcoming. Things like, "Something is going to happen, but I can't say what it is, because all of it is not in place." They were basically delivered to us by persons of an older black generation in Greensboro who were very confident that the white community would deliver on whatever they promised, no matter how vague. We never spoke directly with Mayor Schenck, but we were politically astute enough to know that he had absolutely no power, both in the political structure and within the power structure of Greensboro.

As demonstrations escalated, the elements of the Coordinating Committee of Pro-Integration Groups other than CORE—the NAACP, the Greensboro Citizens Association, and the Ministerial Alliance—negotiated with city officials over the cases of those facing trial. The Greensboro Fellowship Council served a purpose, much of which was group therapy in the community. [Laughs]. It served a good social purpose; it kept people who in ordinary circumstances are in control, from going insane when they are not. The demands of the students, which had taken place in an open, democratic-type of forum were restructured by the Coordinating Committee in a very articulate manner. But at the time we were not able to see that as clearly.

Part of that tension was created by those who left the Movement because they had wished to remain in charge, and they felt threatened by the presence of articulate, substantial, long-term residents of Greensboro who were present at CORE meetings. The students had originally insisted on a Coordinating Committee in which members of the older black community would be represented, but the arrogance of youth also dictated that the students would be in charge of the whole process. The tension developed when that did not take place. The relationship between CORE and the Coordinating Committee was not always as smooth as it was portrayed in the press. CORE took the position that the Coordinating Committee could pass resolutions and do as it pleased, but CORE would maintain control of the demonstrations and go its own way, if necessary. The Committee did not meet that often, and I don't remember a significant meeting with that committee.

But I think that the committee served a good function. The students could not have negotiated substantial changes within the Greensboro racial situation. There is often a time when even to be in dialogue with your allies is detrimental to what you are trying to do, especially if your allies— meaning the Coordinating Committee other than CORE—counseled moderation. Had CORE been moderate, it would have de-escalated the negotiations that the committee participated in, because we understood the attitude of Mayor Schenck, who really didn't understand what the demonstrations were about. He was a very proud man who could not be as flexible in negotiations as Mr. Trotter, which is what ended the demonstrations. To my knowledge, no one from CORE was present at the meeting of the other members of the Coordinating Committee and Mayor Pro Tem Trotter, nor did a CORE representative participate in the Evans Committee that resulted from that meeting. I remember that through the Coordinating Committee "passes" were given to "responsible Negroes" to be admitted to the theaters on an experimental basis. [Laughs]. If they were ever used in any large-scale basis, I am not aware of it.

In the fall of 1963, there was a list of grievances that surfaced from time to time, and it was essentially the same list as before. They were just basic things that had always been made by the adult black community. I think that the real authors of those grievances were George Simkins and Kenneth Lee, because the language is legal. CORE could go along with them, because George Simkins had a greater understanding of students and what they were about than most people. He was never jealous of CORE; he did not have that kind of ego or personality. Nor did George Evans. Dr. Evans was the president of the Greensboro Citizens Association at that time, and he was a wise choice for that position. Nobody would criticize George Evans because of his sincerity.

Bill Thomas and I flew up to New York City to meet with members of the national office of CORE. When we came back, the Greensboro adult community had negotiated the thing down, and made statements that there would not be demonstrations for a while. We felt that they did not have the authority to do that, but there was nothing that we could do, because we did not want to embarrass the adult community, although we thought that they had acted without integrity. But, on the other hand, we could not promise to do anything that was contrary to what they had said, because we did not have the troops; the schools were closed, enthusiasm for the Movement was wanting, and it would have been difficult to have raised ten people. My feeling about the Evans committee was neither negative nor positive. Not positive in the sense that it shouldn't have been set up, but again, what could it do?

Most of the hard negotiating on the matter was with the Governor's office, the powers-that-be, in control of the S&W and so forth. It was really done by McNeill Smith in an ad hoc kind of a way. He had the ear of the governor, and he also had the ear of some persons in the business community, the folk related to the S&W Cafeteria.. He read his conversations with the Governor verbatim at Evans committee meetings; it was always very upbeat. McNeill Smith would, on occasion, develop some quid pro quos. He was terribly upset over the cutting up of seats of the buses that had transported the demonstrators to incarceration centers. There were some white militants in the Greensboro Fellowship Council and McNeill Smith, who wanted us to see that the damage was paid for. I didn't contest McNeill Smith when he said he was pushing for restitution to the city for repairing the damaged seats, and some members of the black community were very embarrassed about it. There were no students there at all. They saw no point or future in discussion with that group. I was disposed to be concerned about it, but two teachers from Woman's College came to me after the meeting and said, "Don't pay for a thing." That resolved it for me.

We didn't take those negotiations seriously. We knew that the business operators and city officials wouldn't negotiate with any haste unless pressure was maintained on them. Despite the rumors of optimism regarding a positive resolution to the impasse, CORE did not anticipate that something would break. As students began to take seriously that school was closing and it was time to go home, there was a dwindling away, and absolute fatigue after sustaining a movement like that for a period of time, and much of what was being said in the press at that time, is to create illusions. And the illusion intended there was, that if you say that something is about to break through, then the powers-that-be, if they want to be the "nice guys," have got to come through with something, since I had already announced that they were supposed to do something very wonderful. [Laughs]. The quotes in the media attributed to me were just rhetoric. It's very interesting that I used the word "enlightened." That doesn't quite describe anything. [Laughs]. I made that statement to set up the powers-that-be as nice guys so that they had to do something to look good. And there were members of the Evans committee that would use those kinds of statements to press for positive action, like Bland Worley, John R. Taylor, and Rabbi Joseph Asher.

It is very difficult to do hard negotiation if you are on the front line as one of the troops, and I absented myself from a lot of those things because it would be very difficult to sit across the desk from a person who was hostile to the demonstrations; you needed a person who was neutral in terms of not being a conspicuous figure in the demonstrations themselves, so that you negotiate in some degree of calmness. The persons to follow me on my invitation to serve on the Human Relations Commission were attorney Kenneth Lee and George Simkins. I resigned early on. Not in protest; I just had other things that I wanted to move onto, and my experience with the committee basically was in the organizational phases. I was replaced by Dr. Gladys Royall, who was then on the faculty with her husband at A&T College. During my tenure I was chairman of the subcommittee on Progress and Information. My initial function was to receive from other cities from across the country laws pertaining to regulations relevant to the operation of the Human Relations Commission: how they functioned, how they were comprised, what kind of subcommittee and so on, that they had. I received a lot of correspondence, but they had not processed it before I resigned, and that committee was given to my successor, Dr. Royall.

In the short time that I served on that committee, there were really no issues; they were just organizational meetings. I only got together with Dr. Simkins by telephone because he was chairperson of the subcommittee. Kenneth Lee was Secretary, and W. O. Conrad was chairman. My subcommittee [focused] on information or whatever it was. Some materials we had received from other cities, but we never dealt with issues. My impression at the time was that the mandate which established it was not a terribly serious one, and it would have been a credibility problem for me, because I had been a leader of the demonstrations and a member of CORE. You can't rush toward the establishment too quickly. I can make no judgment on it because I did not pay it very much attention the months that I had left there, and I did not follow it subsequently, but I certainly was set up to do nothing. I made some comments that were quoted in the newspaper which indicated that I was angry at the slow pace the Commission was taking. The reason that I resigned, is that I had to complain of that in order to remain credible with my comrades in the revolution.

When Arnold Schiffman was quoted in the newspaper as citing the reason that businessmen were reluctant to hire blacks as sales personnel due to their poor command of math and English was just a smoke screen to avoid hiring more black sales personnel, especially with two black colleges here. They could have hired students as sales personnel. When Conrad made a speech in which he stated that it was the responsibility of the black academic institutions to properly educate students to qualify as sales personnel, rather than a responsibility to hire more black sales personnel, he was always trying to throw the ball back onto our court. He was a nice guy, but he didn't understand either side of the South, white or black. I'm sure that he took some severe criticism from both sides, but you always felt definitely spanked by what he said: "If you all will be nice, everything will be all right." He was a nice guy; he was just not a part of the Southern tradition. But he was sincere. I am sure that some of the other members of the Commission were not sincere, because the idea of the members was that what you must do is represent all points of view, and it was my contention that there was but one: that there should be a city of complete racial equality. It wasn't a forum to debate whether blacks were equal.

CORE continued to meet after the demonstrations ended, but much of the membership after that were rebels without a cause. We understood plainly that the battle had to be fought subsequently on the economic front in terms of jobs, and we did not have the strength to do it, so it was very depressing. I don't recall a CORE meeting after our termination in June, when Bill Thomas and I flew off to New York, and Reverend Douglas called the whole thing off. There was no one to demonstrate anyhow, but Bill and I had told the city, "You'd better be straight by the time that we get back." But you can't demonstrate unless you have large numbers. Our trip to New York was basically "rest and relaxation." [Laughs]. So was the Bill Thomas and James Farmer trip to Washington. We had grown very weary. The newspaper played it up as substantive meetings with representatives of the federal government, but it wasn't. I don't know if they played up the New York trip, but we wanted to lend the impression that we were going to New York to bring back all kinds of new strategy, new people and orders from Jim Farmer, but it was "R&R."

Other cities were beginning to desegregate. I think it is important to point out, on the basis of what was happening in Greensboro, because in Greensboro I think that history will indicate that at a given point we had more people in jails because of civil rights demonstrations than any other location in the country, including Birmingham, and it was because of the intensity of the Greensboro Movement that Charlotte and all of these other places began to open up.

Much of that had to do with Terry Sanford's commitment, which he did not state in the press, but he was quite committed, and I knew it for a fact. One of his aides had been in the Yale Law School when I had been in the Divinity School at Yale, I knew where he stood and I knew it through McNeill Smith. What got things moving were these telephone calls. McNeill Smith was quite strategic in all of that. I have said on many friendly occasions, where I sat in McNeill Smith's house with Attorney Sapp, who was a delightful fellow. If he had a problem, it was not that he was racist at all, but he represented his clients and they had gotten to him early on, because he is quite a liberal fellow and most brilliant. But a lot went on in situations like that. McNeill Smith was very strategic in all of that, and the Governor of North Carolina called and said "cut that out. Everybody else is doing right, so straighten the man [Schenck] out." He [Schenck] didn't know which end was up.

Tart Bell was the Director of the American Friends Service Committee, Southeast Regional Office over in High Point. Dick Ramsay was a field representative for the American Friends Service Committee, who at a point in time became almost exclusively related to CORE, although his assignment with them was peace. CORE worked closely with the AFSC.

By the time that the theaters desegregated in June 1963, there were few to rejoice, because the students had gone home, and they were the heart of our Movement. I left Greensboro in 1966.

## William Thomas

The reason that there was such a positive response to Mayor Schenck's largely noncommittal statement on June 8, which effectively ended the demonstrations, was that the mayor made a big thing about reading it in a news conference, then met with a number of black leaders at the Hayes-Taylor Y. Basically it said that he and the City Council would work toward supporting the demands of the demonstrators by establishing a permanent Human Relations Commission. A temporary committee was established and empowered to work to achieve a solution, although it wasn't going to pass any resolutions requiring integration, of course. But I can almost assure you some deal was made somewhere along that line. And we felt strong enough to know that the way we turned the demonstrations off, we could turn them back on.

After the summer of 1963 CORE turned its efforts to voter registration and voter education drives. They were probably involved in a lot of the employment efforts. I left Greensboro following my junior year at the end of 1963, then came back to finish in 1966. So I was not really involved after that. My brother Alvin was then elected president of the CORE chapter.

The committee under Dr. Evans was a vehicle by which discussions could take place. I was on Dr. Evans' committee, and I was involved in all of the negotiations. But it wasn't the committee that finally produced results. What happened was, the business community decided that it wanted these black people out of the street so it could make a dollar. That's what brought it about: the business community realized that it was losing money. And it was embarrassed by what was going on, because the demonstrations showed the world that Greensboro was not the nice little quaint town that the business community wanted it to be. You had big industry here: Burlington Mills, Cone Mills, other major industries that had an economic stake in maintaining some semblance of peace in Greensboro. So it was the whole disruptive tactic that we were able to bring about that created an atmosphere where these people that were on the committees could sit down and began to intelligently work out the problems.

The reason that mass demonstrations did not resume in the fall of 1963 had to do with what was happening throughout the country. People are basically crisis-oriented, and at that particular time there was no real crisis. It's very difficult to maintain the level of intensity that we had during the peak of those mass demonstrations. The only way that would happen again was that it would have to be a response to a crisis, to create that high level of emotionalism. It's very difficult for people to stop what they're doing. In other words, to function in a normal way—to go to work, to come home, to cook, to cut their lawn, to go to the barbershop, to shop—in order to participate in that. That's abnormal. And because it was abnormal, you had to have something to motivate you. Unless it was a crisis, it would be impossible to maintain that level of intensity. We did not have a Bull Connor [Birmingham, Alabama, Police Commissioner] that kept something going, or just kept black folk angry as hell all the time. There was no crisis.

After that, we began to focus in on employment in these types of places, specifically employment in the areas where we were spending our money. Not only in terms of five-and-dime stores, but also in major department stores, where you had a large number of minority people patronizing the stores. And from that, other types of goals along that line began to evolve. Our goals expanded from just the desegregation of public accommodations to employment, to increased voting rights, to the whole area of human rights that we now focus on. There were no alternative strategies that we considered, other than what we employed. In terms of action, things went pretty much according to plan. The basic form of action was through economic withdrawal, another name for boycotting, and through actual physical street demonstrations. Those were the two main types of direct action that we were involved in. Little litigation went on at that time, other than defending those people that were arrested. And we were able to get all of those cases thrown out. But nothing was planned that really did not go off.

Representatives of Greensboro CORE made several trips to Washington during the spring and summer of 1963, at which members of the Kennedy Administration Justice Department spoke to a number of individuals in the Civil Rights Movement, as well as the officials of chain stores, chain restaurants and hotels in the South. I remember one meeting in Washington with an assistant of Bobby Kennedy, one of the U.S. attorneys, but it was inconclusive. I don't think that the Federal Government could have been very active in resolving the situation in Greensboro. Looking at what was actually happening in Greensboro, other than using its influence to force these national outfits to go ahead and desegregate their facilities, I really don't know what role they could have played in Greensboro. I think in some of the communities where it was more of a violent atmosphere, they in fact could have played more.

By 1964 CORE had served its usefulness. It was basically made up of young people, and it responded to a particular need at the time, which was an organization that believed in the tactic of nonviolent direct action. It merged rather than dissipated, into other organizations in Greensboro; the Greensboro Citizens Association, the NAACP were still there. There were other committees that these people actively functioned on. Their goals and their activities were the same, and there was really no need for CORE at that time. There was still a lot of activity by the national office, but not in Greensboro. That's the key. Greensboro was unique in that way, because while we had national ties, we were not that nationally involved.

## Frank Sherrill, Jr.

My father went up to Washington and met with John and Robert Kennedy. What I heard from my father was that Bobby Kennedy was rather ruthless about the whole thing. [Kennedy] was cut-and-dried and very ugly to them when he went up there. He hardly even wanted to speak to them, and was very rude—he hardly acknowledged that they were there. They seemed to like John Kennedy very much, and he talked to them very nicely. John and Bobby Kennedy both wanted them to integrate, naturally, but Bobby Kennedy was very ugly about it.

Bobby Kennedy called Mr. Marriott in Washington; he was the president of the Hot Shoppes and the Marriott Hotels, and was president of the National Restaurant Association. Mr. Marriott and my father were good friends, and they would talk things over. Mr. Marriott had some business in the government buildings at that time, and it was about one or two million dollars worth of business a year. Bobby Kennedy told Mr. Marriott that if he didn't feed the colored people down here in Greensboro, that he would take the government contracts away. In other words, political blackmail. So, Mr. Marriott started feeding the blacks, and that was the first time here in Greensboro, to my knowledge.

What really changed the S&W's policy was that up in Lynchburg, Virginia, we had a group called SNCC [Student Nonviolent Coordinating Committee], and they said that they were getting ready to come into the S&W and wreck the place. It was then that my father decided that the best thing to do was just go ahead and integrate. All of that in Greensboro had an effect on the situation, but it was because of the SNCC group that we integrated. The threat of federal intervention is not what did it for us.

I think that Mayor Schenck finally came to the decision that integration was what we ought to do; to do the best for the whole city. My reaction to the "Open Letter to Greensboro Businessmen" that Mayor Schenck wrote for publication in the newspaper, was that I didn't know what we could do about it. Our policy was still our policy, and we were seeing the people working from the other side. We were on one side, and they were on the other. There was a confrontation and it was in the news. He called the meetings, and we went to them, and it was then that he talked [about the] position that we had been in all along, and it was a pretty good while after that [before] we did integrate.

We functioned independently from the Mayfair. But what Boyd [Morris] was doing, we were doing. We would talk back and forth. I don't think that I attended any meetings in Sapp's office, but I knew that all of that stuff was going on. We felt like that it was communist-inspired at the time, but I'm not really sure. Course, when you have Communists in a group, you begin to wonder. We felt that there was some communism in this. Sapp believed that the Communists do this sort of thing, and [that] they were there. It shows that they were doing something. Armistad had his facts pretty much together; he was always checking into things.

When we desegregated, [Sapp] handled it, that's all I know. He was our legal man, and we worked through him. My father told him how he felt about it, and then Armistad went to work, and he did what we wanted him to do.

How Armistad felt about the whole situation, I never did get that straight. What I really felt like, was that he was not against the colored people, and I wasn't either; I don't think that any of us were against the colored people. We just had a policy that we did not want to feed them, because we felt that we would lose our business. And this is what he went on. He said that he was going to change public opinion, and that he was going to fight this thing and he was going to win it. He felt that he could win it, and I felt like he could win it, after seeing him work the way that he did. He was going to change public opinion by statements and the truth; that he was fighting for those businesses. I really felt that we had them licked until the SNCC thing came along, and Armistad had nothing to do with that. That was my father. I remember the day that Dad called Armistad and told him that we were going to integrate because of that particular thing. Armistad and I were upset about it, because we had worked so hard to do this thing. Armistad was really more so than I was. [But] when Dad said what he wanted to do, Armistad accepted that.

I had talked to the help prior to them coming in, and I told them that now that we were going to feed them, that I felt that we should be just as nice to them as we had to any of our other customers before [because] we were servants of the people. And maybe [we should] go overboard to be nicer to them, since we had to do it, and I wanted to do it the very nicest way that we possibly could. Most of our employees were black. I didn't want to hold anything back from them. I wanted them to know what we were going to do, because I have always felt that if you know what is happening, you can do a little better, but if you didn't know what was going to happen next, you were apprehensive. and I thought that it was best to let them know where we stood, and how they fitted into the picture.

The first customers to desegregate came in—they were well-dressed, and they were as nice as they could possibly be. Most of them were older people with their families, and they looked like they were going to church. I noticed that they tipped the employees, and very well. We tried to look after them the very best that we could. You could see that the black customers were not used to it. I asked them if they liked their meal and that kind of thing, and talked to them. Sometimes I knew them. I think the students came at first, but mostly what we got were families, and they would come in and they were just as nice as they could possibly be.

At first we lost white patronage, and I don't think that it really came back like it was in the past. I think that it was a combination of competition from the shopping centers and integration that caused the fall-off of patrons. The poll conducted by the Evans Committee—I don't think it changed our policy. [*Note: The Evans committee polled a number of restaurants in Greensboro, and reported that the majority expressed a willingness to integrate.*] I don't mean no matter what; but at that time we just were not going to feed blacks.

The public opinion was changing, and my father just decided to do it. There was some talk of desegregating together. I don't think that there were very many that wanted to do that. I remember we would sometimes have a filled-up evening on most nights. When they were demonstrating, we would be two-thirds or one-half filled. So, we were losing business; people would not want to go into something like that. A lot of people would go just for curiosity's sake. But I think that the mothers didn't want to take their children into that.

I was a witness at one of the trials of the arrested demonstrators; I only went to one. They were conducted very nicely. McKissick was one of the lawyers. He cross-examined me, but all that I could say was what our policy was and what I had done. They just asked me about the policy of the company and that kind of thing. I was never asked to identify anyone.

## Neil McGill

Attorney General Robert Kennedy called all of the theater owners in the South to a meeting in Washington. He told them, "I want you to go back home and integrate your theaters." I received word from the president of my company, Mr. Kelsey, of ABC Southeastern Theaters, to desegregate.

Eugene Street [owner of the Cinema Theater], Jimmy Bellows and I were all very close friends. We were segregated; it was the law. We discussed just when and where we would integrate. We decided to do it all at the same time. McNeill Smith met with me on one occasion, but I told him that my company was nationwide and I couldn't authorize the integration myself. When we integrated, it came down from my company. Mr. Sapp represented Gene Street and Jimmy Bellows. I don't think that I attended any of his meetings. We just told them that we were ready to integrate as well as I remember. We met to decide time and date.

I testified at the trials that they had forced their way into the theater. They were brought in individually, and we would have to look at the photographs to see if that was one of the ones arrested. There weren't any convicted because the judge, Herman Enochs, said that it was never proved that they were in the theater without an admission ticket. There was no mention of their entering with a ticket. It puzzled me, but I didn't have any ill-feeling against blacks.

## James McMillan

It was shortly after the mayor announced the formation of the Human Relations Committee that you saw groups of blacks and whites together, particularly professional people. I was invited by a friend, Ed Lowenstein [local architect], to have lunch with him and one of his associates at the S&W. Ed was a very fine gentleman. It was kind of a strange experience for two reasons. One, I had been arrested trying to enter there on one occasion. And two, as a black person to be on the inside of a place that I had always seen as an aloof, foreign place for a black person, and to experience for oneself the nice accommodations that had always been there, but which I had no knowledge of, except from black employees.

It was kind of a traumatic thing, but I had another kind of a feeling; it was kind of like "Gee whiz, I don't know if I even want to go in this place. I don't know if it would be comfortable, if I would feel right." Knowing, too, the attitude of some of the managers and how they responded and reacted in court. I would prefer to see other people enjoy it rather than myself, because I just didn't feel that was the place for me. I would rather go somewhere else, but I did it, mainly as a kind of a gesture.

This has always been a part of [those] who dared to challenge the segregated social order of the day. And this was a special day. But that didn't bother me too much. I guess those of us who had been involved in that kind of thing had always seen stares. You could almost feel the hostile stares as well as the friendly ones. I think, too, that is a kind of thing that one becomes used to. You can almost glance at a person and tell whether they have a sympathetic or a hostile feeling toward you.

In my estimation, the boycott was the most effective protest tactic that we had. Meyer's, Belk's and some of the other large department stores had a substantial black professional clientele, who had a reasonable buying power. Of course, we had to realize that the buying power would not be felt in any great way, but it was, perhaps, the margin of profit and loss for many of these places. I heard that one black patron actually collected a shoebox of charge plates and dumped them on the table of one of the department store managers. This person said that if things did not change, then this is what they could expect from the more affluent black community, unless they integrated their store.

## Lewis Brandon

After the demonstrations, CORE's role changed. There was no real need at that point for mass demonstrations, and hence, we changed our focus. One of the things that we began doing after the demonstrations had ended was to go around to the facilities to make sure that the people were complying. Most of them did open up. The only one that didn't was the Mayfair. In fact, it went out of business. I think that the people that served on the Evans committee, especially Dr. Simkins, were greatly concerned about the employment picture, because the NAACP was already involved in picketing Wachovia to get people hired as tellers.

Another thing was that after we got the accommodations open, it would make it easier to get to the employment and wages issue, because one of the first things that we did upon returning to Greensboro after the summer of 1963 and the March on Washington, was to begin a massive voter registration project. One thing that I worked on in particular with Dr. Laizner was community organizing, which was one of our principal projects that summer. The target area was around Gillespie Street and Gant Street. We conducted a survey of what the people felt needed attention, as part of our "Operation Dialogue" program. This was spearheaded by Dick Ramsay through the College Committee [of the American Friends Service Committee]. He was able to get college students to come in from around the country to help. It was an interracial thing that was headquartered at the St. Stephens Church on Gorrell Street.

With that in place, we also began to meet at Reverend Frank Williams' church on Nance Street. We used it to hold community meetings of members of the Redevelopment Commission to talk about street improvement, because the streets at that time were dirt streets, bringing the houses up to code, putting in streetlights, and the land adjacent to the cemetery, which had been a city dump, converting it to a park. We didn't identify ourselves as just CORE, and the people that took the lead in that project were the people who lived in that community. Our chief role was as facilitators and as resource people in terms of getting the authorities to improve the neighborhood.

At that point, I left to go into the service in 1964. Bill's brother Alvin [Thomas] maintained a remnant of the structure for awhile. On paper we remained an organization, because when I got back out of the service, I maintained it on paper. There was no real effort to do anything as an organization because demonstrations were not the way that things were being done then. Negotiations and other tactics were being used. I was with Elizabeth Laizner when she was arrested in Chapel Hill; we went over there on several occasions to participate in demonstrations. Most of those demonstrations were conducted by white middle-class kids, because the activities at Chapel Hill were white kids. That was true of SNCC; a lot of white kids were involved in it up until the move by Stokely Carmichael toward black power, when they purged all of the white people. Those people formed another organization called COFFO, and I ran into those down in Southwest Georgia. I had relatives in Americus, and I went up for one demonstration, and there were a lot of white people who had been purged from SNCC who were there. But you found a lot of white kids in Chapel Hill in CORE because there wasn't a lot of black kids to draw from. Raymond Mallard was a real bad judge. I don't know if he was intent on breaking the back of CORE, but his sentencing was unbelievable. I wasn't in the state when the sentences were handed out. I didn't get arrested in Chapel Hill, but we went up there for the demonstrations. At that point, there were demonstrations everywhere, and our efforts were concentrated in the downtown area. I think that Dr. Laizner was arrested sitting on a highway.

## Elizabeth Laizner

I left to visit my family in Europe a few days after we were released from the polio hospital, and returned about a month later. We had the Evans committee, but we were sure that the grown-ups would take over, and they did. Besides, to go right back to jail would have ruined the students' finals and graduation. The S&W was open, the movie houses were open, some other little restaurants were open. In fact, we were one of the few towns in the South that had open public facilities before the 1964 Civil Rights Bill demanded it. The things that we had wanted, with one exception, took place. The Mayfair did not come through.

We did not think that we had gotten everything that we wanted, but the main thing was that we had always concentrated on certain places. That fall we did some things, such as the picketing of the Oaks Motel, which was segregated. Then the Civil Rights Bill opened the Oaks Motel, which had seen some of the nastiest picketing, but not so much publicity. That particular place had an interesting sequel. The Oaks Motel had said that they would be open, and in the fall of 1964, [comedian] Dick Gregory was going to give a benefit concert for us, since we needed one badly. We had had enormous expenses; even if the legal fees were borne by the NAACP; there were a lot of other things. We had to maintain an office, for instance.

Mr. Gregory gave the concert in the fall. I was arranging that thing, and somebody called to make reservations for him at the King Cotton Hotel. I talked it over with the leadership, and we came to the conclusion that the best thing to do was register him at the Oaks Motel, because it was then the newest and most elegant. Why not get him in there and see if it would provide a room to a black person? The advance person was hesitant about it, and I assured him that it was an elegant place, that it had a swimming pool and a mini-golf course, and Mr. Gregory was getting what they wanted, and that he would also get quite some publicity. I went out there and made the reservations. I informed the press, and there was a whole page spread about him in the newspaper. It seemed a harmless scene but for the fact that it was the Oaks Motel, which had refused up until then to accept Negroes. We made a big splash of it. We also made sustained daily picketing of the Travelodge downtown for two months, but there was not the same publicity, and we were not successful in desegregating it.

We perhaps could have sustained another major campaign in 1964, but it was very hard on the students and the black community. And it was obvious that the government in Washington was going to do something, so our attitude was, "Let them." We did all sorts of things in the year 1963-1964, but we didn't make the papers very often. In fact, we did quite a lot, but some of it was done quietly. For example, we picketed a small motel downtown. We intervened at Black Cadillac [automobile dealership], where a worker was dismissed because she insisted on calling blacks there "mister." We picketed with the NAACP, and the young lady got a complete apology, but she did not go back to work for them. That was in the papers. We did a lot of things on a smaller scale which were very successful, but not very sensational. We knew that we couldn't [count on] the adults anymore to back us up; everyone knew that the Civil Rights Bill was definitely going to come. We concentrated on small things, sometimes in cooperation with the NAACP. There was no animosity between CORE and the NAACP. In the spring of '64 the NAACP wanted to integrate the banks, especially Wachovia. "We don't have people to picket, can you lend us some?" We went over there and did it for them.

Ralph Lee and Pat Patterson ran for chairman in '64, and Ralph was elected. But there was no personal rivalry involved, and there was not a division about what we should do, unless it was in small things. Bill [Thomas] needed time for that. Pat was always with us, and Bill's younger brother [Alvin] was the last chairman. Now, in 1964, when picketing techniques were not so much needed, we switched to social [work] in the neighborhoods. I headed the committee, but Lewis Brandon was the man who had the experience in this. I learned a great deal working with Lewis. One of the neighborhoods where we started working is still cited in sociology texts as an example of people helping themselves. This is the Eastside Park Neighborhood. We deliberately played down CORE's name in the news media on that, because we wanted to stress the efforts of the residents. This was the neighborhood next to Gillespie Street and Morningside Homes, next to the railroad track, which was one of the worst in town. We went in there in force one Saturday afternoon and most of Sunday, to visit from house to house. We told the people living there: "We're from CORE. We're just visiting you, how are you doing?"

Of course, everyone received us; it was fine. We worked up a paper; what we were really after was to document what improvements the city and landlords needed to make; and we had a form that we worked out, but the people never saw it. We handed it out later. It was very simple: it contained such questions as the type of house—frame, brick, wood; how was it heated, etc. And complaints: how was the lighting, how was the landlord, was the street paved, etc. Our purpose was not to do it ourselves, but to aid the neighborhood, and while we did it, there was one crucial question: "Do you consider the person interviewed a potential neighborhood leader?" It took us about three months, but when we were finished, we had surveyed two or three hundred houses. Only two people stayed on, Reverend Marion Jones and myself. We got a group of people that we felt were the right ones, together with CORE, showed them the information that we had as to what most people wanted: better garbage collection, paving of the streets. We presented it to the people downtown, and those things were done. That went on for over a year,.

O. Henry Boulevard, near Gillespie, had no playground for the children living there. The group got together and they got leaflets out to everybody in the neighborhood for a meeting in a church on Nance Street, under the direction of Reverend Frank Williams and Reverend Marion Jones. CORE dropped out after the first few meetings, because we wanted the people to do it for themselves, and they did. Sometimes the younger people were impatient, and the older people would disagree; sometimes, Reverend Jones [had to] ask them to be peaceful. I was not there as a CORE member; I was a secretary at one time, because I had a typewriter. The one who came in and made the Eastside Association a success was Jo Spivey, [who] wrote about it and enabled them to get things, even a playground. [City Manager] George Aull helped on this.

The CORE chapter simply petered out in 1964-1965, but before that we surveyed a few other neighborhoods. By then, there was no support of nonviolent direct action, because the whole Black Movement was going toward greater and greater militancy. I wasn't in as much of a leadership position as I appeared to be. The only actual leadership position that I had was in the Social Action Group. I was mainly an *aulagershield*, which [in German] means "a sign in a shop window." Some members resented the fact that the press focused on me as the only white person when we picketed; they wanted the focus to be on blacks protesting for black issues.

We did one enormous thing in the fall of 1964. Alvin Thomas and I went to the national CORE conference at the time of the murder of the three civil rights workers in Mississippi [Andrew Goodman, Michael Schwerner and James Chaney]. It was tremendously moving. There was also the wife of a minister that was accidentally run over by a bulldozer during a demonstration up north. Alvin promised that our group would collect clothing and food for Mississippi during the summer and fall of 1964. We collected six tons of clothing in Greensboro. Some people brought it to us, and Essa's Bi-Rite on Gorrell Street gave us shopping carts for us to go out and collect more in the neighborhood.

The FBI under President Johnson, was ordered to help when we had some trouble with other shipments to Mississippi. One had been stolen by Klansmen, one had been burned. We sent it to Jackson. The group down there was COCO [Council of Coordinated Organizations]. McKissick suggested that we contact the local Teamster's Union to transport it for us for free, and they did. There were thirty to forty boxes. We repaired and washed clothes; toys were fixed. Then we called the FBI. They followed the trucks through the states to Jackson. I was in constant contact with the COCO office there. After being alerted that men were breaking into our boxes in the warehouse down there, I called the FBI and made a complaint. There were a number of boxes broken into, but nothing had been taken. And they were finally delivered. The story was printed in the *Wall Street Journal*.

I was arrested in Chapel Hill in 1964. It was a mess. The people at Chapel Hill said that they needed some people, and I said okay. This was when we laid down on the street. I had just intended to help. Once again, I was the *aulagershield*. We were supposed to block the road to the airport, which we did. And then we were arrested. I got the book thrown at me, and got the worst sentence of anybody. I was given a $1000 fine and two months in jail, but no probation on one charge, and one-year jail sentence at the discretion of the court. I was in jail until the bail was raised.

## Ralph Lee

I was elected chapter chairman in the latter part of 1963. Before becoming chairman, I attended meetings and made up a few signs, but I did not have any type of heavy administrative responsibility. I was elected chairman really at the pushing of Dr. Laizner, who felt that I would be able to take over, and I would just have to assume that she felt that I would have created a better image for the organization than Mr. Patterson. Whether that's true or not, I have no idea. But, at any rate, I was drafted to run by a contingent who were mainly Bennett students. And I, of course, had A&T support. And that was a very close vote. Pat and I were very close friends, and there was no animosity between the two of us. It was just felt that Pat was a very quiet and reticent guy, and I have to assume that it was felt by the majority that, perhaps, I spoke up more, or had a better voice, or dressed better or whatever. I certainly don't think it had anything to do with who was more capable of running the organization, because at no point did I seek the chairmanship at all. This was just strictly something that I was drafted into doing. Once I got the majority vote, I said, "Well, I'm stuck with it and I'll give it my best," rather than say "Absolutely no" and create further dissension.

The chapter disappeared simply because, at that point, there was a lot of dissension in terms of which way to go. But we had primarily accomplished our goal of desegregating the places of public accommodation in Greensboro. We did not have the sophistication at that time, to pursue more esoteric economic goals. Members said, "I have to look out for myself now," particularly in terms of their studies, because many of us had lost a lot of time out of classes, and, obviously, grades were on the decline.

There were those that wanted to continue direct action activities. Dr. Laizner from Bennett had her contingent as being the more militant. Reverend Stanley took a more conservative approach. A lot of infighting began, and a lot of personality conflicts came about. I got caught in the middle of this, even though all I was trying to do was to straighten out the economic affairs of the chapter, because we were very heavily in debt. There were legal bills that had to be paid, to say nothing about phone bills and rent. We continued to meet on a weekly basis. It was the chapter as a whole—what was left of it. I think toward the end, I would venture to say there were only thirty to thirty-five people.

We talked about new directions, but when I became chairman, we were pretty much closing out things; I think if I got a thousand dollars from the national office, that was the maximum amount of money. We had rent to pay on an office on Gorrell Street with minimal equipment At the time, the Movement was at a very young stage, and the primary concern with us was with opening up public facilities. Of course, as time went on, economic goals became more of a concern. But, we did not address ourselves to that, at least, I didn't during the time I was chairman. I don't think we really had the foresight at that time to talk about economics. I think that this was true of many CORE chapters in Southern cities at the time. It was basically a question that we felt that we had a right to access the public facilities, such as restaurants and theaters.

Rather than venture out into a whole lot of areas where many of us did not have expertise, we decided to do one thing at the time. There was not much support for those kinds of activities among the adult black community, and I think the reason why is because Greensboro, by and large, has a substantial middle class black population, and this was something new to them. I have to assume that a good number of them felt threatened by what we were doing and were quite comfortable with the status quo as it was. We did not get any help from the NAACP chapter here, not at all.

After the demonstrations, and after the federal government and the state legislature passed a number of laws opening public facilities, the problem became: "Where do we go from here" What do we do?" At that point, I recall some of the members indicating that they should petition certain industries in the Greensboro area to hire more blacks and put pressure on them to promote some of the black employees that they had. Of course, at that point, our funds were depleted, and after the initial successes of the demonstrations, support began to wane, and then it became a problem of keeping the members we had. Reverend Stanley was the main one of us on the economic issue, or the employment issue, for some time. My primary concern was with putting our economic house in order before we ventured into other areas.

I did not sit in on Greene Street on June 5th, nor in the Square on June 6th. I left for Virginia on May 31, because I had gotten ill in that year, and on the advice of my doctors, I just needed some rest and recuperation. Some members sat in at the mayor's office, and there was a silent protest march of a very few students in front of the post office. There was some federal legislation pending at that time regarding civil rights, and it seems to me both of the [U.S.] senators from North Carolina, [Everett] Jordan and [Sam] Erwin, opposed it. We had a peaceful march around the federal building, to encourage them to change their positions on the pending civil rights bill. No arrests were made in that demonstration.

The economic issue, or approaching companies to hire blacks, came about. But nothing really got off the ground. I understand that after 1965 the chapter issued a report to the mayor's committee [Human Relations Commission] about the number of businesses that had desegregated. The chapter also sent clothes and food to Mississippi, and occasionally CORE would march or picket with the NAACP on certain very small things. Many of the CORE members remained, since they lived in Greensboro. My presidency ran from the fall of '63 until sometime in '64, and then I resigned due to health issues. There was some dissension within the chapter over goals, and Elizabeth Laizner had a more militant element; Reverend Stanley was the more moderate of the two. When I say militant, I don't mean to imply anything radical and violent. It's just that she insisted on demonstrating almost for the sake of demonstrating.

Comedian and activist Dick Gregory and folk singer Lynn Chandler came down, ostensibly to raise money for the chapter of CORE, as he was doing in a number of other cities. Unfortunately, we ended up spending more money than, in fact, he was able to raise, due to his personal tastes at the time. He ran up close to a six or seven hundred dollar phone bill talking to his wife collect in Chicago, to say nothing about the various outfits that he wanted cleaned immediately. Bill's mother [Mrs. Thomas] had worked at a cleaner's, so we were able to oblige him with getting his clothes cleaned and pressed through her. We had to foot the bill for that; the national chapter paid his transportation. He spent two days in Durham prior to coming over to Greensboro, and then Jesse Jackson and I picked him up and brought him to Greensboro. Mr. Gregory had expensive personal tastes, ordering scotch and cigarettes, and we got stuck with a substantial bill. I would say, after paying his bills, perhaps we showed a profit of three or four hundred dollars. But we got very good publicity, because he got to stay in a place that had not been desegregated. As a matter of fact, he was the first black person to stay at that particular facility.

There was a news conference with some reporters there from the local TV station, but to me, Dick Gregory was a very arrogant, self-centered person. And I just don't deal well with people like that. Had his motives been sincere, there were certain ways he could have saved money. He could have certainly stayed on the campus of A&T in a student's room. He could have certainly eaten a lot cheaper than he did, and if he wanted to make all these calls to his home in Chicago, where he was living at that time, I think he could have [avoided] reversing the charges. Although Dr. Laizner was very supportive of Dick Gregory during that time, she and I had a very close working relationship. She was a tremendous woman.

Soon a more serious problem developed. Some people—perhaps influenced by the Black Power movement—began to question her motives and those of white students from Guilford College who had gotten involved. I don't want to say that anything serious developed, because it didn't; it was just a question of, "This is our battle, and we enjoyed your help, but now we don't need you anymore. Let us fight our own war." And I think that she just became isolated to the point where I was the only one going over to her house. Some others began to feel that there was something wrong, that she was overly aggressive. I know that later when she was involved with activities in Chapel Hill, she says that she had gotten an anonymous phone call that there were attempts to try to have her deported, but they couldn't because she was a naturalized citizen. This is where the Communist label was applied to her. We were all accused of being Communists. It was ridiculous, because I'd venture to say if we were asked to give you a good description of communism as opposed to socialism and Trotskyism and so forth, that none of us would have known what we were talking about. I had heard from another faculty member at A&T, "She's just a 'pinko.'" Nothing developed from that.

The black community in Greensboro, at that time, was extremely conservative. They didn't want to be bothered. And maybe if I had a nice eighty, ninety thousand dollar brick home with two or three Cadillacs in my garage, maybe I wouldn't have wanted to be bothered either. The A&T faculty never really got behind us, not at all. There were a few instructors, assistant professors, lower-echelon faculty members who were involved, but in terms of the top administration, there was no involvement. And, reflecting on it, I can probably understand why. Dr. Dowdy came in at a very crucial time with A&T. And he was looking to develop the university and get federal grants and additional monies from the state legislature, and certainly tried, and from what I hear at alumni meetings before his retirement, he succeeded in attracting a far better faculty there than was there at the time I attended.

The summer of 1965 when I graduated, I worked for the American Friends Service Committee in South Carolina in Rock Hill and worked on a voter registration program down there. At the end of August '65, I came back up to New York, and I've been up here ever since. That pretty much ended my contact with Greensboro and also the CORE chapter.

## Sarah Jones (Outterbridge)

At a mass meeting, it was announced that our representatives had talked with the mayor. He promised to appoint a committee to study the situation, and asked them to cease demonstrations until it could decide on something. They told us at that time that we would cease demonstrations, because we were a nonviolent group, and we tried to conform to this type of thing. They said that they were going to try to work on it and give them a chance to make a deal, but if nothing was done over a certain period of time, then we would go back to the streets and they let that be known.

## Frances Herbin (Lewis)

I participated in other demonstrations, but there weren't too many after that time; they were just marches. We would start out by the Hayes-Taylor Y and march downtown and back to the Y. I did not participate in the sit-down on Greene Street on June 5 or the sit-down on June 6—I don't know why. Although there were no more mass marches, more mass meetings were held, basically to convey information to the community. They would let us know exactly what was going on, what places had integrated, what places were holding back, and that kind of thing. We were told that if there was not progress by the fall, demonstrations would resume. I graduated from Dudley that spring and went to A&T that fall. Everything just ceased. I participated in the picketing of the Kroger on Asheboro Street, but I did it as an individual, not as a CORE activity. The NAACP asked us on several occasions to do things, and that was announced. My father was active with both of them. I did not participate in any civil rights activity in Greensboro after that, although I went to the March on Washington in 1963.

That was arranged through ministers in Greensboro. Floyd McKissick and Reverend Cox let us know that this was taking place, and the offices got together and chartered buses. We left from St. Stephens Church early that morning to go to Washington. We arrived somewhere near lunch time that day. We went directly to the site, and the bus drivers already knew where to park the buses. We went directly to the Lincoln Memorial. I was in the middle of the crowd. I had never seen so many people in all of my life. We boxed our lunches in Greensboro. People brought baskets of food for everybody to take; people that were not participating would bring stuff by the church. I went to different places, walked around and listened and sang; it was long day. We left that evening after dark and got back to Greensboro in the early hours of the morning;

1963-64 was my last year of involvement with the Movement. After graduation I remained in the Greensboro area, but I did not remain in CORE. I don't recall how long we continued to meet past that point, but we all kept in close contact in an informal way, rather than regular meetings. After that, I got married and my first son was born in 1965, and I sort of had my hands full.

## Alvin Thomas

Eventually the demonstrations stopped, and the enthusiasm died down. I guess people thought that we had reached our goals. The numbers shrank; I think that is the normal thing in a dynamic organization like CORE. The Greensboro CORE continued to plan activities, and a lot of our activities dealt with the Human Relations Commission. We tried to work through them when we had certain problems, for these kinds of requests that "We can't find an individual for these positions." and this kind of thing. We would contact the press before things would take place, but the stars were gone, you might say. Generally, the press would only cover our activities when members of the CORE national office would come down to participate.

Ralph Lee was elected chairman of the Greensboro CORE after Bill had left town to go to work. Under Ralph, we concentrated on paying off the debts that had been incurred during the demonstrations and picketing. We generated most of the money ourselves; we never got an awful lot from the national office. I continued to attend CORE meetings that summer [1963], and I did something for SNCC or the NAACP in one of their summer voter registration drives held in North Carolina in the eastern part of the state. Things did not fade away all at once. We tested the Civil Rights Act of 1964; so we had continuous demonstrations. We started the project called "Operation Dialogue," where we went out into the community and knocked on doors, asking people what they thought needed to be done in the black community, and started to solve problems of concern to the community. We were quite successful in doing that, whether it was painting a house to showing someone the way to do the welfare system, that might qualify, but who was not receiving benefits. We held neighborhood meetings relative to that; we participated in voter registration drives to get out the vote; this was a continuous process.

After the passage of the 1964 Civil Rights, we tested places to see if we would be served, and we were turned down quite a bit. We sought to open these hold-outs through negotiations. It took place because we told them that we would write to Washington and take the necessary steps because it was the law, and they gave in. We never had to initiate any suits. Among our last picketing was the Apple Brothers restaurants and the Biff Burger on Lee Street; they were one of the last few to come across. But there were no threats of violence. There was nothing like the police coverage that there had been during the height of the mass demonstrations in 1963. It wasn't that type of coverage, because the numbers were small, and as you really get down to attacking the real problems, the numbers got smaller, and it was not the dramatic action that one had in the height of the demonstrations, which is sort of like a campaign. You can't campaign all of your life. We were dealing with hardcore issues and trying to work through the Human Relations Commission. It was more difficult to work up tactics to protest economic issues than to the desegregation of businesses of public entertainment and accommodation. But, certainly, the economic question was on our minds, because we thought first how we were going to desegregate these places, and how we were going to do that became a problem. But just the day-to-day activities and the arrests still going on and that type of thing, it kind of kept you busy running from pillar to post.

There was not really a serious division of opinion as to which tactics to employ. There was the same commitment to nonviolence that the people had in 1961 through 1963. During the meetings held in my parents' home, we would discuss the running of the organization, particularly our financial status, where we were headed, projects to be selected. Attorney [Floyd] McKissick represented us, and he had to be compensated in some way. Ralph Lee was later elected chairman of the Greensboro CORE; Bill had left town to go to work at that time. Under Ralph, we concentrated on paying off the debts that had been incurred during the demonstrations and picketing. We collected dues, although little was collected. People were basically students, and most students were poor. There were a few fund-raising activities at Dick Ramsey's place. We participated in a freedom songs record being prepared here and in New York. We derived some revenue from that, although most of the money was sent to New York. We generated most of the money ourselves; we never got an awful lot from the national office.

In 1965 I succeeded Ralph Lee as President of the Greensboro CORE. During my tenure as chairman of the Greensboro CORE chapter, there would be an agenda set each night, it would be very organized meetings, a lot of discussions and debate over things that would occur, questions at hand, but few records were kept. But our activities never again approximated the spring demonstrations of 1963, which was the high point of the involvement of the chapter. The membership was getting smaller; I think that it gradually faded away. Although the economic question was on our minds, it was more difficult to work up tactics to protest economic issues than to the desegregation of businesses of public entertainment and accommodation. We operated from a small office off Gorrell Street, but we eventually gave up that office; there was no need for it after a while. Some people came and went as advisors to the chapter, but not like Tony Stanley, Dr. Laizner and Reverend Hatchett, who stayed to the very end. Betty Wall remained as secretary.

I think that it gradually faded away when I went away to graduate school at Rutgers University, because I never heard a word after that. I guess that is one of the things that led me into my major of labor education. I went to graduate school at Rutgers University after leaving A&T because I wanted to make some type of economic contribution, and at the time the labor movement was the only real avenue. I was the first graduate student to receive a masters in that area at Rutgers. I continued to participate in civil rights activities at Rutgers; I was chairman of the Black Graduate Students Association. I eventually worked for the A. Philip Randolph Institute as its Education Coordinator.

I studied under Mr. Randolph. I still work in the field of labor education and relations.

## Lois Lucas (Williams)

After the demonstrations were suspended as part of the arrangement with the Evans committee, the only thing to think about then was to get back to campus and get exams over with, because by then it was time to go home. We met a couple of times after we got out of the polio hospital, but I felt that we had been pre-empted, in a way. All of a sudden, the city was saying, "We're not going to deal with you as students or as a CORE group. Now we are going to go back into the larger community and get the members of the Establishment, and make a deal." In other words, with people that will make compromises. I felt a little bit sold out, but yet at the same time, realizing that it wasn't a movement to get just what young college kids wanted; it was a movement to benefit black people everywhere, including the established black community in Greensboro. So, although we had borne the brunt of the struggle, and been out on the front lines, if the time had come to say, "These are the results" and if they wanted to give it to somebody else, or call somebody else and let them relay it to us, what are you going to do?

It was exam time and I worked my way through college and held down a full time job working at L. Richardson Memorial Hospital as a nurse's aide. So that meant, in addition to exams, I also had to get back to work. Then I was working for the summer, and the only time that I took off was when I went to the March on Washington. I was two miles back. There was an exhilarating feeling of camaraderie that existed between people of all ages and all races. When I got back, the Coordinating Committee was in charge of negotiations. Greensboro CORE continued to play a role, but it was a community effort. A number of more activist people associated with CORE during the demonstrations drifted away for various reasons. I later worked on voter registration. also did training work with some kids from Jackson, Mississippi.

## Jibreel Khazan

I was in Greensboro during the summer of 1963, undecided about what I was going to do. My father was a contractor, and I worked with him painting houses. The first week of September 1963, I got a call from Dr. Samuel Proctor, who asked me what my plans were for the fall of the year. I told him that I was trying to get a job so that I could go to grad school. He said, "How would you like to go to Howard University Law School?" I told him, "It's kind of late," and he said, "School's only been going on for a week. They'll take you there;

how would you like to go right on up?" He wanted me to get a graduate degree. I was having problems with my health and I was just tired, but I wanted to go on to school, because I had taken my pre-law exam back in November of the previous year. I was accepted to Howard Law School, but I had not been able to finance it. So, finally, I agreed to go to law school in the fall of 1963. But, when I got there, school had been going on for almost two weeks and I had to catch up, which was a very difficult to do. I stayed there until April 1964. I had to leave law school; there was too much pressure on me and my health wasn't holding up well. I haven't been back since, because when I left there in 1964, I came back to Greensboro to work for about eight or nine months, then in the spring of 1965, I joined the Job Corps and worked as a teacher in New Bedford, Massachusetts, and I have been there ever since.

## Robert "Pat" Patterson

I believe that the Human Relations Commission deliberately citied the number of seats desegregated in a restaurant, and the number of rooms desegregated in a motel, in order to manipulate the data to make the results appear more progressive than they were. I think that was the design of the group, to dilute the backing of the organizations at that time. I think that this was one of the problems that we ran into in Greensboro. The level of sophistication here was high, and they used all kinds of tactics and techniques. I believe they thought that these are some restless students and, eventually the leadership will move on out, and there doesn't appear to be anyone developing behind them. Jesse Jackson was a senior at that time; I was a senior; Lewis Brandon was about to graduate; Reverend Hatchett had already left. So, a lot of the leadership in the organization was leaving. Most of us were in fields that would take us away from Greensboro.

I remember thinking in the fall of 1964, a lot of things were happening, doors were opening up, and at this time I was close to being graduated and I had to start thinking about what I as going to do with myself. Was I prepared? The last year that I was in school, I had to do some tall studying in order to have any decent grades to offer anybody that wanted to look at my transcript. Quite frankly, after June 7, 1963, I kind of drifted away [from CORE]. I was still actively involved, but I was not part of the leadership after that. I remember one of my professors calling me in and saying, "Pat, I admire you for what you are doing, but you are opening up doors that you won't be able to go through yourself if you don't prepare." By that time I had gotten myself behind, and I had to rededicate myself to getting an education, so that when I got out of A&T, I would be able to get a decent job. I think that kind of thing did happen. My reaction was not disenchantment with CORE so much.

I thought a lot about continuing with civil rights activities. I remember discussing it with Jesse Jackson and Tony Stanley, but I knew that I wasn't the kind of person that could stay in this kind of work, and by this time, I had come to believe that all of us, regardless of what we were doing, could play a part in the civil rights of black people. And I likened it to a stage where not everybody can play the star role. It wasn't that important, and I felt that, at that time, I was ready to move on, and contribute to the improvment of black people in other ways. In my case it was by facilitating economic opportunities through banking and finance policies toward the black community.

I sensed a rise of greater militancy in the black community after 1964. I think it was due to a feeling that not much progress was being made in a short enough period of time. Also, the idea of Dr. King being destroyed in a violent manner seemed to shift the whole thing completely out of focus. I think people began to feel that it no longer mattered; it was no longer sufficient to maintain a low profile of nonviolence, but rather there needed to be a push. My own thoughts tended to go in that direction. People began to question why it all evolved the way that it did.

I think that was part of the case. But I think that the other part was the whole paternalistic attitude that many of the powers-that-be had. And it really disheartened me to constantly hear about vocational training. They didn't train the little white girls to be able to sell hot dogs across the lunch counter or to ring a cash register. No vocational training was needed. The only thing you needed was someone with average intelligence.

I think they were trying to build up a straw man in order to have something to knock down. This has been the history of race relations. Either you don't have qualifications or you're overly qualified. I've actually had people to say, "You're overly qualified. We don't want you." We're trying constantly to find reasons for not doing what we know should be done. This is the greatest country on Earth, and we're qualified to get anything that we want done. Industry constantly trains and retrains. So we don't have to continue to build straw men if we are committed to doing things. The difference was we didn't have that real commitment, at least the timetable that we wanted them to have.

I think the last committee appointed by the Mayor was operating from a genuine spirit of cooperation to achieve positive actions rather than just words, and at the same time trying to accommodate the business and political power structure. I think that basically their orientation was from the business community point of view. But I also think that they realized that some achievements had to be made. But the problem with these types of committees was that they had no teeth, they had no enforcement power. They could only use moral suasion. And I don't think that at that particular time they were really prepared to use any real amount of persuasion. What could they do to Boyd Morris? They were not prepared to call for a boycott by the citizens of Greensboro.

So really they were powerless. And that whole thing of setting up commissions was nothing more than a conciliatory thing on the part of everyone in attempting to create a climate where change could occur. And I think change happened. But at that particular time, we were not willing to listen to more talk and more promises. We wanted action, and we wanted it then. There was a sense of urgency that was there. And we tried to communicate this to the people that made up these committees.

I think that there was some validity to perceiving Greensboro as a moderate Southern city. Take, for instance, how the police responded: it could have been a very explosive situation. But they responded positively, I would say. In many ways, Greensboro is much more moderate than other areas of the country. But that does not mean that we did not have racist attitudes existing. But their reaction to it was a little bit different.

One of the things that helped us was that Greensboro had a local NAACP chapter that was really very strong and very active. George Simkins and some of the other folks had done some things prior to the sit-ins at Woolworth. So a lot of things had gone on prior to some of the things that we were doing. I think that made it a little easier for us to do something here in Greensboro, because there was some very strong leadership in this town. Our strategies began to change, and prior to that it was mostly a student thing. But I think we began to get a lot of older individuals that had been involved in these kinds of things, whether it was a direct confrontation or not, but people that had been involved in these things over a lot of years to bring some organization, some maturity to the group.

By this time we had been involved for about two or three years. And I think that helped a lot, because we had acquired the experience and maturity to warn the younger black population: "You don't change these things overnight. You've got to do some planning. You've got to have good organization. You've got to find a way to keep the community conscious of the fact that these are some things that we want to do." I think that those kinds of groups in the adult black community began to come in, and there was a great deal more organization and experience in how to attack these problems.

## Edward Zane

Sometimes the desegregation of individual restaurants did not come about through negotiations. I was involved in one such occasion, which had a humorous aspect to it. One evening I was exceedingly busy and called home to tell them that I'd eat dinner in town. I went to a restaurant on Summit Avenue. Dr. Evans and Dr. Dowdy and their wives were outside. We greeted each other, and they invited me to eat with them. I said, that I would like to, but I was just going to grab a quick bite before returning to the office, but that I would sit briefly with them.

The hostess knew me well, and she didn't know what to do. That restaurant had not integrated, and she didn't want to embarrass me by refusing service to those that appeared to be eating with me. So, she took them in and sat them down. I spoke to them for a few minutes, and then sat at a different table. The next morning, the owner of the restaurant called me. He said, "Ed, that was a sneaky way of integrating my restaurant." [Laughs] I said, "I had nothing to do with it. They were out there, they came in with me, and the hostess sat them." He says, "Well, there was not a single complaint from any person in the restaurant. So, you tell them any time they want to eat here, they're welcome." That's what happened there; it was just one of those things. That integrated the restaurant. He told me, he said, "You tell them that any time they want to come in, you let them know how we feel here." Well, gradually that's what occurred.

Things went almost that smoothly when I helped to arrange the desegregation of the movie theaters through the distribution of movie tickets to the black community. When the theater operators expressed concern about being overwhelmed by black students, I said, "I'll guarantee that there won't be more than five or eight black youngsters in the movie in any one night." And they told me to go ahead. So, gradually everything simmered down to where everyone realized that segregation was dead. The integration of all facilities is the only answer. And here we are today.

## Otis Hairston, Sr.

As long as we had the balance on the committee under Dr. Evans, and later [W. O.] Conrad, and Tom Storrs on the permanent Human Relations Commission, encouraging progress was made in race relations. Tom Storrs was a very understanding person as to what the problem was, and he was the person who was very helpful in getting the white community to understand what the problem was and what they needed to do about something.

Conrad played a good role as a chairman. He wanted to try to do some things, and yet, he was flexible, he wouldn't move either way too far. He was a good chairman who could get along with everybody. I think that advocating vocational education was an honest perception which he had, and of course, we have said basically, some of the same things today; that if you open the place up and you don't have the money to buy, there is not too much that you are going to get out of that. Of greater importance was upgrading on jobs, and the opportunity to work at different levels where you had not had folk moving up to management, at that level.

Basically, what he was saying is something that we are saying today, that we need to think in terms of economic development and education, along with the voting power that we have. Basically, what he said is what we are saying today. Before he died, Martin Luther King, recognized that this is an area that we have got to move into. He started the Operation Breadbasket-type of thing, where you force people to employ and upgrade people and I think, basically, Conrad's perception was fairly accurate.

We had already done desegregation at that point, so he was thinking in terms of how we would proceed from that point. Some of these things had not been open at this time—you had few places that had not, and recreational facilities some of them at that time—so what Conrad was saying, basically, was that we had to go beyond that, we needed to think in terms of a goal that would really liberate, and I think that education, the power of the ballot and economic development, the things that continued to really liberate us.

## Marion Jones

I remained associated with CORE for quite some time. We were involved in preparatory activities in the event that things were not realized. We never just dropped our guard; we continued to meet and still be alert. I think, in many instances, the reason that demonstrations did not begin again, was that the people got complacent. They thought that the bulk of the things were being achieved and public accommodations were being opened; they saw no need to run it into the ground. However, nobody decided to dissolve. Things began to grow better gradually, and that was just about it. I participated in the March on Washington in August 1963. It was formally organized in Greensboro. We got the buses at St. Stephens United Church of Christ on Gorrell Street, where the buses met and returned. We were all over; I was near the Lincoln Memorial. There really wasn't anything to participate in after we got back, so I went to a church in Ellerbe, North Carolina, and then to Asheboro, North Carolina.

## Leonard Guyes

I was president of the Greensboro Merchants Association in 1963. At the time, our black community felt the need to integrate the retail establishments. They had sent some pretty strong literature to me as president, mostly in the way of threatening boycotts. Since so much of our retail population was black, they felt that an economic boycott would best serve their purpose, if we were not willing to discuss the feasibility and the possibility of integrating. They were mostly after the retail sales staff at the time. We had many meetings with their groups. I think there was unfounded fear on the part of the white citizenry of Greensboro. They became fearful that the demonstrations would begin again, this time with some violence, so they stayed out of the downtown area. It was somewhat of an unpleasant situation for all of the merchants, who were under pressure to hire black salespeople.

Some of us communicated with Mayor Schenck at this time. We had a retail group that went to see him to urge his cooperation and support. What we were trying to do was to "get the monkey off our back" and involve the whole community, since the retailers were the ones that were suffering as a result of this. It did result in some positive measures. Mayor Schenck appointed a Human Relations Committee, of which I was one of the early appointed members with Oscar Burnett, Carson Bain and other members of our community, and we met with certain responsible members of the black community. Back in those days, they had the NAACP and CORE involved, and some of the young members of CORE were outspoken, and I didn't feel acted too responsibly, although we met occasionally with some of the people who represented it that we felt we could communicate with.

I used to get threatening phone calls and nasty letters, and my wife and children did suffer some abuse; it was not a very pleasant time for me. I recall George Simkins, because George has always been a very outspoken member of the NAACP, and was one of the first people that we met with. We also met at one time with some of the young people in CORE and some of the actively involved people with the NAACP. They were very young and very vocal, and very demanding. I don't think any of us felt comfortable talking with those people. They might have had some representation, but most of their spokesmen were represented by what I call more prominent, distinguished members of the black community, who were a little more mature in their thinking and remained cool-headed, people you could sit down and have meaning-ul discussions with.

Most of the pressure against the retail stores subsided when the demonstrations ceased in the spring of 1963. We made a commitment, and those of us who were in a position to do so, made a firm commitment to CORE and the NAACP representatives. And I think we did it with a clear conscience. We did it because we thought that it was the right thing to do. Of course, they put a lot of pressure to bear [on us].. But I don't think there was any resentment after we had done it, or that we were backed up against the wall; we set the timetable. In other words, we agreed to have it done by a certain time to show good faith. And we felt that the only way to accomplish it was to set a deadline for ourselves. I think the demonstrators felt that we acted in good faith and that they believed that we had a willingness to cooperate. And I think that we did open some very good channels of communication in the black community.

There's no doubt that it set business back for a while. A lot of large industries looking at Greensboro might have said, "We're not coming; there's too much unrest." But I think the broader scope is that most businesses or industries that had looked at Greensboro's history had seen that we have met our problems head-on and done everything that we could to solve them, and as a result, had concluded that we were in fact, a good community in which to settle.

## Neil McGill

Eugene Street [owner of the Cinema Theater], Jimmy Bellows [manager of the Center Theater] and I were all very close friends. We discussed just when and where we would integrate. We knew it was coming, and we were going to desegregate all at the same time. We met to decide time, and date.McNeill Smith met with me on one occasion, but I told him that my company was nationwide and I couldn't authorize the integration myself. When we integrated, it came down from my company. We just told them [CORE] that we were ready to integrate. I didn't receive legal advice from my company at all. I received my information and advice from the president of our company.

Attorney General Robert Kennedy called in the executives of the theater companies and told them, "I want you to go back home and integrate." Of course, they didn't have any choice, and they finally came around. The Carolina desegregated in early June 1963, and I was glad to see it. There weren't a lot of black patrons, which surprised us, because they wanted to attend the theater, but when we announced that we had desegregated, they didn't come. In fact, A&T students continued to sit in our balcony, where the admission was less. But we closed the balcony completely due to low attendance.

## J. Kenneth Lee

When the compromise was reached with the theater owners over issuing a certain number of tickets over time to the black community, I thought that three weeks and it will all be over. But the students said, "We want to go there today, or we ain't gonna leave that theater." I went back and told the theater operators, "They said that they either got to go into here today without any limitations or they ain't gonna leave the theater." And they just looked at each other, and they said one word: "Okay." And when they said that, I said, "You know, I am getting so that I am compromising too much. It's time for me to get out of this thing and let somebody else that was raised in a different day take over." They opened it up that same day, right then and there. I had been compromising and I said, "Times have changed. It ain't fifteen years ago now, when I had to take any kind of a compromise that I could take." They were going without compromises; they didn't want any compromises, and I was still willing to accept some compromises.

The students were not aware of the past that made compromises necessary. When we were doing that, they were being born, and this is fifteen or seventeen years later. That didn't mean much to them. Now they were getting things by demanding them and not waiting, and shutting the town down until they got it. It was hard for me to immediately adapt to that, so that was my last time of representing them. They had some new fellows who had come up under a different system, and didn't have any of the problems that I had, who could practice anywhere. So that was my last case, and I haven't taken one since. I am through with it; I think that I have served my purpose as much as I could and somebody else could do it better now.

## James McMillan

The only meeting that I sat in on was one that had been formed by the initial Human Relations Committee set up by Mayor Schenck. It took place in one of the board meeting rooms of the old Wachovia Building. I think that an official with the Wachovia Bank represented that body, and I assume it was a form of the Human Relations Committee that was set up to try to at least give a semblance of resolving some of the concerns that the students and the civil rights groups had brought.

I recall, though, the frustration on the part of the students [who] asked me to go down with them. I think there were some Bennett students, and there happened to be some person from A&T. I went down, and we sat at this long table, and we saw that the city could make a wonderful contribution to race relations if they could make some changes to this segregated pattern that was so insulting and so derogatory to all blacks. Some of our grievances were listed, such as not being able to eat in some of the restaurants, going to the theaters without having to go into the side entrance and having to sit in the so-called "Crow's Roost" and so forth. I remember the steely look of this particular representative, who said that he saw no reason why the attitudes couldn't change by slow process. We said something had to give. We wanted to ensure that he understood our position, but there was a confrontation attitude there.

This is where much of my personal frustration took place, because I simply assumed that most persons [who] had civic roles and responsibilities would be people of reasonably good faith, and one could speak with regard to human dignity, human regard and human respect. But, I guess at that point my entire feeling was somewhat shattered because I began to realize that there was such a thing as official representatives who submerged it for the continuity of the status quo.

This proved to be pretty much the picture that emerged. As the pressure began to mount, and as the boycott proved to be an effective tactic, we saw that it was not the mayor, but the city fathers who had more to lose with their financial investment than it was those persons who had certain official rules in the city. I guess if any one thing became clear to me, it was that the almighty dollar was the ruler in many of these cases that we were attempting to change.

Many things that took place then were appeasement tactics more than anything else. I didn't see anything that was done with regard to any substantial alleviation of the predicament and the problems that we were addressing ourselves to. Everything that I saw came out, more or less, as an appeasement. I did not follow very closely the activities of the Evans committee. We were a little bit skeptical about most of those official organizations and approaches to the kinds of problems that we were talking about. We know that over the years, in most towns and cities, there are those organizations that are set up, primarily with the white city fathers and certain "respectable" blacks, to fit this kind of a role; the real effectiveness of this in terms of making any substantial kind of change was always minimal. We allowed those kinds of things to continue, but we didn't really feel that they were effective in terms of the immediacy of the kinds of things that we wanted to change.

# Boyd Morris

I was not invited to the two meetings with the mayor on June 14 and 15, because I was very outspoken when David Schenck met with the restaurant and theater operators on June 13.. He said, "Well, how much longer do you think that we should protect you?" I said, "As long as you are the mayor of Greensboro." I told him in no uncertain terms that "it is beholden upon you to protect the city and use the police." I think that they thought I was the leader of the group that resisted integration, and I assume that they wanted to deal around me. I presume that is what they did.

Later the Human Relations Commission, headed by Bland Worley, president of Wachovia Bank, called me in singly. I said, "Mr. Worley, gentlemen and ladies, I'll make you a proposition. If you will tell me that you will publicly [state] that you will integrate your offices, I'll integrate the Mayfair Cafeteria tomorrow morning." Well, the subject was changed. They weren't talking about that. They wanted Boyd Morris, to be the guinea pig. Their position was that they wanted me to integrate. But I made them a sporting proposition, and it was not on a whim. It was positive.

I also met with the top corporation leaders of Greensboro, and did the same thing. We met at the West Market Street [United Methodist] Church. There were probably fifty of the top executives there, and I was the only one in the restaurant business. They asked me to integrate. And I said, "Gentlemen, I'll integrate tomorrow morning, if you will let it be publicly known that ten percent of your office staff will be colored from here out." I did it again [with] the ministers,—the Piedmont Baptist Association, the Ministerial Association. This was in '63 and '64. And I told them—the Junior Chamber of Commerce—all of them. I made every one of them the same proposition. None of them even listened wholeheartedly to the suggestion.

I did not hire a lawyer during this; I didn't see any need to. I had not done anything [wrong]. I had complied with all the laws of the land. I wondered why everybody else wanted me to integrate, but at the same time not want to integrate themselves. They wanted me to lead the parade, and I didn't want to go out front. It was not forthcoming. I never received it from the first business, the first church or the first minister, the first lawyer, the first doctor. None of them ever communicated with me on that basis.

The other restaurateurs, we only had one or two meetings. The mayor at that time called us into a meeting. And the mayor was getting as frustrated as we were. But in this meeting, we said no, we would not integrate. And the mayor said, "Well, how much longer do you think the City of Greensboro can protect you people?" And I said, "Mr. Mayor, as long as you're mayor, you represent the law-abiding citizens. And we're law-abiding citizens. You change the law and we'll continue to be law-abiding citizens."

I called my staff together; I had sixty-five employees at this time. And I said, "My name is Boyd Morris. I have been your boss, and I am not going to stand here and tell you that I'm a good man. If you don't know what I am, then I'm lost. I am the same today [as] I was yesterday, and I'm going to be the same tomorrow. If you think I'm wrong, if you'll give me two days notice if you don't want to work for me, I will pay you a week's pay. There'll be no hard feelings. But all I want you to know is that we are experiencing something that is new to America." And they all stood up and said, "Mr. Morris, we understand, and we're with you." I did not lose a single employee during all the confrontation.

The city government was an advocate attempting to persuade me to segregate. I think they were completely frustrated, because it was happening on the buses, it was happening everywhere. There was a planned attack from the black people, and the militant of the black. A lot of it stemmed out of A&T College here, with Jesse and all of those. But I think they were frustrated, and they didn't know anything to do but say, "Let's get it over with and get on with the city," which is what we wanted to do, for goodness sake.

## Clarence Malone

After the momentum of the mass jail-ins had stopped and negotiations had begun, there was no reason for continuing demonstrations; but while the demonstrations stopped, the litigation went on. The litigation went on for months. There were delaying actions on both sides. First of all, the side of it in which

I was involved, which was the side growing directly out of the demonstrations, were all criminal cases, and, obviously, each side is entitled to be a period of preparation and that kind of thing for each level of trial. We slugged it out for many weeks in the Recorder's Court until everybody was exhausted. So finally, I requested jury trials in all of the cases so that we could get up to the Superior Court.

The trials of the persons arrested during the height of the demonstrations went on up into the early fall, which culminated in the Supreme Court opinion in *The State v. Fox* Case, which laid to rest all of the remainder of the cases, and by act of the court, many of the cases after that were dismissed almost en masse. The issue that went up was that involving the street blocking ordinance, but by the time that the Supreme Court decision came down, all of the cases involving the street blocking ordinance and the trespass actions were lumped into the whole pile and flat dismissed to get them out of the court and off the dockets. It was sort of "Let's start all over again; we're negotiating now, we're moving toward a peaceful settlement, and it would serve no purpose to try these cases, so we will dismiss them."

## J. Kenneth Lee

Nobody in Greensboro would take a civil rights case. Conrad Pearson was the State General Counsel for the NAACP; he was the pioneer and leading civil rights advocate among African Americans in North Carolina. I was contacted by Conrad Pearson to assist Clarence Malone in representing the students arrested in the demonstrations. I was in partnership with Major High, and we both preferred to be in the background in an advisory capacity, so that attention would focus on Malone as an out-of-town lawyer. We were in Malone's position in other little towns—Statesville, Lexington or some other little place where the heat wouldn't affect us.

Very few of those people went to court, but somebody had to get every one of them out of jail. They had the old polio hospital out there; I had to get my son out of there three times. They were just piled on top of each other. Somebody had to go out and find people to sign bonds all night long. To that extent, I was the only one involved. I was the only local person.

Mr. Malone called me because, as Assistant Council for the NAACP in the state, I was Conrad Pearson's second-in-command. We had strategy sessions in New York on a monthly basis. They were doing the same thing everywhere. We would get together and say, "This is what they tried on me this week." And they could write sample briefs and cite the law to you, and you'd bring that back, and I had all of that. We knew that there was nothing new under the sun; they had already done everything they could do within a few months, so we knew exactly what they would do, so we would pull out the appropriate brief and duplicate it. He called me at my Greensboro office. Generally, there were just two of us, Conrad and I. McKissick was with CORE, but we never got a penny from CORE.

Herman Enochs was fair, and the trials in Greensboro were fair. But you have to say "fair, compared to what?" If you just take the word "fair" as an objective word, let's put it this way: Greensboro, like every place that I know, sought every way they could to keep from ruling in favor of anybody who was involved in civil rights. Now, they did not get as ridiculous as some of the other communities in the state. They did not just put somebody in jail without a reason, but they actively sought every way that they could that had the appearance of being legal to accomplish the same thing that everybody else was accomplishing. They were far better than most of the smaller communities, because they had some smart folks here. If they were seeking an image of being urban and sophisticated and progressive, it was to attract some industry; it wasn't just because they wanted to avoid losing potential industries, but it wasn't for the purpose of "We want to be fair about it."

I went into court hundreds of times, along with Mr. Malone. There were so many of those cases that no one person could take care of it. I remember specifically representing Jesse Jackson when he was charged with inciting to riot. I spent many a day and night with him in that jailhouse waiting on somebody to come and get him out. It seemed to me that when Malone got into that thing is when they had some kind of agreement that they were going to take sample cases; it was too massive to try them all. I'd say ninety-five percent of those cases were never called.

## Cecil Bishop

After the passage of the 1964 Public Accommodations bill, which opened up everything—there were still a lot of problems in Greensboro. There would be a lot of meetings,—Chamber of Commerce, Community Unity Committee of the Chamber of Commerce, then Human Relations Commission. All of those would provide forums where members of the black and white community would sometimes meet. And sometimes it would be an unofficial, off-the-record meeting. I remember once there was a meeting of members of the Human Relations Commission and members of the City Council. It was like dinner, so the press wouldn't be there. And we talked about a lot of things relative to Greensboro, in a more candid manner. I attended a number of meetings of the Human Relations Commission, and I eventually became a member of the Commission, in 1965-66 I served as chairman for awhile. The Human Relations Commission was established on the insistence of the black community. Many people in the black community felt that it was just a sham, and it would only be a facade, because it had no legal power. It could gather information, and it did a lot of that. And a lot of things it had publicized. And I think therein was a great deal of its power.

But I think there was some effort on the part of the elected officials to do those things that would lessen the tension and hostility that existed at that time. We focused on substandard housing conditions. There were many pockets of substandard housing in Greensboro, pockets of it here and there. And we focused on those. We focused on the way the landlords dealt with tenants. Employment was another matter. But the housing condition was the real focus.

With the ending of school in the summer, the adult black community realized that it would have to take over and keep the ball rolling. It was never with the thought of excluding the student community. But the adult black community did come to grips with the idea that "we're going to be here, and we are going to have to be the ones to work things out, to put up some money, to back these organizations for the Coordinating Committee to work together." We were going to remain here; students may come and go. They could help us, but we really needed to get our act together, because we would be on-going entities in the city.

I think there were many kinds and types of issues that the black community felt had to be addressed on its behalf. One was housing, another was the school situation. The ward system for the elections was a fight. Open housing. On the other hand, many people in the white community felt that too much was being done for the people in the black community, while those in the black communty felt that not enough was being done.

Leaders came out of the public housing community that joined other leaders in the black community in addressing that issue, joining it to the others. The nature of that issue involved several discontents. One, these pockets of housing owned by slum landlords in various parts of town—no relationship to public housing at all—people felt that many times they were lax in the repairs. Sometimes water would be cut off, roofs would be leaking; plumbing would be in a shambles. Yet they were expected to pay the rent. If that housing was condemned, then these people would have to move out, and they may not have anyplace to go. So they had to go along with those conditions. For people who were in public housing, they had the feeling that the delivery of services was inadequate, that the response to needs was much too slow, that the modernization programs in public housing were just inadequate. You had two kinds of concerns coming: one, from the public housing community: these people who were in housing that was owned by members of the private sector.

I think that people tried to take advantage of every possible forum to express these things. The Human Relations Commission, the Citizens Association, the residents' councils within public housing. Perhaps the people who had the least in terms of a forum were those people who lived in substandard housing owned by members of the private sector. People who were in public housing had their own organization and could also petition the Housing Authority itself, as they did many times. The organization itself then could go to the Human Relations Commission, or even to the City Council, as it sometimes did.

But two or three people here or there, scattered all over town with no kind of unity often would have to go along until maybe it would be brought to somebody's attention, somebody in leadership. Connie Raiford, who was always a champion of the underdog, would call to our attention these matters. I went to a place called "Little Korea" and ttook a lot of photographs to record the very substandard conditions that people were living in.

The Coordinating Committee did do strategy planning. But by its very composition, the Coordinating Committee had student input in that strategizing and planning. The idea was that the Coordinating Committee would be representative of the total black community. And that there would not be spurious and tangential efforts going in different directions. But that there would be some unity in terms of what was being said, in the strategy and the planning. That's why these different entities were included in the Coordinating Committee.

I later served on the Greensboro Housing Authority. A few months before I came on board a new director was employed. The previous director had a background as a prison warden. So that orientation transferred into the way that he executed his role as the executive director of the Housing Authority. In my opinion, he was quite insensitive to many of the needs of people in public housing. There were some people who were board members who were not as sensitive as I would like them to be. With the change in directors, I was able to address the needs of the public housing communities and tried to do that, even in the midst of great criticism from both the private sector of the community and residents of the public housing communities themselves.

We were in the middle. One side of the community said, "You're doing too much." Members of the public housing community, said we weren't doing anything. But there was a very serious attempt to do that. The Commission itself requested that the City Council to enlarge the board to include a voting member from the housing community itself., and the public housing organizations would determine who that person would be. It wouldn't be somebody picked by us or by the mayor. they would have at least that little bit of self-determination in saying that "X, Y or Z will represent us." That proved quite helpful.

*Civil rights activities in Greensboro were not limited to the years from 1960 to 1965. The pattern of race relations settled into an on-going dialogue between the African community and the white power structure, sometimes through quiet negotiations, sometimes through civil suits. Issues such as more rapid school integration and calls for a ward sysem, which would* substantially increase the representation of the African American community on the City Council, remained high on the political agenda.

On occasion, tensions resulted in isolated instances of violence. When Dr. Martin Luther King was Dr. Martin Luther King, Jr., was assassinated, rioting erupted downtown and in the black community.

Members of the Communist Workers Party and the Ku Klux Klan exchanged gunfire at an anti-Klan rally on November 3, 1979, in which five members of the CWP were killed. The Klansmen were found not guilty of murder, but were later convicted of violating the deceased CWP members' civil rights. The tragedy was not specifically race-related, and the African American community chose not to rally behind the incident to any great extent.

Claude Barnes, a student at Dudley High School, was elected president of the student body. The administration at Dudley considered him a Black Power radical and negated the election. The students at Dudley conducted a demonstration in protest, forcing the principal to order another election, which Barnes won. The unrest spread to the A&T campus, resulting in gunfire between snipers at Scott Hall and the National Guard and police. A student, Willie Grimes, was shot from a passing automobile, and the murder was never solved Order was restored, but a simmering distrust persisted between radical young African Americas and the police.

The adult African American community was chary of identifiying with the radicals, but resented the fact that city and state officials failed to consult them regarding their own community, indicative of a reversion to a more traditionally conservative stance on race relations.

## Lewis Brandon

I was a member of the Chamber when the disturbances at Dudley High School and A&T [occurred] in the spring of 1969. There were so many contributing factors that it mushroomed into a lot of other things. And I think it did that because there were some animosities residual in the community on both sides. The report supported the call by the Dudley High School administration to have another election for student body president, which was adopted, and the same individual was re-elected. That became the spark that set off the big fire. I think that the use of force was excessive on the part of the city and the state. It didn't have to grow to those proportions, not at all. It wasn't necessary to have the National Guard out there and to bring all of the guns. They had some big guns aimed at Scott Hall, ready to shoot.

I think that this was a signal from the white power structure to the black and student community that enough concessions had been granted, as a result of the demonstrations, at least for the time being. It was like the white community saying, "Okay, boy, now you've said enough. I've heard you, now sit down and be quiet." I think that was the message.

# Chapter 9

## In Retrospect

For African Americans in Greensboro, the focus of the Civil Rights Movement remained the sit-ins and the marches, which they perceived as an ongoing movement for civil, political and economic rights. Those events proved to be crucial to the participants and the society at large. For some, it was but one moment in an ongoing career. For others, it became a central commitment for their lives. It is significant that so many remained in Greensboro, thus providing a perspective upon the events, and sometimes the ability to effect the changes they sought. Regardless of the stand each person took at the time, all acknowledged that the city would never be the same. Looking back from a perspective of twenty years, many participants recognized that the Greensboro Movement had significantly influenced the course upon which the South had been set.

## George Evans

The interaction between the races was not immediately improved in Greensboro in 1963; the immediate after-effect was perhaps a widening of some of the feelings between the races, because there were so many people in the community who didn't agree with the objectives of the demonstrations. But I think in the long run, relationships were improved quite a bit.

The short-term results of the demonstrations were the opening of doors at the time. Later, long-range results became evident in terms of more and better employment opportunities for black people working in white-collar positions in many of the industries in the area. I believe that the opportunities that have been given to black people to participate in the work of these large organizations perhaps would not have come along as early had it not been for the work of the demonstrators, all of whom participated in the opening of doors, opening up of polls to voter registration and to voting, and to economic opportunities in general. This has been fostered a great deal by better educational opportunities. For example, by admission of black kids to some of the larger institutions of learning, where they could not attend before that time. They've had opportunities to get into fields of training and education that were not available in the predominantly black schools prior to the demonstration days. So that the long-range objectives have been things of that kind: better educational opportunities and better industry-related positions of white-collar nature.

When the permanent Human Relations Commission was established under W. O. Conrad [Western Electric executive and member of the Evans committee], it stressed improving black schools and job training for blacks. Attention was given to opening other doors besides those of restaurants, movie houses and motels. I think that some consideration needed to be given to professional education opportunities, in order that people could prepare themselves for better employment.

But I believe also that the approach to these problems probably was more successful by starting slowly, as we did with these merchants. That, in turn, opened some minds to let people see that a number of people in the black community were capable of handling other than menial jobs. In the past, they had had little opportunity to prove themselves qualified to do these jobs, so that somebody had to take the lead in giving them an opportunity to train for these jobs. They couldn't find any blacks qualified to fill these positions. Well, that was because no efforts had been made to find anybody. Once they decided that they would open the doors, they found all the people they wanted, without any problem, to do the same jobs that had been denied them all along.

Because of the demonstrations, you have seen many black people as telephone operators, bank tellers, and bank executives. I know of instances of vice-presidents of the local branches of large chain banks with black people. I think Mr. Conrad's position was a very strong statement that, "We need to give these people better working opportunities, better schools and better facilities at the schools," which at the time was resisted to a great degree. But I feel that the gradual approach to it, which started with the work of our committee, was the thing that led up to the opening of other doors farther down the line. I don't think that it could have been done on an instant basis, but I think it evolved in a natural manner as a result of concerted efforts by some key people in the community, that was stimulated by the demonstrations.

## Pat Patterson

I think that we still have a long way to go in achieving satisfactory race relations in Greensboro and the rest of the country. For example, I have been in banking for a number of years. I think that it's, personally, another ten years off before you really start to see blacks move in the upper echelon of the different institutions that we have in this country. I think you are going to see it quicker in certain places than you will in others, for example, in government. But in private industry, I have some really mixed emotions about Affirmative Action. I wish there was a way that blacks could catch up overnight. I know that Affirmative Action had to be, but I just don't see how anybody in their own mind, could think that we've reached a point where reverse discrimination is going on.

My reaction was not disenchantment with CORE so much. I think that after Farmer stepped down, CORE was probably looked upon as being a very radical group; it did some things different from SCLC and the NAACP, but the kinds of people that were beginning to infiltrate CORE then were getting involved in some things, and there were some people in the Civil Rights Movement that were crisis-oriented. You'd have a lull and then you'd have to just go out and do something to let people know we were still around.

But I think that out of all of that, what really happened was that, after the big push in 1963, Martin Luther King and the NAACP were the ones that weathered the storm. They were the ones that had the grassroots backing, because CORE was considered very radical in terms of the civil rights groups at that time. We were bolder; we weren't willing to wait long years. But the groups that have survived have been the ones that appeared less radical. SCLC made it. The groups that were primarily student-based tended to pass away. All I can relate it to is the chapter here in Greensboro. I remember as our people began to graduate, there weren't people stepping into the slots, because in Greensboro the students that were involved at that time, just didn't have the same motivation as those who were in the demonstrations.

Obviously, the committee headed by George Evans got some results, so you'd have to say that they did all right. But, as a whole, I don't think the negotiating committees during that time got very much done. I think that it was the mass demonstrations that achieved results. They became so massive that people in the white power structure said, "It's going to be easier for us to open these places up." I don't know why they didn't figure out that ninety-five percent of those marching were not going to be able to come into those establishments and eat anyway. And the ones that could were going to be the doctors and the lawyers, and they're all "nice people."

I think that for one time in Greensboro, especially, it was something that the black community could rally around, and they weren't splintered about. I think up until that time, the NAACP voiced the sentiments of the community. Before the demonstrations, I don't know whether the white community really believed him when George [Simkins] said that he spoke for all of the blacks in the community. After the mass demonstrations they really believed that there were things that black people in Greensboro and the rest of the country really wanted, and that when these things were being said, you had to believe them.

I would say that the results achieved by the mass demonstrations were a mixed success for many reasons, and when these places opened, we recognized right away that now that we had them open, what could we do about it in terms of economic issues?

The things that were accomplished during that time could only have been done by the black students. It was something that I think a lot of people finally realized: that we have a generation of blacks that were just not going to tolerate the current situation. The NAACP was a group that had good financial backing and had lawyers and could go through the courts. At the same time, there was a group of people that was getting out of school with degrees, and they operated a little bit differently; they were going to push harder. Although most places in Greensboro were desegregated because of the 1964 Civil Rights Act, I think that the demonstrations had a lot to do with the passage of that act by focusing attention on the injustice and absurdity of segregation.

I am in banking, a part of the "Establishment," so I think that I have made contributions. I am a little older than most of the youngsters coming into banking now, and I know some of the things that they are going to run up against. For example, I go out to A&T and talk to different classes. I try to advise them and tell them the kind of things to expect in the corporate world; what kind of courses they ought to take to get into banking, if that is their thing.

I wasn't a Jesse Jackson, and there was no point in thinking that I was. I am basically a loner. I mix well with people when I have to, although I try to get away and I am by myself most of the time. But I'm glad that I got caught up in the Civil Rights Movement when I was at A&T. I grew up in a very quiet, lazy town, and when I got here, these things became so clear to me what had happened and what was happening; I didn't have any choice but to get involved, and it set the course of my whole life. Even today, I find myself thinking back and wondering what I would be doing if I hadn't gotten involved in those things.

## A. Knighton Stanley

It's difficult to assess what the demonstrations were able to accomplish without looking at what had occurred earlier. I think the demonstrations created a situation where it was possible for positive things to happen. I think that through the demonstrations, we created a climate where people were more willing to sit down and talk, because they knew that if they didn't, then they were going to be confronted with a type of situation that they didn't want.

[W. O] Conrad gave periodic statements or speeches to various business and civic groups in which he emphasized an economic point of view: vocational training. He seemed to be ignoring the importance of civil rights to the black community. Or it may be that he was just being pragmatic and practical and saying, "Well, the important thing is to change the economic situation."

But by advocating that black students in the high schools should be enrolled in more vocational training, and return to restructuring, put the blame on the black community and turning the burden back to the black community and the still predominantly black schools. I think that was part of the case. But I think that the other part is the whole paternalistic attitude that many of those in power had.

I think that for what we set out to accomplish, we, in fact, accomplished. The demonstrations not only led to a desegregation of lunch counters and other eating facilities in Greensboro, but it led to employment opportunities for blacks. It was a snowball in terms of black awareness, in terms of the political arena and for the registration for minorities. From where we started and what happened, I think it was very successful. And we did have the black community involved. Not only lay people, but the so-called middle class blacks were involved. They were not out front all the time, but they were involved, and we did get support from them. But it wasn't given up voluntarily by the white business community or the city government. They didn't give up anything; they were forced to give up whatever was accomplished. I think it was economic sanctions and the potentially violent situation that existed. They didn't want that in Greensboro. Even so, it was a slow process. If you're talking about Woolworth, you had a few salespeople hired. But if you're talking about Cone Mills and other major companies, then it took the civil rights legislation of 1964 to achieve large-scale desegregation in terms of employment.

Our goals developed, or evolved, you might say. Initially with the sit-ins, the specific goal was to desegregate the lunch counter facilities. That spread from lunch counters in five-and-dime stores and other types of facilities to all types of public eating facilities within the Greensboro area. Greensboro was fortunate in that it had quite a few progressive people that were involved at different times of the entire era that we're talking about.

W.O. Conrad's best contribution was the establishment of the Human Relaions Commission. It seems to me that the initial persons on that from the black community included Kenneth Lee, George Simkins, Gladys Royall and me; we were all on that first Commission. A formal vote was not taken; no formal votes were taken in most of these commissions, because it was basically for discussion. I think the last committee appointed by the Mayor was operating from a genuine spirit of co-operation to achieve positive actions rather than just words, and at the same time trying to accommodate the business and political power structure. Their orientation was from the business community point of view. But I also think that they realized that some achievements had to be made.

## Lewis Brandon

CORE was very effective in bringing about social change in Greensboro, and this is what I think that we did. I think that it was effective enough to the point that we were able to desegregate public facilities in Greensboro. In terms of bringing about changes in social attitudes, no organization, up to this point, has been able to do that. Greensboro still tends to be a racist city, still tends to be controlled by the mill interests. To that end, we were not successful, but in terms of our primary goal of desegregating public facilities, we did that. We were able to organize communities and set up networks for communicating and disseminating information. I have been in Greensboro since 1957, and I have not seen any instance of change that was not the result of some direct action. I think that the Chamber and the leadership decided that there wasn't going to be any violence. Where violence occurs, I think that it is a conscious decision that it should occur. It was not to their advantage to have violence in Greensboro at that time, because there had been too much negative publicity already around what happened in 1969 and some of the other demonstrations that they had.

The guy that made me aware of that was a poet from South Carolina, James McBryde. He was at Greensboro College during the initial phase of the 1962 demonstrations. Dick Ramsay had invited him to come up to speak to the kids, and he said that the decision was not whether or not people will be violent, [but] is based on how the power structure wants people to move, and they have certain key phrases to incite people to make those moves.

They [demonstrations] were necessary. If these events had not taken place, I'm not sure when the laws that were enforced at that time of separation would have changed. Because one of the things that happened was we were immediately criticized for going too fast, that Greensboro was a good place, and in time it would work these things out. That was kind of the position of the busi-ness community and the media: that we should go slow and that we were affecting good race relations in the community, even though there was this great divide between blacks and whites.

This is how I explained it to some students at A&T once. We were at the Carolina Theater. They were getting ready to put on the performance "Bullet Holes in the Walls [Reflections on Acts of Courage in the Struggle for Liberation]" at the Carolina Theatre. We were sitting on the stage and I said, "You know, if we backtrack to 1960, we wouldn't be here on this stage. If we were in this facility, we would be [up there]"—and I pointed to the area in the balcony where we would be sitting. And then I said to them, "The social climate is that today when we came into this building we came in through the front door, and we'll be sitting downstairs, and we're now in this room where we're having a reception." So I guess that sort of highlights where we are with this whole thing. But then I went on to say to them that even though that is occurring and has occurred, that we still have all these social ills, inequities that exist in the community that we have to work on.

## Frances Herbin (Lewis)

I think that the demonstrations accomplished the point that we were making at the time: the desegregation of certain facilities. I think it gave the black community an opportunity to take advantage of some of the places of entertainment here in the city. The most important thing that they accomplished for black citizens in Greensboro, was the fact that at least you feel that you can take advantage of them, whether you do or not. I did attend the cafeterias and the theaters that we picketed, but only if I wanted to go, not as a matter of principle or victory. I don't think that the students were so concerned that, "If I want to sit down and eat, I can." We were tired of spending our money and having to stand there at a lunch counter and eat a hot dog if you were hungry. You could shop all day, but there was no place for you to sit and eat a hot dog and drink a soda, when two counters over, other people were allowed the same privilege.

I think that we have accomplished a lot in terms of race relations in Greensboro, but I think we still have a long way to go. It's far from being totally solved. I think today, it's a little hard to say. I have some ideas about the general feelings, but I don't think they are as good as the general city or officials would project that they are. I think that the general attitudes control most of the educational and vocational opportunities. I think that it still exists in the attitudes toward minority participation in city and county governments. I still think that it exists on a token basis.

Public officials were compelled to meet certain requirements, and once they had met those requirements, they did not feel compelled to do more. They just did the bare minimum, and I think this is where we are now. Generally, I think that with the pressures that have been placed in certain areas, say minority participation in city and county government. I don't think that there is a wide-open range of opportunities for us even now. You have to be a "super-black" to be accepted. You have to be twice as good, twice as prepared, to be hired. It's not on an equal basis, and I think until we get to that point, we will never have total equality.

## Lois Lucas (Williams)

I think that our purpose and our accomplishments were just as important as the original sit-ins. It was just another phase that we went through in trying to establish equality. As I said before, at that time, my thinking then was a little narrow because of my age, and I probably didn't realize the purpose then as I do now, as to what was trying to be done. There were some people who burned themselves out as a result of the Movement, and then ended up with no place to go. There were also people who lost jobs who found it difficult to secure a position later on. Twenty years ago, you lose a job teaching and it was like you had a bad record that branded you forever.

Those were the people who helped to make the Movement a success: the man out on the street, waiting for a truck to take him to a job and saw a group of people on the picket line, and stepped in and took a cigarette in his face, or a mouth of saliva that someone was spitting. That's the kind of support that we got from the regular people in the community that were doing menial jobs, who may have saved our lives or prevented us from being permanently disfigured. As people were assimilating the gains of the Movement, those were the people who got nothing out of it. There were people who suffered. People who, when it was time for people to say, "Okay, this is going to be given out, and you can have this share of the pie," they couldn't qualify. They didn't have the skills to be promoted from floor sweeper to clerk and nobody was prepared to give that to them.

There were a lot of such people after the Movement of the Sixties died down. People said, "All right, we'll give you these jobs if you are qualified." But it turned out that you had to be twice as qualified as your white counterpart; you had to have twice the education and twice the experience, then if you did get into the door, it turned out to be that you were basically still just a step above menial labor, in many instances. It was all dressed up and it was all a fancy title, but that's all it was. The racism became more subtle. One thing that black people used to say about the South versus the North—and one of the reasons that they felt more comfortable living in the South—is that you knew where you stood in the South. You knew that there was a certain section of town where you couldn't buy a house in or you couldn't have an apartment, there were certain stores that you didn't go into because of the way you were treated. There were restaurants that you didn't go into because no blacks were allowed.

The North was far more subtle. I remember in 1965-1967, I trained as a medical technologist at Public Health Service Hospital at Staten Island, and I worked there for a while. When I left there to work for a large international corporation in New Jersey, I had to get out and find a place to live. After a week of looking, I was physically ill. I broke out in hives because I didn't know how to deal with the stress. There were all these ads in the paper "equal opportunity housing," but then you call someone up on the phone, you experienced a subtle racism. I don't have what people consider a discernable black accent over the telephone. When I got there they'd say, "The apartment has just been rented." Or you would go into a restaurant, and you get a table that is next to the kitchen. You don't go back again, so the place is, in effect, segregated.

So, these were the people who did not get their share of that dream. These are the younger ones that were part of the riots in Watts and Newark and the other large cities. Those are the people who have seen the last twenty years go by with very little hope. They are a part of the next confrontation that this country may find itself in, because they have paid their dues and followed the proper procedures step-by-step. They are owed something because they gave up their lives so that all of this could go on. You could have this picture of Americans working side-by-side irrespective of their color, but it's not a reality for them.

I made my roles as a CORE officer a part of my role as a college student. It didn't supersede the fact that my primary purpose was that I was there to get an education. Getting an education would certainly mean that I would be able to move a lot easier in the larger society, and that when the changes came, as they had to come, I would then be prepared to take advantage of it. But I didn't make the Movement my life; I didn't make it a career, as did a lot of students throughout the country. They became the Movement; there was no separation of where the Movement ended and where their own lives began. When the Movement was over, and when jobs opened up, these were people who were still out there; their only job was the Movement. Their only education was the Movement, and when it came time to need an education or to move ahead or to use skills that they should have acquired, during that time, they didn't have the skills. These are the people that the Movement burned out. They gave their all to it, and they have not been able to get anything in return.

Some of them have gone back to school. At that time we had this other great big American whitewash of "Black Studies," setting up programs and degrees in Black Studies at some of the best universities across the country. You found a lot of these people saying, "Oh well, here I go, I've had all of this for the last ten years and now I can channel all of it right back in here and I am comfortable and I am at home." That is one of the biggest hoaxes that has ever been perpetuated against blacks. Black history has to be taught in the schools and in the home, but there was no viable job market for a person who had majored in black history unless he intends to teach. I think that the hoax was in the way that the program was designed. I think that you had lots of universities and lots of liberal-minded people who said, "Well, we need a certain number of blacks in certain universities. One of the ways that we can have blacks in our universities and not have them is to set up something that's for them, and for them only. We're going to make them feel great; we're going to set up this whole program with a complete degree in black studies.

And it looks good, and you get a lot of press, "We're teaching Swahili, we're teaching all of this," but what can you do with a degree in black studies or black history unless you intend to teach it? If you want to say, "Okay, we're going to offer black history, we're going to offer a program in black economics, we're going to offer a program about African nations, and we are going to offer it so that you will know something about yourself."

So a lot of people went into that and there are a lot of people that are still just out there. By the time that the colleges opened up with these programs, they were either married, they had a family, or they couldn't go back to school. So they were out here with two or three years of college and very bitter, with a right to be bitter, because the Movement was over, because people in the North started to find out that they had just as many problems as Southerners with school integration and with all of these other problems. These problems were becoming very evident, so they couldn't jump on television and talk about "that ignorant Southerner, he didn't know what he was doing," because they had to face the problems that were in their own back yards. So they started retrenching and pulling back.

By 1965, 1966, 1967, there was little or no activism in terms of where blacks were coming from in the South. The Voting Rights Bill was passed, and everybody started to go home. The Northerners, the kids who came down South, they started to go back home. People were able to vote, people started to assimilate the gains that had been made by the Movement. There were promotions in job areas, blacks were being hired in areas that they had so those people who were able to move and capitalize on the gains that been made by 1965 and 1966, were starting to sit back and enjoy that.

But most people tended to find that they were at a dead-end. You found that there were blacks who had titles and sat in offices, but still couldn't make decisions. You found blacks being hired for corporate jobs and that's all it was, window dressing. There was still someone above them who made the decisions that they should have been making. And that is still happening today. You find that there are a lot of places, restaurants and hotels, that are still segregated. There are no "white only" policies or "white only" signs written on the doors, but money-wise, there are all kinds of ways of achieving segregation. You talk about equality in the schools, and whites simply move to the suburbs.

## Sarah Jones (Outterbridge)

I think that many blacks have become dissatisfied with the situation now. There is so much confusion and conflict on the part of certain leaders, for instance, the problem which is now involved with leadership. Perhaps we have become more concerned with our own personal goals than with the more general goals that might benefit the community as a whole. I think there is a lack of cohesion and unity in the black community on a local and national level. I think we have gotten a piece of the pie; we're able to live in Starmount Forest and buy Cadillacs, if we have the money. We have been told that "You're different from these other people." For instance, "You're the kind of people we like." Let's say, the black person that has arrived, the "successful black." So that sets you apart and maybe, we get to feel that we are a little better than some other people. Better off, surely, but just a little better and not really wanting to get involved, not wanting to put anything on the line, not wanting to put forth any effort to organize activities in the community, to improve baseball fields that are in black communities, for instance, that could be done very easily by a few leaders getting together.

On the other hand, there is quite a bit of interaction between the races, although much of it is simply surface interaction. Now the prevailing mood of the black community is to be able to go and do what other people do. I think some things have happened that have made us realize that maybe this coming together has not been quite as beneficial we thought that it would be. For instance, the desegregation of schools, the switching about of, white teachers into formerly all black schools and vice versa. It gets back to the attitudinal problem, so that even though black students can go to formerly white schools, there is an attitude that is still there, and we may find that desegregation was not all that great after all. I'd like to hope that it has had a beneficial effect on both black and white students to go through the entire school system integrated, because I feel like that whole thing was to be a leading thing for both parties.

It's difficult now to make younger blacks think of the years gone by and say, "Well, this is what happened at such-and-such a time. Can you believe that there was such a time that you couldn't go to McDonald's or when Dudley was all black?" It is difficult to get into that; the students may not be concerned or not thinking about what was, but only of what is right now. In a way that is good, but in another sense it was one of the goals of the Civil Rights Movement. I don't mean that the results have backfired, or that they don't appreciate it. They are not aware of it, it's so far removed from their minds. But it has backfired because of what we thought would come.

## William Thomas

The Civil Rights Movement was a perpetual, ongoing thing, but it did not maintain the same level of intensity, of sensationalism that it did during the demonstrations. In many ways, there was still a movement going. It took on different shapes and different forms. Once the goals of desegregation of public accommodations and the hiring of a few salespeople were achieved, the emotionalism was gone. That didn't mean people stopped working to achieve a better standard of living in the black community, but the dynamic nature of the Movement was gone.

Other things were happening in the country that black people were involved in. But, because you don't read about black people constantly marching, picketing, demonstrating, doesn't mean that people were not out there working to try to correct a wrong situation. To do that, I would have to assume that there was a demise in the Civil Rights Movement, and I don't accept that premise. I think that it changed. It merged into other things, as part of what was occurring. And that occurred from frustration by people who said, "Nonviolentce did not accomplish what we thought. It's not occurring at the rate that it should." But by that time, the mass demonstrations had subsided anyway.

## Clyde Marsh

Although I did not feel any hostility from the demonstrators, I knew that there was resentment toward the Fire Department in the black community, which hurt us deeply. I am sure that there are those who felt that I shouldn't have had all of these students arrested; I had no other choice. I think that some of the other Fire Department officers felt that I should have been more aggressive and arrested more people or something of this nature.

Assistant Fire Chief Robert L. Powell and I, along with some other instructors, had just trained twenty-eight black men, and they were assigned in the Fire Department at Station Four down on Gorrell Street, and a lot of them were A&T graduates, and I was in charge of them. But we did get some resentment from them, because the Fire Department was not integrated. These twenty-eight blacks were put down in one station by themselves. Both Chief Powell and I requested that they be integrated with the whites throughout the city rather than being put down in one station in a black neighborhood. So the city did not really understand or move as fast as it should to meet what the blacks were really asking for: complete desegregation of city services.

I think that Greensboro was more progressive in accepting the black community than other cities, but we still were slow. We still didn't progress as fast as we could have. This had been going on for a long time, and I'm sure that it's something the black community couldn't get over quickly, and they still haven't gotten over it, because it still isn't completely settled.

## William Jackson

I don't think that there was any additional animosity between the black community and the police force at all. If anything, it might have mellowed the black community towards the Police Department. A couple of years after that we had another situation at the [A&T] college, and things were not as easy as they had been prior to this incident. But as far as the 1963 doings, I'm going to say it might have helped some.

## Otis Hairston, Sr.

I think that the demonstrations led to a lot of things that were, and perhaps still are, happening as a result of the demonstrations. Of course, it called attention to an evil which had not been demonstrated in that manner. Just like any demonstration is designed to do, to call attention to an evil, and to try to get people to try to look at it and see it as an evil, and as a result, to convince them to use their influence to do away with whatever it is. Despite the demonstrations, some of the theaters and restaurants were hard-core and refused to desegregate. Some of them were forced out of business as a result of not cooperating. I would say that, perhaps, the majority were hard-core persons who wanted to hold out. Of course, the [1964] Civil Rights Act forced them to do what demonstrations could not force them to do.

Not everything opened at once, but I don't think that I would say that the demonstrations failed, because if you pave the way for something to happen, it is certainly not a failure. Of course, perhaps there are other forces that will lead to it, too, but you certainly determine the effect of demonstrations or whatever the effort is, will have on ten ultimate opening of whatever you are trying to achieve. If it is achieved, then it is very difficult to measure just what factor was primary.

The demonstrations were necessary because of the kind of political leadership we had in Greensboro at that time. In any community you can have people who are willing to do the right thing, but if the leadership is not willing to do those things, then you are held back, and I think it is the kind of leadership that we had at that time in Greensboro. You had liberal, moderate folk, but you had a leadership that was stubborn; they always tried to evade rather than comply. I think that the moderate leadership forced the stubborn leadership on the part of the mayor and others to do what the community really needed to do. I don't think that the mayor really wanted to do anything. He was stubborn and he had really gotten pretty angry as a result of the demonstrations, and I think that the other folk in the community, the business elite, just forced him to do what was best for the community.

Once the restaurants and theaters had been opened to black patrons, the local Civil Rights Movement had to be directed toward the ballot and economic power. We had an extensive voting registration effort as a result of that, so a large number of blacks registered. The other effort was through economic boycott, to at times force institutions to do was what we felt that they ought to do. I remember Wachovia Bank had not employed a black teller and, of course, we had folks who had accounts there. We had one demonstration for an hour one day at lunch, and then folk were urged not to have accounts there. Well, the next day they had a black person from Winston-Salem as a teller. So we shifted to those areas.

I'm sure that some of the things that we secured after that resulted from the ballot and economic pressure. I'm sure that the ballot was a threat in that we had the votes and we were listened to. A lot of the things that we got as a result of the threat of being able to vote and being able to [politically]defeat folk who would not go along with some things.

## Joseph McNeil

Being one of the "Greensboro Four" has not had an overwhelming impact on my life. We never wanted to be "professional civil righters." Each of us had chosen careers: mine in finance, McCain's in chemistry, Blair's in education. But involvement in the Movement has given me a real sense of pride and confidence. When I was in the military and I would be confronted with moments of fear, it was advantageous for me to have been involved in a movement where I had seen people who were ready to kill me, and this was true of many other people, I am sure, who participated in the Civil Rights Movement, who later faced danger.

I never understood how Southern cities could see themselves as being "All-American," but Greensboro perceived of itself in that way, and needed to preserve that image. With five academic institutions, it was progressive in that sense. We were aware of the political reality; we were not going to come in and force integration overnight, but we knew that the city was vulnerable in that regard. Nevertheless, the city dragged its heels, and I don't think that it gave anything willingly. But gains were certainly made.

I do think that we succeeded in maintaining a continuing economic pressure on the city administration. We could literally break city government by filling the jail, if it came to that point. We could stay in jail for six months, and it would become a problem for the city government to handle that. In addition, there was the economic pressure that we could apply to the business community. This is not to mention the bad press and world opinion. It was a combination of the economic factor involved and the public sympathy for the moral issue that eventually brought about a public accommodations law. Economic pressure by the sit-ins and marches on the stores were our most effective tactics, but I don't think that they alone could have achieved the goals we sought. It also took the resolve of the black community and individuals in the white community to follow through on the promises made after 1963.

## Franklin McCain

At about the end of our junior year, Joe [McNeil] and I had begun to think about other things, but still things that would concern civil rights. Things like employment or housing discrimination. We spent considerable time looking into the plans for what was called "urban renewal" of the area on Market Street down by the underpass. We knew that this was going to happen; our goal at that time was to develop a plan of our own for urban renewal, which would avoid tearing down people's houses and pushing them off their property. We wanted to rehabilitate the places that they were in, and let them stay where they had their birthright and had their neighbors of long-standing, and that sort of thing. Our ultimate goal was to make a presentation to the City Council, but we never made a complete plan. It was overwhelming for full-time students. But we continued to spend a lot of time in thinking about things on that order, and moving away from the more activist types of things in terms of total involvement. Not that we lost commitment, by any means, but I think that we were looking at discrimination and segregation at a different level, on looking into ways to achieve or restore full rights to people.

The experience of the demonstrations gave many of the students involved the resolve and vision to pursue careers that would contribute to solving problems such as urban renewal and other issues that continued to hamper improved race relations and other economic and social difficulties in this country.

## Arnold Schiffman

I thought the demonstrations were unnecessary, because these matters could be and should be considered in a calm manner and listen to the problems and find a solution. Demonstrations do no good, except to raise tempers, and that's never good.

I think there were other factors besides the demonstrations that caused Mr. [Boyd] Morris to give up his business at that time. I had no part in making those decisions. I was very friendly with Neil McGill and talked with him at the time of the 1963 demonstrations. He and I would walk down the street together and exchange ideas. I knew he was struggling with the matter and trying to find a calm and sensible way to solve it. I think he felt that the public wouldn't stand for integrating the theaters, and that his white patronage would drop away very rapidly if it were not done over a period of time and calmly. But when desegregation did occur, there was practically no loss of white patronage by any of the stores or restaurants that did so. The public needed to get used to it. I wouldn't say that the fears of the owners and managers were groundless, but I would say they were exaggerated.

We must remember that there were not near as many people downtown to observe it. And those who did come down to see them came out of cursity. I don't think that I was in total agreement that the police should make those arrests, as long as the demonstrators were not doing anything violent or destroying property. Trespassing is another story, but as to blocking the store traffic or exits, you don't want the entrance to your business blocked. But this dwindled away. The positive work of our committee was on the desegregation of the eating places, period. After that time there was nothing for us to do, really, other than observe. We did not put any pressure on the managers or owners to desegregate. Our function was merely to give voice to the various sides, and to listen, hopefully with intelligence, to be able to reason with all concerned to find the right solution. There was certainly no pressure, but just reasoning together as to what was the right thing to do and when. I still maintained the opinion that we could open the door, but blacks couldn't enjoy it until they earned it with their actions and their way of life.

I don't think that the higher echelon of the black community ever put real pressure on the business community. I think that some of them did have to take public stands. But I do not think that the black boycott had any adverse effect on the business community downtown. I think that desegregation had to come. I'm glad that we got it early and were able to solve it calmly. And It's to the advantage of all concerned that everybody had the same rights.

It's only right that a person has a right to go into any establishment and spend his dollars, which are just as good to their merchant as somebody else's, and be treated exactly the same. And I think it's going the right way. I think that desegregation in the long run was good in the sense that the black community could come downtown in comfort and spend their dollars like anybody else. It's unfortunate that there is abroad some feeling that there are many more blacks on the streets than whites, which is a fact on the weekends. It's unfortunate that some of those people misbehave in the remarks that they make to other people on the street and are loud-mouthed. But who's to say that you can't shout while I talk calmly?

I stayed on the committee as long as it existed. Our committee worked to meet various crises until the permanent Human Relations Commission was established, and I think that it was an excellent thing. I think that it serves a vital function in the community. We need to be able to exchange ideas to eliminate friction and to make life happier for all concerned.

## Ben Wilson

I think, as the years went by, and we had more and more assemblies and rallies, marches, I think that the beginning certainly established a trust between the city government and the colleges and universities that was stretched at times, but I think it certainly seemed to bear fruit. So I think it was an important move, even if it wasn't greatly significant at the time.

We told every member of the faculty what we were doing. The Inter-Faculty Forum wasn't set up to deal with the civil rights crisis, but the civil rights crisis took over the agenda, and I think that was probably the best thing that could have happened. A few of us on the campus had faith in it and saw it through year after year. And essentially it had to reorganize every year. It was somewhat cumbersome to get five colleges and five faculties together. But nevertheless, we established a clear meeting time and we tried to have at least one monthly meeting. It was very fluid, and I think the group was very effective for that very reason. And all of the faculty on every campus knew this. For that reason, some people didn't join because they didn't think we were serious, or they didn't know what to expect, or they couldn't identify with it. So there were other people who were frightened and didn't want to be any part of anything to do with "those people,"—meaning either blacks or people who were interested in civil rights. And we did have people on campus who didn't want to have anything to do with civil rights. There were other people who never made a commitment; they just sat aloof and never said anything.

But I would say probably one third of our faculty were very much interested in what the Inter-Faculty Forum was doing. We'd often have that much attendance in the meeting, especially on this campus. I think the people at the black campuses, you would expect there would be more of a representation, but I think they really didn't want to get us involved with it. They were very conservative about it. And I think it was the younger members who were perhaps members of the Urban League or the Southern Christian Leadership Conference were interested. But it was rather small on the black campus until it began to gather momentum, and I think then more and more people joined in.

In 1963 many of us joined in those marches, not for the reason that we were blindly following what the students said, but that we kept an eye on what was going on, and we made ourselves known to the authority that we were concerned and we wanted those students protected, because there were still many people in the community who were upset about civil rights, and they objected to the students marching through Greensboro. Some of them were very violent, so the students needed protection. I remember one gathering at the City-County Building. We gathered on the courthouse steps for a rally in support of civil rights legislation. People marched that were delegates from various campuses: A&T, Bennett, Greensboro, W.C., and Guilford. We marched in two streams. Those from this side of the city came down West Market Street, and picked up delegations as we went by. They just started at Guilford and picked up W.C., picked up Greensboro College, and then went on. And the same thing from the other direction. It started at A&T, picked up Bennett College people, and came in. There were probably five thousand students in that group. I think from Greensboro College campus we had, probably, one-third to one-half of our students march. There may have been some black students on campus, because we never had a confrontation about admitting black students here. We adjusted to them without any fanfare. I think many white campuses did that.

## Boyd Morris

They wrecked my business. I didn't go bankrupt, but they made me insolvent, owing the government withholding taxes. We had a take in the evening meal of [thousands] of dollars, and after the demonstrations, we fell off to [a few hundred], and we were never able over the next five or six years to get our business over $135,000 a year. I had a real nice fat bank account, and in five years I owed the government sixty thousand dollars in taxes I could not pay. I did finally pay them off. I was sitting there, losing money day after day, and I couldn't get out of my lease. There was nothing I could do about it; I had to carry on.

I considered desegregating from the beginning, but whatever I did would have been wrong with some people. But if I could have perceived that ministers and business leaders would have done what I had asked them to do, it would have been over and done with before that time, and they were talking to me, but they were not talking about themselves. This is the contrariness of the whole thing, the whole situation. They wanted me to sacrifice.

I don't think integration had anything to do with the closing of large cafeterias like the S&W and the Mayfair, other than the fact that, in Greensboro, integration ruined the downtown. We were failing in our business at the Mayfair. We were not doing well because downtown Greensboro was not doing well, and the S&W was not doing well downtown because nobody else was doing well downtown. It was the decay of downtown retail business across America; you'll find this same in Raleigh and Charlotte.

We [businessmen] all fell downtown, due to integration and due to the exodus of businesses from downtown to the shopping centers. We had meetings of the local businesses and churches. When we entered into this strong, militant division of black and white, of wanting to ride in the front of the buses, go in the front door of doctor's offices, lawyer's offices, eat in the restaurants by the front door. Beginning with the Woolworth sit-ins in February 1960, the reaction of the downtown business community was one of fear, anxiety, and doubt. What's next? What are we going to do? I don't think anyone had an answer as to what was going to come. Woolworth is still in business, and it's really the only one. Kress is gone. S&W Cafeteria is gone. The Marriott is gone. Mayfair Cafeteria is gone. Belk's is gone. Thalhimer's is gone. Meyer's Department Store is gone. All multi-million dollar companies.

Two things: the people were scared to come downtown, and then the shopping centers came in and it was a springboard. It certainly helped the shopping centers tremendously to have the fear of people coming downtown. They moved right on in with the nice shopping centers. Very definitely the integration situation helped defeat downtown business. But I would in fairness say that the exodus to the countryside was a big factor, too; the [big] businesses began to move out. All of that combined to pull the plug on downtown Greensboro.

I'd like to think that race relations are better now than in 1963. I think that there are those who still wave red flags that everything that's done is done on a racial basis, which I don't buy. I think if you look at the record and see what has happened and the gains that have been made, you cannot be militant and find fault and throw cold water on everything that's done on a black and white basis. It's going to spill back on you. And when it's all done, They continue to be negative, negative, negative—they are going to defeat themselves. History has proven that, black or white. If black people have the responsibility and have the know-how, they're going to be—they will be elected to office, and they will serve well. But every time something happens—say, "Well, it wouldn't have happened. The only reason it happened is because he's black." I don't buy that. I think that if they have that responsibility and the know-how that they can go anywhere. I think if they could forget the color and just say, "This is the way it is."

## Neil McGill

I remember that my company said that we would integrate, and that was it as far as I was concerned. When integration came, it was sort of a test. There were so few that it wasn't even noticeable. There were no incidents at that time; the incidents came later. There was one occasion that was kind of frightening for me. This was after we integrated. We were having a late show and it was at large crowd made up of about half-white and half-black. Well, before the movie ended, all of the white people had left; the blacks were stationed in the rest rooms and there was violence.

There was another incident that sticks out in my mind: we used to have Saturday morning shows, with combos that appealed to the preteens, and one morning we had three or four hundred white kids, and I saw these same blacks who had given us trouble coming from the corner, with their fist in the air, saying, "Black Power," and I locked the doors. The Police and the Fire Departments got mad about that, but I wasn't going to take any chances [of violence], not with three or four hundred kids in there. We called and the police came down. The blacks left and went over to Elm Street in front of the big department store. It was sort of an exciting time for a little while, but they all settled down. There was a very slow transition as the whites stopped coming to the Carolina, and gradually the audiences became more and more black. Eventually, [this affected] all of the downtown theaters everywhere. We closed the Carolina because the attendance had fallen off to where it wasn't profitable.

## B. Elton Cox

I think that CORE was largely successful, because we got more whites involved than any other civil rights group. North Carolina was important [to CORE] because it was perceived as the most liberal of the Southern states. There was a fairly rapid decline in CORE and CORE influence and activities [from] '63 to '65, such that it was virtually non-existent. Largely because of Stokely Carmichael's comment down in Mississippi on Black Power. When CORE swallowed that, I began to pull away; I could not swallow the philosophy of Black Power: that whites could not lead anymore, but only follow and give financial support. I couldn't go along with that. I'd follow anybody down the street toward the American Dream to freedom. The effectiveness of nonviolent direct action passed away to negotiations that evolved into a wider participation. The nonviolent thing is always there, but the Black Power movement hurt CORE more than anything. I don't think that there were limitations to the effectiveness of nonviolent direct action, because it is best to negotiate rather than demonstrate.

I didn't work with members of the Coordinating Committee of Pro-Integration Groups. I know there were about thirty-five members, and they included members at large of the black community: CORE, the Ministerial Association, and NAACP. There were a lot of groups trying to coordinate and pull together groups. Many people didn't want to come under the flag of the NAACP, and they didn't want to come under the flag of CORE. And they would come up with some local group. And I would work with them, because I was still trying to get something going.

The Greensboro demonstrations had some influence on CORE; subsequent CORE strategies employed the tactics used here in Greensboro a little bit. But basically the action was about the same, however. Blacks and whites—but particularly whites, looked to Greensboro, Durham, Charlotte, Winston-Salem and Chapel Hill for a pattern. I was not present at the sit-down in the Square; I don't know whether I was out in the field somewhere or where. I would have approved of any such action. If it came down that you were not moving at the conference table, then we would take direct nonviolent action—as long as it did not hurt innocent people who may be semi-liberal towards you. I continued in other CORE activities after the outbreak of major demonstrations in the spring of 1963.

## George Simkins

We continued to try to get blacks on city and county boards and commissions. We found out that we had an at-large system here, where whoever got the most votes got to be on the City Council. We asked for a district system, but were denied. So we put in a petition where you get so many voters to sign and you have to have an election; well, we lost the election. But as soon as we'd lose one election, we'd get another petition going, get some more voters to sign, have another election, and lose that one. The third time we lost, we presented a chart showing that it was not a black/white issue. There was nobody on the City Council but people who live in the northwest section of the city, people living in Irving Park and Starmount. Nobody else, black or white, had any representation on boards, nor on the City Council. So the last time we voted, whites in other parts of the city voted with us for the first time.

The city wanted to annex Guilford College. There were fifteen thousand white families out in Guilford College that wanted to be annexed to the city. I called the Justice Department, since we were under the 1965 Voting Rights Act, and tsaid that we didn't have anybody on the City Council now. Putting fifteen thousand more white families on the City Council would only dilute the black vote even more, and we didn't think that they should allow the city to do this until they get a ward system in place. They agreed with me and told the city that in order to get these fifteen thousand white families into the city, they would have to get a district system.

And so we got the five-three-one [district plan].Five from the districts, three at large, and one mayor elected by all the city. The city was losing seventeen thousand dollars a month in tax revenue because they could not bring these white families in. After they got the district system, the Justice Department agreed to allow the families to be brought in. And this is how we got a district system. It took us about seventeen years. Cities around Greensboro had a district system, had had one for years, had had blacks on the City Council. And yet Greensboro was the last to come in. We had to fight to get it.

We also were moving on redevelopment. One of the stipulations for receiving federal redevelopment funds was that if you remove somebody from their house, you had to have some place for them to live. Greensboro Redevelopment was removing them from their homes and had no place for them to go, except the streets. So we looked into it and found out that Henry Lewis Smith Homes had a lot of vacancies over there. So we petitioned the Greensboro Housing Authority to open up Henry Lewis Smith Homes for these blacks from whom redevelopment was taking their homes.

We started a picket line in front of Henry Lewis Smith homes. And the next day, they decided that they had enough of us, and that they opened up one wing just for blacks. We said that we were not standing for any segregation in a public housing project. They had to have blacks all over Henry Lewis Smith Homes to satisfy us, and that we were not going to allow them to be put in just one segment of Henry Lewis Smith Homes. So they finally decided that they would open up the whole place. So we became the second city in the South to integrate public housing. I think Louisville, Kentucky, was the first.

We had to picket the banks to make them hire tellers here. I was on the Human Relations Commission, and we'd been trying to get Wachovia to hire black tellers. They had no blacks in the bank. And they refused. Said they couldn't find anybody qualified. So I left the Human Relations Commission one day and I got a few people that were on the Human Relations Commission, and I said, "Let's go out here and picket this bank." We went out and started picketing the bank. The next day, they called the black bank in Durham and got them to send some black tellers. And then the other banks start following suit. All of them started hiring and training black tellers. This is how the banks got integrated. These are some of the things you have to do in Greensboro to get things done.

It costs you a lot of sleepless nights and threats on your life. It costs you monetarily. I never will forget, one man who had a job with the city, his maid told him she had a toothache, and he told his maid she could go anywhere else but not to me. Well, the lady came to me anyway and told me what the man said, so its little things like that. Looking at it now, I probably would have taken a different approach at Gillespie. Rather than going out there and putting my money down, I probably would've gone to court and gotten an injunction against them. Then I would have avoided all this harassment and this type of thing that I've gone through in the court system. But it's what you're trying to accomplish. It cost Martin Luther King his life, so I'm getting out real cheap.

I don't know whether I had any goals; I'd just go from day to day. I knew that we had to get stronger politically. We had to get more people registered to vote. I think that's one of our shortcomings. And we had to get better organized politically. Our political action committee, organized in 1960, has been sending letters out to the registered voters on every election since 1962. And I feel that we need to be better organized than we are. I feel that we need to probably have a block-to-block organization all over the city in the black community, so that we can get a greater percentage of the people involved in voting. I feel like this is a failure that I admit to. Number one, we are nonpartisan. And we try to get everybody who is running for office to come before us. We have to find out what their platform is. We question them to find out different things about them. After we have questioned all folks running, we have a closed meeting and decide whom to support. We don't care about party. If they're a good person in that party, we're going to support them. This is how we run our political action committee.

## Clarence Malone

The only way I can answer the question of desegregation being achieved any other way than demonstrations is that legally, desegregation was never accomplished through the courts. The final and ultimate blow to segregation was dealt by the passage of the Civil Rights Act of 1964. But we hacked away at it in the courts, bit by bit. Certainly it was weakened and the climate of the times led to the legislation. I don't think that the climate would have been such that the legislation would have passed Congress had there not been the general upheavals that were really the manifestations of these feelings among the blacks against desegregation. I don't think that one would have been possible without the other.

The violation of an unjust law is justified, assuming that the individuals involved have made a commitment to suffer the consequences of their act. Now, where someone goes out and breaks the law on moral grounds and simply says that this is a defense to my action, then I think that he is on a bar of quicksand. But being able to accept whatever consequences are meted out, and where one is doing that as a means of protest to call the attention of the public to what he considers a wrong, I think that he is justified, both morally and legally in breaking it.

However, I don't think that doing it on moral grounds should constitute a legal defense. I can cite tomes of state and local legislation that were designed to prevent those kinds of activities, but I contend that the culmination of the racial unrest that built from the 1930s right on up to the explosion in the mid-Sixties was a direct cause of the passage of what I refer to as "overt legislation." I think that the demonstrations were a catalytic agent of most of the Great Society legislation, bought about in the climate whereby the Congress and the powers-that-be were made conscious for the need for this kind of legislation, but to say a given bill was the result of the demonstrations, no, I don't think so. I think that the tenor of the times were influenced to focus upon the injustices and thereby brought about the passage of the legislation to ameliorate this situation.

As to whether the city could have brought suit against CORE for initiating a boycott, yes, they could have brought suit. I don't think that it would have been possible for it to be successful, because of First Amendment provisions. The idea that the citizen has the right to petition for the redress of grievances, constitutionally, I think that the suit would have been struck down. While it might have run the gamut of the local and state courts, I think that by this time the federal courts were so committed to the enforcement of the Constitution that the bottom rungs would have been cut out from under it. Desegregation in Greensboro had to wait until the passage of the 1964 Civil Rights Act. It brought about statements from the city authorities, but you had spotted compliance; it was more or less done on a voluntary basis, the merchants who became enlightened to the fact that the world isn't going to come to an end, that they were not going to lose their business. But up until then and for some period after the passage of the Civil Rights Bill, you had spotted segregated facilities. I can't say that without the passage of the Civil Rights Act, it would never have come, but it would have been years and years in coming.

## J. Kenneth Lee

Integration did not come about in Greensboro through the law; that had nothing to do with it. Integration came about because they were afraid of what was going to happen if it didn't come. Things had reached the point that the only other options were violence or bankruptcy, like Boyd Morris' experience. They completely stopped downtown, and downtown was the center of trade. Nobody was doing business down there with the streets full of folks. Not only were the demonstrations successful in desegregating the cafeterias and the theaters, but after the demonstrations were over, the few businesses that did not integrate were boycotted and lost money. Greensboro has never done anything because the law dictated it.

## Cecil Bishop

The marches accomplished some limited objectives. Take the S&W Cafeteria situation. The demonstrations resulted in the S&W finally serving black patrons. But that only changed conditions at the S&W; "business as usual" was going on in the rest of the community. The announcements of the number of motel rooms and seats in restaurants desegregated may have been a way of getting around a very slow foot-dragging change on the part of the previously segregated businesses. But the way that the S&W started it, integration was along that line.

Firstly, at the breakfast hour, say, four black people would come to breakfast. And then four black people would come to lunch. And then four would come in the evening hour. That went on for several days, and then it began to pick up. It was almost like saying: if too many black people show up, it might collapse or self-destruct the agreement. It went on as if "we've got to sort of ease this thing into place, because if it just—boom—opens, what will happen?"

So that was the way that happened at that location. The management was afraid that maybe half the student body from A&T would show up and say, "Hey, we want to eat," but that never did happen. The irony of the whole thing was that it came to a point that the biggest clientele that S&W had to help it survive came from students at A&T. It ended up closing in later years, but if you had suddenly subtracted all of the trade from the black student and adult communities, it would have closed sooner.

I don't know what would have happened had it not been for the Public Accommodations Bill of 1964. That's what solved the problem, because there were a lot of places in Greensboro that were operated on a segregated basis. But it was only after the Public Accommodations Bill passed by the Congress in 1964 that everything opened. Had it not been for that, there would have been still an on-going movement in that regard. But when places of public accommodation opened, that still did not touch jobs and housing, or upward mobility in employment. After the Public Accommodations there was a feeling of temporary calm and well-being in the black community. "We're over." But we discovered that we were not over. And so by 1969 we'd gotten into a whole lot of other things so that it became quite clear that public accommodations didn't just do a favor for blacks, because they were spending money for whatever accommodations they were receiving. They weren't getting it free. So it was no favor.

And so people looked at that. And they also began to see that there's a drain on our resources going away from us. Places were open, you could go anyplace to eat or to sleep, or at any lunch counter. But that did not solve these other attendant problems. The 1963 demonstrations did not solve the public accommodations problem in Greensboro; they highlighted it. They opened a few places. But it was the Public Accommodations Act that opened up everything, that then took the winds out of the sails of that Movement in 1963 that was directed toward places of public accommodation.

Then other areas had to be addressed. So this time it started over and picked up another momentum. The Open Housing Act was finally passed. But it demanded and called for a different kind of approach. Because of the difference in focus and the different means of addressing those problems, some people were led to believe that there was no further problem. But there always was a problem. I think it finally got to the point where the marching and the protesting did not really get to the heart of the matter. There had to then be meaningful negotiations of sitting down and talking about these things. And I think that Greensboro got to that point; I think that happened with the schools and, to some degree, with the jobs.

Greensboro did not have the kind of problems, say, that Charlotte had in school integration. School integration went off pretty smoothly in the Greensboro community. In employment and upgrading of teachers' salaries and other educational issues, that movement was not as rapid as it should have been. I remember an opening. And the superintendent made the statement that the black community was trying to get somebody black for that opening, but there was nobody qualified; he couldn't find anybody qualified.

There was a member of the school board who had sent a person with excellent qualifications, a black person, who had the information there when the person applied, what the response was, and their credentials and qualifications which illustrated that point. It's that kind of confrontation that had to take place as on on-going way of dealing with the problems. It still exists today. So direct action had its place and can only do so much. It's not a panacea for all of the ills. You have to have a varied approach to the multitude of problems that are different. People in positions of authority change, and they have different outlooks that must be dealt with differently.

In 1963, I don't think that the black community was exhausted, because the community knew that they still had problems. I think the community was in a holding action, trying to find other ways to address problems. Often we would say, "Hey, look, this demonstrating is not going to change much now." You've got to sit down and talk to somebody, find out some way you can bring some other pressure to bear, other than out there on the street. We recognized that that had limitations and at that time had about run its course. In part, because I think we were making some efforts at meaningful negotiations, sitting down at the conference table and talking things out.

That was the case, because the black community felt that the white community had realized that demonstrations could result in violence, which could have a negative impact on the city. The business community did not want that. So the white community was more open to saying, "Sit down. We'll talk." So everybody came to the conference table, mindful of the fact that it had its shortcomings; there was always the fear that it may just be talk. But it did move us away from direct action as being the panacea for all of the civil rights ills that were bothering us.

## George Evans

I can't say that I wholly agreed with some of the methods that were used. And yet, it's pretty hard to argue against what was done in the light of the results that they helped produce. Many stressful situations are resolved only after some pretty forceful protesting, not necessarily including violence. But I think that if this protesting had not been done on a rather prominent and very definite note, that we might not have reached the solutions that we did reach. In other words, my philosophy has been ever since those days, that when you're confronted with problems such as we were confronted with, that I don't think either of two methods of approaching the problem—protest marches and demonstrations on the one hand, and negotiations on the other hand—could have solved the problems or brought this to the conclusion that it came to.

My personal feeling is that a mixture of both approaches was a much more successful approach to the problem than either one alone. If there wasn't the pressure of the mass demonstrations, there wouldn't have been any pressure for the members of the white power structure to compromise. I don't think that the resumption of the mass demonstrations hampered our negotiating efforts. The managers of the targeted businesses and city officials might have been more intransigent to some degree, but not to any great extent. And certainly, not to the extent where that intransigence interferred with a willingness to do something about the situation. I think they had reached the point where they felt that something had to be done to resolve the problems, or else we might have been subjected to more violence than there was. So I think they were anxious to get something done to solve it.

I believe that the boycott of black patrons to downtown businesses was an effective protest instrument, because there was a significant amount of black patronage of the businesses downtown. And I believe that it was a significant factor in the compromises that were eventually worked out. In fact, I know quite a few people who left Greensboro to go to places close by— High Point, Kernersville, Burlington, Reidsville—to do some of the shopping that they normally would have done right here in the city, including the chairman.

We feel that we were successful, through negotiation, in getting a peaceful settlement to many of the longstanding situations: refusal to serve our people at restaurant counters, refusal to let them into the movie houses except in the balcony three floors up, which at times were rat-infested and which were not kept very clean at times. And we felt that we were able to get people to see that there were lots of black people in the community who were not criminals, and that opening the doors to these people was not going to ruin their businesses as they feared. So all in all, we were able to do a lot of changing of the climate that had been persistent through the community all through the years—a climate of standoffishness demonstrated by lots of merchants who did not want to listen to reason when it came to the matter of accommodating Negro patrons. The committee was able to accomplish quite a little bit in this regard, and to quiet the situation that probably would have led to a lot of violence if something hadn't been done to get it resolved.

There are still a number of people in the community who feel that the city's image was tarnished way back in 1963, by their not moving as rapidly and as quickly as they might have in these matters of protesting. But there are a good many others who feel that the job was accomplished perhaps in as good a manner as it could have been accomplished, although not as rapidly.

There was a shift to more long-term legal channels—voter registration and the 1965 Voting Rights Act. Voter registration was and still is a large part of that push, not only to voter registration but with efforts following the registration of voters to get them to go to the polls and vote. There's quite a bit of apathy, not just in the black community but in the voters generally, toward going to the polls for election, for voting instead of just registering and forgetting it.

I think the mass demonstrations had declined nationwide, because it's felt by most of the members of the black community that I've heard express themselves that those demonstrations served their purpose. That is, as a catalyst to broader opportunities than just sitting down in a restaurant or in a theater. Now, the push is to more voter participation in the elections, and the election of people who voters believe are amenable to opportunities for political participation and thereby better economic status generally. And demonstrations, it is believed now, are not the way to opening such doors. Rather, it is more through the avenue of negotiations and better training and wider opportunities for participation in things other than just eating in a restaurant.

For example, we have people now who have the opportunity to get into positions where they can earn, say, twenty thousand dollars a year instead of five thousand dollars a year. I say more power to them. This has come about largely as a result of the beginning of door-opening through demonstrations. Now it comes down to a matter of better education, better preparation and more opportunities for participation in these higher-level things than earlier.

It's easy to see how patronage of downtown businesses was given a big push by the black community from the very fact that the black population of Greensboro stays around twenty-seven or twenty-eight percent, which is more than a fourth of the population, needing to buy clothing, automobiles, television sets, radios, whatever. You can see how that constitutes quite a bit of the income of downtown businesses.

My personal belief is that I realize that there isn't any way for sixteen members of the university system to be equal in every respect such has been talked about. However, I believe, also, that some of the larger black institutions which have better facilities should be preserved and upgraded, in facilities, equipment and trained faculty to push these efforts forward should be maintained. If there's a merger, then many identities and job opportunities will be lost. There is room for both black and integrated institutions, involving communication and exchange of facilities and programs without merging. The same thing is true of the local public schools.

## Gordon Carey

North Carolina, as a whole, including Greensboro, was very important to CORE. From 1960 until I left CORE in 1965. Those states where CORE was most active in the South were North Carolina, Louisiana and Florida; these three states had a major, on-going presence and structure. They provided the bulk of the volunteers, activities, energy, wisdom and genius that came from the kids.

I don't think that it was due to the skill of the field secretaries. It was that North Carolina in particular, had a long history of good government and that it prided itself on not being backward like Mississippi and other states.

You had a state government that wanted to be somewhat progressive. The fact that you had a lot of universities and colleges in North Carolina was important; you had more black colleges in North Carolina than anyplace else. A lot of them were independent, church-related, and that was important. You had a lot of major businesses and banks that were big on a national scale. These things tend to make a state more cognizant of its image. They didn't have any direct role; they didn't even talk with us in those days. But when you have a business community that wants to be responsible, and you had a governor that wanted to be responsible; there was a progressive environment for change. There good newspapers—the *Charlotte Observer* and the *Greensboro Daily News*. There were a lot of good local people like George Simkins in Greensboro, Floyd McKissick in Durham and Kelly Alexander in Charolotte.

Is it too bad that CORE no longer exists now as it did back then? I would say no. I'm sure that it was temporary in the sense that organizations have a life and death like people do, especially if you're talking about cause-oriented organizations; they ought to grow and they ought to die. I don't judge success in the same way that some others do. I was primarily a social activist. You don't count success in terms of numbers of restaurant desegregated, nor in terms of stability of an organization; numbers of chapters, or the fact that they die out two years later. I judge success by the kinds of things that happen to the people that are involved in the thing, what happens to them as individuals.

To what extent did [the Greensboro Movement] affect history in its own community? We're feeling today the results of the Movement of the Sixties; Greensboro and North Carolina are different places today and this did not come about primarily because of legislation. It came about because of those college kids who suffered and were in those organizations. The Civil Rights Movement is now a part of history, and it should be. It accomplished significant political and social changes, and then history moved on to other issues.

A major factor in the success of the Greensboro Movement and North Carolina was that public accommodations were easily amenable to a direct action thrust. Another factor was that our society was ready for change. The nation has moods and it goes through phases. I'm not saying that there won't be, at some point, renewed activism in the field of civil rights, but I think that it will be very different. I just don't think that you will get the same kind of nonviolent direct action. I don't think that the problems are amenable to that kind of approach. They are mainly economic problems, not solvable through nonviolent direct action.

Many of the field secretaries were college students in those days, so they got into the Movement, and then at some point they were encouraged by their friends and associates in CORE to return to college and that "this is not a lifetime position." Back in those days, people were in and out of the Civil Rights Movement. It was just a very changing and dynamic situation.

## James McMillan

I had to recognize that out of all this, the worst thing that could happen was that someone could be killed. We knew that this happens, but when you are committed to a notion that racism is one of the most degrading things that exists, life is not of much value when you have to live in a system where these kinds of things exist.

So, that was the prevailing thing, that when my respect of the human person tends to not be likewise reflected, obviously it does invite a certain kind of a defensive position, and I guess it is that [which] begins to rally whenever the kind of positions we have to take in order to do some of the things we have to do. We do it because it has to be done, and personal safety is not even considered. As I think back about that person that had the knife on that rainy day, the kinds of things that flashed through my mind were not so much that I would be lying there dead, [but that the most] important thing is what we were doing. I think it is that kind of thing that tends to dominate, it's not the negative; it's the positive. We know of all the hurts that are a product of this segregated society. I think that this thing becomes more imperative that changes take place, because we don't want to see our children treated the way that we had to be treated.

This was at a time that I had two young children, and in many of the occasions of the marches, I carried my children with me. I wanted them to experience something that I felt was an extremely important part in their experience as being black Americans. And that has certainly been borne out. I have a daughter and she constantly speaks about this strange time when she was looking up at all these people and the commotion and the sounds and the songs that were being sung. And my son constantly speaks about this same period, not always with great affection. There is still, of course, a kind of resentment that those kinds of things had to be, and still are in so many ways, perhaps in a subtle and pernicious way, but I think that during that time at least, it was a very concrete opportunity to speak to some of these ills we know on the American scene.

To me, there were all kinds of things that were accomplished. From 1947, when I first came to Greensboro, through the Sixties, and into the Eighties, I have an interesting kind of perspective. Since the Sixties, there is no question in my mind that Greensboro is a much better place to live for everyone. The kinds of things that have taken place, and we speak primarily about our own contacts, professional and otherwise. We've seen the colleges and the universities move in a direction whereby everyone could have the opportunities and benefits that higher education offers. There have been all kinds of wonderful coordinated programs, consortia arrangements, that could not have been done as effectively had this not taken place.

Obviously, we could talk of the kind of immediate things, like restaurants that are available, and movies, motels and all of these kinds of things; those are just incidentals. But in terms of quality of life, I think that many people feel that Greensboro is one of the better cities in the South. I'm sure that it has much to do with the activities that took place during the Sixties. I would say that Greensboro has, through its crisis, come to deal with, in a rather honest way, the problems that are inherent in a multi-racial society. These problems have not been resolved; they have been spoken to with some honesty and, unfortunately, it was a case of having to be pressed upon the minds of those who were in positions to do something. But at least it has begun. If nothing more, I think that this is a very positive thing.

What was attacked in the Sixties was the overtness of segregated society; we are talking about those kinds of things that are most obvious. When you talk about those things that are more fundamental, such as attitudes, we're not talking about official policy and law; we're talking about attitudes. It takes a long time for attitudes to change, and we certainly understand that if attitudes don't change in a positive way, then many negative kinds of things can be very easily perpetrated.

I believe that we are now in a stage where this is the thing that has to be resolved. It has to do with interpersonal relationships; it has to do with ingrained attitudes. It's much more difficult to put your finger on. I would say, though, that the questions of jobs, perhaps, is the most significant area that still has to be resolved, because once that happens, perhaps other things can change. It may mean that people can buy houses and move to another neighborhood. Moving into other neighborhoods allows people to know each other better, form a relationship, and that can help to change attitudes.

I think that massive busing was a necessary activity that had to occur. I know that there is a sense of futility in the black community in terms of the effects about busing black kids out of the black neighborhoods into some of the white schools. There are also attitudes of the whites who had to be bused into the black communities, but I think that this was a necessary alternative that had to take place. I think there are still problems, but I think that those problems go back to attitudes. Some of these attitudes may have positive effects. I think that where young people are able to meet each other on a personal level, they are able to deal with them as individuals rather than as groups. They can overcome many of the stereotype concepts that have been provided by their parents and others who would prefer to remain as they are. But I think that in the long run, we still have some serious problems in the school situation and it may be that busing is not the final answer.

I think that some substantive changes have taken place. But I think those have taken place only where there has been direct contact, where there have been interpersonal relationships that have allowed various racial groups to know each other directly. I think, perhaps, in government levels this has taken place, I would say that those are the areas [where] most of the substantive changes have taken place.

When it comes down to it, it's an interpersonal thing; this thing called "human relationship" is the key to much interracial relations. I think it behooves us all, to maintain the kind of attitude that helps to promote a congenial interracial relationship. I don't think that it always has to be done as organized confrontations, and I guess that personal feelings tend to promote that kind of way of feeling with this whole question.

## John Hatchett

I think that basically what we were able to achieve was a welding together of a number of diverse groups in Greensboro, that by dent of very hard work and perseverance, we were able to convince the community that what we were doing—limited though it may have been at that time—was important enough to merit their direct participation.

As I stated before, we were at that time very idealistic, very optimistic, very hopeful that a nonviolent but direct confrontation-type of demonstration would be able to beat down the walls of segregation and discrimination. Looking back in hindsight, I would say that, although we did achieve a modicum of success, the deeply ingrained racism that permeates our entire society was not dented that much, and that one of the lessons that emerged from such a movement is that you have to begin to develop some very sophisticated tactics to deal with an economic power structure that is quite widespread and formidable.

The marching and the other demonstrations served the purpose of calling attention to many of the problems that we felt were important. What I mean by more sophisticated tactics would have been a sustained boycott, not only of places of public accommodation, but of business establishments, sustained to the point that it would achieve the goals that we had in mind. That was initially done, primarily in connection with the five-and-dime chain stores. And it was done so effectively that they eventually capitulated—not necessarily because we were sitting-in, but because we were also encouraging people not to buy. Once we took that turn, then tthose who govern Woolworth and Kress made a decision that, if this is what they want, then we'll open up.

I think that if we had extended that kind of tactic into other areas, in the long run it would have been far more effective. Demonstrations are exciting. Demonstrations get press headlines. When people are arrested, people sit up and take notice, but then they soon forget. But it's an age-old adage that in a country that is based on a free enterprise system, if you want to make certain basic changes, you hit the free enterprise system in its pocketbook, and then it will yield. But you cannot appeal to that system's sense of morality or fair play, because that's not how it works. And I think that this is part of what I'm talking about. I don't want this to be interpreted as a blanket criticism of sit-in demonstrations, because I certainly am not criticizing that which I myself participated in. But I'm saying that there were deeper issues involved. Those deeper issues called for more structured tactics in order to deal with them. What I'm calling an economic boycott would have been such a tactic.

What transpired in Greensboro between 1960 and 1963 was very good. I just think, looking back in retrospect, that there were a number of things that all of us could have done in general and that certain people could have done specifically, to further the gains that already had been made. And this was not done. Part of the reason for it was because people were too easily side-tracked into areas that were of dubious importance, such as being entertained.

I think the power structure manipulated CORE into accepting short-term goals that did not result in significant breakthroughs, by getting through to the leadership, and convincing them that the gains that they had made were quite significant, and that, to a large extent, they could rest on their laurels. And I think that the events that took place in the latter part of 1963 would bear this sort of observation out. The employment gains and certain other various substantive gains were not made even two and three years after that time.

They also agreed with the national leadership that certain demonstrations should be called off. And later on, they were involved in the demonstrations that led to the mass arrests, which I believe was a very tactical mistake, because the number of people arrested almost literally comprised the number of people involved. And once they were arrested, the momentum of the demonstrations was slowed to a standstill. The city was not really put into a very bad position. There was a great deal of talk about the lack of adequate facilities where the arrested persons were housed. There were a lot of complaints centered around that. But, in all honesty, I don't recall the city really being put in a very compromising position.

I think the massive arrests, the cooling down of the demonstrations, and the lack of focus on the more substantive issues, all of this, I believe, came about as a result of a leadership and advice that did not realize the kind of ballpark they were in. This has happened to many of us. But I think that given the fact that just prior to those massive demonstrations we had begun to involve in a very effective manner the citizens of Greensboro, the adults and people who were not connected with either college said that we were moving in the right direction. But I think much of that was lost after the massive arrests. We had some sympathetic support from the white community, but, to my knowledge, very little active involvement in terms of actual demonstrations.

We were not advocating precipitous and non-rewarding demonstrations. We were talking about the very keen need to keep a certain kind of momentum going to let people know that we would not fade into the background and then re-emerge at another point when it seemed to be convenient to do so. It was this kind of activism that characterized our involvement. We were not activists and irresponsible; we were committed activists, and highly responsible. Reverend Busch and Lois Lucas basically shared that point of view. I think that perhaps in some cases, some of the people may have been caught up in situations over which they had no control, so that at earlier and later points, it would appear that we were completely at odds with one another. It wasn't that. I think that other things were operative here that would bring such a picture to the forefront. I think that the persons that disagreed with us were very committed to one another. We had our differences, of course. But we were very committed to one another and very committed to doing some very positive things in terms of black people and their livelihood in the city of Greensboro.

There were a lot of students that were shocked and asking the question, "What do you hope to gain?" The administration didn't try to stop us from doing it. But it surely wasn't helping them, because you had people down in Raleigh feeling like they didn't understand why the president couldn't control those students and keep them from going downtown and sitting there. But during the time that Dr. Dowdy was president over there, he never really asked us not to do it. I think Dr. Dowdy took the position that we were adults and that to that extent he couldn't control us.

But I think at the time that happened, it was a shock to a lot of people. I think the kids that went down there were shocked that we did it. And after we got through, after the first fear of doing it, more people got involved. The Bennett College and A&T kids got involved. And we got backing from some of the faculty at A&T and Bennett College, and some of the people in the [black] community. George Simkins, Reverend [Marion] Jones and those professionals whose incomes were not predicated on working for the state or working for somebody here locally. Most of the people who had their own dental practices or medical practices, and a lot of the pastors of various churches in Greensboro supported us. There wasn't but so much pressure that could be put on those people.

And I think that the college kids had enough savvy to know who could be affected by what we were doing, and we tried as best as we could to not draw those people into that. We didn't want kids going around saying, "Well, so-and-so was not involved." We understood why they weren't involved. Those teaching for the City of Greensboro could be put under a lot of pressure. After all, we were talking about their livelihood. So we knew at that time what we were up against, and the kinds of people that we probably could draw into the demonstrations during that time.

There was a certain amount of comfort level that a lot of people got with the thing, because the Greensboro Police Department protected us very well. When we would have these big marches downtown, we had a lot of the very influential blacks in town— school teachers and what have you—that got involved in that. They didn't go to jail, but we did show a kind of oneness in the black community that there was more than some college kids over there who had a lot of stored up energy just looking to get their kicks from demonstrating. So I think that might have been part of the reason why some things in Greensboro went a little smoother than they did in some other cities, because they knew the kids who were involved. And if you remember, once the sit-ins started in Greensboro, it spread to practically every city in North Carolina where there was a black college. It kind of spread like a wildfire. It became contagious. And I think that was the thing that kind let the people know that the college kids were going to have to be reckoned with.

And I think that for the first time, college kids were able to make an assessment that this is something we can do that our parents can't do, as long as we use some good common sense about it. I think that for the first time college kids saw that there was an opportunity where they could do something that could help a lot of people. And I think that a lot of them just boiled it down to that. "This is something that I just got to do. The time has come. Something has to be done, and this is the way, this is the part I can play."

I didn't like the idea of going to jail, but it was something that you accepted each time you got more involved. And you had to start using some other techniques, because just marching and singing; the Greensboro city officials got used to that. It was the kind of thing that you were trying to use something to get them off dead center. I remember we used to have negotiating committees. You'd sit down with the business people from Greensboro, and I think they were sincere, but we just didn't agree. But I think things began to move, and when we started having all those arrests, the city fathers thought that these kids come from middle-class families and although they didn't want to go to jail, they were willing to do so for their principles.

## David Schenck, Jr.

The importance of civilities in political discourse is often underplayed. When they break down, then you reach a crisis point in your community. My father felt that setting aside civilities was a bad thing; that certain basic rules of discourse are important, or the whole situation breaks down into conflict. But, I believe that the demonstrations were the only way for the black community to get what was just and right was to do what they did to challenge the civilities and demand a reformulation of civilities and the rules of political discourse and order. I think that my father was so concerned with his responsibility to maintain social order that he didn't see the moral importance of the black movement, and I think that was a flaw in his own moral vision. I say that with a great deal of love and understanding, and yet I think that he was wrong or missed some of the significance of the whole thing.

## Hal Sieber

A lot of changes that seemed to be taking place in race relations in North Carolina wasn't a change of revolution in any pronounced way, but a subtle change, a stepping out here and a reaching out and participation there. We now brag about the sit-ins, as if we invented the Civil Rights Movement here in Greensboro.

On behalf of the Chamber, Skipper Bowles and Allen Wanamaker hired me to bring Greensboro into the 1960s without hurting its progressive reputation, someone who had an idea of how the business community operated, but also felt at home in the whole community. I became a member of Omega Psi Phi, which is an African American fraternity. I helped to organize a new chapter of the Sertoma Club and made sure that exactly one-half of the members were African American. I went to all the community meetings in the African American community. But more than that, I found in the Chamber an opportunity, in all sorts of subtle ways, to get things to happen. For instance, we championed school integration.

Greensboro was a model community in the way it undertook school desegregation. But school desegregation isn't "integration," and did not truly "integrate" the African American community with the white community. The African American community was sort of tolerated by the white community. Since there was no reciprocity, there was no real integration. And so we are suffering some of the problems now, for example, that derived from that earlier manipulation of school assignments.

I knew that what was going on was wrong and that it needed to be corrected, and that it meant some risks had to be taken. Of course, members of the Chamber didn't talk about that; it was just something that wasn't discussed. But I felt confident, because Bill Little, Executive Vice President of the Chamber of Commerce, had an uncanny sense for what was coming historically. He was good at bridging the gap between the Old South and what had not yet arrived: the New South. And he backed me until about the time that I left. I felt comfortable that Al Lineberry, Sr., Herbert Falk, Bland Worley, and L. Richardson Preyer, while they did not have all the philosophical experiences and insights in terms of the dilemma that we faced, I think in their own way, were sincere, and genuine contributors to change. L. Richardson Preyer, in particular, had tremendous insights, was a highly literate and sensitive person, and a very gentle human being. McNeill Smith, while not quite as comfortable with being open, had done a lot of important things in Greensboro. Others, more revolutionary, like Sol Jacobs, was obviously very sincere.

Even individuals who had more traditional Southern perspectives, proved amenable to change. I remember a high-ranking law enforcement officer in the community, who after a black/white encounter session, made the comment that he had learned something. He had learned that the "niggers" don't want to be called by their first names, and so he was going to tell the policemen to refer to people as "Mr." or "Miss" or "Mrs." But by saying "niggers"—and he wasn't even aware that he was doing it—he showed the contradiction in his life. And I would hear enlightened people say, "We're not talking about change in our personal lives; we're saying in our public life. You can still marry whom you want to, and you can still socialize with whom you want to, but when you're doing business, you do such-and-such . . ." [This was] the rationalization that kept so many good people from being involved in the timely change that we should have had. They didn't talk about it very much.

I would say that most Chamber members felt very uncomfortable with what I was doing. Caesar Cone resigned from the Chamber because he believed that I was going too far, at that particular time. And it was difficult even for Bill Little to handle, because that involved a good hunk of money every year, as far as dues were concerned. But there were people such as Carson Bain, who, while they weren't liberals, produced some change in their behavior and in the environment. There were in Greensboro some very important African American leaders, such as Otis Hairston, Sr., Cecil Bishop, and Lewis Dowdy.

I'm not saying the people who supported segregation were evil; I think that segregation itself was evil, but I think people, obviously, are products of their times and there's so many things that make them be what they are. But you had some very important people in Greensboro, such as Orten Boren, and others, who were very conservative, and they didn't want the Chamber to make any of these moves.

I wrote a list for myself of about fifty propositions. I said that I would arrange for no meeting and participate, to the extent that I could control that, where there was not at least one African American, because I knew that the presence of one African American would intimidate the extreme "rednecks," to the point where they would not say some of the things that they might otherwise say. I used them later on when I was teaching race relations at Guilford College for several years. There were no textbooks back then for race-related community relations. Most of the things that I had to do or did, I didn't have many models. I had some people who were willing to talk to me and give me ideas, and I also knew that if I could do some innovative things for several reasons, then, the conservatives could see some conservative reasons for what I as doing and those who were less conservative could see some progressive reasons. And it wouldn't be devious. It would be exactly what the situation was.

But most people didn't expect the Chamber of Commerce, of all places, to be a civil rights-type of organization. I thought the first thing I had to do was to get people around me who were supportive of what I was trying to do, and also had some expertise to give me and the Chamber. So one of the first things that I wanted to do was to bring in through the membership programs as many African Americans as I could. Within a very short period of time we had several hundred black members of the Greensboro Chamber of Commerce, more black members than all of the 3000 Chambers of Commerce in the United States put together.

I couldn't bring them all in by myself. Mike Fleming, who was a very enthusiastic membership recruiter. He was a businessman, and he zealously collected referrals, people that I would suggest to bring into the Chamber. And brought in well over a hundred African American members. Those members became members of committees, some of them became committee chairmen, some of them became board members, as early as 1966, '67, '68, well ahead of most organizations in the South. And their presence made a tremendous difference.

I think that they felt that I would protect their participation so it wouldn't be a waste of time. I edited the publications. And when they got the magazines, what have you, there were all these articles that related to African American history. There was an openness or forthrightness that they hadn't seen before. I also wrote speeches for the president of the Chamber, and I always sneaked things in there that would sound like the Fourth of July, that when people heard it over here, they'd say, "What a patriot." When people heard it over there [the black community], they said, "What an emphasis on everybody being equal."

The second thing was that I wanted to have discussions. And within two months after arriving, I started the first what I call "discussion cells." Discussion cells being little dialogue groups of a small number of people which would meet ever single week, where the moderator was told that he could never take sides, but he had to restate every opinion given, particularly those things that related to race relations. And I used the term "discussion cells," because it sounded revolutionary and yet, you know, the word "cell" isn't so terrible. And at one time, we had a number of cells. And then as time went on, I used those same people in black/white encounter groups. I made sure that black people showed up at these discussion cell meetings. I made sure that the subjects were those that people didn't want to confront. I made sure, on special occasions, that there were people like the mayor or the county commissioners, or if there was a political campaign going on, The lieutenant governor, whoever it was, visiting. For example, on April 5, the day after Martin Luther King's assassination in 1968, we had a scheduled discussion cell meeting. Early in the morning—at six o'clock—I called several African American ministers and white ministers, and we had, at a little restaurant here in town, on the morning of the day after Martin Luther King's assassination, I believe, one of the first memorial program in the country. It was just a natural group.

Another thing we did to symbolize interracial cooperation in the community, was to portray African Americans as a part of the past and present of Greensboro. I invented a lively, modern, sleek cartoon character named Nat Greene. Then one day he showed up in the cartoon being African American. And then one day you saw the African American Nat Greene shaking hands with the white Nat Greene. And then we had blacks who dressed up like Nat Greene and were in photographs at special events and so on. And we made people feel comfortable about the fact that we were a multi-cultural community. Before I got here, Chamber literature stressed that Edward R. Murrow, Dolly Madison and Uncle Joe Cannon [former Speaker Of the U. S. House of Representatives] were born here, but made no mention that the Underground Railroad began here. And if you go back to 1808 when Greensboro was incorporated, there were blacks as part of the community almost immediately, because blacks were slaves. We had slavery here. But we had a lot of Quakers here too.

An important part of this effort was to emphasize the significant amount of cooperation between the races in the past. So you had Charles Moore collaborate with the Richardson family to start L. Richardson Hospital, the hospital for African Americans. You had Charles Moore collaborate with Dr. DeWitt Clinton Benbow, in raising the money to acquire the land for what is now A&T University. you might almost say the serial collaborators—moved us into the mid-20th century, when Ralph Johns brought George Simkins into the NAACP and collaborated with the sit-ins; where I collaborated with the African American community. African American members in bringing about certain changes. And I think that made Greensboro a little bit different. I think that there was not only the early Quaker influence, by the early pattern of interracial activity I think Greensboro was just a little bit further down the road toward tolerance and justice than most other Southern communities.

And so we've had a lot of interesting things happen in Greensboro. Now, Greensboro is a place that let civility sometimes carry the day. It's a serious matter. I think you need to confront the evils in our society in a timely way. And civility pays until you're ready to confront. But when you confront, you can't be too civil. Justice requires us to look at African Americans and Native Americans as our equals. And so it's been a running battle over the years.

I think Greensboro is a unique kind of place. It's sort of horizontal, not a single pyramid kind of power structure; there are a lot of little pyramids. There is a pyramid for the arts; there is a pyramid for civil rights; a pyramid for business; a pyramid for industry; a pyramid for religion and a pyramid for education. And there's nobody at the top that can pass the word. down

Over the years there have been people that have been rumored as being extremely powerful, and they certainly are, but not as powerful as they would be if they had a similar role in, say, Winston-Salem. Well, the African American community was quite similar to that. You had the A&T structure, very clearly defined. You had the Bennett College structure, which didn't overlap, a different structure. You had the clergy, again separate. You had the African American business community, which was quite different from the business community in general. And in fact, when we talked about membership to bring in business and professional people into the Chamber of Commerce, I had to teach the recruiters that we were emphasizing professional people. We had to bring in educators and physicians, because there weren't too many strong business people.

Now, in the civil rights pyramid you actually had a lot of little pyramids again. You had the NAACP-type of leadership. And you had the Black Nationalist or Pan-African leaderships. You had some conflicts of enthusiasm, but we all sort of appreciated that, if we were living in the marketplace of ideas, that was good, even in the civil rights arena. And it certainly helped show that the African American community was not monolithic. There wasn't even universal respect for Martin Luther King. When he came to Greensboro in 1958, they couldn't find a place for him, couldn't find a pulpit for him, until Bennett College opened up its chapel to allow him to speak. That was 1958.

Well, you had these different enthusiasms for different approaches to bring about change, but I would say that most of these groups, with the exception of a few people who believed in a more abrupt confrontation, were of the same mind back then in the African American community that they had to bring about by the desegregation started crumbling that the other subtleties and the political and quasi-military type of confrontation and legal confrontation even became more pronounced in their extreme elements. I also remember that I came one time to a community meeting that had been broadcast as being open to the community, but actually it meant only the black community. Some people looked as if they were suspicious that I was a representative of a traditional Chamber of Commerce, or I was someone that came to bring about change in some devious manner. I tried to go to another meeting, and I was told that it was for the black community only. Since they were meeting in a church, I went to the pastor and I said: "Why don't you and I step into the meeting?" He and I went into the meeting. That caused a lot of hostility, but I played it very even-handedly during that period. So if somebody said it was a public meeting, I went, even if I was the only white person there.

And I always made sure that African Americans were at any functions that I attended that were predominantly white in character. But I still saw, among most of the established institutions, a sea of white faces when I came, except for the people that I brought along with me, or had to really call several times to get them to come.

A generation earlier, the Chamber had its first black member, but it was a weird sort of situation. A dry cleaner in the city received a letter from the Chamber offering membership, and he joined. Lo and behold, the Chamber discovered that the man was African American. They wanted to refund his money, but the man refused to quit the Chamber. And so, for a time, in 1948, this man was the first black member in the Greensboro Chamber of Commerce.

I thought progress was coming very rapidly. We got the first black board members within six months to a year. We got the discussion cells going almost immediately. We had black faces showing up in the Chamber magazine almost immediately. We got certain policy changes in the board's policy. We brought in quite a few black members in a very short period of time. We started speaking up about the need for racial change. We had banquets where we had heavy black invitation lists, because we had a large number of black members.

We had very little discussion of something being abnormal in the sense that I tried to do everything in the "do-it-for-many-reasons" way. And I think most people felt fairly comfortable at that point, until I started becoming more specific and talked about schools and funeral homes and barber shops and what have you. And the barbers would say, "I don't know how to cut black hair," and the undertakers would say, "A time of grief is no time for social experimentation." And the school teachers would say, "Well, they have their own schools and that's what they want. And the fathers and mothers would talk about, "Would want your daughter to marry a black person?"

I thought that the Chamber quickly got a reputation for being at least progressive and open-minded. Then there was a man named Charles Smith from the Department of Defense who came to Greensboro to investigate something, and he suddenly discovered what was happening at the Chamber, and he wrote somebody about the Chamber being very unique. We were invited to Atlanta and Detroit to receive awards, and we got one from the Freedom Foundation. He was helpful in putting pleasantness into what was happening, because Chamber officials were happy to get all these awards. They got the recognition. They got invitations, what have you.

But then there were some things that happened. There were the heartbreaking shrieks for attention and change after the death of Martin Luther King. And then, ultimately we saw what happened at A&T and the death of a young man, and we saw what happened in 1969 at Dudley High school and the conflict that developed over a student election. and an organization that we had developed, called the Community Unity Division, suddenly had its first real test.

Here was the division with a board and leadership that cut across the city. Dave Richmond, one of the original four who sat-in a Woolworth, was a member of the Community Unity Division. Henry Frye was a member. You also had some of the top industrialists in the city as members of the Unity Division. And Reverend Otis Hairston. And you had connections all over the place. And we always made sure that certain African Americans were invited to come. We also had members of GAPP [Greensboro Association of Poor People] who were members of the Community Unity Division and other organizations that the Chamber had developed.

Ultimately Al Lineberry of the Chamber and Otis Hairston had negotiations and discussions that resolved the problem at Dudley High School and brought about some very basic changes in the school system. And Al Lineberry, as the school board chairman, and W. A. Pitt, as president of the Chamber of Commerce at that time, who succeeded Al Lineberry, became a solid front for the community for what was known as a peaceful transition than a transition to what. So the people were more concerned about having a peaceful transition than a transition to what. And it, of course, produced some positive changes. But also, I suppose, in the rush to be caught in the action of doing a good thing, the integration that was produced did not have as strong a roots here as I think that it should have had, although the roots were stronger than they were in most communities.

What were the failures? Too much accommodation of the whites who did not want to send their kids into the black neighborhoods. And it was felt, "All right, we'll just let the mixture take place in the white neighborhoods. Too much of an acknowledgement of something that wasn't really true, and that was that the hlack neighborhoods weren't safe. One example, in later years, of the kind of thing that this "civil" Greensboro did, where the African American community contributed to this recognition that I'm talking about. Mattye Reed started the African Heritage Center. Well, here hundreds of thousands of African artifacts and art works, masks and all sorts of things African were collected at the Heritage Center. It was my thinking that this was a wonderful museum which would allow whites to come onto the campus, which was deep in the heart of the black community where whites stayed away and they were scared to death.. Whites didn't come to A&T campus very often.

So A&T set up a satellite for the museum in the Cultural Center in Greensboro downtown so that it would have more exposure to the total community. Well, I think it would have had more exposure to the total community if it had had that so-called satellite right on the campus so that it would have forced whites to come. And those that didn't come just didn't come.

Anyhow, it might sound somewhat crude, but it would be similar to a heart surgery section in the hospital not putting whites and blacks after surgery in the same room for fear that they would wake up from their surgery and suddenly have a heart attack and die. I somehow felt, if that's what's going to cause people to have that kind of emotional response, I suppose nature should take its course.

Now, that sounds somewhat cruel and hard, but I don't believe in accommodating, making it easier for people to tolerate. And I never did particularly care for the National Conference of Christians and Jews talking about tolerance and brotherhood, because I think, first of all, brotherhood was an extreme expression which never quite got down to the neighborhood of Christian spiritual writings, for example. And I also thought the tolerance is not what we need in our society.

What we need is total acceptance, with people being willing to be part of each other. I think that, for instance, when Stanley Frank, who is considered in Greensboro as a person who has contributed greatly to human relations improvement, became president, I think he showed awkwardness in becoming the leader of the Chamber that had gone through a metamorphosis that it had during the previous six, seven years, when he set up a the meeting at the Country Club, thinking that he was doing a good thing and taking it personally. That's the meeting that the Chamber had of staff to get to know the new president, and it was considered urgent that I be there to orient him to my area of responsibility. I refused to go because I felt that it was a segregated facility and I did not want to go to a Country Club for the meeting. In fact, I thought it was highly inappropriate to schedule it there. His approach to change was to bring people along and to meet them on their terms, and it was a different approach, but it happened to be one that I did not go along with.

It was similar differences of approach among whites who were equally committed to change, but some were not as willing to expose their true feelings because their true feelings were much more conservative, and some were not willing to expose their true feelings because some would be considered revolutionary by the others. At the same time I visited a jailed inmate in the Guilford County jail., who had charged police brutality. I had just gone up to the jail and I said, "I'm with the Chamber of Commerce." And the jailer thought that that meant I was a city official. And I was criticized, saying that I had posed as a city official. No, not at all. You know, just a matter of my going there and being admitted to see this We had a Mr. Lay, who was with the White Citizens Council, American Party leadership in the county, who had written a letter to the *Greensboro Daily News* or the *Record*, saying that I should resign because I was distorting the purpose of the business organization. And I refused to. You know, that was in the back of his head.

The city is neither white nor black. And nothing is too cut and dry—the arguments that we're having about neighborhood schools and other things right now are not easily denied as arguments presented by blacks or by whites, but rather because of the trauma of thirty, forty years, in some respects, are arguments that have found attachments in both major communities in a city that is no longer white nor black, because of the fact that we have a large contingence of Montagnards and Native Americans and Thai and Vietnamese and Koreans and Nigerians. And they're not just Nigerians, but Uruba and Ebo, and on and on and on. And so it could be said that things are more complicated now. And the world "complicated" as used at the time that I left the Chamber of Commerce

I think that the so-called modified ward plan, that is, the districting plan for the City Council works fairly well for Greensboro. A third of the city's population is African American. I think that the mayors and City Council members in the time since that plan was adopted—and the discussions of that plan developed during my tenure at the Chamber with Bland Worley's committee. I think that the City Council members and mayors have become more and more attuned to the potential of a district representation, living more and more comfortable, as if it had always been that way. We've had very good leadership from the mayor, who believes in the consensus-building approach to leadership.

There are people who criticize us, but I think that any democratic leadership approach in any city is going to have its critics, because that's how our political mentality has developed over the decades. But I think Greensboro has had very progressive city leadership. We have not had a very progressive county leadership. We've not only had, from my integrationist perspective, some rascals on the County Commission, we've also had some people who are clumsy and can't rise above their clumsiness. On the other hand, we've had some very remarkable people as County Commissioners and they've saved the day for us many a time. That is the kind of Greensboro I'd like to see, where people are free to develop as they wish within an environment of music and art, poetry and education, and with a celebration of diversity, of international participation with a recognition of the greatness that really is Greensboro in some ways, particularly in understanding the history of Greensboro.

## Lewis Dowdy

I think the entire country was impressed by the nonviolent nature of the sit-ins and the demonstrations impressed the entire nation. I think the students still pass this down from one class generation to another. And I think they feel proud of the fact that they have assisted Americans to fulfill at least one or two of the dreams of America. And if we can continue to do this all over the country, then we'll have the kind of country that we wanted all the time.

In the final analysis I believe that they were part of a process which was necessary at the time.

# Afterword

I have chosen to end the history of the Greensboro Movement in 1966, which marked the dissolution of the CORE chapter and when direct action gave way to ongoing, low-key negotiations with the white power structure. This is in keeping with the trend of the Civil Rights Movement nationally. As the 1964 Civil Rights Act and the 1965 Voting Rights Act led to gradual empowerment of African American communities, the tactics of the Movement evolved from direct action to sometimes glacial negotiations in both northern and southern communities. But just as the urban riots of the late 1960s characterized continued racial tensions nationally, so too did Greensboro experience outbreaks of violence. While these events reflected the ongoing racial turmoil in Greensboro, they were not part of a dynamic student movement whose success both reflected and influenced the early Civil Rights Movement.

In the course of reading these accounts of the Greensboro Movement, one comes to understand the complexity of the perspectives of those involved. Their diversity reveals much about the times and its culture. While there are attitudes recorded that may disturb some, it is a representative account of a community that was forced to closely examine its most cherished beliefs and traditions. The revelations are not always pleasant, but they are honest, and all of them contribute to an understanding of the tortuous process by which one community struggled to cope with perhaps the most daunting social issue in 20th century American history. One comes to understand the values that motivated the participants. Leaders of the white political and business establishments were faced with a perplexing restructuring of a society with which they and their forebears had been content for generations. African Americans would no longer accept a denial of their fundamental rights as human beings and citizens. And white citizens were forced to confront an irrevocable change to their society, disturbing to many, requiring a faith that it would be for the better. Above all, they reveal the convoluted process by which a culture addresses and slowly changes its prevailing mores.

What makes the Greensboro Movement virtually unique is an absence of the violence that is a tragic part of the Civil Rights Movement. Certainly there were individual instances of violence, and the potential existed for a great deal more. But there was a concerted effort in both the white and black communities to avoid that path. As one reads these oral histories, it becomes clear that this was no accident. Liberals and moderates provided a climate conducive to social change through patient efforts to maintain crucial channels of communication between the races. The city administration, although attempting to minimize radical social change, sincerely desired to maintain law and order without abusing basic human rights. The black community had a tradition of strong leadership for generations, which gave the Movement a cohesive sense of purpose. This tradition enabled the black adult and student communities to exercise responsible discipline in a desire to achieve civil rights in such a way as to evoke admiration and a reasoned, if reluctant, cooperation from the power structure and the entire white community. Police forces conducted themselves with a restraint that stood in marked contrast to their counterparts in other Southern communities. The owners and managers of the targeted businesses struggled with ingrained attitudes and pragmatic decisions vital to their livelihood.

The widespread desegregation of Greensboro businesses had to await federal legislation, but the process was begun by a grudging voluntary acceptance of change for the greater public good by most of the targeted businesses. The experience proved to be a learning process in which individuals had to continually broaden the limitations of their perspectives. Repeatedly, people of good will displayed enlightened leadership that averted tragedy. Perhaps most of all, the reaction of the local society at large is the most heartening aspect of the Greensboro experience. Although the community, on the whole, appeared determined to maintain the segregated status quo, when confronted with the choice of acceptance of dramatic social change or violent resistance, the community chose nonviolent compliance. Although crowds contained an intransigent racist element, most of those that witnessed the demonstrations were more curious than hostile, and the community accepted the compromises annnounced by the white power structure with surprising readiness.

Certainly the history of the Greensboro Movement is not one of an idealistic solution to the dilemma of opposing rights. In many cases, attitudes remained unchanged. City officials and businessmen resented pressures from the national and state governments that seemed to ignore their rights; African Americans and white sympathizers seethed at what they regarded as subtle pre-empting of substantive change through a veneer of civility by the white power structure. Meaningful accession to the demands of African Americans awaited the Civil Rights Act of 1964, and the more complex economic issues continued to confront the city for many years. Rather, it is a story of how people can address crucial issues that divide them, and find a means to live with each other in relative harmony.

The transition of fundamental values in a society is never simple; it is an evolving, frequently painful process of progressive and regressive effort. Social mores based on concepts of race, class and property rights, inevitably came into conflict. But the citizens of Greensboro successfully accepted that daunting challenge. Perhaps its ultimate legacy may lie in being a testament to the peaceful resolution of conflicting ideologies, and how ordinary people can work together to achieve goals of enduring value.

# Sources

Most of the information contained in this book is from interviews conducted by the author under the auspices of the Greensboro Public Library Oral History Program. Those interviews conducted by other individuals are so designated. All interviews are housed at the Greensboro (N.C) Public Library and the Walter Clinton Jackson Library, University of North Carolina at Greensboro. Those wishing to access them may do so on the internet as part of the "Community Voices Project" of the Jackson Library through www.uncg.edu/libraies Background material was derived from the following sources:

## Newspapers

*The Greensboro Daily News*
*The Greensboro Record*

## Books, Dissertations and Pamphlets

Bradley, Josephine Boyd. "Wearing My Name: School Desegregation, Greensboro, N.C., 1954-1958." (Ph.D. dissertation, Emory University, 1996.
Chafe, William C. *Civilities and Civil Rights, Greensboro, North Carolina and the Struggle for Black Freedom.* Oxford University Press: N.Y., 1980.
Wolff, Miles Jr. *Lunch at the Five and Ten: The Greensboro Sit-ins: A Contemporary History.* Stein & Day: N.Y., 1970.

## Interviews

Helen Ashby  [William Link]  3/25/87
Warren Ashby  5/15/81
Joseph Asher  4/22/82
Pattie E. Banks  6/14/79
Cecil Bishop  2/5/85
Ezell A. Blair, Sr.  1979
Ezell A. Blair, Jr. (see Jibreel Khazan)
Gloria Jean Blair (Howard)  9/15/82
Lewis A. Brandon  6/3/81
Gordon Carey  7/15/81
Vance C. Chavis  11/21/79
B. Elton Cox  5/15/82
Ann Dearsley (-Vernon)  [Herman Trojanowski]  5/21/2007

Lewis C. Dowdy  2/21/77
Ima Edwards  [Jim Schlosser] 1988
Herman Enochs   1980
George Evans  4/27/79; [William Link] 11/3/89
James Farmer   12/10/81
Warmoth T. Gibbs  5/17/77
Evander Gilmer  6/10/82
William L. "Lody" Glenn  [William Link] 4/16/87
Leonard Guyes  9/21/82
Otis L. Hairston, Sr.  6/1/79
Otis L. Hairston, Jr  1980
Clarence L. Harris  [Jim Schlosser]  1988
John F. Hatchett  1980;  5/2/81
Frances Herbin (Lewis)  1/17/81
Sarah Herbin  12/14/83 ; [William Link]  6/5/90
Howard Holderness   8/13/82
William H. Jackson  5/18/79; [Glen Jordan]  10/1/87
Hobart Jarrett  1980; [William Link]  2/3/90
Ralph Johns  1/17/79
Marion Jones  10/14/79
Sarah Jones (Outterbridge)  7/24/82
Jibreel Khazan (Ezell A. Blair, Jr.)  12/4/80; 10/20/79
John Marshall Kilimanjaro [ n. d.]
Elizabeth Laizner  6/19/79
J. Kenneth Lee  1980; [Kathleen Hoke]  6/6/90
Ulysses Ralph Lee   7/29/82
Lois Lucas (Williams)  12/27/80
Clarence C. Malone  1980
Clyde Marsh  4/13/79
Franklin McCain  10/20/79 ; [Jim Schlosser|  12/17/90
Neil McGill  1980
Floyd McKissick  8/9/82
James C. McMillan  8/15/79
Joseph McNeil  10/14/79
Furman M. Melton  4/12/79
Jack Moebes  4/18/79
David H. Morehead. [William Link.]  6/5/90
Boyd Morris  1980; [William Link]  12/9/86
Franklin Parker [William Link]  3/8/87
Jennie Parker [William Link]  3/8/87
Robert Tyrone (Pat) Patterson   7/17/79
Willa B. Player   12/3/79

David Richmond 10/14/79
George Roach 11/17/78
David Schenck, Jr. 5/26/81
Arnold A. Schiffman 4/11/79
Eugenie Seamans (Marks) [Herman J. Trojanowski] 6/17/2007
Frank O. Sherrill, Jr 1980
Hal Sieber [William Link] [n. d.]
George S. Simkins, Jr. [ Jim Schlosser]
McNeill Smith [Kevin Costello] 1/3/87
Willliam L. Snider 4/19/79; [William Link] 10/1/87
Jo J. Spivey 5/30/79; [Glen Jordan] 6/90
A.Knighton (Tony) Stanley 1/26/82
Marvin Sykes [Kathleen Hoke]; 2/12/90
Alvin Thomas 8/12/82
William A. Thomas 7/5/79; 8/13/82
Geneva Tisdale [Jim Schlosser] 1998
Elizabeth (Betsy) Toth [Herman J. Trojanowski] 6/17/2007
James R. Townsend 11/22/78
Ben Wilson [Kathleen Carter] 5/17/89
Edward R. Zane [William Link] 2/13/87